WILDLAND
RECREATION
POLICY

WILDLAND RECREATION POLICY

AN INTRODUCTION

SECOND EDITION

J. DOUGLAS WELLMAN
North Carolina State University

DENNIS B. PROPST
Michigan State University

KRIEGER PUBLISHING COMPANY
MALABAR, FLORIDA
2004

Original Edition 1987
Reprint Edition 1992
Second Edition 2004

Printed and Published by
KRIEGER PUBLISHING COMPANY
KRIEGER DRIVE
MALABAR, FLORIDA 32950

**FROM A DECLARATION OF PRINCIPLES JOINTLY ADOPTED BY A
COMMITTEE OF THE AMERICAN BAR ASSOCIATION AND A COM-
MITTEE OF PUBLISHERS:**
This publication is designed to provide accurate and authoritative information in
regard to the subject matter covered. It is sold with the understanding that the pub-
lisher is not engaged in rendering legal, accounting, or other professional service.
If legal advice or other expert assistance is required, the services of a competent
professional person should be sought.

Library of Congress Cataloging-in-Publication Data

Wellman, John D.
  Wildland recreation policy : an introduction / J. Douglas Wellman, Dennis B.
Propst.—2nd ed.
    p. cm.
  Includes bibliographical references and index.
  ISBN 1-57524-173-0 (alk. paper) — ISBN 1-57524-243-5 (pbk. : alk. paper)
    1. Wilderness areas—Recreation use—United States. 2. Wilderness areas—
Government policy—United States. I. Propst, Dennis B. II. Title.

GV191.67.W5W45 2004
333.78'0973—dc22

                                                            2003060624

10 9 8 7 6 5 4 3 2

CONTENTS

v

CONTENTS

PREFACE TO THE FIRST EDITION

This book has emerged from 10 years' experience teaching an introductory outdoor recreation course to juniors and seniors in natural resources (forestry, fisheries, and wildlife), education (health, physical education, and recreation), and other disciplines including biology, landscape architecture, business, political science, and agriculture.

When I began teaching this class, I adopted the method with which I was most familiar from my own schooling—lecturing. Where more gifted public speakers might have succeeded, I had difficulty. Presenting historical information on laws and agencies to classes of over a hundred students, most of whom were there because they were required to be, was trying for all of us. Learning more about my subject didn't help matters directly, since it gave me so many more seemingly important facts to "cover." And efforts to improve my stage presence and delivery failed to remove the glazed looks from my students' eyes. It became obvious that I had to reconsider my approach.

I began by thinking about my students, who they were and what they should be getting from the class. Only a few in each year's class were majoring in wildland recreation. After graduation, most would work in forest management or community recreation, and some would go on to graduate school. However, even though wildland recreation was peripheral to most of their career interests, it was not unimportant to them. For personal as well as hazily perceived professional reasons, many cared about parks, wilderness, trails, and rivers. My challenge was to work with this interest, bearing in mind that for all but a few students mine would be their only class in wildland recreation.

I decided that my educational goal would be to help students develop their own models of the policy process as it operates for wildland recreation in America. If they could leave my class with some understanding of how wildland recreation areas come to be and why they are managed as they are, together with an interest in knowing more, I felt I would have succeeded. The few who would go on to careers in wildland recreation management would have a foundation on which to build technical expertise; those who would manage forest, fishery, and wildlife resources would have a better understanding of the human dimensions of their work; those in community recreation would have a feel for the rest of the recreation spectrum; and those whose careers in no way directly related to wildland recreation might have a basis for becoming informed and perhaps involved in emerging issues.

With this goal in mind, I realized that I was lecturing too much. By hogging the stage I was encouraging student passivity and emphasizing facts at the expense of the mental engagement and sustained interest that produces understanding and concern. The most troublesome lectures were those on policy history; yet, the more history I read, the more convinced I became that it was essential to understanding present and future events. I had to find a better way to present it.

The outcome was the first draft of this book, which consisted essentially of my class notes on the history of the national parks and wilderness areas. I asked my students to read the notes on their own, with the help of a study guide. I did not "go over" the notes in any systematic way during class, but I attempted to reference them frequently in the course of other class activities. Class time was largely given over to more free-flowing and interactive pursuits like case studies, special issues, student presentations of individual and group projects, and debates about controversial ideas.

The transformation of the class was dramatic. Most of the glazed looks disappeared, and class meetings became lively and enjoyable. Student's essays, projects, and discussions gained new depth. At the same time, students displayed an improved command of the historical material. They understood history better, and they were more adept at using it to analyze and interpret contemporary issues. I attribute these gains largely to the notes. Instead of transcribing lectures, inevitably missing much in the process since I tend to lecture in a conversational style, they read the notes at their own pace. Many told me they read them two or three times.

In developing the lecture notes into this book, I have tried to retain the essence of the notes as something students can and will read on their own. I have avoided "academic" material and language, since I view it as counterproductive for my purposes. I have tried to indicate the depth of the ideas involved in wildland recreation as a way of demonstrating that it is an important component of American life. While I have tried to persuade readers of wildland recreation's importance, I have tried to do so in an enjoyable way, so that the "lessons" would be lasting.

One way I have sought to make the text readable was by being selective. If I wanted my students to develop their own thoughts about wildland recreation and its place in American life, I felt it would be more effective to concentrate on a few representative events rather than to attempt to tell all. I see little lasting value in trying to teach my students all the details of laws, agencies, regulation, persons, and so on. The half-life of these details is exceedingly short, and such details as they might need at some future time can readily be found in any number of thorough reference books. On the other hand, a limited number of more complete policy stories would be something students could carry with them long after the class was over. Therefore, I have maintained my original focus on the early national parks. I have included only so much other historical information as is necessary to provide context and linkages. Similarly, I have resisted expanding coverage beyond the U.S. Forest Service and National Park Service, because I think these two agencies sufficiently represent public sector activity in providing wildland recreation experiences.

In this book I devote much attention to the lives and ideas of a few key people. In doing this, I risk being seen as having a "great man" view of history. As I hope will be evident in the text, this is not the case. I believe individuals are necessary but not sufficient cause of historical events, and that in many instances their contributions are overshadowed by much larger social and economic forces. Nevertheless, to a significant degree, I have written this book about people. My thinking in doing this is that the biographies I have chosen, in addition to being important in their own right, are representative of important themes in wildland recreation policy. I think innate human interest in other people gives biography unique memorability. Long after factual accounts of any given policy have faded from memory, readers will recall something of George Perkins Marsh, Emerson and Thoreau, John Muir, Gifford Pinchot, Aldo Leopold, and Bob Marshall and their ideas and struggles. As a way of enhancing the biographical approach, I have relied heavily on extended direct quotations of original writing.

I have presented policy as the outcome of social conflict, and have chosen to build the book around the theme of nature preservation versus economic development. I realize that policy conflicts are more complex than they may appear in the text, and that many conflicts in addition to preservation/development are involved in the emergence of any given policy. I have chosen to illustrate the many layers of issues and concerns intertwined in the emergence of policies, rather than to attempt a rigorous policy analysis for each. This choice, once again, stems from my purpose in writing this book. I felt that a conception of policy as the product of struggle between use (man-centered) and preservation (nature-centered) was sufficient burden for an introductory book to bear. In portraying the use/preservation conflict in its many manifestations, I have offered ample glimpses into the ambiguity that prevents easy good guy versus bad guy explanations. Preservation/development is a familiar dialectic, one that is found throughout the literature on wildland recreation. My hope is that after completing this text, readers will recognize the dichotomy in reading and in life, and will understand its usefulness, as well as its limitations, as a way of structuring thinking about conflict and policy in resource management.

ACKNOWLEDGMENTS

During my work on this book, I have benefitted from hundreds of kindnesses, large and small. In my attempt to thank those who have helped me, I hope those I may inadvertently overlook will forgive my faulty memory, and those who I do mention will realize that I do not hold them responsible for the book's failures, but only its successes.

First and foremost, I want to thank Lyle Craine for introducing me to natural resource policy, and for providing me with the historical and analytical foundation on which this book rests. Ross Tocher and Bev Driver introduced me to wildland recreation and its role in American culture and politics. I am deeply indebted to Greg Buhyoff for his friendship and scholarly collaboration since 1976, and for his encouragement when I decided to shift my academic focus to policy. Ed Hampton helped me reach the original decision to substitute written notes for lecturing. Greg Buhyoff, John Hosner, and Mark Paddock encouraged me to consider publishing the notes. Reviews of the orginal notes by Ben Twight, Bob Becker, Hanna Cortner, Burce Hull, Lyle Craine, and Sally Fairfax were instrumental in leading me to restructure my thinking and to embark on the reading I needed to do. I am particularly grateful to Lyle Craine, and Sally Fairfax for challenging me to rethink my overall approach to the book, and to Ben Twight for the sustained sharing of his encyclopedic store of knowledge and references.

Thanks to my students for their honest reactions throughout this learning experience; their positive response to the new direction supplied me with essential motivation. Others who reviewed the entire manuscript or parts of it, and who provided helpful insights, corrections, and encouragement, included Dorothy Anderson, Janine Benyus, Perry Brown, David Cockrell, Bev Driver, Jim Fazio, Jim Herndon, Rick Knopf, Floyd Kregenow, Bob Lucas, Len McKenzie, Susan Oliver, Joe Roggenbuck, Bill Shands, George Stankey, and Terry Tipple. Others who helped in various ways, directly or indirectly, include Pete Bromley, Marilyn Buhyoff, Ken Cordell, Dan Dustin, Ken Farrar, Roy Feuchter, Charles Goodsell, John Heerwald, John Hendee, Destry Jarvis, Bill Leuschner, Leo McAvoy, Tom More, Frank Noe, Mark Reisch, Lynn Rogers, Joe Roggenbuck, Judy Schwab, Terry Sharik, George Siehl, and Hal Wisdom.

Tom DuRant, Bill Hauser, and Tome Watkins were exceedingly helpful in securing the photographs. In addition, I appreciate the services of the staffs at the Library of Congress Prints and Photographs Division, the Bancroft Library at the University of California at Berkeley, the National Portrait Gallery, the National Museum of Natural History, and the Architecture and Special Collections divisions of the Newman Library at Virginia Tech.

Thanks to Don Deneck of John Wiley & Sons, Inc., for his willingness to take a chance on me and my book, and for the editorial guidance he gave this novice book author in the early stages of the project. My thanks, also, to Cliff Mills for his editorial responsiveness in the latter part of the project, and to Richard Christopher, Susan Winick, Connie Rende, Gilda Stahl, Glenn Petry, and Christopher Cosentino of John Wiley for their help on particular aspects of the project.

Janine Benyus helped me solve the mysteries of the first chapter and develop a coherent introduction appropriate to the rest of the text. For transforming my handwritten hieroglyphics into readable typescript and for maintaining her good humor through repeated drafts, I am sincerely grateful to Carol Sheppard; her effort in the latter stages of this project went beyond the call of duty. Kendra Kohl bore the brunt of the work in the early stages; I am very thankful for her cheerful and tireless help transcribing notes and typing the early chapter drafts. Darrell Nicholas, Peggy Quarterman, Mariette Dawson and Ann Day also helped with the typing. Thanks, too, to the friendly people at the North Central Forest Experiment Station for their hospitality during my sabbatical leave, during which much of the final composition was completed.

Finally, I want to thank my family for their support throughout the project. I could not have completed it without them. Liza and Sam were patient with me in my preoccupation, and their skill in managing their own lives freed me to focus on my own. Janet, my own "best friend and severest critic," was too busy with her own professional challenges to provide her customary review and reminder that "brevity is the soul of wit," but I hope the text will reveal some traces of wisdom she has imparted on me over the years.

J. Douglas Wellman

PREFACE TO THE SECOND EDITION

As a graduate student in the 1970s, when the environmental movement was first showing its muscle, I found the subject of natural resource policy to be particularly fascinating. New policies were emerging, debates about clearcutting and recreational use of public lands were vigorous and stimulating, and we were worried as a nation about resource scarcity. In addition, the social sciences were beginning to make a mark on the natural resource management profession by adding scholarship from diverse disciplines, such as political science and social psychology. The dynamism and seeming chaos in the policy process kept me interested and even entertained, if one can recall the political satire that went along with the James Watt era.

Later, as a reviewer of portions of Doug Wellman's original *Wildland Recreation Policy,* and as an assistant professor teaching natural resource policy for the first time and living close enough to Washington, DC, to introduce my students to the players in the policy process, I maintained my enthusiasm for trying to understand more about natural resources policies, how they come about, and their historic antecedents.

My graduate students and I at Michigan State University continue the debates and curiosity that Doug Wellman, and later, Lou Twardzik at Michigan State University, engendered in me at various points in my career. The current debate about U.S. energy policy along with the Vice President Dick Cheney's publicized epiphany that conservation was a waste of everyone's time keep me engaged in the policy process at both intellectual and emotional levels.

When I first suggested the idea of revising *Wildland Recreation Policy,* Doug wondered if there was still a demand for such a book. I argued that there was, but as a reality check I asked a number of colleagues at various conferences over the years, particularly the semi-annual Symposium on Society and Natural Resources, their views on the demand. I got enough encouragement to persuade Doug that there was a need, he acquiesced, and here we are with a revised edition.

Doug and I had long and difficult discussions initially about what to keep, what to delete, what to revise, and how. One thing we agreed on was to keep chapters three through eight from the original book largely intact. Doug had received so many compliments on the clear, interesting, and concise manner in which he had told the story of the utilitarian conservation and romantic preservation movements and the history of the U.S. Forest Service, the National Park Service, and the National Wilderness Preservation System that we decided major surgery was not necessary. We expanded the treatment of history in these early chapters by incorporating recent scholarship on many of the featured historical figures. We also added, with the help of works by Dorceta Taylor at the University of Michigan, Carolyn Merchant at Berkeley, and Polly Kaufman at the University of Southern Maine, scholarship on the contributions to the conservation movement of women, the working class, and persons of color. Dorceta Taylor was particularly helpful in the early stages of revision by providing her thoughts on how to integrate this rich and growing literature and by providing critical references. We updated the chapter on current wilderness policy (chapter 8) through the Aldo Leopold Institute's extensive website: www.wilderness.net, the assistance of Chad Dawson at Syracuse University, and our own research.

To add breadth and depth to the original discussion of the policy formation process based on new scholarship since the first edition was printed, we split the original first chapter into two. Chapter one of this edition sets the stage by describing the extent and value of wildland recreation in America and discussing why we kept the term "wildland recreation." We agree with environmental historians and other colleagues that the term "wildland" is a social construction. At least from the standpoint of programmatic initiatives within the federal resource management agencies, the term has evolved to become more inclusive of urban issues and resources. Chapter two is now completely devoted to describing the policy making process in the United States. For this, we are indebted to Michael Mintron of Michigan State University, whose book, *Policy Entrepreneurs and School Choice,* provided an excellent review of the political science literature on policy formation, and stimulated us to explore in our book the concept of the wildland recreation manager as policy entrepreneur. As policy entrepreneurs, wildland recreation managers have a more active role in the policy process than has been portrayed in much natural resource policy literature, which typically defines the manager's role as implementer of policy, rather than one who also directs and creates policy. Robert Reich, Ronald Heifitz, and others from Harvard's Kennedy School of Government, and Gary Wamsley and his colleagues at Virginia Tech provided evidence and justification of the evolution and need for these more active public managers across all domains. In the early '90s, Doug Wellman, Terry Tipple, Margaret Shannon, Hanna Cortner, and others brought this lesson into the literature and scholarship of the natural resources profession. We attempt to capture all these scholarly contributions in the revised chapter two.

For the new section on urban wildland initiatives and programs of the U.S. Forest Service and USDI National Park Service (chapter 9), we profited greatly from the comments and documents provided by John Dwyer and Paul Gobster (USFS, North Central Experiment Station, Chicago), Ed Dickerhoof (USFS, Washington, DC), Barbara Nelson-Jamieson (NPS, Midwest Region, Omaha), and John Debo (Cuyahoga Valley NRA Superintendent). Our interactions at two professional conferences: The 8th International Society and Natural Resources Symposium (Bellingham, WA, June 2000) and the George Wright Forum (Denver, CO, April 2001) yielded additional agency contacts and perspectives on urban recreation policy initiatives and trends.

Our most radical revisions involved the last chapters of the book. Doug Wellman ended the first edition with current (1980s) policy directions in the National Park Service and an attempt at linking policy with management. This idea of linking policy with management—of demonstrating the challenges managers face in the "free fire zone" of public policy development—is where readers who make comparisons will find the most significant changes between the first and second editions. Although there are significant updates in all chapters, chapters 10 through 12 contain the most new material.

Reviewing the literature in natural resource-based outdoor recreation, we discovered only broad and often superficial attempts to link policy and management. We wanted to add some substance to this linkage, to flesh out the role and importance of public managers in the policy process, and indicate to students how managers cope on a day-to-day basis with life in the fishbowl of public scrutiny. We wanted students and other readers to know that managers play an absolutely pivotal role in the policy process regarding wildland recreation and other natural resources in the United States, that persistence pays off in policy formation, and that some managers find the development and implementation of policy to be one of the most challenging and dynamic aspects of their careers. We set the stage in chapter 10 by examining current issues in wildland recreation management. We did this by focusing in detail on the changes that took place in the 20-year period from 1980 to 2000 in the planning process for Yosemite National Park and in an overview of the internal and external "threats" facing all national parks. John Reynolds (Director, Southwest Region, NPS) helped us greatly with historical and technical details of the Yosemite planning process and we wish to acknowledge his assistance.

Recreation managers respond to the challenges and threats they face in innovative ways, and we wanted to tell some of those stories. To do this, we conducted in-depth interviews with a number of recreation managers and planners in the U.S. Forest Service in western and midwestern states. We simply asked individuals what some of their current policy implementation challenges were and how they were dealing with them. After numerous phone conversations, emails and reviews of background documents, we boiled the stories down to four "policy-management vignettes," which we feel exemplify well the realities of policy implementation (Chapter 11). We acknowledge their contributions in Chapter 11, but again, for helping us add a personal touch to some abstract concepts, we express our gratitude to Therese O'Rourke (then, program leader, Southern California Conservation Strategy, Cleveland National Forest), Raina Fulton (recreation officer, Angeles National Forest), Janna Larson (then, landscape architect and recreation planner, San Bernardino National Forest), and Les Wadzinski (recreation program manager, Hoosier National Forest). Their personal experiences in implementing the Endangered Species Act, the Americans with Disabilities Act, and agency carrying capacity mandates provide valuable lessons to current and future wildland recreation managers.

Chapter 11 ends with a discussion of the policy implementation frameworks and tools that managers have at their disposal—some old (recreation opportunity spectrum, limits of acceptable change, and user fees) and some new (benefits-based management, public participation, and collaborative management). In chapter 12, the final chapter, we summarize major themes, but more importantly, we reaffirm the critical and changing role of the manager in the policy process. In so doing, we highlight the important skills that wildland recreation managers of today and of the future will need to resolve increasingly "wicked problems."

In addition to those already mentioned, there are others whose contributions we wish to acknowledge:

- Joyce Parks, Bill Page, and Krieger Publishing Company for their expert assistance in editing and overseeing the production of the final product
- Debra Chavez (Research Social Scientist, USDA Forest Service, Pacific Southwest Research Station, for getting us started with contacts for the policy-management vignettes)
- National Park Service staff: Earlene Malloy (Realty Specialist, Washington, DC) and Butch Street (Public Use Statistics Coordinator, Denver) for providing updated statistics on everything from visitation to the number of acres under easements
- Brian Feeney (Public Affairs Officer, Gateway National Recreation Area) for helping us get the story and numbers straight concerning public transportation to Gateway
- Dave Mihalic (Superintendent, Yosemite National Park) for updates on Yosemite planning and for providing contacts concerning the history of the Yosemite Valley Plan's evolution
- Chad Dawson (Professor, Syracuse University) for reviewing drafts of the chapters on wilderness
- Ken Elwert (graduate student, Michigan State University) for reviewing early drafts of chapter one
- Patte Hahn (staff assistant, Michigan State University) for her expert assistance in keeping all the files organized and creating the index; I cannot underscore enough the importance of these often thankless tasks and the amount of effort that goes into them

I wish to thank my son and daughter, Blake and Bridget, for putting up with my surly moods and odd hours as I agonized over changes and additions and, in my obsession, forgot important family events and dates. My wife, Maureen McDonough, deserves special credit, not only for putting up with my eccentricities and moods while working on this revision, but also for her scholarly contributions in the areas of urban and community forestry, public participation, and collaborative conservation.

Finally, I wish to thank Doug Wellman for having enough confidence in me to allow me to tamper with his original creation. Readers in particular will profit from the English teacher in Doug who would frequently chop off my long sentences and eliminate unnecessary wordiness. With Doug on board as editor, motivator, and scholarly contributor, I did not once falter in my belief that we would complete this revision in a quality manner.

Dennis B. Propst
Michigan State University
May 2003

CHAPTER 1

INTRODUCTION

ABOUT THIS BOOK

Twenty-first century Americans are endowed with a vast number of places where they can experience the benefits of nature. In a little over 120 years, America has managed to set aside a publicly owned outdoor recreation domain of a size and variety never before seen on earth. To care for these lands and to ensure that visitors can enjoy what they have to offer, Americans have built a network of management institutions. Associated with these management institutions are countless citizen and business groups, all of which have a say in how visitors use America's wildland estate.

How did all this come to be? How did we as a nation decide to create these areas and institutions? How, once we have set aside an area, do we determine how it will be used and what can and cannot be done with it? Once we have given an agency responsibility for an area, how do we make sure it will be responsive to diverse and changing values in an increasingly heterogeneous society? These questions and their answers fall into the realm of policy.

This book is about the ever-changing, never-ending process of policy-making in wildland recreation. We focus on the issues that trigger policy, the political system that produces it, and the people who defend or fight to change it. A unique feature of this book is the explicit link between policy and management. Public managers not only play a critical role in implementing broad policies, but they also can be instrumental in creating the climate in which public ideas become new policies.[1]

1

Four policy developments are featured: the Yosemite Grant of 1864, the Wilderness Act of 1964, Gateway and Golden Gate National Recreation Areas of 1972, and the urban forestry programs of the 1990s. These developments represent key turning points in wildland recreation history, span the continuum from remote to urban wildland resources, and are good places to start understanding the policy debates that continue today. As these stories unfold, you will learn how policies emerge and are shaped by social forces, and how important the ideas and actions of individuals can be. You will also see the virtues of persistence and developing a long-range vision.

Our discussion will concentrate on the two federal agencies that have had starring roles in these policy developments, namely the Forest Service (in the U.S. Department of Agriculture) and the National Park Service (in the U.S. Department of the Interior). Both provide recreation, which, for the purposes of this book, will be defined as things people do in their free time to refresh themselves from work and other obligations or to expand their personal horizons. The term wildland, as used here, refers not only to wilderness, but to any lands where the works of nature, rather than those of people, are the main attractions. Our definition of wildland includes urban environments and other environments close to where people live. As such, we use the term "wildland recreation" primarily to mean outdoor resource-based activities that specifically require a natural resource environment for the activity. Our primary focus is on federal outdoor recreation resources, though we acknowledge that backyards, neighborhood parks and streets, outdoor concerts, golf courses, and the like all contain elements of what various individuals and groups would define as "natural."[2] Our definition includes most forms of water-based, winter, and trail-related recreation activities.

Americans haven't always assigned great value to wildland recreation resources. Before we begin our story of how and why forest and park recreation policies emerged, we first consider some of the factors that have added to the value society places on these resources.

VALUE OF WILDLAND RECREATION IN AMERICA

American Culture and Wildland Recreation

"Resources are not, they become," wrote E.W. Zimmerman some 50 years ago.[3] Whether or not people value natural landscapes depends on their culture—their knowledge, attitudes and technology. Uranium deposits in the Amazon basin are not resources for the indigenous peoples living there, just as naturally occurring roots, herbs, and grubs are not resources for most twenty-first century Americans. In America, lands that early in our national history were considered worthless, even inimical to our collective well-being, are now celebrated in literature, painting, and photography.[4] This shift from viewing wildlands as worthless obstacles, to seeing them as national treasures was brought on by many factors.

Scarcity has played a large role in the cultural creation of wildland resources. As long as natural landscapes were abundant, they had little value. As the American population increased, open space became a valued resource.[5] A second factor was the growth of the national economy. The emergence of American business and industry produced an abundance of wealth and leisure time for the majority of the population, along with the mobility to reach wildland areas. A third factor contributing to the creation of wildland recreation resources in America was Euro-Americans' need for distinctive symbols of their national identity.[6] In the nineteenth century, Euro-Americans in the New World found in spectacular natural landscapes something they could compare with pride to the castles and cathedrals of the Old World.

A fourth factor creating wildland recreation resources is found in the inventive genius and creative vigor of private enterprise. Before the development and mass marketing of snowmobiles and ski equipment, winter was a burden to be endured; now, bumper stickers encourage us to "Think Snow!" Ordinary mortals can now experience the wild water of the Grand Canyon (where explorer and scientist John Wesley Powell once risked his life), thanks to the development of rubber rafts and the commercial packaging of raft trips. Mountain climbing and mountain biking have developed into major recreation activities, in part because enterprising businesses have adapted space age technologies to reduce the sports' risks and increase their pleasures. Buttressing the development of recreation equipment has been the growth of a fifth factor: information about wildland recreation. Hundreds of books, thousands of articles, and numerous websites capture our interest and instruct us in the delights of the great outdoors, and in so doing, they reaffirm the value of wildland recreation to many people.

These factors—scarcity, economic development, nationalism, technology, and information—are among the many changes in American society that have helped create wildland recreation resources. These resources have allowed many Americans to participate in forms of recreation that honor their pioneering heritage, respond to their desire to take risks, allow them temporarily to move from their complex everyday environments into quieter and greener places, and offer special opportunities for them to discover things about themselves and their surroundings. They have also enhanced the quality of life for countless others who enjoy them vicariously and appreciate their value for wildlife and other valued features of the natural world.

The Role of Wildland Recreation in Our Lives Today

By almost any measure, wildland recreation is important in American life. Since the first edition of this book was published, there have been three national outdoor recreation and tourism trends symposia (1990, 1995, and 2000). The purpose of these symposia is to bring together the nation's best analysts and forecasters of outdoor recreation and tourism trends. An overriding theme of the 2000 Trends Symposium was that travel in pursuit of outdoor recreation and other opportunities to learn about the natural world grew throughout the 1990s and is expected to be a dominant force in future travel markets.[7] In addition, the "National Survey on Recreation and the Environment" (a series of national recreation surveys begun in 1960) found that nearly 95 percent of all Americans reported engaging in some form of outdoor recreation during the 12 months prior to being interviewed. The survey also reported that the overall growth in outdoor recreation participation (13.4 percent) exceeded the rate of population expansion between 1982 and 1994.[8]

Both the supply and demand for outdoor recreation are growing and will continue to do so. The following sampling of statistics may help to convey just how devoted Americans are to wildland recreation. Where figures were available, we compare current data with data from the 1980s when the first edition was published.

Supply[9]

1. Excluding Alaska, federal and state governments managed a total of 381.9 million acres of designated public recreation lands in 1980. By 1996, this figure had grown to 429.1 million acres, an increase of 47.2 million acres in 16 years. Alaska contributes an additional 246.5 million acres, or 36.5 percent, to the grand total of 675.6 million acres in federal and state public lands.

2. As of 2003, 105 million acres were included in the National Wilderness Preservation System (NWPS), up from 80 million in 1982, a 33 percent increase. Alaska contains 56 percent of the total NWPS acreage.

3. In 1996, the National Wild and Scenic Rivers System included parts of 154 rivers totaling 10,817 river miles, an increase of 55 percent in river miles since 1983.

4. In 1995, American governments at all levels maintained 9989 miles of "National Recreation Trails," an increase of 1229 miles, or 14 percent since 1987. This figure does not include the 2157-mile Appalachian Trail, the 2638-mile Pacific Crest Trail, National Historic Trails, or side or connecting trails. Separate state trail systems totaled 15,390 miles in 1996.

5. In 2002, state public lands (parks, forests, wildlife areas, natural areas, etc.) totaled almost 13 million acres, up 20 percent since 1975. Furthermore, in the 1990s, more than 1267 new state areas were added to state park systems nationwide, a 30 percent expansion.

6. In 1995, there were 18,980 year-round state park employees and 29,861 part-time state park employees, representing expansions of 5 percent and 22 percent, respectively since 1984.

7. In 1996, a total of 4091 campgrounds were managed by public agencies, an increase of 2.4 percent from 1987.

8. There were 4528 local governmental park and recreation departments in the United States in 1993; of these, 73 percent were municipal and 19 percent were county agencies.

9. The number of selected recreation businesses (marinas, boat rental, bicycle rental and tours, organized camps, public and private golf courses, archery ranges, guide/outfitter services, and rifle/pistol ranges) grew from 29,050 to 32,462 such businesses between 1985 and 1996, a 12 percent increase.

Participation[10]

1. In 1996, approximately 759 million visitor days (1 visitor day equals 1 person for 12 hours) were recorded on federal recreation areas, an increase of 40 percent since 1981. *(By comparison, attendance at major league baseball games and motion pictures was 71 million and 1.5 billion, respectively in 1999[11]; from 1980 to 2000, the U.S. population increased by 24.2 percent).*

2. In 2002, state parks counted 766 million recreational visits (a visit equals any part of a day for day users or an overnight stay of any length), a 46 percent increase since 1975 *(from 1970 to 2000, the U.S. population increased by 38.4 percent).*

3. In 1995, among Americans 12 years old or older, 63.3 million fished (46 percent increase since 1982), 58.5 million camped (114 percent increase), 20.6 million hunted (9 percent decrease), 16.2 million rode horseback (no change), and 17.5 million canoed/kayaked (no change).

4. In 1996, 133.7 million Americans walked outdoors and 57 million went bicycling. *(By comparison, 57.3 million persons visited Disney's theme parks in 2001).*[12]

5. From 1990 to 2000, participation (more than one occasion per year) increased in the following activities: exercise walking (15 percent increase), camping (3.7 percent), fishing (2.4 percent), hiking (2.3 percent), backpacking (4.6 percent), and snowboarding (2.8 percent)

6. In 2001, 66 million people fed, observed, or photographed wildlife around their homes and on trips away from home, a 5 percent increase since 1996.

7. In 2001, total expenditures for hunting and fishing were estimated at $71 billion; and for wildlife watching (persons who feed, observe, or photograph wildlife), $38 billion. *(By comparison, in 2001, Americans spent $106 billion on new autos; $73 billion on audio and video goods; including musical instruments; $33 billion on computers, peripherals, and software; and $35 billion on books and maps).*[13]

Impressive as figures like these may be, statistics don't tell the whole story about the value of wildland recreation in American life. Americans' enthusiasm for wildland recreation is also evident in the extensive record of federal legislation dating from at least as early as the 1864 Yosemite Park Grant. National parks and forests created through this legislation have been a source of pride to generations of Americans and the inspiration of legions of artists, from Albert Bierstadt and Thomas Moran in the nineteenth century to Ansel Adams and Eliot Porter in the twentieth.[14] Leading newspapers like the New York Times and the Christian Science Monitor, intellectual journals like Harpers and Atlantic, and popular magazines like Newsweek and Sports Illustrated regularly carry articles about wildland recreation. Extended photo essays adorn the pages of Life, Sunset, and National Geographic. Contemporary writers carry on the long tradition of examining nature and human existence as revealed in natural settings. Writers like Wendell Berry, Annie Dillard, Anne LaBastille, John McPhee, Ann Zwinger, Terry Tempest Williams, Barry Lopez, and Peter Matthiessen help us discover and interpret nature's ways and meanings. Thus, in law, art, and literature Americans repeatedly affirm that wildland recreation is a vital component of national life.

As our population and economy continue to expand, wildland recreation is likely to become even more important to us. Open space near cities is threatened by urban sprawl, and mineral development, water projects, and hazardous waste disposal sites endanger remote areas. In addition, most observers expect that more people will use wildland recreation areas and there will be more conflicts between incompatible types of recreation and between recreation development and the environmental community. All signs point to an intensifying debate over how we manage our wildland recreation estate.

WILDLAND RECREATION AS PUBLIC POLICY

In *Preserving Nature in the National Parks: A History* (1997) NPS historian Richard Sellars reports on his study of natural resource management policies in the national parks since early in the 20th Century. Sellars tries to answer the question, "Why hasn't science been used more often and more explicitly to make decisions regarding the management of natural resources in national parks?" He cites scientific study after scientific study that indicate some fairly clear policy directions that the NPS should take regarding wildlife, forests, water, minerals, and other natural resources. In his concluding chapter, Sellars laments the fact that the NPS still does not use science to guide many of its decisions. Why not? This book provides one answer, that all the science in the world does not negate the power of politics and the policy-making process in the United States. This is not to say that science does not or should not play a role in policy making. Nothing could be further from the truth. However, Sellars concludes that policy and management decisions are often governed by political concerns, and science often plays only a limited role in how those decisions are made.[15] Therefore, it is imperative that students of wildland recreation policy understand how the policy process in the United States works. Understanding the history of current policies and institutions sheds valuable light on the process by which they have emerged and the underlying forces that continue to influence natural resource management.

In America, decisions about how to allocate resources are made primarily in the private marketplace. Wildland recreation on public lands, however, has not traditionally been part of that marketplace. Recreationists are seldom charged fair market value for their experiences. The kayaker plunging down a mountain cascade pays little or nothing directly to the agency responsible for its management. Yet, maintaining that river in its free-flowing state may have meant foregoing many things, including clean hydroelectric power, greater regional economic development, flatwater boating opportunities, and the cold-water fishery created below the dam. The sightseer in a forested area enjoys the sense of untouched nature provided by aesthetically sensitive timber harvesting, while in no direct way paying the price of the extra management care and the opportunity costs of the trees not sent to the mill.

We subsidize wildland recreation for a variety of reasons, including economic logic, democratic theory, practical politics, and sheer inertia. Philosophically, many Americans have thought it healthy and socially beneficial to come in contact with natural landscapes. Many have felt that the benefits of nature should not be restricted to those who can pay for them, and so we have provided wildland recreation opportunities at zero or near-zero cost to all who could find their way to them. Subsidies for wildland recreation have not been unchallenged, however. Arguments for realistic pricing have flared at various times throughout our history. Recently, for example, concern over governmental size and accountability once again brought the issue under intense scrutiny, a subject we address in detail in chapter 11.

The benefits of wildland recreation are being subjected to more and more scientific scrutiny in order to ensure that public expenditures are indeed enhancing societal welfare. For example, an increasing number of park and recreation professionals are advocating the Benefits Approach to Leisure (BAL) as a system for using objective data to guide policy and management decisions.[16] Whatever the arguments for or against subsidizing wildland recreation, the fact remains that many opportunities are provided by government agencies at little or no direct cost to the consumer. If wildland recreation opportunities are essentially unpriced, and if the marketplace does not operate to allocate these resources, choices about them must be made through the political process. In this arena, advocates from many segments of our society openly debate issues. The issues involve basic values and tend, therefore, to be controversial. To provide a framework for understanding the policy arena for wildland recreation, we introduce the issues, ideas, and participants in the policy-making process in the next chapter.

NOTES

1. Reich, *The Power of Public Ideas,* Chapters 1 and 6.
2. The authors agree with Kaplan and Kaplan (1989), Cronon (1995), and Brunson (2000) that naturalness can be conceived as a spectrum. In Brunson's words (p. 231), "naturalness can be seen as a kind of continuum that describes the form of the nature-culture relationship at any given place."

Thus, nature is as important a feature of culture in urban areas as it is in other places. The term "wildland" can be misleading and distracting if it is construed to mean nature that it is "out there"—i.e., somehow separated from urban areas and influences. We feel that the term "wildland" is a state of mind similar to Nash's (1973) definition of the term "wilderness." As such wildlands and wildland recreation can exist at any point on the naturalness continuum from urban to remote. To maintain identity with the first edition of this book, we decided to continue using the term wildland recreation, though at times we use the term outdoor recreation interchangeably.

3. Zimmerman, *World Resources and Industries.*

4. Nash, *Wilderness and the American Mind,* documents early American negativism toward wilderness and traces its old-world antecedents, particularly in Judeo-Christian religion. Irland, *Wilderness Economics and Policy,* attributes these attitudes not to Judeo-Christian religion, but to the Greek scientific tradition and the growth of private property and the market economy in Europe at the end of the middle ages. Bratton, "Battling Satan in the Wilderness," employs a content analysis of the four gospels to demonstrate that wilderness was viewed as a place of great potential for either good or evil, but that overall, wilderness was viewed less negatively than cities.

5. Nash, *Wilderness and the American Mind.*

6. Runte, *National Parks: The American Experience.*

7. Based on data gathered by the Travel Industry Association (TIA) and presented in a keynote address by Suzanne Cook (Senior Vice President for Research and Technology Planning) at the 2000 Outdoor Recreation and Tourism Trends Symposium, Lansing, MI, September 17–19, 2000. The September 11, 2001, terrorist attacks in New York City appeared to dampen the demand for outdoor recreation only termporarily. The tragedy even stimulated certain types of outdoor recreation uses—there were anecdotal reports of Americans purposefully visiting public parks and forests after the September 11 attacks in order to seek respite, sanctuary, and places of contemplation. Furthermore, RoperASW recently released the results of its 2002 "Summer Travel" survey, which revealed that while two-thirds of Americans are planning spring and summer vacations in 2002, the overwhelming majority (82%) plan to stay within the Continental United States ("RoperASW Summer Travel Survey Finds Sharp Rebound in Domestic Vacation Plans", *http://www.roperasw.com/newsroom/news/n0204001.html,* accessed 4/18/2002).

8. From Cordell et al. (1999), *Outdoor Recreation in American Life: A National Assessment of Demand and Supply Trends.*

9. Item 1 is from Cordell et al. (1999), item 2 is from the Wilderness Information Network (2003), "National Wilderness Preservation System" (*http://www.wilderness.net/nwps/db/table_4.cfm*), items 3, 4, and 6–9 are from Cordell et al. (1999). Item 5 is from the National Association of State Park Directors, *http://www.naspd.org/,* "Inventory Statistics," accessed 4/18/02.

10. Item 1 is from Cordell et al. (1999) and item 2 is from the National Association of State Park Directors, *http://www.naspd.org/*, "Visitation Statistics," accessed 4/18/02. Items 3 and 4 are from Cordell et al. (1999) and Kelly and Warnick (1999) *Recreation Trends and Markets: The 21st Century.* Item 5 is from the National Sporting Goods Association, "Ten-Year History of Selected Sports Participation," (*http://www.nsga.org/public/pages/index.cfm?pageid=153*, accessed 4/18/02). Items 6 and 7 are from U.S. Fish and Wildlife Service (2001), "Survey of Fishing, Hunting and Wildlife-Associated Recreation" (*http://info.fws.gov/s.html*).

11. Statistical Abstracts of the United States, Section 26: Arts, Entertainment and Recreation, accessed 4/18/02 from *http://www.census.gov/prod/2002pubs/01statab/arts.pdf*

12. Park Attendance, accessed 4/18/02 from *http://www.saferparks.org/attendance.htm*

13. U.S. Bureau of Economic Analysis, "Personal Consumption Expenditures by Type of Product, 1996–2001."

14. Huth, *Nature and the American,* is especially good on American nature appreciation as shown in art.

15. Hartzog, *Battling for the National Parks,* agrees.

16. See Chapter 11 for further discussion.

CHAPTER 2

THE POLICY PROCESS

THE NATURE OF POLICY

Like truth and beauty, policy is a concept that is subject to diverse interpretations and meanings. We know what a policy is when we see or hear
one or feel its effects. For example, students understand that most instructors have written policies related to late assignments and that the
risks of not living by these policies can be serious. Over numerous years
and instructors, students have come to expect that late work policies are
not open to much debate or subject to substantial change. This example
points out one of the manifestations of policy—a sense of permanence.
Even without reading the syllabus, most students expect that there is a
policy related to late assignments. Once policies have been adopted they
tend to lend stability and predictability to how institutions and individuals act in certain situations, whether that involves turning in late assignments, driving an automobile, or backpacking in a national park. The example also underscores one of the nagging qualities of policy. The
inherent nature of policies to lend order and predictability to how we act
also makes them slow to change. New policies or radical reforms might
be seen as breaking habits that we as a society or as instructors do not want
to break. Therefore, not only are substantial changes in policy slow in
coming, when they do come, changes usually affect only portions of a
given policy.

So, what then is policy? Our interpretation of the term is most nearly captured in the following statement by Heinz Eulau and Kenneth Prewitt.

> Policy is defined as a "standing decision" characterized by behavioral consistency and repetitiveness on the part of both those who make it and those who abide by it.[1]

There are many places one might look for indications of the "behavioral consistency and repetitiveness" that constitute policy for wildland recreation. What come to mind first are public laws, but policy is not limited to laws. Laws are one of the official acts of policy making, but there are other official acts as well. A comprehensive accounting of wildland recreation policy ranges from the macro-level public laws that announce substantive policy goals, congressional appropriations bills, presidential budgets, and executive orders to micro-level management plans and operational policies and procedures established in the field. Between the macro and micro levels are agency rules and court decisions that affect the manner in which macro- and micro-level policies are implemented. In chapters 5 through 9, we concentrate on public laws for forests, parks, wilderness, and urban recreation areas since they are explicit and traceable markers of wildland recreation policy at the macro-level.

In considering these public laws, however, it must be remembered that understanding them is necessary but not sufficient for understanding public policy. The explicit policy statements in public laws may be only loosely related to the actions they are intended to influence.[2] In attempting to carry out congressional mandates, agencies develop rules and management guidelines to clarify their legal mandates and add consistency to their implementation. However, public land managers often discover that the world does not work the way the lawmakers and agency leaders assumed it would, and interpretations and adjustments must be made.

We provide examples of these interpretations and adjustments in chapters 10 and 11. In chapter 10, we show how the application and interpretation of a plethora of federal policy has sculpted planning decisions at Yosemite National Park for over 20 years. In chapter 11, we provide some policy-management "vignettes" based on interviews with wildland recreation managers. These vignettes illustrate how policy implementation is often more an art than a science. Sometimes, presented with only vague policy guidelines or insufficient funding, managers must follow their professional lights and interpret and implement policies to the best of their abilities, enjoying accolades when things go well and, more often, taking the heat when critics find fault.

At the macro level, the executive branch frequently pursues goals in conflict with legislative goals. In the 1970s, for example, in the Federal Water Pollution Control Act, Congress called for extensive federal grants to local governments for the construction of wastewater treatment facilities, but President Nixon refused to spend congressionally authorized funds because he wanted to slow the growth of the federal budget. Under President Reagan, a broad array of environmental policies was unsupported for reasons both of budget-balancing and political ideology.[3] More recently, President Clinton set aside numerous public lands as national monuments despite the protests of Republican lawmakers who supported private property rights initiatives and wanted to reduce federal land acquisition. President George W. Bush is emphasizing federal government expenditures for repairs and maintenance over increased funding for land acquisition even though numerous proposals for new parks are on legislators' agendas.

Conflicts between legislative and executive policy goals are not the only sources of slippage in policy implementation. Within the Congress, as well, incompatible goals are frequently featured. For example, in the 1980s and 1990s, under the leadership of Representative Phillip Burton, Representative Bruce Vento, and other legislators, Congress added many new units to the National Park System. To translate ideas into reality, the legislation authorized expenditure of government funds for land acquisition and development. However, congressional purse strings are in the hands of a different set of committees with different motivations, and appropriations for the national parks lagged far behind authorizations.[4] A third source of the looseness between governmental policy goals and actions arises from litigation brought by those who believe their interests are suffering under the new policy. In the 1970s, the procedural requirements of the National Environmental Policy Act of 1969 joined with relaxed rules on standing to sue to produce a flurry of environmentalist lawsuits. Judicial decisions resulting from this litigation, combined with the threat of additional legal actions, strongly shaped federal environmental policy.[5] From the 1990s to the present, legal actions pertaining to the takings clause of the Constitution have resulted in legislative proposals that would expand the definition of "takings" to include compensation for regulations (e.g., the Endangered Species Act) that inhibit private, commercial development.[6]

Policies, whether in the form of public laws, court verdicts, or administrative decisions, do not arise in a vacuum. They are the result of group and individual struggle for control of scarce resources. Because each group has its own goals, actions that favor one interest often threaten another. The evolution of policy over time reflects the changing balance of this group struggle. Thus, any given policy is only a temporary course of action, which can be amended and even reversed.

This is particularly true for wildland recreation policies. As the national economy waxes and wanes, as the structure of our population changes, as new recreation technologies emerge, as fads arise and fade, and as basic attitudes toward nature change, wildland recreation policy changes. The specific rules of the game can be altered very quickly. For example, in 1972 President Nixon responded to mounting environmentalist pressure by issuing Executive Order 11644. This order directed federal land managers to regulate off-road vehicle use of their properties. With the stroke of the presidential pen, the freedoms of off-road vehicle enthusiasts were suddenly and significantly restricted. Similarly, the National Park Service issued a proposed rule in 1999 that would significantly restrict or eliminate altogether the use of personal watercraft (PWCs) and snowmobiles in national parks. That same year, President Clinton issued an executive ruling that imposed a ban on road building in roadless areas of national forests. As this book is being written, the Bush administration is attempting to soften or eliminate both the road building and the snowmobile/PWC restrictions ordered by President Clinton.

If such fundamental changes in policy are not to continually take us by surprise, we must have a sense of how the policy process works and an awareness of some of the broader issues involved.

AN ONGOING DEBATE—THE SCRIPT

Basic Issues

We view the policy process as an ongoing debate about particular enduring issues. The names of the debaters may change, but the essence of what is said—the script—remains fairly constant throughout the years. New rounds of debate are prompted by shifts in social and economic conditions, the flowering of new recreation activities, and by dissatisfaction with those who hold the power at the time. Despite the diversity of their origins, there is remarkable continuity in the arguments.

The major long-standing argument in wildland recreation is between those who want to develop natural landscapes for economic or other forms of personal gain and those who see value in preserving landscapes as nature made them. Controversies over river development projects are good examples of the preservation/development argument. In these battles, the virtues of a free-flowing river are weighed against the benefits of electric power, flood control, and other economic goods. These arguments have their parallels in controversies over timber harvesting, oil exploration, highway and airport construction, navigation projects, aircraft overflights, solid waste dumps, urban expansion and other forms of economic development in wildlands.

In the course of these struggles, it is often tempting to identify one side as the "good guys" and the other as the "bad guys."[7] In most of the rhetorical flourishes that accompany these debates, in fact, both sides claim to represent the public interest.[8] A less partisan viewpoint is that most of the conflicts represent public choices between two goods.[9] Dams, roads, and reservoirs are one kind of public good, part of the drive for economically useful internal improvement which has been with us since colonial days. However, choosing these improvements means foregoing another sort of public good represented by untouched waterways.

This preservation/development struggle was evident during the 1973–74 oil crisis, when we were made acutely aware of our dependency on foreign oil. Lawmakers tried to spark local ingenuity by requiring electric companies to purchase power from small hydroelectric projects. Congress's intent in this legislation was to encourage entrepreneurs to retrofit old dams, especially in the Northeast where fuel costs were high and old mill towns were in decline. Along with the applications for retrofitting, however, came requests from business leaders wishing to tap into these guaranteed profits by building new dams. This prospect brought howls of protest from anglers, canoeists, and other river lovers. Thus, the conflict between one set of public goods—business activity and cheap, domestic energy—became pitted against another set associated with free-flowing streams.[10] The current controversy over attempts to explore for oil in the Arctic National Wildlife Refuge is another example of the public goods debate. In this case, those who want to tap the oil as a way to decrease our dependency on foreign sources are pitted against those who see the refuge as a fragile biological resource that protects wildlife and unspoiled nature.

Struggles like these have been with us since the early days of our country. The general historical trend has been toward a strengthening of the preservation side, as growing urbanization and industrialization have imposed human forms on natural landscapes, while giving many the time, money, and perspective to appreciate what is left. The trend, however, is not unidirectional. In the 1970s, the preservation side achieved a high-water mark, while in the early 1980s concern over America's economy shifted the initiative back toward development. In the 1990s, the emphasis was more of a middle-of-the-road approach. With tremendous economic prosperity based on international trade and the explosion of growth in the technology sector, development increased, but some forms of development (e.g., information technology) were relatively clean. At the same time, as previously noted, the Clinton administration was successful in protecting additional public lands from further development. As we enter the twenty-first century, advocates of fossil fuel development are in control of the national administration, and growing turbulence in the Middle East is being offered as justification for expanding domestic energy production.

A related conflict exists between different forms of wildland recreation. Struggles along this philosophical fault line are found between those who want to promote mass recreation, encouraging all who can to enjoy the outdoors, and those who seek intense personal contact with undisturbed nature.[11] Mass recreation advocates argue that America is a democracy, and that if the wildlands belong to all the people, then all the people should be able to use them. This position calls for the development of roads, lodging, campgrounds, picnic areas, sports facilities, and other developments that will reduce the inconvenience of "roughing it" and entice people from all walks of life to visit natural areas. Advocates of purist recreation, on the other hand, think that mass recreation use and its accompanying tourist trappings destroy the very thing the wildlands are supposed to offer. Purists would like to restrict the number of wildland visitors and, if necessary, regulate their behavior to protect nature and the experiences it provides.

As with the preservation/development debate, both mass and purist recreation advocates claim to speak for the public interest. The middle-ground position is that neither "industrial tourism" nor "contemplative recreation" is wholly good or bad, but that decisions must be made on a site-by-site basis to provide for a reasonable balance of different opportunities.[12] In addition, such decisions must somehow accommodate the unknown recreational interests of future generations.[13]

These major lines of values conflict have, to some extent, been embodied in our leading wildland recreation agencies. The Forest Service was founded on a clearly articulated utilitarian philosophy; America's national forests were to be used for human benefit. Preservation of nature for nature's sake was anathema for Gifford Pinchot and others who established the Forest Service. The primary mission of the Park Service, on the other hand, has been to protect scenic and historic resources from economic exploitation and to encourage people to enjoy them.

The picture is not without its complications, however. Political and social forces cause both agencies to sway with the times. From the mid-1960s to the early-1990s, the Park Service developed visitor facilities that sometimes threatened to overwhelm nature,[14] whereas the timber-minded Forest Service assumed the role of one the world's leading wilderness management agencies. Recently, changing environmental values and ecosystem thinking have led the Forest Service to emphasize forest health, biodiversity, water conservation and urban programs over timber production.[15] Likewise, the Park Service is moving back toward a preservationist stance, restricting motorized recreation and private automobiles and moving developments away from fragile areas,[16] while simultaneously increasing its assemblage of historic and cultural parks.

Behind the evolving struggle over particular wildland policy issues lay some fundamental ideas about how land should be used. These ideas, eloquently argued at various times in history, have provided the intellectual framework for the public policy debates and serve as the basis for chapters 3 through 9.

THE IMPORTANCE OF IDEAS

The social actions, laws, and other policies relating to wildland recreation have clearly been shaped, at least in part, by ideas. Ideas reflect important values, and the debates about the relative merits of these ideas have a profound influence on policy making.[17] Thinkers and writers such as George Perkins Marsh, Henry David Thoreau, Frederick Law Olmsted, Marjory Stoneman Douglas, and Rachel Carson have influenced the way we as a nation think about nature and wilderness. As important as ideas are, however, direct links between policies and their intellectual origins are often obscure. Many years and many layers of influence may come between an idea and its expression in policy. Writing in 1936, with World War II looming, British economist John Maynard Keynes stressed the import of ideas for the course of public affairs:

. . . madmen in authority, who hear voices in the air, are distilling their
frenzy from some academic scribbler of a few years back . . . Soon or late,
it is ideas, not vested interests, which are dangerous for good or evil.[18]

The time span between the expression of ideas and their policy effects
can be relatively short. Rachel Carson's powerful descriptions about the
effects of pesticides in *Silent Spring* (1962) helped spark the environmental movement in less than a decade. Usually, however, ideas have
been articulated many years before actions are taken, and they have had
time to spread through influential sectors of the society. Here, they lie in
wait for a favorable alignment of social and economic conditions. Powerful ideas not only spread but also grow; they attain a life of their own,
and others develop them beyond their original conception. George
Perkins Marsh's ideas about watersheds seeped into the collective consciousness of scientists, resource managers, and politicians over the
course of nearly half a century before they were employed in the drive to
establish the eastern national forests.[19] Henry Thoreau's ideas about
mankind and nature, expressed in the mid-1800s, became potent ammunition in the conservation battles of the 1970s and beyond. Frederick Law
Olmsted's conceptions of outdoor recreation's role in democracy helped
to redefine the purposes of America's national parks almost a century after they were first expressed.[20] Marjory Stoneman Douglas's ideas about
protecting the Everglades were first expressed in the 1930s and '40s, but
they prevented certain commercial developments in the 1970s and influenced recent Congressional action regarding the restoration of water quality in the area.[21]

Once ideas have been developed by spirited thinkers, who brings them
into the public consciousness? Who debates the issues and decides directions for wildland recreation? There are two ways to answer these questions. The first way flows from the traditional model of government in
which government officials are rather passive recipients of information
about citizen wants via the usual democratic processes (e.g., votes and
phone calls) and provide solutions to problems where there is some consensus about the nature and definition of the problems, the range of possible solutions, and who is to solve them. In the second, more ideal way,
public managers have a bigger responsibility—not just to provide what
they are told citizens want for themselves, but to engage citizens in re-
thinking how problems are defined, alternative solutions developed, and
responsibilities for actions allocated.[22] As such, "spirited thinkers" do not

have to be famous historical figures.[23] They may be legislators or members of their staffs, agency officials, or public natural resource managers. They may emerge, and indeed are expected to emerge, during the process of capacity building, collaboration, idea generation, and public discourse. This latter, more ideal model is especially critical in dealing with natural resource problems, which are typically messy and where consensus is elusive. We address the ideal way at the end of this chapter and again in chapter 11. In the next section, we meet the players who shape public policy and help it to evolve—that is to say, the more traditional model of how the policy process works.

SHAPING WILDLAND RECREATION POLICY— THE PLAYERS

Congress

A number of standing committees in the Senate and the House of Representatives shape congressional policy for wildland recreation. Substantive legislation for the Forest Service is written in the House by the Committee on Resources and, in the Senate, jointly by the Agriculture, Nutrition and Forestry Committee and the Committee on Energy and Natural Resources. Substantive legislation for the National Park Service is written in the House by the Committee on Resources and, in the Senate, by the Committee on Energy and Natural Resources. The substantive committees are joined in shaping legislative policy by the appropriations committees, which decide how federal funds will be spent (see Figure 2–1). In addition, the actions of other procedural and substantive committees may strongly influence congressional action for wildland recreation; the Rules Committee decides how bills will be considered and by whom, and committees on public works pursue many policies which impact wildland resources.[24]

Congressional standing committees are often organized into subcommittees that have jurisdiction over the policies and programs of an executive agency. Both national forests and national parks have such subcommittees as shown in Figure 2–1. It is in these subcommittees where legislation, such as the proposal for a new park or restrictions on aircraft overflights, is initially considered before it goes to the full committee.[25] We do not want to understate the importance of these subcommittees in

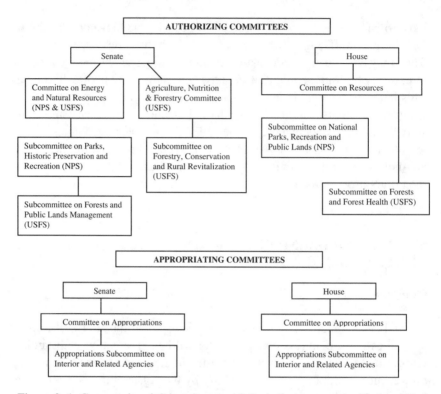

Figure 2–1. Congressional Committees with Jurisdiction over the National Park Service (NPS) and U.S. Forest Service (USFS), 107th Congress

the policy process, for it is at this level that substantial changes or delays can, and often do, occur. Depending on which party, Republican or Democratic, controls the majority, and whether or not the majority is the same as the president's party, the makeup of the subcommittees governs which policies move forward and which do not. Subcommittees also take and request testimony from experts and representatives of various lobby groups in the process of making decisions and amending legislation. In short, once a bill is placed on their agenda, the subcommittees become the first line in the gauntlet a bill must run to become law.

Congress not only enacts laws, raises revenues, and appropriates funds, it also has the power of oversight. After passing legislation, Congress may conduct oversight hearings or request special studies, such as those conducted by the Government Affairs Office, to make certain the agencies are carrying out policies and programs as intended. Oversight is part of the checks and balances system provided by the Constitution between the legislative and executive branches. Committees or subcommittees may invite testimony or subpoena witnesses as part of the oversight process. In this way, legislators hear directly from constituents of the agencies. The results may include changing enabling legislation, modifying the administrative rules used to implement broad legislation, or appropriating or not appropriating funds for the agencies.[26] According to George B. Hartzog, Jr., Director of the National Park Service from 1964–1973, oversight hearings "are unglamorous and difficult but indispensable tasks, if government is to be efficient, responsive and responsible."[27]

It is sometimes assumed that Congress functions essentially as a sounding board and broker for others' initiatives, and that individual senators and representatives have few ideas and goals of their own. On the contrary, however, individuals in the legislative branch often display the expertise and sustained commitment that constitutes policy leadership.[28] To cite a few illustrative cases, Senator Edmund Muskie made a personal contribution to shaping air and water pollution control legislation, as did Senator Hubert Humphrey for forestry, Senators Dianne Feinstein and Russell Feingold for wilderness and other protected areas, Senators John Culver and Max Baucus for endangered species, Representatives Phillip Burton and Bruce Vento for parks, Representative Morris Udall for public lands, Representative Sidney Yates for urban forestry initiatives, and Representative John Dingell for fisheries and wildlife.

More obscure but still vital to the policy process are the hundreds of men and women who serve Congress in legislative and administrative staff positions, and as subject matter experts in the Congressional Research Service, the Congressional Budget Office, and the General Accounting Office. Taken together, the legislative branch commands a wealth of expertise and institutional memory, which it brings to bear in exercising policy leadership.[29]

Agencies

Our system of public wildlands is managed by a host of agencies at all levels of government.[30] At the federal level, the Forest Service and the Park Service represent two types of management: multiple use and limited use. The Forest Service is representative of multiple use land management agencies where the primary challenge is to balance economic use and preservation. The other major multiple use agencies are the Bureau of Reclamation, Corps of Engineers, and Tennessee Valley Authority, all of which offer outdoor recreation opportunities as part of their water projects, and the Bureau of Land Management. The Park Service represents agencies that must seek a balance between preservation and limited human use. For the Park Service, the primary questions concern the types and amount of recreational use to permit. The other federal land management agency with a limited human use mandate is the U.S. Fish and Wildlife Service, which provides highly regulated wildlife-related recreation associated with its wildlife refuges. In addition to these federal land-management agencies, there are numerous other agencies at different levels of government that provide wildland recreation opportunities.

The Forest Service, located in the Department of Agriculture, manages over 192 million acres of land in 177 units: 155 national forests (188 million acres) and 22 national grasslands (4 million acres). Most Forest Service land is in the mountainous West, with smaller acreage in the East. The western National Forests were established first, by reservation from the public domain lands.[31] The eastern National Forests were acquired later, largely by purchase of properties that had been badly abused. In addition to outdoor recreation, the National Forests are managed to produce other renewable natural resources—wood, forage, water, fish, and wildlife—on a sustained yield basis. Recreation on the National Forests tends to be dispersed across the landscape rather than concentrated around particular attractions. Popular activities include driving for pleasure, hunting, fishing, hiking, horseback riding, camping, canoeing, off-road vehicle use, picnicking, snowmobiling, and cross-country skiing. The National Forests also include areas that are leased to ski resorts, youth camps, and cabin owners. Total recreational use on the National Forests in 1996 was over 859 million visits.[32]

The Bureau of Land Management (BLM), located in the Department of the Interior, is in charge of the nation's remaining public domain lands. These lands, most of which are in the arid and semiarid West, are primarily what was left over after years of transferring economically valuable lands to individuals and other agencies. Today they are mainly used for mining, grazing, and recreation. As a result of past political machinations, BLM also manages some outstanding timberlands in Oregon and California. At its height in the 1970s, BLM was responsible for over 450 million acres of land.[33] Now, following settlement of the Alaska lands issue and other land transfers, the figure is 262 million acres. Until recently, there was little interest in what happened on the majority of BLM's arid lands. Lately, however, mineral exploration and off-road vehicle use on these lands, coupled with growing environmentalist interest in deserts, has led to vigorous controversy, particularly in the California Desert east of Los Angeles and in the State of Utah. Recreation on BLM lands is dispersed; in fact, simply contacting recreationists has been a major challenge for the agency with its extensive holdings and small staff. Altogether, BLM lands received almost 54 million recreation visits in 2000.[34]

Three water development agencies producing recreation opportunities for millions of people across the nation are the Bureau of Reclamation, Corps of Engineers, and Tennessee Valley Authority. The Bureau of Reclamation, housed in the Department of the Interior, is engaged primarily in administering 348 multiple-purpose reservoirs to supply irrigation water in the 17 western states. The Bureau's 308 recreation sites were visited by 90 million people in 2000.[35] The Corps of Engineers (CE or Corps) is located in the Department of Defense. The Corps was originally concerned primarily with navigation, but it has since broadened its scope and is now engaged in a wide variety of waterway modification and environmental restoration projects. In terms of recreation, the most important of these are the multiple purpose reservoirs. These impoundments, ubiquitous in the South, provide water, power, downstream flow augmentation, and flood control in addition to fishing, boating, and camping on adjoining lands. The Corps manages 4,330 recreation sites at 456 lakes and reservoirs. In 1999 there were 385 million recreation visits on Corps' projects,[36] making it the leader in water-based recreation in the United States and second only to the Forest Service in terms of total visitation.[37] The Tennessee Valley Authority (TVA) also offers water-based and related recreation on its 29 multiple purpose reservoirs, which are located along 650 miles of the Tennessee River and its tributaries in seven south central states. The TVA hosted 604,000 visits in 1996.[38] All three water development agencies are now struggling to redefine their missions as reservoir proposals are increasingly challenged, as economically viable sites disappear, and as competing uses (e.g., hydroelectric power versus free-flowing rivers for recreation and wildlife) must be reconciled.

The National Park Service, located in the Department of the Interior, manages 379 units totaling 83 million acres of land. The Park Service does not attempt to produce economic benefits directly from the natural resources it manages, so activities like logging and mining are excluded. Economic activity does exist on NPS lands, however, in the form of concessionaires. Concessionaires provide visitor services such as food and lodging. Although the National Park Service includes an incredible diversity of resources, the large, western nature parks like Yellowstone, Glacier, Yosemite, and Grand Canyon have historically set the tone for the Service. These areas were the scenic spectaculars of the developing West, and the Park Service's original mission was to protect them from economic despoliation and encourage Americans to visit them. From that starting point, the agency's responsibilities have grown to include urban parks, historic monuments, parkways, seashores and lakeshores, Civil War battlefields, trails, scenic rivers, nature preserves, and heritage corridors. In 2002, all these places received more than 278 million recreation visits.[39]

The U.S. Fish and Wildlife Service (FWS), also in the Department of the Interior, is responsible for enhancing fish and wildlife populations on nearly 700 field units (national wildlife refuges, national fish hatcheries, etc.), which comprise nearly 93 million acres of land and water. Primary recreational uses of the refuge system are hunting, fishing, wildlife viewing, photography, and nature study. In 2000, FWS areas accommodated 38 million recreation visits.[40]

In addition to these federal land and water management agencies, the separate states are heavily involved in providing wildland recreation opportunities. In 2002, state departments of parks managed a total of 8.5 million acres. State forests provide a variety of recreation opportunities on their 1.36 million acres of land, and use of the 350,000 acres of state fish and wildlife areas is growing. Adding recreation, natural, historic, wildlife, forest, environmental, and miscellaneous areas, the state system contained more than 4,644 operating areas in 2002, an estate of just over 13 million acres.[41] There were more than 766 million recreation visits to state park systems in the United States in 2001.[42]

Responsibility for coordinating outdoor recreation planning across all the agencies currently rests with the National Park Service. The Park Service was originally given this task in 1936, but dissatisfaction with their efforts led to the creation of the Bureau of Outdoor Recreation (BOR) in the early 1960s. BOR worked for 17 years to improve and bring coherence to the nation's outdoor recreation service system. Among BOR's most important accomplishments were managing the Land and Water Conservation Fund,[43] directing statewide outdoor recreation planning efforts, and providing technical planning assistance to states and localities. BOR also produced several nationwide outdoor recreation plans, but their impact was limited. In the late 1970s, BOR was expanded into the Heritage Conservation and Recreation Service, and in the early 1980s, HCRS was dismantled for a variety of political reasons.

BOR's fate is indicative of our consistent inability as a nation to develop a coherent overall program for outdoor recreation.[44] One reason may be the multitude of players in the game. Some have looked with horror at the apparent chaos in outdoor recreation and have been prompted to advocate centralized authority. Others have looked at the same chaos with a sense of equanimity, seeing in the diffusion of responsibility a resilient system, stable against unidirectional stupidity and full of potential for creatively responding to local needs and changing times.[45]

Whatever your overall judgment, you should recognize that none of the agencies mentioned are passive recipients of policy directives from legislative or executive bodies.[46] Agencies, like individuals, try to protect themselves from constant buffeting by external forces. They seek to control their environments and to shape them to their purposes. Unfortunately, perhaps, their own purposes are not always clear or consistent. Neither of the agencies highlighted in this book, the Forest Service or the Park Service, has enjoyed an unambiguous and steady sense of purpose. The Forest Service has had to try to balance the mix of economic and noneconomic benefits flowing from its lands, while the Park Service has had to balance its mandate to preserve nature against its mandate to accommodate visitors. For both agencies, the balancing act is a perpetual challenge forced by changing conditions in the larger society they serve. Just as individuals must continually reassess their goals if they are to be successful, agencies must also reexamine their missions in order to satisfy the public.

The Courts

What happens when citizens, organizations, or industries are dissatisfied with the manner in which legislative bodies or executive agencies carry out their agendas? In these instances, the third branch of government, the judiciary, often becomes involved. In fact, courts have played an increasing role in influencing forest, wilderness, and park policy.[47] Cubbage et al. provide a succinct summary of the means and structure by which courts exert their influence:

> They (the courts) hear cases regarding public laws—the general rules that govern social life. Courts have the authority to settle controversies between individuals who bring suit and those who respond or defend themselves. They also may review legislative acts to determine if they are constitutional.

The federal and most state courts have a three-tier system for civil and criminal cases. The lowest level consists of district courts, the intermediate level of appellate courts, and the highest of a supreme court. In civil cases, judges may issue temporary or permanent stop work orders (injunctions), order corrective action, or assess fines.[48]

Most suits are filed either by industry groups challenging natural resource agency policies as too restrictive or by environmentalists contending they are too lax. Individuals may also file suits against agencies, as in recent cases involving private property rights controversies. Judicial review of agency management actions can cause significant delays or stalemates, and slowing or stalling unwanted actions may constitute a "victory" for a litigant. Thus, litigation is a tactic often used today by all sides in natural resources disputes.[49] We will see examples of the power of the courts in delaying and changing agency management decisions in chapter 11 where we discuss case studies pertaining to endangered species, wilderness management, and recreation accessibility.

Interest Groups and Industry

Other influential players in the creation of wildland recreation policy are interest groups and businesses. Speaking for the preservation interests are groups like The Wilderness Society, Izaak Walton League, National Audubon Society, Sierra Club, National Wildlife Federation, Trout Unlimited, National Parks Conservation Association, and Save the Redwoods League. Commercial recreation interests are represented by groups like the National Campground Owners Association, Eastern Professional River Outfitters, Recreational Vehicle Industry Association, American Recreation Coalition, and National Sporting Goods Association, along with equipment manufacturers like Coleman and Evinrude. Economic development interests are well represented by organizations like the National Association of Manufacturers, the National Forest Products Association, and the American Mining Congress.

It is a mistake simply to label these groups "special interests" and assume that the policy process is distorted by their lobbying activities. These interests play a vital role in developing information and articulating the concerns of our multifaceted society.[50] Nor are they the monolithic institutions they are sometimes made out to be. For example, within the environmental groups there is often extreme conflict over strategies and between those who want to expand the agenda and those who believe in focusing on a limited number of issues. Though the internal struggles of business and industrial interests are less public than those of environmental groups, they are just as real. Like the agencies, interest groups and industries are engaged in continual reassessment of purposes and strategies.[51]

Professional Organizations

Professional resource management organizations are active participants in the policy process as well. The Society of American Foresters, the Wildlife Society, the National Parks Conservation Association, and the National Recreation and Parks Association are among a host of professional organizations active in the ongoing wildland recreation debate. These organizations, like other interest groups, develop information and feed ideas to Congress and other players. Like the other players, professional organizations are engaged in a steady stream of internal debate and interaction with their political environment. One need only look at a few issues of the *Journal of Forestry* to discover how vigorous the internal debate can be.

Individuals

It has been said that nothing important happens unless individuals are willing to throw their energies into the cause.[52] Certainly this has been true in the history of wildland recreation policy.[53] In the historical account that follows, you will be introduced to a handful of the thousands of people who have contributed their intelligence and effort to the building and shaping of America's wildland estate. Most of those to whom we are indebted as we enjoy these places have been ignored by history. Particularly obscure are the many contributions made by women and minorities.[54] Yet, historians have documented how women and womens' organizations of the early twentieth century stopped the exploitation of bird species for plumage in women's hats, helped save the redwoods from extinction, lobbied successfully for the creation the first forestry schools, and were instrumental in the protection of forests and parks.[55] Native Americans, who gave up or were forced to evacuate many of their lands that then became national parks and forests, are beginning to regain access to sacred sites within these federal lands and influencing how they are managed.[56] They have also influenced the development of earth-centered spirituality among some environmental groups and religious organizations and the development of certain outdoor skills and practices among youth-serving organizations, like the Boy Scouts of America.[57]

The Media

Throughout history, the media have played a powerful role in shaping Americans' images about natural landscapes and in bringing attention to areas of societal debate. Sometimes the media attention becomes so pervasive and attracts so much attention that politicians, bureaucrats, and managers have no choice but to take some sort of policy action. When you read about John Muir and Hetch Hetchy, you will see how his powerful and persistent writings about the controversial dam in Yosemite attracted national media attention and eventually forced a political decision that continues to have repercussions in national park policy even today. At the same time, Gifford Pinchot was equally as successful with the media:

> Pinchot's aggressive use of government resources to present his conservation policy to newspapers and magazines in a form acceptable as news allowed Pinchot to dominate natural resources management discussions at the beginning of the twentieth century and to remain an influence in those discussions today.[58]

David Brower effectively used the media in his campaign to end dam building in the Grand Canyon. Marjory Stoneman Douglas's media relationship helped put an end to the destruction of the Everglades. Edward Neeman, editor of the *Memphis Press Scimitar,* almost single-handedly led the campaign to create the Great Smokey Mountains National Park[59]. Earth Day, the environmental movement, and many of the outdoor recreation and land management laws of the 1960s and '70s were born out of societal conflicts that were amplified by the media. In addition to these high profile issues, the media can also be effective in assisting management agencies to develop positive public images, explain policy decisions, and advertise public programs. Poor media relations can result in negative images, misunderstandings of policies and regulations, and lack of attention to critical resource matters.

SETTING THE STAGE FOR POLICY

In addition to issues, ideas, and a willing cast of characters, other elements must be in place before major policy actions will occur. One of the most important elements is discontent. Someone must be sufficiently annoyed with the status quo to be willing to work to change it. Policy actions result from discontent, conflict, and the desire to resolve that conflict. Much of American public policy develops incrementally, not as an effort to reach desired future states, but rather to solve known problems.[60]

Discontent can lead to specific policy changes only because our political system is designed to adapt and adjust. This underlying potential for responsiveness is something we can come to take for granted. In certain countries, control of some specific behavior like irresponsible timber harvesting may not be possible except as part of more sweeping social and governmental change.

A responsive political system and some unhappy people are not enough to elicit policy, of course. There must be some degree of agreement on the causes of and solutions to the problem. Once again, the work of intellectuals and "policy entrepreneurs"[61] is important here, together with the practical experiences of managers and the concerns of interest groups. The media are vital to creating some collective sense of purpose. Frequently, blue-ribbon commissions are called into service, such as the Outdoor Recreation Resources Review Commission in the early 1960s and the President's Commission on American Outdoors that concluded its formal work in 1987.[62] The academic community may contribute scientific and historical research to these consciousness-raising exercises. Sometimes, the experience of other nations is imported; the concepts of scientific forestry, pastoral urban parks, and governmental action to preserve landscape values on privately owned land all were imports. All of these sources are tapped in our search for possible ways to solve problems.

Even when we have acknowledged a problem and identified a proposed remedy, it sometimes takes a dramatic event to capture our collective attention long enough to bring the problem to government.[63] We tend to operate with a crisis mentality, whether the crisis is real or only perceived. For example, scientific reports since Rachel Carson's 1962 book *Silent Spring* had prepared the ground for increasingly stronger pesticide regulation, but it took the discoveries at Love Canal to prompt passage of the so-called Superfund toxic waste disposal program. Occasionally, one crisis may be so dramatic that later policy actions can be directly attributed to it. More often, events and information build up until the time is ripe, and then the dissatisfied parties use the next crisis to advance their cause. Old crises have a way of resurfacing in these situations, as in the case of the Hetch Hetchy dam in Yosemite National Park, which was used as a rallying point in preservation struggles half a century after it was built.

PRODUCING POLICY

Various authors have described the policy formation process as consisting of six steps—problem formation, policy agenda, policy formulation,
policy adoption, policy implementation, and policy evaluation (see Figure 2–2). Each step constitutes a subsystem of players for a given issue at
a given time.

Once we have a recognized problem (step one), the problem must make
its way to the political agenda where it can be scrutinized and debated
(step two). Placing the problem on a political body's agenda is not always
an easy task. At various times, the media, advocacy groups, individuals,
government agencies, and even catalytic crises are responsible for the
problem's being placed on the agenda. Powerless and underrepresented
groups struggle or frequently fail to get past this step. Once the problem
is on the agenda, the political system officially comes into play. Ideas

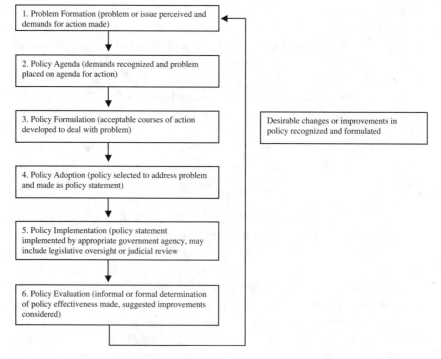

Figure 2–2. Six-Step Policy Process[64]

about workable solutions to the problem are formulated (step three) and formal policies are adopted (step four). The primary actors in steps three and four are the "subgovernments" comprised of congressional subcommittees, agency specialists, interest group leaders, and others with a direct interest in the issue.[65] There are subgovernments for each major issue area, such as defense, transportation, banking, housing, and environment. The tendency for these subgovernments to operate in relative isolation from others and to resist outside influence has led political scientists to call them "iron triangles."[66]

If the pressure for new policy is strong and sustained, and if a course of action can be agreed upon, the political system is likely to adopt (step four) a policy. At this point, however, the policy process is far from finished. The signing of a new law is little more than a temporary cease-fire among competing forces. In all likelihood, the social conflicts associated with the problem have not been finally resolved, nor is the law itself free from continued conflict. Congressional laws are cast broadly and must be translated into more detailed agency regulations (step five). These regulations are subject to public review, and discussions concerning their interpretation are often heated. Then, the law must be implemented by agencies in the field (step five). These actions, carried out under congressional and administrative policy guidance, are also subject to public review and court challenge (step six).

This cycle may repeat itself again and again as policies evolve. We "muddle through," in the words of political scientist Charles Lindblom, in an evolutionary process:

> It is decision-making through small or incremental moves on particular problems rather than through a comprehensive reform program. It is also endless; it takes the form of an indefinite sequence of policy moves. Moreover, it is exploratory in that the goals of policy-making continue to change as new experience with policy throws new light on what is possible and desirable.[67]

Policy cycles have varying time frames, depending on a multitude of conditions. While some policies have very long histories, as in the case of the ecological restoration of the Everglades, others arise relatively quickly, as in the case of the National Environmental Policy Act. Whether the policy time frame is short or long, the process is continuous and dynamic. Even as the Congressional committees finish their markup of new legislation, changing social and economic conditions begin to cause the dissatisfaction that prompts a new round of policy-making. One need not be a prophet to predict that even as the President ceremoniously signs a new bill into law, efforts to amend, enlarge, or repeal it will sooner or later be made. The competing interests, who have compromised to permit the new policy, will search for ways to achieve more of their goals. Then, when the timing is right and the issues and players are once again in place, the cycle of policy-making will begin anew.

Like most models, the stage model presented in Figure 2–2 is an oversimplification of how the policy process works in real life and has its share of critics.[68] Nonetheless, it has survived the test of time because of its usefulness in obtaining a beginning level of understanding of how policies evolve. Furthermore, dividing the process into stages permits clarity in where various authors focus their scholarly attention. In this book, we stress the importance of the problem formation and policy implementation stages of Figure 2–2. Other authors focus more on how agenda setting occurs or the role of the courts in evaluating and re-interpreting policy.[69]

One of the focal points of this book is the explicit linkage between policy and management, which has typically been represented by step five of Figure 2–2. Because of this critical implementation step in the policy process, professional resource managers must develop a basic grasp of natural resource policies and the workings of the policy process. They must understand congressional, administrative, and judicial intent in the policies governing their activities. They must testify when challenged, and they must develop and defend budgets in a policy context.[70] Managers must facilitate public discourse about the resources for which they are responsible, and rather than simply providing forums where those with power can express their concerns, managers must also seek ways of involving disenfranchised, neglected, or underrepresented interests.[71] This facilitation step is not shown in the stage model, and it is a good example of how the model is an oversimplification of the policy process. Problem definition may not be restricted to the beginning of the process, but may be continued by agency bureaucrats and managers at the policy implementation stage. This implies a nontraditional role for management in setting the policy-making agenda and it argues for managers ". . . to engage the public in an ongoing dialogue over what problems should be addressed, what is at stake in such decisions, and how to strengthen the public's capacities to deal with similar problems in the future."[72]

The most successful government leaders have been those who have purposefully sculpted public visions about what is desirable and possible for society to accomplish.[73] We argue that the same holds true for wildland recreation managers, and in chapters 10 and 11 of the book we will illustrate how. In the next seven chapters, we present some of the historical events that helped set the stage for current wildland recreation policy actions and debates in America.

NOTES

1. Eulau and Prewitt, *Labyrinths in Democracy,* Indianapolis: Bobbs-Merrill, as found in Jones, *An Introduction to the Study of Public Policy,* 2nd ed., p. 5.
2. Jenkins, *Policy Analysis,* Chapter 6.
3. Odell, "Congress Tells It Like It's Supposed to Be." Clarke and McCool, *Staking out the Terrain,* agree.
4. Clarke and McCool (p. 90) provide data that support this phenomenon.
5. Dana and Fairfax, *Forest and Range Policy,* 2nd ed., p. 312, discuss the Scenic Hudson and Mineral King cases, which expanded legal standing to sue beyond those who personally claim injury.
6. Meltz et al., *The Takings Issue: Constitutional Limits on Land Use Control and Environmental Regulations.*
7. Nash, *American Environmentalism: Readings in Conservation History,* p. 7.
8. Susskind and Weinstein, "Towards a Theory of Environmental Dispute Resolution."
9. An engaging account of the good vs. good conflict in environmental matters is McPhee, *Encounters with the Archdruid.*
10. Reisner, "Power, Profit and Preservation."
11. Foresta, *America's National Parks and Their Keepers;* Sax, *Mountains without Handrails.*
12. The phrase "industrial tourism" is from Abbey, *Desert Solitaire;* "contemplative recreation" is from Sax, *Mountains without Handrails.*
13. A classic illustration of such a balancing act is found in the history of Central Park. Park professionals, led by Frederick Law Olmsted and Charles Vaux designed Central Park for contemplative, passive forms of recreation to soothe and civilize the masses who were subjected to the industrial blight of the time (Roy Rosenzweig and Elizabeth Blackmar, *The Park and the People: A History of Central Park*). Over time, members of the working class socially reconstructed the park to have more of their needs for active recreation met. The implication is that outdoor recreation areas can gravitate toward a balance between passive and active types of development even in the face of direct attempts to swing the pendulum one way or the other

(Dorceta Taylor, "Central Park as a model for social control: Urban parks, social class and leisure behavior in nineteenth-century America," and "The urban environment: The intersection of white middle-class and white working-class environmentalism (1820–1950s)").

14. Alfred Runte, *National Parks: The American Experience* (3rd edition) and Richard Sellars, *Preserving Nature in the National Parks.*

15. Clarke and McCool (p. 129); also see *www.fs.fed.gov*, "Press Releases" and "U.S. Forest Service chief develops new priorities," Lansing State Journal, March 9, 1998, 5A.

16. Grand Canyon National Park, 1995 General Management Plan (available online at: *http://www.nps.gov/grca/gmp/index.htm*); Yellowstone National Park, "Winter Use Planning in the National Parks of the Greater Yellowstone Area" (*http://www.nps.gov/yell/technical/planning/winteruse/plan/index.htm*);Yose mite National Park, 2001 Yosemite Valley Plan, (available online at: *http://www.nps.gov/yose/planning/yvp/*); Zion National Park, "Zion Valley Shuttle System" (http://www.nps.gov/zion/ShuttleSystem.htm).

17. Robert Reich, *The Power of Public Ideas*, pp. 1–12.

18. Keynes' quotation found in Socolow, "Failures of Discourse," p. 29.

19. Udall, *The Quiet Crisis.*

20. Sax, *Mountains without Handrails.*

21. Kaufman, *National Parks and the Woman's Voice: A History*, pp. 190–191.

22. Reich, *Power of Public Ideas*, ch. 6.

23. Mintron, *Policy Entrepreneurs and School Choice*, ch. 5.

24. Ripley, *Congress: Process and Policy*, 2nd ed., p. 155; Cubbage et al., *Forest Resource Policy*, p. 145.

25. George B. Hartzog, Jr., *Battling for the National Parks*, p. 115.

26. Cubbage et al., p. 139; Hartzog, p. 115.

27. Hartzog, p. 250.

28. This is a point made frequently in Mintron's, *Policy Entrepreneurs and School Choice.*

29. Ripley, p. 155; Cubbage et al., Chapter 6.

30. Our description of wildland recreation management agencies is primarily from Ibrahim and Cordes, *Outdoor Recreation.* We have updated the statistics from the agencies' websites and from Cordell et al., *Outdoor Recreation in American Life: A National Assessment of Demand and Supply Trends.*

31. Clawson and Held, p. 22; Dana and Fairfax, p. 8; Adams, p. 61, agree on the following definition of public domain (from Dana and Fairfax): "unentered, unreserved, unoccupied lands of the original public domain which were or are in public ownership and were subject to disposition under the general land laws until 1976 and are managed by the Bureau of Land Management." These are or were lands acquired from other nations and those received in

exchange for such lands (e.g., Alaska, Florida, parts of Oregon—see Adams, p. 60, for a full listing).

32. Cordell et al., *Outdoor Recreation in American Life,* p. 46. However, note that recent changes in procedures for estimating the amount of recreation use on Forest Service lands makes this figure suspect. It is likely highly exaggerated. A recent report accessed online on March 10, 2003, reports "214 million national forest visits" in 2002 (*http://www.fs.fed.us/recreation/programs/nvum/,* "2002 National Visitor Use Report"). This apparent shrinkage in national forest visitation by a factor of four is likely the result of the more accurate sampling and survey procedures implemented by the Forest Service in 2001.

33. Dana and Fairfax, p. 342.

34. *http://www.blm.gov/recreation/,* accessed March 10, 2003.

35. *http://www.usbr.gov/main/what/fact.html,* accessed March 10, 2003.

36. *http://www.corpsresults.us/recreation/default.htm,* accessed March 10, 2003.

37. See note #32. Because of changes in the manner in which the various agencies measure and report recreation use figures, comparisons like these can be misleading. Depending on whose numbers are used, the Corps of Engineers is either first or second in terms of total recreation visitation in the United States.

38. Cordell et al., *Outdoor Recreation in American Life,* p. 283.

39. *http://www2.nature.nps.gov/stats/,* accessed March 10, 2003.

40. *http://planning.fws.gov/,* accessed March 10, 2003.

41. National Association of State Park Directors, *http://www.naspd.org/,* "Inventory Statistics," accessed 4/19/02.

42. National Association of State Park Directors, *http://www.naspd.org/,* "Visitation and Use Statistics," accessed 4/19/02.

43. We provide a detailed discussion of the history of the LWCF and its current status in Chapter 11.

44. President Reagan's Commission on Americans Outdoors (PCAO) was another attempt at coordination but the recommendations have largely fallen by the wayside (George Siehl, "U.S. Recreation Policies Since World War II"). Some hope for stability may be seen in the substantive increase in funding for the LWCF, which Congress approved in 2002 with the urging of the Bush administration. However, as of the February 2003, with growing budget deficits and mounting military expenditures, the amount that Congress is recommending for the LWCF continues to erode.

45. Grodzins, "The Many American Governments and Outdoor Recreation."

46. An excellent theoretical statement on how agencies function as part of the larger society is Lyden, "Using Parson's Functional Analysis in the Study of Public Organizations." Twight, in *Organizational Values and Political Power,* provides a detailed illustration of an agency unable or unwilling to innovate in response to environmental challenge. Twight's second chapter

is a clear, theoretical explication of how public agencies interact with out-side social forces. See also Cubbage et al. and Clarke and McCool for fur-ther analysis.

47. See Cubbage et al. and Adams for support for this trend and for overviews of the roles and responsibilities of the U.S. judicial branch in the natural re-sources policy process; see Clarke and McCool for examples of judicial in-fluence in the policy process for the seven federal land and water manage-ment agencies; see Freedman, E., "UP wilderness battle may have wide impact," Capital News Service, April 28, 2000, for a current example of the power of the courts in setting policy for the Forest Service regarding wilder-ness management.

48. Cubbage et al., p. 198.

49. Clarke and McCool, *Staking Out the Terrain,* give numerous examples.

50. While political theorists may reach some agreement on pluralism as a de-scription of how policy is made, there is strong disagreement as to whether the group struggle should be relied on to produce policy in the public inter-est. Some argue that, much as the marketplace is supposed to produce opti-mal welfare by allocating goods and services to those who value them most, so group struggle works to allocate political goods and services optimally. Increasingly, however, strong dissent against pluralism as a normative pre-scription is heard. Jenkins presents an excellent review of the contending ap-proaches. See also Cubbage et al. for a discussion of the role of interest group politics.

51. See Schrepfer, "Perspectives on Conservation." Also, it is important to con-sider whose purposes and strategies interest groups represent. For example, Taylor ("The urban environment: The intersection of white middle-class and white working-class environmentalism") found that the mainstream envi-ronmental groups have mostly been responsive only to national issues, like saving whales and wilderness, and are dominated primarily by white, mid-dle-class values and leaders. Taylor also found that some organizations are trying to reach out to wider audiences with mixed success. Though the sta-tus quo may be changing in some isolated cases, by and large the environ-mental interest groups that exert the most influence on public land decisions are not inclusive of people of color or the working class.

52. Mintron, *Policy Entrepreneurs and School Choice;* Reich, p. 4.

53. Fox, *John Muir and His Legacy.*

54. Ibid., pp. 341–345.

55. Merchant, *Problems in American Environmental History;* Kaufman, *National Parks and the Woman's Voice: A History.*

56. Burnham, Indian *Country, God's Country: Native Americans and the National Parks.*

57. Cornell, "The Influence of Native Americans on Modern Conservationists."

58. Cubbage et al., p. 272.

59. Personal communications, Jim Detjen, professor of journalism, Michigan State University, March, 1999.

60. Jones, *An Introduction to the Study of Public Policy,* p. 7.; Cubbage et al., pp. 90–93; Mintron, p. 41. In his review of the literature on policy making processes, Mintron (ch. 2) acknowledges the wide acceptance among political scientists that policy making is primarily an incremental process; however, he also provides conditions and cases in which policy change takes the form of an innovation that breaks from the status quo.

61. In *Policy Entrepreneurs and School Choice,* Mintron notes that there are many subsystems or "players" in the policy making arena at a given time and for a given issue. Any of these subsystems may include individuals that Mintron refers to as "policy entrepreneurs" or "energetic, creative individuals" that "help stimulate or redirect debate about policy issues" (p. 57). These people play an important role in the policy process sometimes by disrupting the status quo and turning policy ideas into policies or fostering policy change. Dorceta Taylor, in her analysis of working class environmentalism ("The Urban Environment"), agrees—she says this is why the middle class wildland, wilderness, preservation movement was much more effective than the urban, working class, recreation movement. Mintron emphasizes that policy entrepreneurs can be in or out of government. He credits Kingdon (1984) and Baumgartner and Jones (1993) with original reference to policy entrepreneurs. See also, Shannon, "Resource managers as policy entrepreneurs . . ."

62. Op. cit. Siehl, U.S. Recreation Policies since World War II.

63. Downs, "Up and Down with Ecology."

64. Cubbage et al., p. 32; Baumgartner and Jones; original source is Anderson et al. (1984).

65. Ripley, *Congress: Process and Policy,* 2nd ed.

66. Mintron (pp. 54–55) notes that there is "a large amount of fragmentation in terms of policy involvement" (i.e., any individual citizen or "proximate" decision maker can devote to only a small range of public policies that they feel will most affect their daily lives or political careers). "Realizing this, scholars commonly argue that each area of public policy is dominated by relatively small gatherings of actors. These gatherings have been variously described as iron triangles, issue networks, policy monopolies, or advocacy coalitions" (p. 55). See also Sabatier, "An Avocacy Coalition Framework . . ."

67. In Jones, p. 7; Lindblom, *The Policymaking Process.*

68. Mintron (ch. 2), for example, notes that there is no evidence that the stages are causal. Also, problem definition may not be the beginning of the process, but may be continued by bureaucrats and managers during the policy implementation stage. Cubbage et al. (p. 38) point out additional limitations of the stage model, noting that it does not capture the complexities or messiness of a policy decision (firings, threats, deals, hard behind the scenes work, etc.). Also, the steps may not be followed in the order implied. Some steps

may be done simultaneously. It is not clear when a policy action is complete. The government, not just the private sector, also places problems on the agenda. "Policy implementation is not performed solely by bureaucrats, nor is legislation developed only by legislators." Yet, Cubbage et al. feel that the model does help reveal the "rules of the political game" and the choices that must be made by competing interests. They feel the model helps managers understand the process by which resource policies are "initiated, proposed, deliberated, and resolved" and that makes managers "more effective participants in the making and implementing of policy decisions" (pp. 38–39).

69. Mintron (Ch. 2) evaluates competing efforts to conceptualize the policy making process: proximate policy makers and incremental policy change (Lindblom, 1968), process streams and windows of opportunity (Kingdon, 1984, 1995), agency, and structure (Marsh and Olsen, 1989), policy images and venues (Baumgartner and Jones, 1993), and advocacy coalitions (Sabatier, 1988). He concludes that all the conceptualizations as-a-whole, including the stage model, "present a reasonably coherent portrait of the policy-cymaking process." All have strengths and weaknesses and thus complement each other. In the interest of space and clarity of presentation of our intent in this book, we present only the linear or stage model in detail, and we encourage advanced policy students and others to become familiar with the competing explanations.

70. Hartzog, *Battling for the National Parks,* warns that without appropriations, nothing happens.

71. Reich, *Power of Public Ideas,* p. 6.

72. Ibid.

73. Ibid., p. 4.

CHAPTER 3

ROOTS OF POLICY: UTILITARIAN CONSERVATION

In 1864, in the midst of the Civil War, two significant events for wildland recreation policy occurred: George Perkins Marsh published his monumental treatise on the environmental impacts of human activities, and the federal government granted the Yosemite Valley and Mariposa Grove of sequoias to the state of California for "public use, resort and recreation." Marsh's book laid the foundation for utilitarian conservation, the wise use of natural resources for the benefit—especially the economic benefit—of mankind, while the Yosemite Grant was the first major action in federal wildland preservation for recreational purposes. The book and the grant signalled the start of a new era in American land policy, one in which abundant resources were no longer taken for granted, and in which active steps were increasingly taken to secure both economic and aesthetic benefits from our land.

The conflict between preserving natural resources for their intrinsic or noneconomic values and developing them for economic gain has been the primary motive force in the development of wildland recreation policy. The use/preservation conflict, while symbolized by Marsh's book and Congress' grant to California, did not begin with those events. The lines of contention were drawn from the beginning of white settlement of America.[1]

In framing our treatment of recreation policy in terms of the use/preservation conflict, we want to acknowledge at the outset that this conflict is more complex than it is sometimes portrayed, especially by advocates seeking to paint the opposition in negative terms. Many of those who have played roles in this history express sympathy with both use and preservation, and many of the historical events we will discuss have both use and preservation dimensions. Marsh's book (this chapter) and the Yosemite Grant(next chapter) demonstrate the ambiguity and complexity that make up the policy history of wildland recreation. *Man and Nature,* while strongly scientific and utilitarian, offers ample evidence that Marsh both knew and loved pristine landscapes. The Yosemite Grant, which most commentators view as arising primarily from nature appreciation combined with democratic idealism, is also the product of economic and political interests. While we recognize the risks of over-simplification that come with presenting wildland policy history in terms of the use vs. preservation dichotomy, we believe that the intellectual structure provided by this eternal struggle is sufficiently helpful to make risk-taking worthwhile.

EARLY ATTITUDES TOWARD NATURE

The views of nature held by the colonists cannot be characterized simply. A full range of feeling about the landscape can be found in their correspondence and journals.[2] The attitudinal framework for both economic and noneconomic resource policy actions existed from the beginning. What was not present until much later was a sense of alarm sufficiently strong to bring forth policy actions.[3]

One thing common to the thinking of European-American settlers was their sense of the abundance of American natural resources. European explorers and settlers were dazzled by the abundance of nature. First, and most important, was the land base itself. To men and women from lands long occupied and controlled, often by nobility, the vastness of available land was miraculous. Nature's abundance expressed in other forms also amazed early European explorers. The journals of visitors to Cape Cod in the early 1600s, for example, reported fish measuring 5 feet in length and 3 feet in girth, schooling so thickly their backs appeared to be the sea bottom, oysters with shells a foot long, 2-foot trout in coastal streams, and 18-foot sturgeon.[4]

From the first explorations until the latter half of the nineteenth century, the "myth of superabundance" of natural resources held sway.[5]

Value derives from scarcity, and it would take several centuries of accelerating exploitation until wildlife and woods, fisheries and fresh air would be sufficiently scarce to arouse the collective will to policy actions.

The story of our treatment of the deciduous forest, as told by Robert Petty, provides a capsule history of Americans' relationship with the land. The following selection vividly captures the sense of abundance and the challenge of taming nature, followed by actions taken to restore values lost in the process of settling the land.

> In the late 1700s, settlers reaching a crest of the Wilderness Road in a notch of the Cumberlands stood blinking into the western light across the greatest deciduous forest that ever was.
>
> How do you make a cornfield out of a forest? How do you make a town? How do you clear away trees five feet through and towering one hundred and fifty feet? Forty acres, eighty, a section, a county—how do you "cut the top off" all the flat land between the Cumberlands and the Mississippi?
>
> Our minds can only ache to comprehend.
>
> Looking west from the Appalachians men spoke of an "ocean of trees" rolling on and on until it met a "sea of grass." There remains the image of a man cutting a tree in that green ocean—all around him is the damp hush when the wind dies into miles of towering shadows and green-filtered light. The ringing of his axe, his shout to no one, the creaking collapse and crash of the tree, the rustle of drifting leaves—all vanish into a sudden stillness that slowly yields to the late summer drone of insects. He squints at the immense circle of light as the silence rolls over him again. And again he is alone with the pounding of his heart and the noise of his own mind. He has marked the wilderness and he has heard its answer.
>
> Oak and hickory; beech, maple and elm; poplar and walnut—chip by chip, the stutter of axes echoed in the winter hills. Year after year, men felled the small trees and girdled the barks of the larger ones to kill them. Eighty trees to an acre was the average. First-year corn was planted under a lattice of dead branches, and remnant wild flowers crowded the stump-twisted rows. More winters, more trees girdled and some of the dead ones felled or burned where they stood; cold, seasoned wood was split into rails to fence the cattle out. With enough sons and neighbors a man might make a stumpland farm in a score of years, but battling the trees consumed three generations. Life was a long-handled axe and crosscut saw.
>
> "Sugar and Walnut Land" read the plat books of the original land surveyors; it meant the soil was calcium-rich. The pragmatic frontier farmer

quickly learned that sugar maple and walnut meant rich loam, prized as potential cropland. Government Land Offices set these sections of ground as much as fifty cents to a dollar higher per acre—which might double the price.

We can only imagine the confusion, the boisterous promise of those early days. We can hear the thudding of axes, the songs, the shouts of log-rolling fellowship around incessant fires.

For the rich, clearing crews "made land" and sold back timbers. Cabin logs were a penny a foot, hewn square. In time, water-powered sawmills would rip the trees to lumber. Yellow poplar, white oak, white ash and hickory—a wood for every need—for buildings, tools and wagons; for furnishings, maple, cherry and walnut; burnished "curly maple" for the stocks of the frontier rifles; oak, walnut and locust for fence rails—a wood for every purpose from cradles to coffins. Never had civilization been so rich in wood. By necessity, wood was used for every fashioned article of living. Even so, most of the trees were rolled together and burned. The greatest resource need was land for crops.

Like the first farmstead, towns of the frontier were built in stumpland meadows. The trees were gone. The civic landscapes sweltered in the sun. Never so quick an afterthought: fast-growing black locust trees were imported and planted everywhere, from college campuses to courthouse squares, to provide a promise of shade. What irony—the sons of the world's most incredible axemen planting seedlings in the shadow of stumps five feet across.[6]

Coupled with the rich natural resource base was a set of social conditions which, for early European-American settlers, strongly countered control over their exploitation.[7] Above all was the widespread demand for land. Social norms favoring careful resource use were weak among the settlers, and the external controls that might have been imposed by a strong government were absent in those formative years. There was little inclination toward the creation of a strong central government, since escape from authoritarian central government had led many to America in the first place and prompted the break from England. Not only were there few restraints on development, but there were strong incentives favoring rapid settlement, since powerful foreign countries were ready to fill any power vacuums. England was the most important threat, but France and Spain claimed vast tracts of land, and Russia maintained colonies in the Pacific Northwest.[8]

The fundamental conditions of available land and uncontrolled demand provided the background for a variety of ideological and attitudinal responses. Salesmen of the New World lured prospective European immigrants with descriptions of an earthly paradise, the realization of the ancient dream of a comfortable existence, free from want and from extremes of crowding and solitude.[8] At the other end of the spectrum were the New England Puritans. They looked on untamed nature as a dangerous place, a moral vacuum where innate human sinfulness might burst forth.[10] The Puritan's negative opinion of nature may have had functional value, as well; depicting their surroundings as threatening helped maintain focus on their mission and discipline for its accomplishment.[11] Even among the Puritans, though, there was a diversity of opinion about nature; Jonathan Edwards, the prominent Calvinist pastor, delighted in nature throughout his life.[12]

The New World had political, as well as economic and religious significance. Thomas Jefferson was one of a number of thinkers who saw in the American land a unique opportunity to bring democratic idealism into reality. Jefferson sought policies which would transfer land from the federal government to small farmers, for he believed the democratic ideals of the new republic could best be nurtured by a nation of small, independent farmers with a strong commitment to the land. Jefferson feared the industrial capitalism he had watched begin to grow, of necessity, during the Revolutionary War, and he hoped Americans would leave future manufacturing, together with its urban masses dependent on the marketplace, to Europeans. Jefferson believed that individual freedom and the permanence of democratic governance were of paramount concern, not economic development. At the same time Jefferson held his pastoral ideal in mind, he also recognized that America would inevitably develop its commerce and industry. Ironically, the only way to prevent economic growth of the sort Jefferson feared would be through a strong central government, something this man who so prized individual liberty feared even more than industrialism. Thirty years after a passionate defense of the plowman in his *Notes on Virginia,* Jefferson argued that changing conditions necessitated American economic development. The ideal of the sturdy, independent farmer served Jefferson as a model against which the events of the real world could be measured and judged.[13]

The American landscape meant many things to many people. Common to all the settlers was the sense of opportunity it provided. Dreams could be realized in this new land, whether they were economic, religious, or political.

EARLY LAND USE POLICIES

America in its early years was fabulously wealthy in land and resources, but correspondingly impoverished in labor and capital. This situation encouraged free and wasteful use of resources, since it made no sense to expend scarce labor and money in order to carefully manage abundant land, timber, fish, and wildlife. Nevertheless, since the means of getting resources to market were poor, local resource shortages existed or were threatened almost from the outset of white settlement. These shortages led to policies designed to curb exploitation. For example, only six years after its establishment in 1670, the Plymouth Colony passed a law which required the approval of the governor and the council for any sale or transfer of timber out of the colony. This policy action was meant to protect the colony against the future loss of readily accessible wood.[14]

In like manner, policy actions to protect local natural resources were taken throughout the colonial period. In addition to restrictions on the cutting of accessible timber, fire control and timber poaching legislation was enacted in nine of the colonies by the time of the Revolutionary War. The most notable effort to protect especially valuable resources, and one that exemplifies the challenges of controlling resource use in Colonial America, was the Broad Arrow Policy, enacted in 1691.[15]

The name of the Broad Arrow policy derives from the three blazes, symbolic of the British navy, used to mark potential mast trees. The navy was crucial to Britain's national security and imperial goals, and the navy needed masts. Before the opening of the North American colonies, Britain had relied on Scotch pine from northern and central Europe. However, the British were not happy with that source of masts because there was little reciprocal trade and because the supply of masts might be interrupted during war. The American colonies, with their rich timber resource, provided the answer to the British need for a secure source of masts—or so the British thought.

Ideal mast trees were 40 inches in diameter at the butt and 40 yards tall. To assure future mast supplies, the Broad Arrow policy reserved to the Crown all trees on public land in the Massachusetts Colony 24 inches or larger at one foot above the ground. Trees were marked, and penalties for illegal cutting were established. Unfortunately for the British navy, the policy largely failed. The colonists resented the distant authority and poached mast trees freely. Even the premium prices paid for intact trees did not overcome the special difficulties involved in felling and delivering such large timbers, and colonial loggers diverted many mast trees into other, less demanding uses. One estimate was that for every mast sent to England, 500 trees of equal value were cut for other purposes. The three-years supply of masts held by the British navy at the start of the Revolutionary War was not sufficient to prevent a number of naval breakdowns due to mast shortages.

Like the Broad Arrow Policy, measures were taken in the colonial period to protect oak for shipbuilding, pitch pine for naval stores, and mulberry trees for silk making. However, there is no evidence that these and other restrictions on resource use reflected a general awareness of broad-scale environmental or economic disruption due to uncontrolled exploitation.

At the close of the Revolutionary War, the non-native American population consisted of approximately 4 million people living along the Atlantic Seaboard.[16] To the west lay a vast wilderness, the claiming and subduing of which would occupy much of the nation's attention for the next hundred years. The rapidity and severity of resource exploitation during that time led eventually to Marsh's concerns expressed at the time of the Civil War and to the conservation actions taken around the end of the nineteenth century.

In less than 100 years after the Revolutionary War, the national government obtained control over more than 1.9 billion acres of land and water. Beginning with the cessions of the western lands claimed by the original 13 states following the Continental Congress of 1780, and continuing through the Alaska Purchase in 1867, the immense original public domain was acquired. From the first, the major topic of debate about the public domain was not whether but how the land should be disposed of. The essential question was whether the public domain should be sold or given away. Arguing for sales were those, like Alexander Hamilton, who saw land sales as the best way of raising revenues for the fragile new federal government. On the other side were those who, with Thomas Jefferson, believed that the first step toward national strength was to get settlers on the land.

Hamilton and his followers held sway at first, but the sales policy failed either to provide much revenue or to regulate settlement. "Squatting," or illegal settlement, was commonplace. The practice was supported by much of the public and justified by Jeffersonian democratic idealism. Increasingly there was pressure for giving land to settlers. The efforts to transfer public land to small farmers culminated in the landmark Homestead Act of 1862. This law, described as "the common man's greatest day," provided that 160 acres of public domain land could be claimed for free by citizens who had lived on and cultivated the land for five years. In addition to sales and grants of land to settlers, there were grants to states to support public education and improve transportation, grants to railroads to encourage expansion of the transportation system, grants to veterans in payment for their service, and miscellaneous other grants and sales. All told, these disposal policies transferred over 1 billion acres out of federal control.[17]

The Indians who lived on lands in the path of the growing American empire suffered grievous losses. In their push to occupy the continent, U.S. governmental leaders signed myriad treaties, but they then ignored many of the treaties' provisions. In the rationale of the time, because the Indians were treated like children in the face of the spread of European-American society, government leaders felt that Indians should be protected until they could be assimilated into white society.

Protection took the form of agency trusteeship and Indian reservations. Trusteeship responsibility was assigned to the Bureau of Indian Affairs (BIA).[18] The BIA was given "plenary power" over Indian affairs, ostensibly so that states or other political entities would not dominate tribal matters.[19] According to legal scholar Charles Wilkinson, "the phrase 'plenary power' became a pejorative byword among Indians and their advocates for unreviewable, and potentially autocratic, federal legislation and administrative authority".[20] It was not until the 1960s, under law and policies enacted beginning with the Indian Reorganization Act of 1934, that tribes began to be able to assert their inherent powers of self-rule.[21]

Indian reservations were set aside, but for the most part these lands had low agricultural potential; like the early national parks, the Indian reservations were "worthless lands." In addition, even as the government created large western Indian reservations, they assumed that " . . . once Indians became farmers and ranchers, they would need a smaller land base for sustenance and the reservations would shrink".[22] Most Indian reservations were opened to settlement by non-Indians by the so-called Dawes (General Allotment) Act of 1887, with the result that Indian landholdings, some of which would later become national parks and forests, fell by 62 percent in 47 years, from 138 million acres in 1887 to 52 million in 1934.[23]

In the years between the Revolutionary and Civil wars, then, an immense land area was acquired and much of it was transferred into private, non-tribal hands. Much of the land was conveyed in small parcels, since the prevalent ideology was to support the concept of Jefferson's yeoman farmers. Resources were used and abused freely, under the guiding myth of superabundance. Much of the land abuse resulted from attempts to clear and farm land unsuited for agriculture. Resource abuse was especially prevalent in the period between 1840 and 1860, when the industrial revolution in America reached the "take-off" point.[24] The extreme rapidity of resource development during those two decades set the stage for *Man and Nature,* the Yosemite Grant, and for the dramatic forest and park reservations that followed.

GEORGE PERKINS MARSH

Man and Nature: or Physical Geography as Modified by Human Action was Marsh's attempt to bring together the wisdom of the Western World concerning the unanticipated consequences of human activities, and to prompt concern and action toward wiser use of natural resources. Marsh himself was driven by a strong sense of alarm. His writing is a passionate academic review.

> The earth is fast becoming an unfit home for its noblest inhabitant, and another era of equal human crime and human improvidence, and of like duration with that through which traces of that crime and that improvidence extend, would reduce it to such a condition of impoverished productiveness, of shattered surface, of climatic excess, as to threaten the depravation, barbarism, and perhaps even the extinction of the species.[25]

Man and Nature is a long book filled with scientific fact, theory, speculation and nomenclature. Yet it was immediately successful and within a decade had attained an international reputation.[26] The real impacts of the book would not be felt for at least 25 years after it was published, but leading figures in American natural resource history have called it "epoch making," a "fountainhead," and "the beginning of land wisdom in this country."[27] Part of the book's success stems from the keenness of Marsh's insight, the breadth of his scholarship, the clarity of his writing, and the intensity of his concern. The other part of its success, at least in America, stems from its timeliness. *Man and Nature* appeared at a time of extreme resource exploitation. White civilization was sweeping westward across the continent in a first-come, first-served spirit of personal and corporate freedom that we view today as incredibly exploitative and wasteful. New territory was attacked with new technology to produce what Stuart Udall has called "the Big Raid."[28]

Historian Robert Dorman points out that it was the forests that most clearly showed the impacts of the antebellum economic expansion:

> Sawmills dotted the landscape everywhere. Wood was utilized for building purposes, and it remained the principal source of heat and fuel for most Americans throughout the period. Huge amounts of wood were needed to construct railroads—an estimated 2,500 wooden ties per mile. Steamboats burned several hundred cords of timber on each round-trip, altogether consuming hundreds of thousands of cords annually on the nation's riverways. The railing-style fences used by farmers required thousands of wooden rails to encircle even a modest field, and there were more than three million miles of such fencing around the country by 1850. In addition, broad areas of land were cleared by frontier farmers as well as those engaged in more modern, mechanized production that demanded extra pastureland for draft animals. The consequence of this unlimited wood consumption was startling. During the 1850's alone, deforestation in America amounted to some 40 million acres, one-third of the total that had occurred over the previous two centuries.[29]

Dorman reports that deforestation was especially pronounced in the New England region Marsh called home. In 1620, New England had been as much as 95 percent forested, but by 1850, Vermont had less than 45 percent forest cover.[30] Beginning in New England, the raid on America's forests moved across New York and Pennsylvania, into the pineries of the Great Lakes states, through the yellow pine stands of the South and on to the great conifers of the Northwest. In addition to their tree removal, careless loggers caused fires that burned an estimated 25 million acres per year. According to Udall:

> Lumbering, in its raider phase, was a strip-and-run business: the waste of wood was enormous, and when the best stands had been cut, the operator dismantled his mill and moved it farther west, letting the raped land go back into public ownership because the taxes went unpaid. In some areas sawmill ghost towns still clutter the landscape. Trees, like gold or silver, were "mined," for the land-skinners wanted the quickest profits the system would allow.[31]

Other forms of resource exploitation also reached new heights about the time of the Civil War. Hydraulic mining, invented in 1852 by a California miner, involved washing gold-bearing gravel banks with water.

The pressurized water broke up the banks and carried material into placer pits where the traces of gold could be separated out. By 1870, this technology had evolved into huge and powerful hydraulic systems that tore up whole hillsides and overwhelmed rivers with debris and silt, ruining fisheries and burying farmland. Oil and gas development began in the 1860s, and ignorance of geology led to appalling waste; gushers in Pennsylvania in the 1860s wasted oil at the rate of 3,000 barrels per day, and that rate was regularly exceeded in subsequent years. The record for wasteful gushers was set in Texas in 1901 when Spindletop ran wild for nine days at the rate of 110,000 barrels a day. Wildlife and fisheries were also ruthlessly exploited; the fate suffered by the passenger pigeon is one of the most notorious cases. About 1810, ornithologist Alexander Wilson reported seeing a flock of these birds which was a mile wide and 240 miles long; by the end of the nineteenth century, the combination of hunting and habitat loss exterminated the passenger pigeon as a species.[32]

By the time of the Civil War, enough resource abuse had occurred that conditions were right for a thorough review of the dangers posed by the "raid on resources." In addition to amassing evidence of resource abuse in America, Marsh's book informed readers of the hard-earned lessons of Europe and the Middle East. *Man and Nature* warned that America's growing national identity and strength might be shortlived if we continued our uncontrolled exploitation of our natural resources.

Who was this prophet whose words came "with the force of a revelation"?[33] Marsh was a native Vermonter, born in 1801, and raised in the small Green Mountains town of Woodstock.[34] In 1800, Woodstock consisted of 41 houses and 250 people, while another 2,000 people lived in the surrounding township. The Marshes were one of the area's leading families; George's father was the town's leading lawyer and the U.S. District Attorney for Vermont, as well as a major landowner. With his natural curiosity encouraged by his father's expectations, George was an avid reader. He read everything he could get his hands on, but his favorite was a huge encyclopedia, full of facts he delighted in sharing with his father. His obsessive reading strained his eyes to the extent that at age 7 or 8 he almost went blind. Until he was 11 or 12 years old, he could hardly read at all; during his convalescence, others read to him. Careful listening helped attune his ear to foreign languages, and he became one of the leading linguists of his era. During the years when his reading was restricted, he explored nearby nature with the same zeal he had applied to his books. Through direct observation, he came to understand the negative impacts of forest clearing such as soil erosion, flooding, and changes in fish and bird populations.

In addition to being a keen observer of nature, Marsh developed a life-long romantic attraction to the outdoors. He was attracted to the writings of Thoreau and influenced by Transcendentalist thinking. Late in life, Marsh reminisced that he was "forest born":

> . . . the bubbling brook, the trees, the wild animals were to me persons, not things . . . (and, as a boy, he had) . . . sympathized with those beings, as I have never done since with the general society of men, too many of whom would find it hard to make out as good a claim to personality as a respectable oak.[35]

In choosing a career, Marsh yielded to family pressure and became a lawyer and businessman, but he found little success or pleasure in these lines of work. In a time of rampant entrepreneurship, Marsh tried his hand at many ventures. At various times he was a lawyer, lumberman, railroad speculator, sheep rancher, mill owner, and mine owner, among other things. For the most part, he met with failure. Marsh biographer Lowenthal documents this late-bloomer's long and futile struggle to find a career:

> Sampling a dozen careers (from age 26–44), Marsh was no nearer knowing what to do with his life than at the start; indeed, only after eighteen years more, at the age of sixty, was his course clear to him. Meanwhile he vacillated: law and politics he found dull and degrading, scholarship ill-paying. Business for its own sake never suited Marsh; he hated dealing with men whose sole concern was money. Forays into finance, manufacturing, railroad and land speculation invariably proved disastrous, miring him further in callings he abhorred. Pursued by some evil genius, he shifted course time and again. In law Marsh was crippled by the untimely death of his first partner, and enmeshed in calamity by his second. In politics he made two false local starts before finding his way on the national stage (as elected representative beginning in 1843); in business all went wrong whenever Marsh took a hand.[36]

Marsh's real talent stemmed from his intense curiosity about the world, the breadth of his accumulated learning, and his ability to see the connections between disparate phenomena. While he struggled to find a way to make a living, his restless intellectual energy led him to read large numbers of great books and scientific papers, to master 20 languages by the time he was 30, and to probe the developments in European silviculture, among other pursuits. Based on his reading of history and science and his own observations of the ways land misuse degraded the fertility of Vermont's valleys, Marsh began to question the notion that our natural resources were inexhaustible.

Marsh was persuaded to run for Congress, won the election and went to Washington in 1842. There he was strongly influenced by John Quincy Adams, then serving in Congress after having been defeated by Andrew Jackson in the presidential election of 1828. In his belief that the public lands should not be transferred rapidly and indiscriminately to private ownership, Adams ran against prevailing opinion. Adams sought an active government which would develop the public lands so as to promote the general welfare. In those times of laissez-faire capitalism and minimalist government, his was a lonely position. It would be nearly 80 years before our collective sense of need for an active, positive government would be sufficient to prompt land use policy actions.[37] One of the most important forces in bringing about that revolution in thinking was Adams' young friend George Perkins Marsh.

Historian Robert Dorman asserts that to understand the origins of Marsh's ideas in *Man and Nature* it is essential to understand his political orientation. Marsh's political ideas arose from his family—especially his strong-willed, politically active father, a staunch conservative who was strongly concerned with social stability and believed in leadership by an enlightened elite. Concerned about the democratizing tendencies of the Jacksonian era, and thwarted in his efforts to reform election laws as a way of controlling the "inconsiderate, violent rabble" of the Popular Assembly, Marsh's father pursued the social stability he treasured through strict religion and personal moral self-development.

> Marsh was, by one account, "every inch a Whig," and the Whigs were preeminently a part of men like himself—striving, upstanding, native-born middle- and upper-class entrepreneurs, advocates of economic progress and industrial development. They were in addition the party of Protestant moral reform, upholding personal piety and social order as chief national goals.[38]

> Whigs equated material progress and moral progress very literally. Individual striving and ambition, if turned in constructive directions, contributed to the greater social good. Conversely, a prosperous, growing economy provided a setting in which invidivual faculties and talents could be realized, where self-improvement could occur.[39]

The major ideas of *Man and Nature* were in place 17 years before the book's publication. In an 1847 address to the Agricultural Society of Rutland County, Marsh warned of the dangers of extensive forest clearing in Vermont.[40] In the 1850s Marsh served as Vermont's fish commissioner, and his official duties led him to conclude that deforestation was harming fish populations by causing extremes of stream flow and temperature and by reducing insect populations.[41]

Marsh's ideas based on conditions in Vermont were supported by his experiences abroad. In 1849, President Taylor appointed him as Minister to Turkey, the first of a succession of ambassadorial postings. Marsh seized the opportunity to travel widely in the Middle East and Europe:

> He inspected much of the Nile Valley, took a camel caravan to the Holy Land, saw 'Aquaba and the ancient ruins of Petra, went mountaineering in the Alps, studied glaciers, scrutinized Vesuvius in eruption, traveled through the desolate Adriatic Karst, walked in the eroded Tuscan hills, and saw the ravaged islands of Greece. Here were ancient lands that revealed the successes—and failures—of the 'husbandry of hundreds of generations.' For Marsh, every violated valley and hillside was pregnant with meaning.[42]

Marsh returned from Turkey to more failure and financial trouble, including a long, nasty struggle to get Congress to reimburse him for expenses he had incurred in Turkey. It was with great relief that he accepted the appointment as Minister to Italy offered by President Lincoln in 1861. Marsh held this post until 1882, one of the most enduring foreign service records in American history. He wrote *Man and Nature* during his early years in Italy, and he continued to revise and refine his book to the day he died.

One of Marsh's central tenets in *Man and Nature* is that humanity is not a part of nature and does not act wholly according to nature's laws. Instead, as Marsh expressed himself:

> The fact that of all organic beings, man alone is to be regarded as essentially a destructive power, and that he wields energies to resist which nature—that nature whom all material life and all inorganic substance obey—is wholly impotent, tends to prove that, through living in physical nature, he is not of her, that he is of more exalted parentage, and belongs to a higher order of existences than those born of her womb and submissive to her dictates.[43]

Since humans are independent of nature and do not simply follow its rules, their actions toward nature have moral dimensions. In Marsh's view, not only were people independent of nature, but they were morally justified in changing natural features for their benefit:

. . . man, the domestic animals that serve him, the field and garden plants the products of which supply him with food and clothing, cannot subsist and rise to the full development of their higher properties, unless brute and unconscious nature be effectually combated, and, in a degree, vanquished by human art. Hence, a certain measure of transformation of terrestrial surface, of suppression of natural, and stimulation of artificially modified productivity becomes necessary.[44]

Although he felt a "certain measure of transformation" of the earth was necessary and justified, Marsh felt that humans had gone too far in changing nature to suit their needs. Admittedly, many destructive actions were accidental rather than deliberate, but in the aggregate their unintended consequences threatened the earth and humanity's future. One reason for Marsh's sense of alarm was his conclusion that since we were independent of nature, the natural balancing forces leading to a state of equilibrium would not operate to heal the wounds we caused. In reaching these conclusions, Marsh came to reject the self-correcting view of nature that was the prevailing wisdom of his time.

Despite strong evidence about the damage people caused when they had power to do so, Marsh did not favor turning away from the use of power. Instead, he optimistically described how the development of science was enhancing future prospects for restoring damaged nature:

Among the mysteries which science is yet to reveal, there may be still undiscovered methods of accomplishing even grander wonders . . . Mechanical philosophers have suggested the possibility of accumulating and treasuring up for human use some of the greater natural forces, which the action of the elements puts forth with such astonishing energy. Could we gather, and bind, and make subservient to our control, the power which a West Indian hurricane exerts through a small area in one continuous blast, or the momentum expended by the waves, in a tempestuous winter, upon the breakwater at Cherbourg, or the lifting power of the tide, for a month, at the head of the Bay of Fundy, or the pressure of a square mile of sea water at the depth of five thousand fathoms, or a moment of the might of an earthquake or a volcano, our age—which moves no mountains and casts them into the sea by faith alone—might hope to scarp the rugged walls of the Alps and Pyrenees and Mount Taurus, robe them once more in a vegetation as rich as that of their pristine woods, and turn their wasting torrents into refreshing streams.[45]

It is Marsh's belief in using our power over nature to improve humans' lot on earth that most clearly establishes him as the fountainhead of the progressive conservation movement. This movement would be most fully institutionalized in the U.S. Forest Service under Gifford Pinchot. Conversely, this belief distinguishes Marsh and his intellectual heirs from the romantic preservation movement that reached institutional fulfillment in the National Park Service under Stephen Mather. The competition between the Forest Service and the Park Service that has been a major feature of wildland recreation over the years thus reflects the dominant American culture's fundamental ambivalence toward their land.[46]

In establishing major themes, we must be careful not to overstate the case. Marsh's utilitarian beliefs did not mean he had no sympathy for the romantic perspective. As Marsh biographer David Lowenthal notes, ". . . for all Marsh's praise of human agency, *Man and Nature* is suffused with partiality for untamed nature." After dismissing the economic value of the small forest plants lost in converting forest to agricultural land, Marsh comments:

> He whose sympathies with nature have taught him to feel that there is a fellowship between all God's creatures; to love the brilliant ore better than the dull ingot, iodic silver and crystallized red copper better than the shillings and the pennies forged from them by the coiner's cunning; a venerable oak tree than the brandy cask whose staves are split out from its heartwood; a bed of anemones, hepaticas, or wood violets than the leeks and onions which he may grow on the soil they have enriched and in the air they made fragrant—he who has enjoyed that special training of the heart and intellect which can be acquired only in the unviolated sanctuaries of nature, "where man is distant, but God is near"—will not rashly assert his right to extirpate a tribe of harmless vegetables, barely because their products neither tickle his palate nor fill his pocket; and his regret at the dwindling area of the forest solitude will be augmented by the reflection that the nurslings of the woodland perish with the pines, the oaks, and the beeches that sheltered them.[47]

To this point we have concentrated on Marsh's philosophy. Yet *Man and Nature* overflows with state-of-the-art science. Historian Thomas Cox credits *Man and Nature* with introducing science to natural resource management in America. Before Marsh's book, the two major concepts determining land use policy were agrarianism, based on Jefferson's ideas about the importance to democracy of small, independent farmers, and romanticism, a complex assemblage of aesthetic and religious ideas imported from Europe and transformed to fit the American landscape.[48]

Amidst the welter of fact and hypothesis in *Man and Nature,* one subset of scientific knowledge stands out, both in terms of the prominent role it plays in Marsh's book and in terms of its impact on American science and land use policy. We refer to Marsh's treatment of the watershed problems caused by forest clearing in headwater regions. Marsh devoted the largest part of his book to the impacts of human activities on forests. Demonstrating sensitivity to nature's subtle interconnectedness that anticipates twentieth century ecology, he hammers home his theme of the evils of unregulated forest clearing:

With the disappearance of the forest, all is changed. At one season, the earth parts with its warmth by radiation to an open sky—receives, at another, an immoderate heat from the unobstructed rays of the sun. Hence the climate becomes excessive, and the soil is alternately parched by the fervors of summer, and seared by the rigors of winter. Bleak winds sweep unresisted over its surface, drift away the snow that sheltered it from the frost, and dry up its scanty moisture. The precipitation becomes as irregular as the temperature; the melting snows and vernal rains, no longer absorbed by a loose and bibulous vegetable mould, rush over the frozen surface, and pour down the valleys seaward, instead of filling a retentive bed of absorbent earth, and storing up a supply of moisture to feed perennial springs. The soil is bared of its covering of leaves, broken and loosened by the plough, deprived of the fibrous rootlets which held it together, dried and pulverized by sun and wind, and at last exhausted by new combinations. The face of the earth is no longer a sponge, but a dust heap, and the floods which the waters of the sky pour over it hurry swiftly along its slopes, carrying in suspension vast quantities of earthy particles which increase the abrading power and mechanical force of the current, and augmented by the sand and gravel of falling banks, fill the beds of the streams, divert them into new channels and obstruct their outlets. The rivulets, wanting their former regularity of supply and deprived of the protecting shade of the woods, are heated, evaporated, and thus reduced in their summer currents, but swollen to raging torrents in autumn and in spring. From these causes, there is a constant degradation of the uplands, and a consequent elevation of the beds of watercourses and of lakes by the deposition of the mineral and vegetable matter carried down by the waters. The channels of great rivers become unnavigable, their estuaries are choked up, and harbors which once sheltered large navies are shoaled by dangerous sandbars. The earth, stripped of its vegetable glebe, grows less and less productive, and, consequently, less able to protect itself by weaving a new network of roots to bind its particles together, a new carpeting of turf to shield it from wind and sun and scouring rain. Gradually it becomes altogether barren. The washing of the soil from the mountains leaves bare ridges of sterile rock, and the rich organic mould which covered them, now swept down into the dank low grounds,

promotes a luxuriance of aquatic vegetation that breeds fever, and more in-
sidious forms of mortal disease, by its decay, and thus the earth is rendered
no longer fit for the habitation of man.

To the general truth of this sad picture there are many exceptions, even in
countries of excessive climates. Some of these are due to favorable conditions of surface, of geological structure, and of the distribution of rain; in
many others, the evil consequences of man's improvidence have not yet
been experienced, only because a sufficient time has not elapsed, since the
felling of the forest, to allow them to develop themselves. But the
vengeance of nature for the violation of her harmonies, though slow, is sure,
and the gradual deterioration of soil and climate in such exceptional regions
is as certain to result from the destruction of the woods as is any natural effect to follow its cause.[49]

The relationship between forest cover and streamflow, as described by
Marsh, provided the constitutional lynchpin for the acquisition of the eastern national forests. If the destruction of forest cover in a river's headwaters altered streamflow in such a way that interstate commerce might be
harmed, the federal government was enabled, under the commerce clause
of the U.S. Constitution, to intervene in what otherwise was considered
strictly a state government matter. The 1911 Weeks Act and the 1924
Clarke-McNary Act, justified in part by the sponge theory, led to creation
of the eastern national forests. These forest lands, once badly abused, now
constitute an extremely important wildland recreation resource.

Marsh struggled with the question of how best to make humans' use
of natural resources less destructive. His travels in Europe and his study
of early restoration efforts in France and Germany showed him a positive leadership role for government, but he understood that what worked
in long-settled Europe would not play well in America, and in so doing
he confronted one of the fundamental dilemmas in U.S. conservation
history:

Marsh well knew that European statist, interventionist models could not be
adopted in frontier, laissez-faire America, where resources seemed limit-
less and there was no sentiment that might favor government interference
with free economic individualism—the highest social good for both American political parties . . . To what degree could conservation practices be left
to the discretion of the individual landowner, and to what extent did such
measures require public intervention and regulation? Individuals could be
counted on to put their personal greed and self-interest ahead of the good
of the environment and the community, or they might abuse the land out of

plain ignorance. Conversely, public regulations could be by turns onerous, or, if unenforced, ineffective, particularly if there were no concomitant change in attitude and practice on the part of landowners. Already, in this originative book of American conservation, Marsh was grappling with such issues.[50]

In the end, Marsh was forced to abandon his whiggish preference for relying on enlightened self interest to solve the environmental problems he documented. He concluded that for major issues like transportation, communication, and watershed protection, some form of larger societal control was needed. If he had grave concerns about governmental corruption and paternalism, he had even deeper misgivings about leaving such important matters in the hands of private corporations, based on his negative experiences with the railroads. In this way, this deeply conservative man came to provide justification for the aggressive governmental intervention under Roosevelt and Pinchot, which we review in Chapter 5.

David Lowenthal, whose first biography of Marsh was published in 1958 and his second almost half a century later, considers Marsh's *Man and Nature* and Darwin's *The Origin of Species* to be the nineteenth century's two seminal works on nature. When it was published, Marsh's book challenged conventional wisdom in many ways. Now, over 135 years later, *Man and Nature* continues to run against much of prevailing thinking, according to Lowenthal. He offers the following illustrations of ways that Marsh's ideas remain germane:

- Human impacts are inevitable and growing. Wishful thinking based on yearning for pristine nature is misguided and dangerous. "To Marsh, the thought of relinquishing dominion over nature was a nightmare. It meant regression to a heedless, amoral life ruled by hunger, fear, and superstition . . . Growing human might demands not relaxing, but intensifying, purposive global manipulation."

- Unintended consequences predominate, yet ". . . we have not yet schooled ourselves to accept the humbling awareness of uncertainty that pervades the pages and informs the insights of *Man and Nature*. In Marsh's words, "The equation of animal and vegetable life is too complicated a problem for human intelligence to solve, and we can never know how wide a circle of circumstance we produce in the harmonies of nature when we throw the smallest pebble into the ocean of organic life."

- Marsh believed humans were above nature. He would have been incredulous at the notion of according rights to non-human nature. Humans alone exercise conscious will, and therefore humans alone operate in a moral sphere. In Lowenthal's words, "To shoulder responsibility for our own actions and ambitions is more honest, and in the end probably more environmentally and socially efficacious, than to reify and take refuge in voiceless nature."

• If we are not accountable to nature itself for how we behave, we are accountable to ourselves and our descendants. Environmental stewardship is a necessity, and it requires limiting private property rights: "Man has too long forgotten that the earth was given to him for usufruct alone, not for consumption, still less for profligate waste." Stewardship must be nurtured by education and dedication to the public good.

• "In the end only amateurs make sane decisions." Specialization works to limit our understanding. While the world demands specialists, their very strength of focus demands that others transcend their narrow ways of looking at the world. Per Lowenthal: "Once it is realized that experts are often more irrational, defensive, and culture-bound than generalists, we amateurs may gain confidence in our ability, as it is clearly our need, to assess the most arcane and abstruse enigmas confronting us."[51]

As Marsh's 1864 book laid the foundation for the utilitarian conservation movement, so did the Yosemite Grant in the same year provide the first major policy breakthrough for the romantic preservation movement, as we describe in the next chapter. Just as Marsh brought together and sharpened preexisting ideas in a way that had great impact on the course of history, so the act granting the Yosemite Valley and Mariposa Grove to California brought years of preservationist thinking together in legislation that set precedent for the development of our wildland recreation system. And just as Marsh's book was not based on unalloyed utilitarianism, so the Yosemite grant was prompted by economic and political, as well as philosophical, concerns.

NOTES

1. Nash, *Wilderness and the American Mind;* Marx, *The Machine in the Garden.*

2. Merchant, *Major Problems in American Environmental History,* provides an excellent compendium of examples of the diversity of colonists' writings on nature.

3. Nash, *Wilderness and the American Mind;* Huth, *Nature and the American;* Udall, *The Quiet Crisis.*

4. MacLeish, *The Day Before America,* pp. 165–166; Cronon, *Changes in the Land,* chapter 2, notes that early European explorers were prone to exaggeration and likely saw nature's abundance during the "strawberry season."

5. The expression "myth of superabundance" is Udall's, although many others have noted the belief that American resources were inexhaustible.

6. From *Wild Plants in Flower III: Deciduous Forest* by Torkel Korling, with essay by Robert O. Petty. Reprinted with permission of Robert O. Petty.

7. This synopsis of social conditions favoring resource exploitation is based on Prof. Lyle Craine's lectures in natural resource policy at The University of Michigan, as supplemented by the work of Hays, Udall, Nash, and Merchant, among others.

8. Hibbard, *A History of the Public Land Policies,* pp. 554–566; Dana, *Forest and Range Policy,* Chapters 1 and 2; Merchant, *Major Problems in American Environmental History,* pp. 65–93.

9. Marx, *The Machine in the Garden.*

10. Nash, *Wilderness and the American Mind,* pp. 34–40.

11. Marx, *The Machine in the Garden,* p. 43.

12. Huth, *Nature and the American,* pp. 7–9.

13. Marx, *The Machine in the Garden,* pp. 116–144.

14. Dana, *Forest and Range Policy,* p. 4.

15. Ibid, pp. 11–14.

16. Ibid., p. 18; MacLeish, *The Day Before America,* pp. 167–168, reports that at the time of "contact," the native American population was approximately 1.9 million across North America.

17. Ibid., pp. 18–45; Clawson and Held, *The Federal Lands.*

18. Clow and Sutton, *Trusteeship in Change: Toward Tribal Autonomy in Resource Management,* pp. xxx–xxxii, 316–317. Since this time, the role of trustee has diffused from just the BIA to other agencies, including the National Park Service, U.S. Forest Service, and Environmental Protection Agency, who act as "surrogate trustees" of the federal government. Because these other agencies have multiple mandates and serve diverse and often conflicting constituencies, Clow and Sutton point out that the trustee management relationship is a delicate one with high potential for conflict.

19. Ibid., p. xxx.

20. Wilkinson, *American Indians, Time and Law,* p. 78.

21. Ibid., p. 21.

22. Burnham, *Indian Country, God's Country,* pp. 26–28. However, the problem was that forcing Indian tribes, some of which were nomadic, to turn to farming and ranching on marginal lands institutionalized poverty on many of the reservations, thus increasing tribes' vulnerability to pressure to sell their land.

23. Wilkinson, *American Indians, Time and Law,* p. 21. Despite American's negative treatment of Indian tribes, Wilkinson depicts U.S. Native American as relatively progressive by world standards, and particularly so for judicial decisions during the 1960s to 1980s (pp. 5, 82–83). Nonetheless, Clow and Sutton (*Trusteeship in Change,* p. 315) conclude that despite recent gains in tribal autonomy and tribal and trustee attempts to manage resources better, only some Indian communities have witnessed modest gains from the conservation and environmental movements. Frequently gains in one area are offset by losses in another. For example, "productive tribal management of the tribes' own parks does not compensate for the tremendous loss of former lands now part of the national parks and national forests where tribal access means less than full restoration of sites to the tribes."

24. Marx, *The Machine in the Garden,* pp. 26–27.

25. From *Man and Nature,* by George Perkins Marsh, edited by David Lowenthal, copyright 1965 by Harvard University Press. Reprinted by permission.

26. Lowenthal, *Man and Nature,* p. xxii; Dorman, *A Word for Nature,* pp. 42–43.

27. Dorman, *A Word for Nature,* p. 44.

28. Udall, *The Quiet Crisis,* p. 66.

29. Dorman, *A Word for Nature,* p. 11.

30. Ibid., p. 11.

31. Udall, *The Quiet Crisis,* p. 66.

32. Ibid., pp. 70–76.

33. Lowenthal, *Man and Nature,* p. xxii.

34. Lowenthal, *George Perkins Marsh* (2000), and Dorman, *A Word for Nature,* chapter 1, are our primary sources for Marsh.

35. Lowenthal, *George Perkins Marsh,* p. 30.

36. Ibid., p. 31.

37. Udall, *The Quiet Crisis,* p. 85.

38. Dorman, *A Word for Nature,* p. 13.

39. Ibid., p. 15.

40. Lowenthal, *Man and Nature,* p. xxii.

41. Cox, "Americans and Their Forests," p. 163.

42. Udall, *The Quiet Crisis,* p 87.

43. Marsh, *Man and Nature,* p. 36. Compare Marsh's ideas with those of Chief Seattle, written about the same time: "We are part of the earth and it is part of us. The perfumed flowers are our sisters; the deer, the horse, the great eagle, these are our brothers. The rock crests, the juices in the meadows, the body heat of the pony and man—all belong in the same family."

44. Marsh, *Man and Nature,* p. 38.

45. Ibid., p. 45.

46. Nye, "The American View of Nature," p. 302.

47. Marsh, *Man and Nature,* p. 249. The absence of unidimensionality in feeling and action toward nature is found throughout the literature. One of the most striking examples comes in John McPhee's account of the geologist who accompanies leading preservationist David Brower on a trip into a wilderness area rich with copper ore. At the same time the geologist relentlessly presses the utilitarian value of copper mining over wilderness preservation, his apparent interest in nature rivals Brower's; in fact, he is more adept at identifying the butterflies sighted on the trek than is the "archdruid" Brower. See John McPhee, *Encounters with the Archdruid.*

48. Cox, *The Americans and Their Forests.*

49. Marsh, *Man and Nature,* pp. 186–188.

50. Dorman, *A Word for Nature,* pp. 38–39.

51. Lowenthal, *George Perkins Marsh,* pp. 425–429.

CHAPTER 4

ROOTS OF POLICY: ROMANTIC PRESERVATION

INTRODUCTION

Just as there were utilitarian concerns with resource protection from colonial times onward, so also were there nonutilitarian concerns. Granted, neither concern was voiced by the majority, which was eager to tame the wilderness, but both existed, and both found more and more receptivity as cities expanded, farmland was opened, and we began more and more to dominate the landscape.

This chapter traces the growth of the preservation movement from colonial days to the 1864 Yosemite Grant. Building on the foundation developed in Europe, intellectuals developed a philosophy of nature appreciation with a uniquely American flavor. This philosophy was supported by growing American nationalism, which sought through the preservation of spectacular natural landscapes to demonstrate our country's equality with Europe. Frederick Law Olmsted, the driving force behind New York City's Central Park and chief architect of the Yosemite Plan, was instrumental in transforming the idea of nature preservation into the reality of national parks.

THE INTELLECTUAL FRAMEWORK FOR
NATURE APPRECIATION

The intellectual framework for American nature appreciation was drawn from European Romanticism, itself a product of the Renaissance and the transition from medieval to modern thinking.[1] Advances in science (astronomers' discovery that the earth was not the center of the universe), religion (the Protestant Reformation's assertion of direct, personal faith), and economics (the theory that individual and corporate pursuit of wealth would lead to the common good) led, by the end of the eighteenth century, to the collapse of the highly organized, hierarchical medieval world view. Without the strong hierarchical framework of institutions and associations that shaped the lives of previous generations, the individual was left to search alone for purpose and meaning in life.[2]

Along with a new perspective on the importance of the individual, the Romantics developed a new perspective on nature. As advancing science revealed astonishing facts about the world and the solar system, earthly features that had been ignored because humans could not use them or cursed because they blocked our desires came to be seen as evidence of God's handiwork. It followed that if God were evident in nature, the deity was most readily apparent in wild nature. The New World was a perfect setting for the romantic imagination. European Romantics were especially fascinated by the reports of American Indians. At a time when American pioneers feared the woods because they concealed dangerous Indians, European Romantics like Montaigne and Rousseau were extolling the virtues of the noble savage uncontaminated by decadent society.

The new concept of nature also had a new aesthetic and a new vocabulary. Rebelling against the formality of the classical definition of beauty, thinkers like Burke and Kant ascribed beauty to vast and apparently chaotic scenes, describing them as "sublime" and "picturesque." This vocabulary, and the attitudes toward nature it connotes, was widely shared by early American explorers, scientists, and men of letters. Most of them adopted the rhetorical convention of the day and described the natural landscapes they encountered as "sublime" or "picturesque" and themselves as overwhelmed with feelings of awe, wonder, and exaltation.

By the early years of the nineteenth century many urban, educated elites shared positive feelings toward America's natural landscapes. The stage was thus set for the entrance of thinkers who brought new power and substance to the nature preservation movement. Ralph Waldo Emerson and Henry David Thoreau were leading voices in a group of literary figures that established the intellectual framework for future nature preservation in this country.

EMERSON AND THOREAU

Emerson and Thoreau were the founders of a group that came to be known as the New England Transcendentalists. They believed that there is a reality higher than the physical reality we see and that the human soul enables us to transcend our physical existence in the material world; intuition or imagination, not rigorous deductive logic, enable us to discern spiritual truths.[3] For the Transcendentalists, natural objects were important because they reflect, however imperfectly, universal spiritual truths. In natural areas, in contrast to the city, these spiritual truths are least obscured by human activity and therefore most easily perceived. In this way, nature was crucial to the search for the new moral order—a moral order built on an ethos of freedom and individuality—needed to replace the outmoded moral order of the Middle Ages.[4]

Transcendentalist philosophy was formally initiated in 1836 with the publication of Emerson's first book, *Nature*. The book was full of optimism, reflecting Emerson's belief in the possibilities of new lives in the New World:

> Embosomed for a season in nature, whose floods of life stream around and through us, and invite us, by the powers they supply, to action proportioned to nature, why should we grope among the dry bones of the past, or put the living generation into masquerade out of its faded wardrobe? The sun shines today also. There is more wool and flax in the fields. There are new lands, new men, new thoughts. Let us demand our own works and laws and worship.[5]

Nature is one of the foundational documents of American culture. It obtains its driving force from the elements of individualism, nature, and the future. These three elements particularly characterized the thinking of elites in Emerson's time. They separated nineteenth century America dramatically from Europe, which we pictured as the home of long-tamed nature and huddled masses of people chained by the shackles of history.[6] Emerson wove these elements into a call for spiritual revitalization that drew many followers in his time and has resonated down through the history of wildland preservation.

A disaffected ex-minister of the Unitarian church, Emerson adopted as his life's mission to awaken his countrymen from their spiritual slumber.[7] He urged his audiences to look on the world as children do:

> To speak truly, few adult persons can see nature. Most persons do not see the sun. At least they have a very superficial seeing. The sun illuminates only the eye of man, but shines into the eye and the heart of the child. The lover of nature is he whose inward and outward senses are truly adjusted to each other; who has retained the spirit of infancy even into the era of manhood.[8]

Looking at nature with the openness of a child best prompted the development of innate goodness and capacity for spiritual growth:

> In the woods, too, a man casts off his years, as the snake his slough, and at what period soever of life is always a child. In the woods is perpetual youth. Within these plantations of God, a decorum and sanctity reign, a perennial festival is dressed, and the guest sees not how he should tire of them in a thousand years. In the woods, we return to reason and faith. There I feel that nothing can befall me in life,—no disgrace, no calamity (leaving me my eyes), which nature cannot repair. Standing on the bare ground,—my head bathed by the blithe air and uplifted into infinite space,—all mean egotism vanishes. I become a transparent eyeball; I am nothing; I see all; I am part or parcel of God. The name of the nearest friend sounds then foreign and accidental: to be brothers, to be acquaintances, master or servant, is then a trifle and a disturbance. I am the lover of uncontaminated and immortal beauty. In the wilderness, I find something more dear and connate than in streets and villages. In the tranquil landscape, and especially in the distant line of the horizon, man beholds somewhat as beautiful as his own nature.[9]

The closing lines of *Nature* capture the excitement and promise Emerson's vision of spiritual rebirth offered to those independent and self-reliant enough to follow him:

> All that Adam had, all that Caesar could, you have and can do. Adam called his house, heaven and earth; Caesar called his house, Rome; you perhaps call yours, a cobbler's trade; a hundred acres of ploughed land; or a scholar's garret. Yet line for line and point for point your dominion is as great as theirs, though without fine names. Build therefore your own world. As fast as you conform your life to the pure idea in your mind, that will unfold its great proportions. A correspondent revolution in things will attend the influx of the spirit. So fast will disagreeable appearances, swine, spi-

ders, snakes, pests, mad-houses, prisons, enemies, vanish; they are temporary and shall no more be seen. The sordor and filths of nature, the sun shall
dry up and the wind exhale. As when the summer comes from the south the
snow-banks melt and the face of the earth becomes green before it, so shall
the advancing spirit create its ornaments along its path, and carry with it the
beauty it visits and the song which enchants it; it shall draw beautiful faces,
warm hearts, wise discourse, and heroic acts, around its way, until evil is
no more seen. The kingdom of man over nature, which cometh not with observation,—a dominion such as now is beyond his dream of God,—he shall
enter without more wonder than the blind man feels who is gradually restored to perfect sight.[10]

Emerson's ideas were widely circulated among the intelligentsia of his
time, but they were brought most fully to realization by his younger friend
Henry David Thoreau. Through his life and writing Thoreau left his mark
indelibly on American culture, and his work has been one of the touch-
stones of the preservation movement. In his lifetime, though, Thoreau
would have been judged a failure. Making a living was a problem he never
solved, and he never developed a close friendship or love. He died in
1862, at age 44, of tuberculosis, with few worldly possessions and scant
recognition of the value of his thinking and writing.[11]

When Thoreau graduated from Harvard in 1837, his major career alternatives were the ministry, business, or a profession. With his contempt
for business and his distrust of the church, he was left to choose a profession, and at that time the choice was limited to medicine, law, or teaching. He had no interest in either of the first two paths, and so he was left
with teaching. He obtained a position in Concord, his hometown and that
of Emerson, but resigned within a month because he did not believe in
flogging the students and the school board did. Thus, in his first formal
job experience, Thoreau demonstrated the importance he attached to
moral principles and his willingness to accept the penalties that came
from challenging authority.

Thoreau's libertarian views gave rise to some of his most powerful
writing. In an early incident the state of Massachusetts attempted to ex-
tract from Thoreau payment to a clergyman whose sermons his father had
attended. Thoreau, thinking it equally fair that the clergy be taxed to support his own lectures at the Lyceum, refused to pay, and in the process,
publicly "signed off" from what he considered an unjust society: "Know
all men by these presents, that I, Henry Thoreau, do not wish to be regarded as a member of any incorporated society which I have not

joined."[12] Later, he spent a night in jail for refusing to pay taxes he declared went to support the unjust Mexican War, and that experience led his essay on "Civil Disobedience," a work which influenced Ghandi and the American Civil Rights movement.[13]

Several years after the 1849 publication of "Civil Disobedience," Thoreau demonstrated his willingness to work more actively against unjust authority. He became a public opponent of slavery, lecturing and writing for the abolitionist cause, including a ringing eulogy on the martyrdom of John Brown. Thoreau's opposition to slavery was a natural outgrowth of his family's longstanding abolitionist activity (their home was a stop on the underground railway), but it represented more than family influence. Thoreau's lifelong opposition to slavery arose from that system's opposition to individual freedom: "It abrogated the God-given moral free will of the slave's soul, denying the possibility of self-perfection."[14]

When Thoreau, in words widely quoted in the late twentieth century, stated ". . . in Wildness is the preservation of the world," he was thinking of things far more profound than recreation in the usual sense.

"In its open-ended vastness and mutability, its wildness, nature thus symbolized for Thoreau the spiritual truth of freedom, including, above all, human freedom."[15] Nature—particularly wilderness—served as a resource through which Thoreau could resist the societal forces that threatened individuality and freedom: "Wilderness, for him, was not only 'free,' it was also—in a personal, social, and political sense—liberating and subversive."[16]

Thoreau worked at a wide variety of jobs—teacher, lecturer, laborer, handyman, tutor, editor, and pencil-maker (he invented a way of purifying the graphite used in his father's pencil factory.[17])—but his true, self-proclaimed calling was to be a poet. Thoreau's conception of the poet's role was exalted; he wanted, in his life and writing, to lead the world to new philosophical and moral heights. His major difficulty was getting paid for this job. He tried lecturing, following Emerson's successful example, but he did not project well; a short, retiring person, he did not create much excitement in his presentations. Since he could not seem to enlarge his income, Thoreau decided to reduce his costs. His benefactor Emerson had some land on Walden Pond near Concord, and he was willing to let Thoreau use it. So in the spring of 1845 Thoreau built a small and deliberately simple cabin there and moved in to record the events and thoughts that led to his masterpiece.

Walden is Thoreau's account of his attempt to find the essence of life:

> I went to the woods because I wished to live deliberately, to front only the essential facts of life, and see if I could not learn what it had to teach, and not, when I came to die, discover that I had not lived. I did not wish to live what was not life, living is so dear, nor did I wish to practice resignation, unless it was quite necessary. I wanted to live deep and suck out all the marrow of life, to live so sturdily and Spartan-like as to put to rout all that was not life, to cut a broad swath and shave close, to drive life into a corner, and reduce it to its lowest terms, and, if it proved to be mean, why then to get the whole and genuine meanness of it, and publish its meanness to the world; or if it were sublime, to know it by experience, and be able to give a true account of it in my next excursion.[18]

Walden is a profound source of preservationist philosophy. The wholesomeness of the simple life close to nature is set again and again in sharp contrast to the superficiality and destructiveness of social and economic life, as illustrated by the following selections:

> Flint's Pond! Such is the poverty of our nomenclature. What right had the unclean and stupid farmer, whose farm abutted on this sky water, whose shores he has ruthlessly laid bare, to give his name to it? Some skinflint, who loved better the reflecting surface of a dollar, or a bright cent, in which he could see his own brazen face; who regarded even the wild ducks which settled in it as trespassers; his fingers grown into crooked and horny talons from the long habit of grasping harpy-like; so it is not named for me. I go not there to see him nor to hear of him; who never saw, who never bathed in it, who never loved it, who never protected it, who never spoke a good word for it, nor thanked God that He had made it. Rather let it be named from the fishes that swim in it, the wild fowl or quadrupeds which frequent it, the wild flowers which grow by its shores, or some wild man or child the thread of whose history is interwoven with its own; not from him who could show no title to it but the deed which a like-minded neighbor or legislature gave him—him who thought only of its money value; whose presence perchance cursed all the shore; who exhausted the land around it, and would fain have exhausted the waters within it; who regretted only that it was not English hay or cranberry meadow—there was nothing to redeem it, forsooth, in his eyes—and would have drained it and sold it for the mud at its bottom. It did not turn his moll, and it was no privilege to him to behold it. I respect not his labors, his farm where everything has its price, who would carry the landscape, who would carry his God, to market, if he could get anything for him; who goes to market for his God as it is; on whose farm nothing grows free, whose fields bear no crops, whose meadows no flowers,

whose trees no fruits, but dollars; who loves not the beauty of his fruits, whose fruits are not ripe for him until they are turned to dollars. Give me the poverty that enjoys true wealth. Farmers are respectable and interesting to me in proportion as they are poor—poor farmers. A model farm! where the house stands like a fungus in a muck-heap, chambers for men, horses, oxen, and swine, cleansed and uncleansed, all contiguous to one another! Stocked with men! A great grease-spot, redolent of manures and butter-milk! Under a high state of cultivation, being manured with the hearts and brains of men! As if you were to raise your potatoes in the churchyard! Such is a model farm.[19]

Cultivate poverty like a garden herb, like sage. Do not trouble yourself much to get new things, whether clothes or friends. Turn the old; return to them. Things do not change, we change. Sell your clothes and keep your thoughts. God will see that you do not want society. If I were confined to a corner of a garret all my days, like a spider, the world would be just as large to me while I had my thoughts about me.[20]

Still we live meanly, like ants; though the fable tells us that we were long ago changed into men; like pygmies we fight with cranes; it is error upon error, and clout upon clout, and our best virtue has for its occasion a super-fluous and evitable wretchedness. Our life is frittered away by detail. An honest man has hardly need to count more than his ten fingers, or in extreme cases he may add his ten toes, and lump the rest. Simplicity, simplicity, sim-plicity! I say, let your affairs be as two or three, and not a hundred or a thou-sand; instead of a million count half a dozen, and keep your accounts on your thumb nail. In the midst of this chopping sea of civilized life, such are the clouds and storms and quicksands and thousand-and-one items to be al-lowed for, that a man has to live, if he would not founder and go to the bot-tom and not make his port at all, by dead reckoning, and he must be a great calculator indeed who succeeds. Simplify, simplify. Instead of three meals a day, if it be necessary eat but one; instead of a hundred dishes, five; and reduce other things in proportion. Our life is like a German Confederacy, made up of petty states, with its boundary forever fluctuating, so that even a German cannot tell you how it is bounded at any moment. The nation it-self, with all its so-called internal improvements, which, by the way, are all external and superficial, is just such an unwieldy and overgrown establish-ment, cluttered with furniture and tripped up by its own traps, ruined by lux-ury and heedless expense, by want of calculation and a worthy aim, as the million households in the land; and the only cure for it as for them is in a rigid economy, a stern and more than Spartan simplicity of life and eleva-tion of purpose. It lives too fast.[21]

Although he wrote, "We can never have enough of Nature," Thoreau's frame of reference was not the wilderness modern adventurers seek in remote and mountainous country, but the semi-domesticated nature of Walden Pond. In this Thoreau lived out Emerson's famous aphorism, "The inevitable mark of wisdom is to see the miraculous in the common." The wilderness ideal embodied in the 1964 Wilderness Act postulates vast areas of untouched nature meant to be appreciated in solitude. The landscape Thoreau wrote of at Walden featured high-graded woods and abandoned farms and was populated with visitors from town, travelers, ice-cutters and other workers.[22] It was on his trip to Maine in 1846 that Thoreau encountered something more nearly approaching today's wilderness ideal, and he found it overwhelming. His experience on Mt. Katahdin was anything but transcendent.

> Aeschylus had no doubt visited such scenery as this. It was vast, titanic, and such as man never inhabits. Some part of the beholder, even some vital part, seems to escape through the loose grating of his ribs as he ascends. He is more alone than you can imagine. There is less of substantial thought and fair understanding in him, than in the plains where men inhabit. His reason is dispersed and shadowy, more thin and subtle, like the air. Vast, Titanic, Inhuman Nature has got him at disadvantage, caught him alone, and pilfers him of some of his divine faculty. She does not smile on him as in the plains. She seems to say sternly, why come ye here before your time? This ground is not prepared for you. Is it not enough that I smile in the valleys? I have never made this soil for thy feet, this air for thy breathing, these rocks for thy neighbors. I cannot pity nor fondle thee here, but forever relentlessly drive thee hence to where I am kind. Why seek me where I have not called thee, and then complain because you find me but a stepmother? Shouldst thou freeze, or starve, or shudder thy life away, here is no shrine, no altar, nor any access to my ear.[23]

Thoreau resolved the philosophical confusion into which his Maine experience had thrust him by insisting on the value of balance. He decided he wanted to be half-cultivated. Continuing the agrarian analogy, he viewed wilderness as a potent fertilizer to be added to cultivated soil. For Thoreau, one of nature's major benefits is the contrast it provides to daily life:

> Our village life would stagnate if it were not for the unexplored forests and meadows which surround it. We need the tonic of wildness — to wade sometimes in marshes where the bittern and the meadow-hen lurk, and hear the

booming of the snipe; to smell the whispering sedge where only some wilder and more solitary fowl builds her nest, and the mink crawls with its belly close to the ground. At the same time that we are earnest to explore and learn all things, we require that all things be mysterious and unexplorable, that land and sea be infinitely wild, unsurveyed and unfathomed by us because unfathomable. We can never have enough of Nature. We must be refreshed by the sight of inexhaustible vigor, vast and Titanic features, the seacoast with its wrecks, the wilderness with its living and its decaying trees, the thundercloud, and the rain which lasts three weeks and produces freshets. We need to witness our own limits transgressed, and some life pasturing freely where we never wander.[24]

The relationship between wilderness and cities has continued to engage thinkers. Philosopher John Hammond suggests that we should not view wilderness and cities as unconnected and think of wilderness only as a place in which we can escape the oppressive city. He points out that the intellectual apparatus that enables us to enjoy wilderness—the aesthetic, scientific, and philosophical foundations—was developed in urban areas.[25] Historian William Cronon takes this argument one step further and argues that wilderness is, in fact, a human cultural invention, a product of civilization, and not a nature sanctuary uncontaminated by humans.[26]

AMERICAN NATIONALISM

By the time of the Civil War, the attitudinal foundation and much of the philosophical framework necessary for wildland preservation policy-making had been completed. Nature-love was still not a perspective shared by a majority of Americans, but it had permeated far enough into the urban-intellectual class to have an impact. Nevertheless, it would be an overstatement to claim that these ideas led to the Yosemite Grant of 1864. Among other important factors contributing to the Yosemite Grant was growing American nationalism.[27]

The middle of the nineteenth century brought growing awareness of the environmental problems caused by settlement, industrialization, and unregulated economic enterprise. The sense of nationalism was linked to this emerging environmental consciousness. Nationalism had been connected to nature since colonial times. For example, Thomas Jefferson asserted that viewing the Potomac Gorge and Natural Bridge were worth a trip across the Atlantic, and artists like Thomas Cole and Asher Durand of the Hudson River School had attempted in their landscape paintings to glorify the wild natural scenery so abundant in America. Their efforts did not always have the impact desired, however, as indicated by the following comment from John Ruskin, the leading English art critic of his day: "I have just been seeing a number of landscapes by an American painter of some repute; and the ugliness of them is wonderful. I see that they are true studies and that the ugliness of the country must be unfathomable."[28]

The natural feature which drew the greatest number of European visitors was Niagara Falls, and commercial exploitation there had been a serious embarrassment to American intellectuals since the 1830s. Suffering from a cultural inferiority complex, American elites were striving for a sense of national identity. We looked to Europe and saw the products of centuries of cultural attainment in their cathedrals, literature, painting, and other arts and sciences. America, by contrast, was a fledgling nation with little to boast of save our monumental natural resources. At Niagara Falls we had allowed one of our most magnificent natural landscape features to be turned into a mass of claptrap viewing stands and other commercial trappings designed to fleece the tourist, and visitors had to pay the landowners for permission to view the falls.[29] The mid-century settlement of the West presented Americans with other magnificent scenic wonders in the Rockies and in California, and with them came an opportunity to redeem ourselves for the shame of Niagara Falls. The comments of the western publicists illustrate clearly the sense of nationalism in the appraisal of these western resources. According to Samuel Bowles, "only the whole of Switzerland" eclipsed Yosemite. Albert Richardson contended that "In grand natural curiosities and wonders, all other countries combined fall far below it (the American West)." And Clarence King offered his opinion that no "fragment of human work, broken pillar or sandworn image half lifted over pathetic desert—none of these link the past and today with anything like the power of these monuments of living antiquity [the Sierra redwoods]."[30]

PARKS PROPOSED AND PARKS REALIZED

Park proposals had been made for many years before the Yosemite Grant. The first call for a large, wildland park was made by George Catlin, a lawyer turned painter who traveled in the upper Missouri River area during the summers of 1829–1832. The American Indians fascinated Catlin.

In 1832 on his trip to the headwaters of the Missouri River, Catlin witnessed Sioux Indians slaughtering buffalo in order to trade their tongues for whiskey. The waste of beast and man prompted him to consider ways of protecting the Indians and their land from advancing civilization. He proposed that the area he had traveled be made into a huge and magnificent national park that would preserve the Indian culture, together with their mainstay, the bison.[31] Articulating an argument that would be critical to most of the major wildland recreation preservation actions, Catlin justified removing lands from economic exploitation on the grounds that they were "useless to cultivating man." Presciently, he argued that the value of this proposed park would grow with time and the inevitable separation from nature that would come with progress.[32]

Thoreau, too, advanced wildland park proposals. Unlike Catlin's grand scheme, however, Thoreau proposed small nature preserves located near where people lived. People could repair to these accessible preserves for temporary escape from urban and industrial stresses, for the enhancement of their physical, emotional, and intellectual power, for companionate sharing of nature's benefits, for nurturance of distinctively American individuality, and for relief from a materialistic society.[33]

Curiously enough, it was an urban, not a wildland park, that may have been most important to the Yosemite Grant and the future national parks that the grant presaged. This is because that urban park provided one of America's great public servants his first opportunity at park design. The urban park was Central Park in New York City, and the man was Frederick Law Olmsted. Based on the development of his ideas during ten years of work on Central Park, he developed the first plan for Yosemite. After his work at Yosemite, Olmsted went on to become a founder of the profession of landscape architecture, one of America's most influential park designers.

FREDERICK LAW OLMSTED

Olmsted was born in 1822 in Hartford, Connecticut. At the time Hartford was a bustling small city surrounded by a charming rural landscape. Olmsted's father was a well-to-do businessman who loved and supported him. One of his family's favorite activities was taking leisurely drives in the countryside. Vacations and holidays were often the occasion for foreign travel. As a young man, he was influenced by the Hudson River School of painters, the romanticism of Emerson, and the progressive conservation philosophy of Marsh. From these early experiences Olmsted developed a love of quiet, pastoral scenery that defined his mature aesthetic sense and shaped his professional work.[34]

Another formative element of Olmsted's early life involved the application of power by authority, and it was as negative as the country rambles were positive. From age 10 to 14, Olmsted was sent to be tutored by a minister. The conditions of life and education were rough, with hard work, primitive living conditions, and frequent beatings. Olmsted developed a lasting resentment toward his tutor, which grew into a lifelong dislike of authority figures.[35] Later, at age 21, Olmsted shipped out in the China trade as an able-bodied seaman. He was outraged by the absolute power exercised by the ship's officers.[36] His experiences as a sailor joined with his experiences as a student to confirm Olmsted as a lifelong lover of democracy; his belief in the abilities of common people and his commitment to improving their lot are found throughout his life. In his journalistic analysis of slavery, for example, he concluded that the system was a failure because it treated people as animals and provided no incentive for productive work, while at the same time corrupting the masters with absolute power.[37] His management of the work force at Central Park was marked by his respect for his subordinates and his willingness to entrust them with responsibility. Most importantly for our purposes, his concepts for public parks were grounded in democratic idealism.

Olmsted's democratic idealism was of religious proportions, and such a strong faith demanded his service to his country. He was almost possessed by a sense of duty. Virtually every decision he made in his professional life was guided by his judgment of its value for the common welfare. He did not accept the prevailing laissez-faire thinking of his time, and he did not believe that government should watch quietly as economic forces decided the country's course of action. If he was going to give his life in public service, he expected that government should be an active force working to improve life. Not only was the improvement of life good for the citizens, it was necessary for the survival of the country. Olmsted believed that democratic government required the "capacity for liberty" in its citizens, all of them. Therefore, democracy required that government bring all citizens to the level where they could contribute something positive. In these beliefs Olmsted ran a course absolutely contrary to the prevalent thinking of his day, which held that "that government is best which governs least."[38]

Seeing Birkenhead Park in Liverpool, England, brought together Olmsted's love of quiet nature and his democratic idealism. Built in 1844, Birkenhead was laid out as a rural park. Two things about the park particularly impressed Olmsted. First, the park's romantic, pastoral scenery was man-made; in the original flat land a lake had been dug, and the earth taken from it was used to create a gently rolling landscape. Second, the park was explicitly designed for public use; this was in contrast with most English parks which were originally the private reserves of the wealthy.[39] Birkenhead Park reminded Olmsted of the restful Connecticut countryside he had enjoyed in his youth and the rural England he loved from his travels. He was enchanted with the park. He saw in Birkenhead Park not only beauty, but the opportunity to enrich the lives of the poorer citizens of the area who used the park. Furthermore, since both the poor and the well-to-do used the park, Olmsted saw it as a vehicle for combating class definitions. In bringing people together in a beautiful setting, this quiet little park was, in Olmsted's eyes, a powerful engine of democracy.[40]

Central Park

Several years after his return from England, during which time he pursued a career as a journalist, Olmsted was at a seaside inn in Connecticut, where he had gone to work on a book. At tea one day he happened to meet a commissioner of the newly authorized Central Park in New York City. The commissioner lamented the poor quality of the candidates for park superintendent, a position they were to fill at their next meeting. He urged Olmsted to apply, and Olmsted, remembering his interest in the English urban parks, decided he would.[41] In this happenstance way, Olmsted became associated with Central Park.

In 1853, responding to agitation for parks voiced since 1785, the New York legislature had authorized the city to acquire the land for Central Park. In the years between the legislative authorization and Olmsted's arrival, the land had been acquired and a preliminary plan drafted, but development of the park was tied up in political maneuvering. For a salary of $1,500 a year, Olmsted was given the formidable job of transforming the park dream into a reality.[42] As biographer Laura Wood Roper reports, Olmsted took charge of the largest public works project in New York City at a time when the social order necessary for such an undertaking was "in dark eclipse":

(The social order) had been declining all through the 1840s when a million and a half European immigrants had poured into the city, many of them to crowd and stagnate in its sordid and degrading slums. There gangs, native and foreign born, fought and slaughtered each other; in better neighborhoods footpads, pickpockets, prostitutes, and beggars operated busily; at fires, companies of volunteer firemen brawled with rival companies and other rowdies. Gang members, firemen, criminals, each with his vote to sell, had palpable influence in the political organization of the city, especially Tammany Hall, and were little disturbed by the police. The state government, moving finally in June 1857 to curb some of the local administration's much-abused powers, sought to replace the corrupt police with a new force under five commissioners appointed by the governor; and the governor appointed a new street commissioner. Lawlessness for a time increased: Wood (the Tammany-backed Mayor) and his police defied the new police commissioners and threw the new police commissioner out of City Hall. Even after the authority of the new police was established, order was not: on July 4 the Dead Rabbits, an east-side gang, attacked a Bowery saloon and precipitated two days of murdering violence in which other gangs and members of the old police enthusiastically joined; and less than two weeks later an armed mob, alleged to have been mostly recent Irish immigrants, attacked the police. In both instances the militia had to be called. These disturbances pointed to grievous conditions of dense ignorance, cruel poverty, reckless despair — conditions that were aggravated by a far-reaching catastrophe, which had been slowly building, the panic of 1857.[43]

In these times Olmsted had ample opportunity to observe the effects of poverty and ignorance, and to further develop his thoughts on barbarism, civilization, and democracy. These thoughts would help lead him to California and to Yosemite.

Despite the degraded and chaotic state of public affairs in New York at the time, there was political support for the development of Central Park. Taxpayers, having already sunk $5 million into the project, wanted to see progress, and with the worsening economic situation the working population was eager for the jobs park construction would provide.[44]

When Olmsted first visited the park site, according to biographer Laura Wood Roper, he found a "mess." There were shacks, pigpens, slaughterhouses, and bone-boiling works, situated on a difficult piece of land with thin topsoil, rock outcrops, and bogs. The challenge was to create an area of charming scenery that related fully to the city developing around it. It was a task without precedent in this country.[45]

Olmsted was hired to supervise the park's construction. A design competition was used to determine the plan for the park. Fortunately, architect Calvert Vaux invited Olmsted to join him in preparing a plan. For Olmsted the partnership provided an opening into the design professions; for Vaux the partnership provided a first-hand, detailed familiarity with the site.

Vaux and Olmsted's winning plan, modeled on Birkenhead Park, called for the creation of "contrasting and varying passages of scenery, all tending to suggest to the imagination a great range of rural conditions."[46] Understanding clearly that the working class, the poor, and ethnic minorities had no alternative access to nature other than public parks close to where they lived, Vaux and Olmsted's plan was to create a pastoral, rural, therapeutic sanctuary in the midst of the nation's largest city.[47] To accommodate the passage of commercial traffic, as the competition required, the plan called for sinking four transverse roads below the level of the park; pleasure roads and trails in the park could then pass over these thoroughfares on bridges without interference. Sinking the business roads would also nullify their impact on the pastoral scenery within the park. Within the park, the same principle of reducing user conflict was applied; carriage roads crossed footpaths and bridle paths on bridges, and bridle paths and footpaths did not cross.[48] As biographer Laura Wood Roper states, Vaux and Olmsted reinterpreted landscape architecture from "a polite art oriented toward horticulture, which could be competently practiced by skilled and intelligent amateurs, to an exacting professional discipline embracing various aspects of the arrangement of land for human use and enjoyment."[49]

Forty years' work were needed to build out the Olmsted-Vaux plan, and continuing vigilance was required to protect the park's integrity from myriad public and commercial development schemes. Olmsted struggled with the task for a decade, motivated by his democratic idealism, stoically moving forward in the face of innumerable personal and professional difficulties. His health was not good. He suffered chronically from insomnia and upset stomach; he was bedeviled by debts; he had to bear many family responsibilities; an accident on a horse broke his leg and nearly killed him; his infant son died of cholera; and he was constantly vexed by the man who controlled the Central Park budget.[50] Though he would suffer greatly in creating Central Park, in the end he was proudest of it among all his works, because it anticipated the growth of an immense urban population and provided for public needs that would not be recognized for many decades after the park was built.

With the advent of the Civil War, Olmsted pondered how he might serve his country in its great crisis. Unfit for active duty as a result of his accident, he accepted the position of executive secretary of the newly formed Sanitary Commission, with responsibility for improving general hygiene in the Union army.[51] He brought to this important job the same administrative genius he had shown at Central Park. Nevertheless, after almost 3 years of intense effort, the political aspects of the job frustrated Olmsted. Returning to his post at Central Park was not inviting after his years of struggling with its money manager. He was in poor health, he had a number of substantial debts, and he felt the need to build his private fortune if he were to play the public leadership role he aspired to. Thus, when he was invited to California to manage the Mariposa Estate, a gold mining operation, he jumped at the chance.

The Mariposa Estate, located in the western foothills of the Sierra Nevada Mountains near what is now Yosemite National Park, was described at the time as "one of the most gigantic mining operations in the world."[52] Soldier-adventurer John C. Fremont had founded the Mariposa Estate in 1847.[53] The property included the famed "mother lode" and Fremont made a fortune, but he spent it on political activities. In 1863 and with a debt of more than $1.5 million, Fremont sold the estate to a New York banker. "The property covered 70 square miles and included six mines, two towns, a railroad, and a tenant population of about seven thousand."[54] It was truly a "wild west" environment. Managing this large group of rough people was a severe challenge for Olmsted. More challenging, and ultimately defeating, were the legal and financial tangles left from years of poor management.

Olmsted did not simply escape to California; he looked on the job as an opportunity to accomplish something tangible that would support American democracy.[55] Olmsted wanted to refute the English critics who, favoring an aristocracy, suggested that the crude, raw aspects of life they observed in America were a natural outgrowth of democracy. Olmsted felt these conditions were attributable not to our form of government, but to the pioneer conditions still found in much of the country. Along with Herbert Spencer he believed in social evolution, but unlike the English philosopher who provided such comfort to the rich, Olmsted believed an active government could and should take steps to help the poor become more fit for a life of freedom. The primitive, lawless community at Mariposa provided Olmsted with an opportunity for "social engineering," a chance:

. . . to transfigure a semiarid, barbarous principality into a well-watered, fertile garden; to turn its economy from dangerous dependence on a single industry to thrifty reliance on diversified enterprise; and to shape from its transient and semi-barbarous population a stable and civilized community in which should prevail "an all-embracing relationship based on the confidence, respect and interest of each citizen in all and all in each."[56]

Success did not come to Olmsted at Mariposa; the legacy of previous mismanagement undercut his vigorous efforts at every turn. But his dream for Mariposa's transfiguration is instructive of the idealism underlying his park designs. He referred to his overarching goal as "communicativeness," which he defined as a "combination of qualities which fit (a person) to serve others and to be served by others in the most intimate, complete and extended degree possible."[57]

At Mariposa, we see Olmsted working on the same theory of social class integration he had seen at Birkenhead Park in Liverpool. This theme—creating attractive environments that promote healthy, democratic mixing of the social classes—was prominent in Olmsted's goals in Central Park. At Central Park, luxurious facilities were provided to attract the upper crust to join other social classes in enjoying the park.[58]

However well-intentioned Olmsted may have been in planning parks for social improvement, some modern scholars have called attention to its inherent paternalism. In this interpretation, Olmsted and other elites decided what types of settings and experiences would best elevate the poor and help them become more civilized. The opinions of the working class were seldom sought or incorporated into park design.[59] Moreover, they question the extent to which Olmsted's vision was realized. According to Dorceta Taylor, encounters between middle and working classes in city parks were "awkward and sometimes hostile." The middle class established "rules of behavior and decorum, thus setting the stage for greater confrontations and rebellion." Working class park users' resistance to being told how to use public parks led to the creation of multiple-use urban parks designed to accommodate both passive and active recreation.[60]

These criticisms may be valid, but they should not diminish Olmsted's contributions. In an era when prevailing opinion favored reliance on the market economy and social "survival of the fittest," Olmsted argued steadfastly that government had a responsibility for improving the lives of all citizens by providing public parks. In championing this cause, Olmsted forced leaders in New York and elsewhere to think about the meaning of the term "public good" and to consider how parks might contribute to it, however it might be defined.[61]

The Yosemite Grant

Working at the Mariposa Estate, Olmsted first saw Yosemite Valley in August 1864:

> Photographs, sketches, the accounts of other travelers, nothing had adequately prepared Olmsted for the awesome, peaceful abyss. Its great cliffs, almost a mile high and backed by the vast Sierras, showed chalky in the morning light softened by the smoke of forest fires and by thunderheads in the east. Down their granite faces threaded the cascades, graceful ornaments to their grandeur. Far below in the serene meadows the green tracery of leaves alternated with grass, and the winking silver stream of the Merced rippled among ferns and rushes and willows. Olmsted thought he was seeing a glorious vision, too wonderful to be believed, a sort of scenic allegory in which the awfulness of the chasm was forgotten in the beauty in which it was clothed.[62]

Only a month before Olmsted first saw the Valley, President Abraham Lincoln had signed into law a bill granting to the state of California 20 square miles of the Yosemite Valley and 4 square miles containing the Mariposa grove of giant sequoias. The land was to be used for "public use, resort and recreation," and was to be held permanently by the state as long as specified conditions were met. The bill Lincoln signed had been introduced by Senator John Conness of California, on behalf of gentlemen "of fortune, of taste and of refinement." In all likelihood, Olmsted was one of these gentlemen. Among the others—the leaders of San Francisco society [63]—was a representative of the Central American Steamship Transit Company, who appears to have first suggested the grant to Senator Conness.[64]

What prompted this policy proposal and enabled legislative action? Whites had first seen the valley in 1833, when a party of trappers traveling westward across the Sierra Nevada under Joseph Walker's leadership viewed it from the rim.[65] The valley was first entered by whites in 1851, by citizen-soldiers pursuing Yosemite Indians who had been provoked into uprising by gold seekers. Journalists first arrived in 1855, and publicity of the valley followed rapidly.[66] Photographer Carleton Watkins produced a popular set of stereoscopic slides, and painter Albert Bierstadt produced two monumental paintings of the valley that were popular successes.[67] White women travelers first visited the valley on horseback around 1857 and journalists' stories about their safe travel encouraged others to make the trip.[68]

By the time of the 1864 grant, the awe-inspiring natural features of the Yosemite Valley and the Mariposa Grove were well known. One of the factors that led to the grant was the fear that these natural wonders would be destroyed. In 1854, in fact, something had happened which made such fear credible. Several enterprising men stripped the bark from a sequoia and charged admission for viewing this wonder of nature, a tree which measured 116 feet to the first limb. The bark was shipped to England and exhibited there at London's famous Crystal Palace. Ironically, the British considered the whole thing impossible and discounted it as a fraud.[69] Still, the affair was controversial, and like the entrepreneurial efforts at Niagara Falls, it became a source of embarrassment to the elites struggling to establish America's cultural identity.[70] The notoriety of the incident helped raise public consciousness of this natural treasure, and soon Yosemite and the threats to it were widely known. As unreserved public land, it was open for entry under a variety of land disposal policies and therefore likely to be damaged.

In Yosemite, America possessed a gem of nature equal to Niagara Falls, and it, too, was threatened by the quick-buck mentality. But threats to landscape beauty were not enough by themselves to prompt the grant. Congressmen had to be persuaded that valuable land was not being lost. Thus, when Senator Conness introduced his bill, he specified, in language reminiscent of George Catlin three decades earlier, that the area to be granted to California was worthless and contained nothing of value to the government.[71]

Finally, as with virtually any federal policy action, we must account for the posture of major industrial and commercial interests. At Yosemite, apparently, politically strong economic interests were not present. Mining, hydroelectric power, and forestry interests did not seek to exploit the resources of the valley and grove.[72] The brittleness of the giant sequoia wood made it unattractive as lumber and thus contributed greatly to forest preservation in the Mariposa Grove. On the positive side, as noted previously, it was a representative of the transportation industry who suggested the legislation, perhaps encouraged by the prospect of future tourism revenues.[73]

Following the grant, Olmsted was installed as one of nine state commissioners charged with developing a plan for the new state park. Olmsted took the lead in this planning, and the plan strongly reflects his democratic idealism.[74] Olmsted's report was the first systematic argument in America favoring governmental leadership in providing parks for people.[75] It linked democratic philosophy and Olmsted's theory of the benefits of encounters with nature. Olmsted felt that the primary value of parks lay in the contrast they provided from people's everyday lives.[76] Rather than human-dominated environments where the individual's agenda was set by others, parks in Olmsted's conception provided a natural scene and permitted visitors to move through them at their own pace and with their own thoughts. Such a setting respected each person's individual responses in a way that packaged commercial recreation—like that found in Olmsted's day at Niagara Falls and in our day at Disney World—did not. Recognition of individualism was proper and, in fact, necessary in a democracy.

In his plan for Yosemite, Olmsted presented his theory of the psychological value of exposure to natural scenery. The temporary relief from workday pressures was not just fun, but a critical restorative for life in modern society. Olmsted lived at a time of rapid urbanization and industrialization, and he feared the loss of such social anchors as the family, church, and tradition. If Americans were to govern themselves well, we needed a permanent standard of value against which our daily tasks could be measured. Ordinary citizens needed the opportunity to exercise the contemplative faculty, an inherent human capacity for absorbed attention. Exercise of the contemplative faculty would free one's mind, at least temporarily, from the achievement motives that typically dominate one's thinking. Natural areas were particularly conducive to contemplative recreation; the visitor's attention was arrested and preoccupation with daily affairs was alleviated. In Olmsted's words:

> It is a scientific fact that the occasional contemplation of natural scenes of an impressive character, particularly if this contemplation occurs in connection with relief from ordinary cares, change of air and change of habits, is favorable to the health and vigor of men and especially to the health and vigor of their intellect beyond any other conditions which can be offered them, that it not only gives pleasure for the time being but increases the subsequent capacity for happiness and the means of securing happiness. The want of such occasional recreation where men and women are habitually pressed by their business or household cares often results in a class of disorders the characteristic quality of which is mental disability, sometimes taking the severe forms of softening of the brain, paralysis, palsy, monomania, or insanity, but more frequently of mental and nervous excitability,

moroseness, melancholy or irascibility, incapacitating the subject for the proper exercise of the intellectual and moral forces.[79]

In a democracy, Olmsted believed, natural scenery should be available to all the people. He did not agree with the apologists of aristocracy that working men and women were incapable of appreciating natural scenery and being improved by its influences. Therefore, in the United States it was the right and the duty of government to protect some natural areas and to make them readily available to all the citizens.

Men who are rich enough and who are sufficiently free from anxiety with regard to their wealth can and do provide places of this needed recreation for themselves. They have done so from the earliest periods known in the history of the world, for the great men of the Babylonians, the Persians and the Hebrews, had their rural retreats, as large and as luxurious as those of the aristocracy of Europe at present. There are in the islands of Great Britain and Ireland more than one thousand private parks and notable grounds devoted to luxury and recreation. The value of these grounds amounts to many millions of dollars and the cost of the annual maintenance is greater than that of the national schools; their only advantage to the commonwealth is obtained through the recreation they afford their owners (except as these extend hospitality to others) and these owners with their families number less than one in six thousand of the whole population. The enjoyment of the choicest natural scenes in the country and the means of recreation connected with them is thus a monopoly, in a very peculiar manner, of a very few, very rich people. The great mass of society, including those to whom it would be of the greatest benefit, is excluded from it. In the nature of the case private parks can never be used by the mass of the people in any country nor by any considerable number even of the rich, except by the favor of a few, and in dependence on them.

Thus without means are taken by government to withhold them from the grasp of individuals, all places favorable in scenery to the recreation of the mind and body will be closed against the great body of the people. For the same reason that the water of rivers should be guarded against private appropriation and the use of it for the purpose of navigation and otherwise protected against obstruction, portions of natural scenery may therefore properly be guarded and cared for by government. To simply reserve them from monopoly by individuals, however, it will be obvious, is not all that is necessary. It is necessary that they should be laid open to the use of the body of the people.

The establishment by government of great public grounds for the free enjoyment of the people under certain circumstances, is thus justified and enforced as a political duty.[78]

At Yosemite, as elsewhere, Olmsted's idealism was far ahead of its time. His report was suppressed, apparently because of fear that the money he sought for implementing it would be diverted by the California state legislature from the Geological Survey, a representative of which served with Olmsted on the Yosemite Board of Commissioners. Olmsted returned to work on Central Park, and the Yosemite Park continued in an essentially unmanaged state for the next half century, with increasing visitation and abuse.[79]

Thus, the Yosemite Grant represents only the start of a policy. It was a crucial breakthrough, though, and served as precedent for establishing future parks. Olmsted's plan, while not immediately implemented, helped provide the philosophical base for the creation of the National Park Service in 1916. Olmsted's ideas in his Yosemite plan and elsewhere have helped to shape the ongoing debate about the meaning and purpose of the national parks in American society.

NOTES

1. This section relies primarily on Nash, *Wilderness and the American Mind,* and Huth, *Nature and the American.*
2. Dorman, *A Word for Nature,* 56–67.
3. Nash, Wilderness and the American Mind, pp. 84–86.
4. Dorman, *A Word for Nature,* 59–61.
5. From *The Portable Emerson,* edited by Carl Bode. Copyright 1946; renewed in 1974 by the Viking Press, Inc. Copyright 1981 by Viking Penguin, Inc. Reprinted by permission of Viking Penguin, Inc.
6. Noble, *The Eternal Adam and the New World Garden.*
7. Bode, *The Portable Emerson,* p. xxix.
8. Emerson, *Nature,* p. 10.
9. Ibid., p. 11.
10. Ibid, p. 50.
11. The biographical background on Thoreau is largely from Bode (ed.), *The Portable Thoreau,* pp. 1–29. See also Richardson, *Henry Thoreau: A Life of the Mind.*
12. Thoreau, "Civil Disobedience," p. 125.
13. Dorman, *A Word for Nature,* p. 97.
14. Ibid., pp. 79–81.
15. Ibid., p. 77.

16. Ibid., p. 82.

17. Botkin, *No Man's Garden,* pp. 87–99.

18. From *The Portable Thoreau,* edited by Carl Bode. Copyright 1947 by the Viking Press, Inc. Copyright in 1962, 1964, by the Viking Press, Inc. Copyright renewed in 1975 by the Viking Press, Inc. Reprinted by permission of Viking Penguin, Inc.

19. Bode, *The Portable Thoreau,* pp. 444–445.

20. Ibid., p. 567.

21. Ibid., p. 344.

22. Richardson, *Henry Thoreau,* pp. 151–153.

23. Thoreau, *The Maine Woods,* pp. 85–86.

24. Bode, *The Portable Thoreau,* p. 557.

25. Hammond, "Wilderness and Life in Cities."

26. Cronon, "The Trouble with Wilderness."

27. Runte, *National Parks,* Chapters 1–2.

28. Huth, *Nature and the American,* p. 3.

29. Runte, *National Parks,* pp. 5–9.

30. Ibid., pp. 20–22.

31. However, in *Dispossessing the Wilderness—Indian Removal and the Making of the National Parks* (pp. 10–11), author Mark Spence makes the point that Catlin's proposal bears little resemblance to the parks that were established later in the 19th century because his vision of a natural preserve included Indian habitation. Spence goes on to explain that, while culturally naïve to assume that native societies would not evolve or to think that these parks would not become more like outdoor museums than wilderness, Catlin's proposal was more than a "historical curiosity." Instead, it reflected antebellum American conceptions of Indians and wildness as being one in the same. Remove one and you remove the other. What is unique is Catlin's desire to set these places aside as preserves and his interest in native people, whereas the majority of his contemporaries viewed "Indian wilderness" as a barrier to progress.

32. Runte, *National Parks,* p. 26.

33. Gilligan, "The Development of Policy.....," pp. 14–15.

34. Roper, *FLO,* p. 6. Other sources on Olmsted include Rybcznski, *A Clearing in the Distance;* Beveridge and Schuyler, *The Papers of Frederick Law Olmsted,* Supplementary Series, Vol. I; Taylor, "Central Park as a Model for Social Control"; and Rosenzweig and Blackmar, *The Park and the People.*

35. Roper, *FLO,* pp. 7–8.

36. Ibid., p. 32.

37. Ibid., pp. 87–88.

38. Ibid., p. 86.
39. Rybczynski, *A Clearing in the Distance*, p. 93.
40. Roper, *FLO*, p. 71.
41. Ibid., p 124.
42. Ibid., p. 129.
43. Ibid., pp. 130–131.
44. Ibid., pp. 127–128.
45. Ibid., p. 136; Rosenzweig and Blackmar, *The Park and its People*, pp. 59–91, report that 1600 families were evicted from the area that became Central Park, including some in neighborhoods with patterns of home ownership and economic stability and where some people had jobs in the city and did not have purely subsistence lifestyles.
46. Ibid., p. 137.
47. Taylor, "The urban environment_," p. 277.
48. Ibid., p. 138.
49. Ibid., p. 144.
50. Ibid., p. 150. Rybczynski, *A Clearing in the Distance*, presents a more positive view of NYC comptroller Andrew Green.
51. Rybczynski, *A Clearing in the Distance*, p. 212–213, reports that the death rate in the Civil War's Peninsular Campaign, served by Olmsted's Sanitary Commission's hospital ships, was 165 per thousand, about half the death rate of British wounded in the Crimean War.
52. Ibid., p. 223.
53. De Voto, *Year of Decision*, offers a frank and uncomplimentary view of Fremont's role in western history.
54. Rybczynski, *A Clearing in the Distance*, p. 223.
55. Roper, *FLO*, p. 235.
56. Ibid., p. 257.
57. Ibid., p. 253.
58. Ibid., p. 141.
59. Rosenzweig and Blackmar, *The Park and the People;* Beveridge and Hoffman, *The Papers of Frederick Law Olmsted;* and Taylor, "Central Park as a Model for Social Control."
60. Taylor, "Central Park as a Model for Social Control."
61. Rosenzweig and Blackmar, *The Park and the People*, p. 58.
62. Roper, *FLO*, p. 267.
63. Sax, "America's National Parks."
64. Roper, *FLO*, p. 282.

65. Gilbert, *Westering Man,* pp. 135–136.

66. Huth, *Nature and the American,* p. 143.

67. Rybczynski, *A Clearing in the Distance,* p. 236.

68. Kaufman, *National Parks and the Woman's Voice,* p. 4. Women continued to visit Yosemite and provide labor for the burgeoning tourist business through 1900 (Kaufman, pp. 5–9). In 1871, Elizabeth Cady Stanton and Susan B. Anthony visited Yosemite as a way of showcasing their California suffrage campaign for women's rights. Jennie and David Curry developed the precursor of the Yosemite Park and Curry Company, the leading provider of visitor lodging and other services in the valley until 1980s.

69. Huth, *Nature and the American,* pp. 142–143.

70. Sax, "America's National Parks."

71. Runte, *National Parks,* pp. 48–49.

72. Ibid., p. 49.

73. Huth, *Nature and the American,* p. 144.

74. Olmsted, "The Yosemite Valley and the Mariposa Big Trees."

75. Roper, *FLO,* p. 285.

76. Sax, *Mountains Without Handrails,* pp. 17–26.

77. Olmsted, "The Yosemite Valley and the Mariposa Big Trees," p. 17. Olmsted's scientific facts are based on 19th century conceptions and are soft by today's standards, although scientific knowledge in support of the connection between nature and mental health is growing (e.g., Kaplan and Kaplan 1989; Ulrich 1993). In passages immediately following those quoted, Olmsted illustrates his 19th century elitism and absence of understanding of American Indian spirituality: "The power of scenery to affect men is, in a large way, proportionate to the degree of their civilization and the degree to which their taste has been cultivated. Among a thousand savages there will be a much smaller number who will show the least sign of being so affected than among a thousand persons taken from a civilized community. This is only one of the many channels in which a similar distinction between civilized and savage men is to be generally observed. The whole body of the susceptibilities of civilized men and with their susceptibilities their powers, are on the whole enlarged."

78. Ibid., p. 21.

79. For an account of how the Yosemite Indians were first tolerated in the park due to their usefulness as tour guides, later denigrated by John Muir and eventually extirpated from the park, see Spence, *Dispossessing the Wilderness.*

CHAPTER 5

INSTITUTIONAL ORIGINS: THE FOREST SERVICE

Although concern over forest depletion had existed since colonial times, efforts to regulate lumbering were sporadic and uncoordinated, and steps to improve the productivity of standing forests were virtually nonexistent. For the two centuries since white settlement of the eastern seaboard, Americans had been content to mine the country's vast timber resource. Timber harvesting methods of the time, like uses of all other natural resources, were incredibly wasteful by today's standards. Under conditions of apparently inexhaustible forest resources and scarce capital and labor, it made little sense to harvest forests with care. Instead, the picture was one of a scramble for riches from a wealth of resources thought to be inexhaustible. The American social system, based on individual enterprise and favoring minimal governmental intervention into the workings of the free-market economy, rationalized and supported the plunder. The pace of exploitation increased until the time of the Civil War when there were calls for reform, most notably in the form of George Perkins Marsh's *Man and Nature*.

The policy process moves from perceived problems to responses, and society's most complex and difficult problems are made the responsibility of complex organizations, or bureaus, devoted to them. Leadership in national security is delegated to the Department of Defense, crime to the Federal Bureau of Investigation, pollution to the Environmental Protection Agency, and so on. There may be overlapping responsibilities and conflicting purposes in the agencies arrayed to attack any given problem.

The lead federal agencies are frequently challenged by sister federal agencies, as is the case of the Bureau of Reclamation and the Corps of Engineers, both of which are involved in water development projects. There are counterpart state, regional, and local agencies providing similar services to differing jurisdictions. However, even though the full institutional structure that evolves around a policy problem may become terribly complex, in most cases there is one particular agency that sets the pace. Nowhere is this more true than for forestry.

The growth of concern over forest resources after the Civil War led eventually to the creation of a new agency, the United States Forest Service (now, USDA Forest Service), to spearhead national efforts in response to existing and predicted problems. This chapter tracks the emergence of the Forest Service and covers the span of time between Marsh's book and 1910. In 1910 Gifford Pinchot, the first Chief of the Forest Service, was fired, leaving a young agency indelibly stamped with his strong beliefs and crusading zeal to carry on the fight for better forest management. The Forest Service has long been noted for its sense of mission and for the strengths and weaknesses that follow from that single-mindedness. Wildland recreation—especially wilderness—has always been a source of difficulty for the Forest Service. Understanding the growth of national parks and wilderness requires understanding the Forest Service, and that necessitates an examination of the agency's origins.

ANTECEDENTS OF THE FOREST SERVICE

Marsh's book (reviewed in Chapter 3) brought focus and weight to the concern over forest destruction that had emerged by the time of the Civil War.[1] Evidence of forest abuse abounded, at least for those with the ability to understand what was happening. For the majority of the population, however, the abuse existed simply as a part of normal life, or did not enter their consciousness at all. A case in point is the Peshtigo, Wisconsin, fire of 1873. This firestorm, which killed 1500 people and destroyed 1.2 million acres of timber in an eight-hour period, was caused in part by months of casual slash burning that helped dry the forest and prepare it for the conflagration. Before the fire, smoke was sometimes so thick that steamers on Green Bay had to navigate by compass during the day. Yet nobody appears to have been much alarmed, presumably because smoke-filled air was part of normal life. The firestorm itself was overshadowed in the public consciousness by the Chicago fire of the same night, although the urban blaze claimed only one-sixth as many victims.[2]

Without widespread public awareness of a problem, policy actions move slowly, and so it was with forestry. Among intellectuals, however, the movement heralded by Marsh's book gained momentum. The year of the Peshtigo fire—an attention-riveting event that helped crystallize policy action—found physician (and historian, naturalist, and statistician) Franklin Hough presenting a paper "On the Duty of Governments in the Preservation of Forests" to the American Association for the Advancement of Science. Hough argued for education of landowners and the general public about forests and their importance to climate, erosion control, and timber supply. He recommended study of the forestry situation in the United States. The study was authorized in 1876 and Hough was hired, for a salary of $2000, including expenses, to conduct the study and report his findings. Congressional authorization for Hough's work came in a rider added to a seed distribution authorization bill. In this way the promotion of forestry became a part of the Department of Agriculture, a position it has held to this day, despite repeated efforts to move it to the Department of the Interior. This important legislative action was carried out without debate, a little-noticed minor part of a large money bill. Hough conducted his investigation and, between 1878 and 1882, produced three monumental reports that provided the foundation for American forestry. In his reports Hough strongly endorsed the reservation of federal forest lands, following the precedent set by park reservations.[3]

In 1887 the first of a number of Germans who would strongly influence American forest policy appeared. Carl Schurz, who fled Prussia after being actively involved in its revolution of 1848–1849, was appointed Secretary of the Interior. A zealous reformer, Schurz attempted to protect the public lands through vigorous enforcement of existing laws, particularly the Timber Trespass Law of 1831, which imposed fines and imprisonment for unlawful cutting.[4] Schurz worked hard but with little effect other than to raise national consciousness of the huge federal forest resource that was legally off-limits. Local citizens living in timber-producing areas tended to think that trees existed to be used, and they recognized that their communities were dependent on the lumbermen's activity, even if it was sometimes illegal. Beyond that, local people resented the intrusions into their affairs by the distant government in Washington.[5]

Congress did respond to Schurz's efforts with several acts intended to make federal timber available to legitimate settlers and others, but these

acts did not serve to protect the forests.[6] In addition to his campaign
against trespassers, Schurz also argued for federal forest reserves, reforestation of cutover lands, user charges, and stiff penalties for setting fires.
For his troubles Schurz was denounced as un-American by a Maine congressman and accused of introducing "Prussian methods" into our democratic system and oppressing honest businessmen. Congress cut off the
modest funding for Interior's law enforcement efforts.[7]

The Adirondack Forest Preserve and Bernhard Fernow

The first policy action to reserve public forest lands from exploitation
came as a result of state, rather than federal, initiative. In 1885 the New
York State legislature established the Forest Preserve, consisting of 12
Adirondack and 4 Catskill counties on which the state-owned land was
to be kept "forever wild." Later policy actions would create an Adirondack Park, comprised of the public land and the intermixed private land
(60 percent of the total) in the Adirondack counties, and firmly fix the
"forever wild" rule by means of an amendment to the New York State
Constitution.[8]

 The initial 1885 action was prompted by reactions to the rapacious logging, primarily the high-grading of pine, hemlock, and spruce, which had
between 1813 and 1850 made New York the top lumber producing state.
A new chemical pulping process introduced in 1860 made cutting small
softwoods profitable, and the advent of the railroads made it possible to
bring hardwoods (which, unlike softwoods, could not easily be floated) to
the mill. The railroads also brought sparks and forest fires, along with a
new element—vacationers. As the Adirondacks became a popular place
to escape the miseries of urban summers, wealthy families built sumptu-
ous "camps" for "rusticating." By 1892 a fourth of the area was owned by
private individuals and clubs. The elites of the Adirondacks became increasingly anxious over the threat of fire created by logging, and they
joined forces with scientists concerned with forest abuse to push for protective legislation. A third and very important source of influence was the
state business community. Businessmen in New York City and elsewhere
worried that continued timber cutting would alter stream runoff and hamper waterborne commerce; if canals and navigable rivers suffered from
droughts and floods as a result of the loss of forest cover, New York City
businessmen would be left at the mercy of the monopolistic and piratical
railroads. Finally, there were concerns about public health, driven by wor-

ries about the effects of over-cutting on water supplies. It was the combination of concerns with trees, watersheds, natural beauty, commerce, and public health that resulted in the Adirondack Forest Preserve.[9]

In 1886 Congress statutorily recognized the Division of Forestry, and Bernhard Fernow was installed as chief. Fernow was the first professionally trained forester to work in the United States. He had studied forestry and law in Germany and had worked in Germany for several years before coming to America in 1875. Prior to his federal appointment, Fernow had been employed in east-central Pennsylvania, as the manager of 15,000 acres of hardwoods used to supply charcoal for ironworks. In addition to observations about American forestry he made as part of his job, Fernow traveled widely observing forest conditions. A paper he read at the 1882 American Forestry Congress brought him to the attention of the growing group interested in improving forest management and led eventually to his position with the Division of Forestry. Under Fernow the Division broadened its scope from education and reforestation to include forest science (biology, timber physics, soil chemistry), forest economics (statistics and policy), and practical forest management (organization and management, regulation and harvesting).[10]

Fernow devoted special attention to research on timber physics. He felt that more efficient manufacture and use of forest products could reduce demand and therefore help avert the widely predicted timber famine. In the formative years of the Forest Service, Fernow's demand-oriented approach would lose out to Gifford Pinchot's supply-oriented approach, and the importance of knowledge as a resource would not be given equal stature with physical wood volumes.[11]

In 1898 Fernow moved to take a position as director of the recently established New York State College of Forestry at Cornell University.[12] In addition to putting the new school on its feet, he was responsible for the conduct of an experiment, the first public test of scientific forestry in America. This test was to take place on a 30,000 acre demonstration forest in the Adirondacks. Half the forest consisted of cutover spruce and pine lands, and half was primarily virgin hardwoods, notably beech. Fernow's plan called for clearcutting the beech and converting those sites to more profitable spruce. A market for the beech was found in a barrel-making firm, which signed a 15-year contract to have the wood delivered in specified quantities. Fernow planned to make use of small and unsound beechwood by building a wood-alcohol distillery and a brick and lime kiln requiring fuelwood.

Fernow's experiment was a disaster. Among other problems, he discovered that 99 percent of the beech trees were unsound, and only part of each could be utilized in barrel-making. Producing the contracted quantity of sound beechwood was therefore very difficult. In addition, delivering the wood they could salvage was made impossible because a proposed railroad line was not built. The debacle ended in 1903 when the governor vetoed an appropriations bill for the College of Forestry.

Yet it was another factor that contributed strongly to the demise of the experiment and the school that is most germane to our discussion. That factor was Fernow's insistence on defining forestry in economic terms, to the exclusion of its recreational and aesthetic components. Despite the fact that the existence of the New York Forest Preserve, and therefore the College of Forestry and the forestry experiment, owed a great deal to the influence of the well-to-do resorters in the Adirondacks, Fernow insisted in downgrading their interests in the management of the forest.

> We must repeat again that forestry is a technical art, wholly utilitarian, and not, except incidentally, concerned in esthetic aspects of the woods: it is engaged in utilizing the soil for the production of wood crops, and thereby of the highest revenue obtainable.[13]

As a forestry expert, Fernow was asked by a group of New Yorkers interested in forest protection what he would recommend as the smallest diameter tree that could legally be harvested. Running headlong against his audience's sentiments, Fernow replied that "any diameter which paid best, even down to the size of the little finger, would satisfy the demands of forestry."[14]

When the proposed railroad lines were not built, Fernow brought the barrel-making plant to the woods. The barrel plant and Fernow's other wood-using installations were unsightly and offended those who saw the Adirondacks as a retreat from civilization. Clearcutting northern hardwoods for cooperage stock went far beyond the concept of forestry held by the people of the area and led to unfavorable legislative review.[15] Moreover, brush burning at the experimental forest got out of hand and spread to neighboring estates, thus bringing to their owners the very threat they had sought to avoid by establishing the Forest Preserve in the first place.

The uproar caused by all this led to the closing of the school, and contract problems with the cooperage firm led to court, where the foresters got a chance to tell their story. In court, expert witnesses for scientific forestry linked arms with businessmen, both using profitability as their sole criterion. But "Does it pay?" is not the appropriate question in the view of all forest users. Those interested in the recreational, aesthetic, and wildlife benefits of forests are slighted if profitability is the only goal in forest management. These interests were important in the Adirondacks then, and they stopped Fernow's demonstration of scientific forestry in its tracks. From that point on, constitutional lawyers have been as influential as foresters in determining how the Adirondack Forest Preserve is used.

Fernow's experience in the Adirondacks is symptomatic of a blind spot toward noneconomic forest uses that has characterized the profession and its institutional embodiment, the USDA Forest Service. In the twentieth century, the Forest Service's insistence on viewing forestry as "tree-farming" (the words of forestry's most prominent spokesman, Gifford Pinchot) would help its rival, the National Park Service, acquire vast acreages through congressional transfers of Forest Service land and prompt passage of wilderness policy to protect remote Forest Service lands from road-building and logging.

Forest Reservation Act

While Fernow's drama was being played out on the state forest of New York, momentous events were under way on the federal lands. Following years of growing concern over the forest abuse on the public lands, Congress in 1891 passed the so-called Forest Reservation Act. This act marks the start of the National Forest System, because presidential actions it authorized provided the essential land base in the West. Later acts permitted the purchase of lands in the East.

The Forest Reservation Act of 1891 consisted of a one-sentence, grammatically incorrect rider to a general land law revision bill:

> Section 24. That the President of the United States may, from time to time, set apart and reserve, in any State or Territory having public lands wholly or in part covered with timber or undergrowth, whether of commercial value or not, as public reservations, and the President shall, by public proclamation, declare the establishment of such reservations and the limits thereof.[16]

Section 24 was added in House-Senate conference, in violation of a congressional rule against the addition of new material at that stage in the legislative process. There was minimal debate on Section 24 before the final vote.[17] Three days later President Benjamin Harrison signed the bill into law. Based on this act, by 1905 three presidents—Harrison, Cleveland, and Roosevelt—had reserved over 100 million acres of the public domain from private entry under various land-disposal laws.[18]

The evident haste surrounding the amendment has been interpreted as signifying that it was a fluke of the legislative process, an accidental law made with no understanding of its potential consequences. The final action may indeed have been hasty, but the ground was well prepared. The Yellowstone Park Reservation of 1872 had established precedent for presidential reservations of land from the public domain. There had been long-standing concern over the exploitation of our forest resources by both nature lovers and commercial interests. Bills to establish forest reserves had been considered by Congress since 1876, so Congress was well aware of the pros and cons of the forest reservation idea. Finally, there was no concerted western opposition; in fact, the early reserves were requested by western spokesmen.[19]

Congress knew what it was doing in passing the Forest Reservation Act. The haste and brevity of the act, and its irregular mode of introduction, may be interpreted as the outcome of a philosophical and legislative struggle, rather than as a surprise. It was the best compromise the opposing interests could come up with, a vague statute which allowed the president to set aside some lands. And Congress took this step in full knowledge of its ability to repeal this presidential power if it was abused.

Within a month after signing the Forest Reservation Act into law, President Harrison established the Yellowstone Park Forest Reservation, thus making the Yellowstone region the official birthplace of both the National Park and National Forest systems.[20] In the next 2 years Harrison set aside 13 million acres. Under existing law, there were no funds for administration, and use of the timber and other resources was not legal. Local resentment began to mount. Fires and trespass were commonplace on the reserves. Settlers and miners felt they had a right to use the resources as they always had and treat the reserves as their own back yards. In 1897 President Cleveland set aside 21 million additional acres of national forests, again with no money for protection. As Cleveland's action came only 10 days before the end of his term in office, his forest reservations were called the "Midnight Reserves." Cleveland's reservations especially irritated those opposed to the reserves, as they were hastily drawn and included some good agricultural lands and even some townsites.[21]

Forest Management Act

Originally, the Department of the Interior's General Land Office was assigned responsibility for the forest reserves. The General Land Office was not a management agency; its primary role was overseeing transfers of the public lands to private citizens, corporations, and state and local units of government under federal land disposal policies. The Division of Forestry, first under Hough and later under Fernow and then Pinchot, was located in the Department of Agriculture. The General Land Office and its field personnel were viewed by those living in the regions of the national forests as overly legalistic, distant dictators wholly out of touch with local forest concerns. They were resented and ignored by those living closest to the reserves.

The opposition that had always been there and had gained strength because of the perceived high-handedness and sloppiness of the withdrawal process eventually led to the next landmark legislative action. The so-called Forest Management Act of 1897, referred to as the "organic" (or organizational) act of the U.S. Forest Service, permitted management of the reserves. Once again a major piece of natural resource legislation was passed as a rider. Again, this law was no surprise, as 27 bills to authorize active management and use of the reserves had been submitted since 1891.[22]

Support for the 1897 act came primarily from those who wanted to exploit the timber resources in the reserves. Interestingly, in this case timber interests were joined by preservationists who feared that unless some use of the reserves was permitted, the whole forest reserve system would be threatened. Opposition to the Forest Management Act came primarily from irrigation interests, who wanted watershed protection. As passed, the act sought a compromise between these competing interests. The purposes of the forest reserves, according to the 1897 act, were to protect the forests within them in order to secure favorable water flows and provide a continuous supply of timber.[23]

One of the 1897 act's major provisions, which would come to haunt forest management in later years, concerned timber harvesting. Timber harvesting was limited to "dead, matured or large growth of trees," which had to be "marked and designated" for cutting. Legal issues in the clearcutting controversy of the 1970s would revolve around this language, and would spur passage of the 1976 National Forest Management Act.[24]

GIFFORD PINCHOT AND THE PROGRESSIVE CONSERVATION MOVEMENT

One of the people most influential in obtaining passage of the Forest Management Act was Gifford Pinchot. Pinchot's involvement reflected his firm conviction that the national forests should be actively managed to benefit the present population, while at the same time protecting the interests of future generations. This belief—one of the central ideas of the conservation movement—differed strongly from the preservationists' proposals for the forest reserves. Preservationists felt that the only way to save the forests and avert the predicted timber famine was to lock up the reserves and send in the army to defend the trees. This conflict presaged later conflicts between Pinchot and the Forest Service, on the one hand, and John Muir and the National Park Service, on the other.

Gifford Pinchot was born in 1867 into a Connecticut family of wealth and social position.[25] Pinchot's grandfather was a successful lumberman who used the environmentally insensitive logging practices of his day. Gifford's father James, a New York City merchant who specialized in interior furnishings—wallpaper, window shades, and curtains—was so successful he was able to retire in his 40s.[26] James Pinchot was fascinated by forestry. He was an early member and one-time vice president of the American Forestry Association, founded in 1874 to promote forest protection in the United States. For his son's twenty-first birthday, he gave Gifford an 1882 edition of Marsh's *Man and* Nature, illustrating both his concerns about human impacts on the environment and his dreams for his son's career.[27] James suggested that Gifford consider forestry as a career. Seeking others' advice, Gifford was told that the profession did not exist in the United States and that following that career would take him into risky new territory. Bernhard Fernow told Pinchot he believed forestry was impracticable in the United States, since the conditions in its countries of origin—Germany, France, and Switzerland—were not found here. As Fernow later wrote:

> If, then, in a country with dense population, where in many places every twig can be marketed, with settled conditions of market, with no virgin woods which could cheaply be exploited and come into advantageous competition with costlier materials produced on managed properties, with the cost of labor low and the prices for wood comparatively high—if under such conditions the return for the expenditure of money, skill, intellect in the production of wood crops is not more promising, it would seem hope-

less to develop the argument of profitableness in a country where all these conditions are the reverse, and a businessman considers 6 percent investment no sufficient inducement.[28]

Far from daunting Pinchot, however, this practical career advice simply spurred his interest, since he could be there at the creation. In his 1889 commencement speech at Yale, he announced his acceptance of a calling to public service on behalf of forestry. As recounted by historian Char Miller, "Pinchot, ever 'eager to bear witness to my faith,' a faith that demanded passionate self-sacrifice, testified that his calling would be to minister to the American Forests."[29]

After his graduation from Yale, he sailed to England, with the intent of speaking to some foresters and purchasing some books on forestry. In London, he met with leaders of the model forest service Britain had established in India and the school in which they were trained.[30] The most important connection he made was with Dietrich Brandis, then the world's most renowned forester. Pinchot seized the opportunity to study under Brandis at Nancy, France. He proved himself an extremely quick and active student, though somewhat restless with desk work. He decided, against the advice of Brandis and others, that after one year's schooling he was ready to return to work as a forester in the United States. He was convinced that French forestry could not be fully applied in the United States and that Yankee forestry problems would have to be solved by Yankees. Specifically, he believed the "Gallic precision" that characterized French forestry was grounded on an " . . . autocratic perspective that would wither in republican terrain."[31]

In France, Pinchot learned to think of trees as a crop. The key to continuous production of timber is to harvest trees in a way that perpetuates the forests. This sustained yield concept was the utilitarian alternative to preservation Pinchot felt was needed in this country. Coupled with the sustained yield concept was Pinchot's conviction that active governmental leadership was needed to regulate timber harvesting on private lands. As his thinking developed, he became increasingly convinced of the importance of governmental intervention to protect the rights of ordinary citizens against large and powerful business interests.

The imagination is staggered by the magnitude of the prize for which we work. If we succeed, there will exist upon the continent a sane strong people, living through the centuries in a land subdued and controlled for the service of the people, its rightful masters, owned by the many and not by the few. If we fail, great interests, increasing their control of our natural resources, will thereby control the country more and more and the rights of the people will fade into the privileges of concentrated wealth.[32]

The primary beneficiary of governmental resource protection was to be the homeowner. In language reminiscent of Thomas Jefferson's hymn of praise to the small farmer, Pinchot wrote:

The most valuable citizen of this or any other country is the man who owns the land from which he makes his living. No other man has such a stake in the country. No other man lends such steadiness and stability to our national life. Therefore no other question concerns us more intimately than the question of homes; permanent homes for ourselves, our children, and our Nation—this is a central problem. . . . The old saying, "whoever heard of a man shouldering his gun to fight for his boarding house?" reflects this great truth, that no man is so ready to defend his country, not only with arms but with his vote and his contribution to public opinion, as the man with the permanent stake in it, as the man who owns the land from which he makes his living.[33]

On his return to America, Pinchot had two major objectives: to develop his personal understanding of forestry conditions here, and to establish a large-scale demonstration of scientific forestry. The first objective was reached through field trips with Fernow, who was wooing Pinchot for an assistant director's position under him, and consultations with industrial forest landowners. The second objective was providentially reached when he was offered the position of forest manager at George Vanderbilt's Biltmore estate near Asheville, North Carolina. Pinchot was recommended for the job and interviewed by Vanderbilt's prime consultant, Frederick Law Olmsted. Olmsted had developed the forest management plan for Biltmore, which called for creating a small park around the house and improving the remaining forest, and convinced the 26-year-old owner, George Vanderbilt, of the wisdom of his plan. Pinchot's job was to carry it out.[34]

At Biltmore, Pinchot halted the regular practice of clearcutting, cut only marked trees, felled them so as not to damage young trees, and left seed trees at regular intervals. One year later Pinchot declared himself satisfied that scientific forestry would pay: expenditures totaled $10,103, while revenues were $4,616 and an estimated $6,708 worth of wood was used on the estate, for a net of $1,221. Pinchot's rendition of this success story may have been unduly self-congratulatory. According to historian Char Miller, Pinchot's bookkeeping was suspect: " . . . much of the income stream was the result of the estate's buying its own wood products, and Pinchot failed to include his salary in his calculation of expenses . . . had he followed better accounting procedures, his project would have been in the red."[35] Beyond the creative accounting, Carl Schenck, who succeeded Pinchot as Biltmore's forest manager, called the efforts of both Pinchot and himself a "debacle."[36]

After leaving Biltmore, Pinchot moved into consulting. He opened his own office in New York, while he continued to consult with Vanderbilt. One of his consulting jobs was in the Adirondacks with Vanderbilt's brother-in-law, who had seen Pinchot's work at Biltmore. Pinchot recommended a light thinning operation, with emphasis on maintaining recreation benefits. This demonstration of scientific forestry caught on somewhat among the wealthy resorters. Forestry's success in this instance is ironic in light of the resorters' role in the "forever wild" decree, on the one hand, and the fundamental assumption of scientific forestry that humans could improve the forest, on the other.

While Pinchot was getting his career established, the Forest Reservation Act was passed. It did not take Pinchot long to become involved in national forest issues. He was instrumental in establishing the National Forest Commission, the first of a long list of commissions he would use to further his purposes. As a member of the commission he was immediately embroiled in conflict when he disagreed with its chairman over the administration of the reserves. The chairman, famed director of Harvard's Arnold Arboretum Charles Sprague Sargent, wanted to lock up the reserves and send in the army to protect the trees, while Pinchot argued vigorously for scientific management. As he later wrote:

> The first great fact about conservation is that it stands for development. There has been a fundamental misconception that conservation means nothing but the husbanding of resources for future generations. There could be no more serious mistake. Conservation does mean provision for the future, but it means also and first of all the recognition of the right of the present generation to the fullest necessary use of all the resources of which this country is so abundantly blessed. Conservation demands the welfare of this generation first, and afterward the welfare of the generations to follow.[37]

The first outcome of the commission's work was President Cleveland's proclamation of 13 new western forest reserves totaling 21 million acres. Pinchot did not like the idea of creating additional reserves without consulting people in the regions affected and making provisions for their use of the resources. As previously noted, the Cleveland reserves had provoked a storm of protest from settlers and other forest users who considered them to be a permanent lock-up, and that protest had led directly to the 1897 Forest Management Act.

Soon after the 1897 act was passed, Pinchot accepted a position as "special forest agent," inventorying the timber resources of the reserves and checking their boundaries. Remembering the problems caused by the Sargent commission's uncommunicative ways, Pinchot discussed his findings and ideas with everyone he could corner. This way of proceeding was an early indicator of his future as chief of the Forest Service, where he was one of the most unquiet bureau heads in Washington history. Under Pinchot's guidance the Forest Service maintained a mailing list of 781,000 people who were regularly informed about the agency's activities, thinking, and needs.[38] Not surprisingly, his final report as "special forest agent" recommended the establishment of a new federal agency to administer the reserves.

When Fernow left in 1898 to head the New York State College of Forestry, Pinchot took over the Division of Forestry in the Department of Agriculture. From the day he took office, Pinchot applied himself untiringly toward wresting control of the reserves from the General Land Office. In addition to his relentless lobbying for the transfer, he took other important steps. He persuaded his family to endow a graduate program in forestry at Yale. It opened in 1900 and provided many of the profession's early leaders. He organized the Society of American Foresters in 1900 and held many of the organization's early meetings at his home. He built up the capabilities of the Division by hiring the best people he could find, regardless of political persuasion, and then giving them great latitude in carrying out their work. The esprit de corps of his agency soared. Manpower expanded in 5 years from 11 to 179 people, and budgets showed parallel growth. The Division, which later became the USDA Forest Service, emerged as a model agency. Employees venerated the hard-working, honest, and frank man at the helm, and their loyalty to him, their agency, and their profession was extreme. On the negative side, Pinchot's zealous pursuit of his ends led him to treat those who challenged him roughly; for example, Pinchot called Schenck an "antichrist" because he had the temerity to advocate lumbering as a central component of forestry, while Pinchot equated forestry with silviculture and portrayed lumbermen as the enemy.[39] Under Pinchot the Forest Service came to be seen as "self-righteous and impervious to criticism," and its strong sense of mission for scientific forestry as Pinchot defined it tended to blind the Service to noneconomic uses of the forest.[40] This weakness would most clearly be seen in the Forest Service's struggles with the Park Service and its difficulties in dealing with demands for wilderness.[41]

Transfer Act of 1905

Despite Pinchot's best efforts, it took until 1905, when Theodore Roosevelt won his first full-term presidency by a landslide, to get the forest reserves transferred to Pinchot's control in the Department of Agriculture. The Transfer Act of 1905, the first major forestry legislation not passed as a rider, not only relocated control of the reserves but also established a special fund for receipts from timber sales on the national forests. That special fund was intended to provide a degree of autonomy from the congressional appropriations process. The fund was an important element in the progressive conservation program, but it would later be repealed as controversy over the Forest Service and its boss increased.

On the same day the Transfer Act became law, Pinchot received from Secretary of Agriculture James Wilson a letter giving broad policy guidance for management of the national forests. This letter, drafted by Pinchot for Wilson's signature, fixed the Forest Service's alignment toward economic use of the forests' resources, guided by principles of scientific forest management. Recreational, aesthetic, wilderness, and other noneconomic benefits of the forests were not mentioned.

In the administration of the forest reserves it must be clearly borne in mind that all land is to be devoted to its most productive use for the permanent good of the whole people, and not for the temporary benefit of individuals or companies. All the resources of the reserves are for use, and this use must be brought about in a thoroughly prompt and businesslike manner, under such restrictions only as will insure the permanence of these resources. The vital importance of forest reserves to the great industries of the Western States will be largely increased in the near future by the continued steady increase in settlement and development. The permanence of the resources of the reserves is therefore indispensable to continued prosperity, and the policy of this department for their protection and use will invariably be guided by this fact, always bearing in mind that the conservative use of these resources in no way conflicts with their permanent value.

You will see to it that the water, wood, and forage of the reserves are conserved and wisely used for the benefit of the home builder first of all, upon whom depends the best permanent use of lands and resources alike. The continued prosperity of the agricultural, lumbering, mining, and livestock interests is directly dependent upon the present and future use of their resources under businesslike regulations, enforced with promptness, effectiveness, and common sense. In the management of each reserve local questions will be decided upon local grounds; the dominant industry will be considered first, but with as little restriction to minor industries as may be possible; sudden changes in industrial conditions will be avoided by gradual adjustment after due notice; and where conflicting interests must be reconciled the question will always be decided from the standpoint of the greatest good of the greatest number in the long run.

These general principles will govern in the protection and use of the water supply, in the disposal of timber and wood, in the use of the range, and in all other matters connected with the management of the reserves. They can be successfully applied only when the administration of each reserve is left very largely in the hands of the local officers, under the eye of thoroughly trained and competent inspectors.[42]

Pinchot's Political and Intellectual Support

The Transfer Act was but one of many of Pinchot's accomplishments that owed much to Theodore Roosevelt. Teddy Roosevelt was one of the most vigorous leaders this country has known, and he frequently adopted an expansive interpretation of the law if it permitted him to take an action he believed was important. For example, in 1903 he established the nation's first wildlife refuge, the 5-acre Pelican Island Wildlife Refuge, without any legislative support. Roosevelt was an avid sport hunter and prominent amateur biologist, and the casual, unsportsmanlike bird-shooting that was taking place on this Florida island prompted his unprecedented action. His action was not sanctioned by law until 1910.

Pinchot first met Theodore Roosevelt in 1894 at a family dinner. Their friendship really began when Roosevelt nominated Pinchot for membership in the prestigious Boone and Crockett Club, an elite sportsman's group Roosevelt had helped found to promote conservation of big-game animals. As governor of New York, Roosevelt obtained Pinchot's advice on state forest management. Their shared commitment to conservation expanded to a personal friendship. These two energetic men shared athletic interests, including boxing; as an older man Pinchot would recall with amusement when he knocked down the future president.

If Pinchot owed a heavy debt to Roosevelt for his political accomplishments, he owed an equally heavy intellectual debt to a group of Washington civil servants who, over a period of 25 years, developed the theoretical underpinnings for the programs he carried to fruition. Although Pinchot credited one of the group, William John ("WJ") McGee, with being "the scientific brains of the new (Conservation) movement," in his autobiography he was not shy about giving himself credit as well:

> In the gathering gloom of an expiring day, in the moody month of February, . . . (1907) . . . a solitary horseman might have been observed pursuing his silent way above a precipitous gorge in the vicinity of the capital city of America. Or so an early Victorian three-volume novelist might have expressed it.

> In plain words, a man by the name of Pinchot was riding a horse by the name of Jim on the Ridge Road in Rock Creek Park near Washington. And while he rode, he thought. He was a forester, and he was taking his problems with him, on that winter's day . . . when he meant to leave them behind.

> The forest and its relation to streams and inland navigation, to water power and flood control; to the soil and its erosion; to coal and oil and other minerals; to fish and game; and many another possible use or waste of natural resources—these questions would not let him be. What had all these to do with Forestry? And what had Forestry to do with them?

> Here were not isolated and separate problems. My work had brought me into touch with all of them. But what was the basic link between them?

> Suddenly the idea flashed through my head that there was a unity in this complication—that the relation of one resource to another was not the end of the story. Here were no longer a lot of different, independent, and often antagonistic questions, each on its own separate little island, as we had been in the habit of thinking. In place of them, here was one single question with many parts. Seen in this new light, all these separate questions fitted into and made up the one great central problem of the use of the earth for the good of man.

> To me it was a good deal like coming out of a dark tunnel. I had been seeing one spot of light ahead. Here, all of a sudden, was a whole landscape. Or it was like lifting the curtain on a great new stage.[43]

Pinchot reported that McGee most quickly grasped the significance of his discovery. McGee's perspicacity is understandable in light of the work of the group of bureaucrat-intellectuals historian Michael Lacey refers to as the Washington National Seminary.[44] To understand the schism between utilitarian conservation and romantic preservation that would be so central to the development of wildland recreation policy, it is important to know something about the intellectual origins of the progressive conservation movement.

In the latter half of the nineteenth century, laissez-faire capitalism threatened not only the environment but also the social fabric in America. Fabulous wealth flowed into the coffers of entrepreneurs like Vanderbilt, Whitney, Carnegie, Rockfeller, and others, while many working men and women suffered in sweatshops. Children were exploited for cheap labor, and workers of all ages were kept in line by the knowledge that there were legions of hungry people waiting to replace them if they complained. The influx of European immigrants provided a large labor supply that kept wages low and working conditions poor. While the poor suffered, the rich displayed their outrageous wealth in many ways, including building resorts like Cornelius Vanderbilt's "Breakers" mansion at Newport, Rhode Island, and his son's Biltmore Estate in North Carolina.[45] It was this combination of the suffering of the poor and the growth of a wealthy aristocracy that had energized Olmsted's urban park designs.

This set of conditions was rationalized in the philosophy of Englishman Herbert Spencer. Taking his lead from Darwin's newly published *The Origin of Species,* Spencer argued that the extremes of poverty and wealth were a necessary and acceptable part of societal progress, and that governmental intervention to change the situation was wrong because it would interfere with the "survival of the fittest" (Spencer's phrase, not Darwin's). These ideas were well received in America. Spencer's work was a thorough and intricately developed justification of the status quo, and it demanded a deep and sustained response. That response came from a group of men, themselves of humble birth and largely self-educated, who were government employees. The patriarch of the group was John Wesley Powell, the one-armed Civil War veteran who led a scientific expedition in the first known boat trip down the Colorado River.[46] Among the 10 others who engaged in "Spencer-smashing" over the years was WJ McGee, who transmitted the results of their thinking to Pinchot, Roosevelt, and the other progressive conservationists.

The Washington National Seminary struggled to develop a rationale for active government. They were driven in this quest not only by their revulsion at Spencer's "Gospel of Inaction," but also by the spectre of a revolution of the masses—the Communist Manifesto, based on Karl

Marx's observations of capitalism in Spencer's England, was published in 1848. Communism, in the opinion of the Washington Seminary, would bring equality at the price of stagnation and paralysis, since it disregarded the role of incentives in human action and ignored the values of autonomy and self-sufficiency. Rather than accepting either unfair inequality or stultifying equality, and fearing that continuation of the former would lead to the latter, the Washington National Seminary sought a way in which governmental leadership could chart a course between these unacceptable extremes.

They seized on natural resource development as the way out of the dilemma. Natural resource development would be governed by, and in turn would support, science and education. By developing our greatest resource, the human mind, we would not simply adapt to nature but transform it through applied science for the benefit of mankind. The most important natural resource in their view was water. Members of the Seminary viewed hydroelectric power development as a clean and inexhaustible source of energy. Governmental control of hydroelectric power development would provide for common wealth that could be used to lift the working classes from their poverty and ignorance. In this way the commons, which had been taken from the common people through fraud, could be restored, and all citizens of our democracy would be presented with equal opportunity. That equality of opportunity—not the levelling of communism or the evolutionary dynamics of Spencerianism—would best ensure innovation and the progressive improvement of the human condition.

Leadership to bring this vision to reality would be supplied by scientific management. Above the political struggle, with their loyalties to their professions rather than to their localities or interest groups, a scientific elite would guide the development of the nation's natural resources. Members of the seminary proposed the development in Washington of two great bureaus, one to direct the nation's dealings with the earth, and one to spearhead the development of knowledge and its application toward the improvement of mankind. A national university would draw students from all regions and train many of them to staff these bureaus.

This was the legacy McGee passed on to Pinchot and Roosevelt. Under their strong political leadership many strides toward the ideal were made. However, to a large extent the progressive conservation movement failed on its own terms. Although water was considered the critical resource, the greatest achievements were made in the management of the national forests, largely because there the government already owned the necessary land. Even there they were hamstrung by a Congress that feared the conservationists were becoming too powerful, and which in 1907 repealed authorization for the Forest Service fund that had provided Pinchot some freedom from Congressional budgetary control.

In 1907, as well, the end of the Forest Reservation Act came. Those in the West who opposed the act, the reservations made under it and the aggressive Roosevelt-Pinchot conservation program, finally succeeded in repealing the 1891 act as it applied to six western states. Seeing this develop, Pinchot and Roosevelt hastily pored over maps and reserved 16 million acres of national forest in Washington, Oregon, Idaho, Montana, Wyoming, and Colorado. Roosevelt then smugly signed the bill repealing his authority to make reservations. These reservations brought the national forests to roughly 150 million total acres and brought western opposition to "Pinchotism" to new heights.[47]

In the end, the conservation movement ran aground on the American grass-roots political tradition. Local interests simply did not believe they would be served by the conservationists' grandiose schemes.[48] Furthermore, the conservation ideology was too socialistic for its time, and the majority of the citizenry was unreceptive to such intense federal governmental involvement and control of the nation's affairs. It would take the severe crisis of the Great Depression, and the leadership of another Roosevelt, before we would be ready for such activist government.

Although its tangible accomplishments fell far short of its dreams, the imprint of progressive conservation on wildland recreation policy has been large and indelible. For the only time in U.S. history, there was a coherent vision of how natural resources should be treated.[49] In its emphasis on resource development for the common good, the progressive conservation movement provided a powerful rationale for the subjugation of nature for social and economic benefits. That rationale was embodied in resource development agencies instituted at the time and later, the most prominent of which was the U.S. Forest Service. Pinchot's philosophy of "wise use" was strongly stamped on his agency and would increasingly clash with the philosophy of preservation, especially as it developed in the wilderness movement. Pinchot's strong focus on production forestry also created a professional culture that has had difficulty accommodating the interests of those living in cities and concerned with open space, public health, and environmental justice.[50]

Of great significance, as well, the progressive conservation movement provided American women the opportunity to become activists for the public interest. As described below, women developed vital educational and political leadership as they sought to build support for the conservation policies of Roosevelt and Pinchot.[51]

ENDGAME FOR THE PROGRESSIVE CONSERVATIONISTS

The defeats of 1907 signaled the beginning of the end for the Roosevelt-Pinchot team. In an effort to recapture momentum, Pinchot suggested and directed a series of well-publicized commissions and conferences.[52] First there was the Inland Waterways Commission, which had the purpose of promoting the integrated water development program central to the ideology of the progressives. From that came the idea for a meeting of broader scope, the Conference on the Conservation of Natural Resources, frequently referred to as the Governor's Conference of 1908. Designed by Pinchot as a chance to showcase conservation ideas, this was the first gathering of the governors in American history. The governors and their representatives were joined by three citizens selected by each governor, the members of Congress, the Supreme Court, the cabinet, the press, and five luminaries at large. In this gala gathering almost nothing about parks, recreation, and preservation appeared on Pinchot's agenda. John Muir, the leading preservation spokesman, was not invited, and not by accident. The Sierra Club, of which Muir was founder and leader, submitted a minority opinion:

> The moral and physical welfare of a nation is not dependent alone upon bread and water. Comprehending these primary necessities is the deeper need for recreation and that which satisfies also the esthetic sense.[53]

From the Governor's Conference came the National Conservation Commission, with Pinchot as head. Congressional dissatisfaction with this ploy led to their refusal to advance even a dollar of the $50,000 he requested for the commission's expenses. The National Conservation Commission did accomplish something of value, though, producing in 6 months the first solid inventory of the nation's natural resources. Pinchot next called a Joint Conservation Conference to present the results of his work to 20 governors and the representatives of national and state conservation groups. The end product of this feverish round of study and meeting was a congressional amendment which stipulated that no payments — whether direct or indirect, as in the case of Pinchot's own time —

would be made for commissions not specifically authorized by Congress. Despite this slap on the wrist, Pinchot convened a North American Conservation Conference three weeks before the end of Roosevelt's term. He also recommended a world meeting, and Roosevelt sent invitations, but that meeting was cancelled.

Pinchot was one of the few Roosevelt appointees retained in the Taft administration. For a while the eternally optimistic Pinchot felt things would work out, but it was not to be. By 1910 he had been fired by Taft for his public denunciations of Secretary of the Interior Richard Ballinger. Although the specific motive concerned Ballinger's role in an allegedly fraudulent claim to some Alaskan coal reserves, the real problem was much larger. The most basic issue was whether the Alaska lands should be sold or leased. Ballinger favored selling the land, while Pinchot, true to his philosophical roots in the Washington Seminary, favored governmental ownership and the leasing of the coal deposits.[54] In addition to this basic policy difference, related stylistic conflicts ensured Pinchot's departure. The Taft administration was far more conservative than Roosevelt's. Although President Taft did not oppose Roosevelt's conservation policies, neither was he as assertive in pursuing them as his predecessor had been. Taft was too cautious to adopt the legal philosophy which guided Roosevelt and his men, which was that the public administrator should do whatever he can to enhance the public welfare, except as specifically prohibited by law.[55]

Pinchot felt the cautious, legalistic Taft administration was undermining the conservation program he and others had built. When questions about Ballinger's handling of the coal claims were raised and it was suggested that Ballinger was involved in a scheme to obtain private control of public resources, Pinchot seized on the opportunity to obtain Ballinger's dismissal and rekindle the conservation flame. At first he thought he would win, but Taft resolutely supported Ballinger, and Pinchot eventually came to view his stance as an opportunity for martyrdom to the conservation cause. Many of his allies warned Pinchot against pushing the president too hard and allowing his strong beliefs in conservation to shape his interpretation of the facts in the coal claims case, but Pinchot had spotted a devil and wanted the fight. He even reported in his diary, after a meeting with Taft, that the president told him "my zeal was so great I tended to think any man who differed with me as to method was corrupt."[56]

In his struggle against Ballinger, as he had earlier in the Hetch Hetchy battle and would later when he worked against the industry-oriented third chief of the Forest Service, Pinchot claimed to work on behalf of ordinary citizens and against wealthy and powerful interests. In the words of historian Char Miller:

This lifelong Republican, raised amid great luxury, advanced a democratic vision that tied conservation to the pursuit of communal responsibility and equal opportunity. 'The man who really counts is the plain American citizen,' Pinchot affirmed, and that is why he stood for 'the Roosevelt policies because they set the common good of us all above the private gain of some of us; because they recognize the livelihood of the small man as more important to the Nation than the profit of the big man.'[57]

Pinchot's final days demonstrated clearly the zealotry that colored his career. As a young man at Yale he had been strongly attracted to religion, and throughout his life he adopted a no-holds-barred approach to the pursuit of strongly held beliefs. Historian Samuel Hays provides the following evaluation of Pinchot's contribution.

One must also reassess Pinchot's wider role in organized conservation affairs. Without question the Chief Forester contributed more than any other individual to public awareness of forestry and water power problems. He firmly planted the idea of conservation in the minds of the American people; he built up the United States Forest Service as a highly effective government agency and almost personally staved off measures which would have granted public utility corporations unlimited franchises. Yet, Pinchot also helped to retard the movement. His vigorous attempt to direct conservation into those limited channels he preferred to stress, and his refusal to compromise with those with whom he differed played a large role in splintering conservation organizations, contributed to conflicts among resource groups and to personal bitterness among their leaders, and alienated many who hesitated to become involved in the tense atmosphere surrounding such a controversial figure. A vigorous attack on resource problems other than national forestry, water power, and mineral leasing affairs suffered from his dominant and inflexible influence.[58]

Pinchot's forcefulness was one of the most important ingredients in setting the Forest Service on its course as an agency with a powerful sense of mission.[59] True believers were welcome, and together they worked wonders for the cause, but apostates—such as those who advanced the value of recreation and wilderness—found life in the Service much less comfortable.

THE ROLE OF WOMEN IN THE PROGRESSIVE CONSERVATION MOVEMENT

The history of women's contributions to the progressive conservation movement has been well documented by Carolyn Merchant and others.[60] Like their male counterparts in the movement, the women who helped advance conservation belonged to the white middle and upper classes. Membership in literary clubs allowed them to continue their intellectual development and form strong bonds with other like-minded women, while increased leisure time provided them with opportunities for botany, gardening, bird watching, and camping, all of which contributed to their impact on conservation policy.

Merchant is clear about the power and extent of women's contributions:

> . . . women transformed the (progressive conservation) crusade from an elite male enterprise into a widely based movement. In so doing, they not only brought hundreds of local natural areas under legal protection, but also promoted legislation aimed at halting pollution, reforesting watersheds, and preserving endangered species.

> . . . without the input of women in nearly every locale in the country, conservation gains in the early decades of the century would have been fewer and far less spectacular.[61]

A few specific examples lend substance to Merchant's claims.

Mrs. Lovell White of San Francisco, founder and president of the California Club, garnered enormous support for forest conservation in the Golden State. In 1900, The California Club merged with other women's clubs throughout the state to form the California Federation of Women's Clubs. The Federation made conservation a focal point of the first meeting:

> While the women of New Jersey are saving the Palisades of the Hudson from utter destruction by men to whose greedy souls Mount Sinai is only a stone quarry, and the women of Colorado are saving the cliff dwellings and pueblo ruins of their state from vandal destruction, the word comes to the women of California that men whose souls are gang-saws are meditating the turning of our world-famous Sequoias into planks and fencing worth so many dollars.[62]

Reflecting a basic tenet of forestry, Mrs. White then proclaimed that forests were the source of Californians' clean water, homes, and health, and the forests must therefore be preserved and, where already destroyed, replanted. In the following years, she personally lobbied every senator and representative in the U.S. Congress until they passed legislation that led to the eventual protection of the Calaveras Grove of Big Trees (*Sequoia gigantea*) in the Sierras. These trees are truly monumental: some measured over 12 feet in diameter and had bark up to 2 feet thick. Mrs. White also worked to save the coastal redwoods (*Sequoia sempervirens*). She served as president of the Sempervirens Club, which later became the Save the Redwoods League and deserves much of the credit for the present-day Redwoods National Park.[63]

Women contributed greatly in urban areas as well as remote natural areas. The General Federation of Women's Clubs, founded in 1890, became active in forestry around 1900. Women who were knowledgeable about forestry principles headed forestry committees in their respective states. Forming coalitions with other civic organizations, these forestry committees succeeded in planting trees and beautifying neighborhoods in cities throughout the country. The General Federation also kept its 800,000 members informed of Roosevelt and Pinchot's conservation policies and lobbied aggressively for legislation to protect forests, water, and birds. The forestry committee of the General Federation of Women's Clubs coordinated much of the support needed for passage of the laws that authorized creation of the eastern national forests.

From an initial focus on forestry, the General Federation of Women's Clubs expanded its interest and influence to other natural resources. In 1909, they formed a Waterways Committee, adding clean water, hydroelectric power, and waterborne transportation to the slate of conservation issues. In 1910, the Forestry and Waterways committees were combined into a Department of Conservation, chaired by Mrs. Marion Crocker of Massachusetts. Representatives of the new Department of Conservation attended the Second National Conservation Congress in 1910. In her speech, Mrs. Crocker addressed the scientific bases of forest conservation. She highlighted the basic life support functions of forests, including the production of humus, conservation of soil minerals, reduction of wind and water erosion, air and water purification, and wood supply. Her closing lines brought forth enthusiastic applause:

> I will say to you this one message, while you are working for this thing of prime importance, the conservation of life, for which this Congress has

stood at this fall meeting, do not forget that the conservation of life itself must be built on the solid foundation of conservation of natural resources, or it will be a house build upon the sands that will be washed away. It will not be lasting.[64]

From about 1909, the General Federation of Women's Clubs, a million members strong, played a key role in the national conservation movement. State chapters passed resolutions in support of the Roosevelt-Pinchot policies and its leading organizations, including the Inland Waterways Commission, Forest Service, Geological Survey, and the American Mining Congress.[65] The General Federation also shaped natural resource policy by influencing other groups, including the Daughters of the American Revolution, which pushed for preservation of Appalachian watersheds, the New Jersey Palisades, and Niagara Falls, and the Audubon Society, where women fought against the fashion industry to protect birds. These efforts produced results. For example, after a 27-year campaign, a tariff act was passed in 1913 which prohibited imports of wild bird feathers into the United States and required women entering the United States from Europe to surrender the feathers from their hats and clothes. In the United States, public opinion shifted to such a degree that populations of egrets, once nearly extinct, rebounded, as did the numbers of little blue herons and ibis.[66]

In assessing the impact of the women of the Progressive Conservation Era, Merchant points out a contradiction. Although they demonstrated substantial power and achieved great successes through their activism,

> . . . they nevertheless accepted the traditional sex roles assigned to them by late nineteenth century American society as caretakers of the nation's homes, husbands, and offspring, supporting rather than challenging the two spheres ideology of the nineteenth century. At the National Congresses, women repeatedly called on the traditions assigned them by society in justifying the public demands they were making. Unwilling and unable to break out of these social roles, and supported by the men of the Congresses, they drew on a trilogy of slogans—conservation of womanhood, the home, and the child.[67]

Characteristic of the Progressive Era itself, these women were feminist and progressive as activists for the public interest, but mostly conservative in their desire to maintain the traditional values and middle class lifestyles rooted in the materialism of the times.

According to political scientist John Freemuth, the apparent contradiction identified by Merchant was also a characteristic and a source of strength of Progressive Era public lands management policies. By linking scientific management to the key democratic values of the time, the progressives were able to forge a vision for resource management that was accepted by the majority of Americans.[68] According to Freemuth, the Progressive Era institutionalized expert-centered public land management by tying professionalism and expertise to the democratic ideal of opportunity for all. Pinchot made it clear that forestry would succeed only if those living in and near the forests had the chance to benefit from forest management practices. Women readily took up the utilitarian conservation cause and made great contributions not only because of their energy and skills but also because they worked within the roles society assigned them.

However, by 1913 women began moving away from conservation and forestry. These had become technical professions, and entry to them was impossible for women of that era. Forestry schools were off limits. The American Forestry Association stopped printing articles about the work of women in forestry. One reason women dropped from the picture may have been the battle to save the Hetch Hetchy Valley in Yosemite National Park. Hetch Hetchy marks the point at which many women formalized their opposition to the tenets of utilitarian conservation, a point addressed further in Chapter 6.[69] After 1913, female members outnumbered their male counterparts in the Sierra Club, Audubon Society, and National Parks Association. The establishment of the National Park Service in 1916 helped draw women away from the Forest Service and other utilitarian conservation agencies. Women lobbied hard for the creation of the National Park Service and for the preservation of Mesa Verde, Rocky Mountain, and Everglades national parks, among others.[70] The source of this shift in women's support is captured in these words from Mary Belle King Sherman, head of the General Federation of Women's Clubs:

> . . . the Forest service "has an important place in the material part of our life: and was "a place where most beauty must be sacrificed." But a national park, she said, "supplies the better, the greater things of life." A park has "some of the characteristics of the museum, the library, the fine arts hall, of the public school, the zoo, and the home."[71]

In this way, in the early decades of the twentieth century, the National Park Service began to provide a significant part of the American public with a more compelling vision of the role and purpose of natural resources than that provided by the USDA Forest Service.

NOTES

1. Runte, *Public Lands. . . .* (p. 28) describes another antecedent. There were a few individuals around the time of Yellowstone, other than the intellectuals, who espoused both the aesthetic and the practical benefits of forest conservation. One of these was Julius Sterling Morton (Nebraska farmer, newspaper editor, politician, and businessman). Morton argued that the planting and care of trees, shrubs, and orchards would not only break up the so-called monotony of the plains but would also help conserve the soil and water needed to improve Nebraska's agricultural productivity. Morton made a resolution, which was adopted by Nebraska's State Board of Agriculture, for a day "set apart and consecrated for tree planting in the state of Nebraska." Thus, on April 10, 1872, Arbor Day was born. By 1882, five more states—Kansas, Minnesota, North Dakota, Tennessee and Ohio—joined Nebraska in the official recognition of this event.

2. Martin, "Peshtigo: The Fire a Nation Forgot."

3. Dana, *Forest and Range Policy,* pp. 80–83.

4. Bonnicksen, "The Development of Forest Policy in the United States."

5. Cox, "Americans and Their Forests," p. 162.

6. Dana and Fairfax, *Forest and Range Policy,* 2nd ed., pp. 47–48.

7. Udall, *The Quiet Crisis,* pp. 99–100.

8. Graham, *The Adirondack Park;* Thompson, "Politics in the Wilderness."

9. Runte, *Public Lands . . . ,* p. 34.

10. Dana and Fairfax, *Forest and Range Policy,* 2nd ed., pp. 51–52.

11. Olson, *The Depletion Myth.*

12. This review of Fernow's forestry experiment is primarily from Thompson, "Politics in the Wilderness." Other sources are Dana, *Forest and Range Policy,* pp. 134–135, and Schenck, *The Biltmore Story,* pp. 106–110.

13. Thompson, "Politics in the Wilderness," p. 18.

14. Rodgers, *Bernhard Eduard Fernow,* p. 254.

15. Dana, *Forest and Range Policy,* p. 135.

16. Section 24, Act of March 3, 1891 (26 Stat. 1095).

17. Runte, *Public Lands . . . ,* p. 45.

18. Dana and Fairfax, *Forest and Range Policy,* 2nd ed. p. 50; Cubbage et al., *Forest Resource Policy,* pp. 290–291.

19. Dana and Fairfax, *Forest and Range Policy,* 2nd ed., pp. 56–58.

20. Dana, *Forest and Range Policy.* p. 102.

21. McCarthy, "The Forest Reserve Controversy."

22. Dana and Fairfax, *Forest and Range Policy,* 2nd ed., pp. 58–64.

23. Sundry Civil Appropriations Act of June 4, 1877 (30 Stat. 11, 34).

24. Dana and Fairfax, *Forest and Range Policy,* 2nd ed., pp. 62–63.

25. Primary reliance for Pinchot's biography has been placed on McGeary, *Gifford Pinchot*.

26. Miller, *Gifford Pinchot and the Making of Modern Environmentalism*, pp. 20–34.

27. Ibid., p. 55.

28. Dana and Fairfax, *Forest and Range Policy*, 2nd ed., p. 53.

29. Miller, *Gifford Pinchot and the Making of Modern Environmentalism*, p. 72.

30. Ibid., p. 79.

31. Ibid., p. 85.

32. From *The Fight for Conservation*, by Gifford Pinchot. Copyright 1910 by the University of Washington Press. Reprinted by permission.

33. Ibid., pp. 21–22.

34. Miller, *Gifford Pinchot and the Making of Modern Environmentalism*, p. 104.

35. Ibid., p. 112.

36. Schenck, *The Biltmore Story*.

37. Pinchot, *The Fight for Conservation*, p. 42.

38. McGeary, *Gifford Pinchot*, p. 88.

39. Schenck, *The Biltmore Story*, p. 118.

40. Dana and Fairfax, *Forest and Range Policy*, 2nd ed., p. 83.

41. Twight, "Organizational Values and Political Power."

42. Dana, *Forest and Range Policy*, p. 82.

43. Pinchot, "Breaking New Ground, 1947," in Nash, *The American Environment*, pp. 40–41.

44. Our account of the Washington National Seminary is from Lacey, "The Mysteries of Earth-Making Dissolve."

45. A vivid portrayal of the excesses of laissez-faire capitalism is provided by "The Manners and Morals of High Capitalism," from the Public Broadcasting System's presentation of *The Age of Uncertainty*.

46. Stegner, *Beyond the Hundredth Meridian;* Worster, *A River Running West*.

47. Dana and Fairfax, *Forest and Range policy*, 2nd ed., pp. 91–92.

48. Hays, *Conservation and the Gospel of Efficiency*.

49. Dana and Fairfax, *Forest and Range Policy*, 2nd ed., pp. 69–71, 96.

50. Taylor, "The Urban Environment . . ."

51. Merchant, "The Women of the Progressive Conservation Crusade, 1900–1015."

52. McGeary, *Gifford Pinchot*, pp. 94–107.

53. Fox, *John Muir and his Legacy*, p. 130.

54. Ise, *Our National Park Policy*, p. 90.

55. McGeary, *Gifford Pinchot*, p. 130.

56. Ibid., p. 147.

57. Miller, *Gifford Pinchot and the Making of Modern Environmentalism*, p. 230.

58. Hays, *Conservation and the Gospel of Efficiency*, p. 198.

59. Watkins, "Father of the Forests"; Clarke and McCool, *Staking out the Terrain*.

60. Merchant, "The Women of the Progressive Conservation Crusade," notes that Gifford Pinchot, in his book *The Fight for Conservation* (1910), and Samuel Hays in *Conservation and the Gospel of Efficiency* (1959), praised these women for their substantial contributions. More recently, Stephen Fox in *John Muir and His Legacy* (1981), Polly Kaufman in *National Parks and the Woman's Voice* (1996), and Carolyn Merchant in *Earthcare: Women and the Environment* (1996) expounded on women's roles in the Audubon faction, hiking clubs, early national parks, and the environmental movement. Beyond these works, most conservation history books make women's contributions invisible. Merchant's work is the primary source of information in this section.

61. Merchant, "Women of the Progressive . . . ," p. 57.

62. Ibid., p. 59.

63. Ibid., pp. 60–61; Schrepfer, *The Fight to Save the Redwoods*.

64. Merchant, *Major Problems in American Environmental History*, pp. 340, 353–355.

65. Merchant, "Women of the Progressive . . . ," p. 66.

66. Ibid., p. 73.

67. Ibid., p. 73.

68. Freemuth, "Emergence of Ecosystem Management."

69. Kaufman, *National Parks and the Woman's Voice*, pp. 30–32.

70. Ibid., pp. 27–35.

71. Ibid., p. 35.

CHAPTER 6

INSTITUTIONAL ORIGINS: THE NATIONAL PARK SERVICE

During the period when scientific forestry emerged, events were also leading toward park preservation. There is remarkable similarity in the early histories of the national forests and national parks. In both cases a solid philosophical foundation joined with effective political leadership to transform events and conditions into policy. The early national parks, like the national forests, were reservations hastily extracted from the public domain, without great apparent forethought, and management policy was developed later in response to real and perceived crises in the use of the land. Both movements produced federal land management agencies. The Park Service, like the Forest Service, had charismatic and effective early leadership, which firmly established its position in the national bureaucratic arena. The early history of the national parks, like the national forests, evolved on a well-lighted public stage, and this publicity was promoted by agency leaders. Both services eventually were plagued with severe policy questions, as their early initiatives were carried out and awareness of policy tradeoffs emerged, and as the underlying climate of public opinion changed toward greater concern about environmental quality.

This chapter covers the period between the Yellowstone Park Act of 1872 and the 1930s. The most important advocate for parks during this time was John Muir, whose writing and political activism were instrumental in the establishment of the National Park Service. In 1928,

Stephen Mather, the Park Service's founding director, suffered a paralyzing stroke and was succeeded by his long-time friend and assistant Horace Albright. The Mather-Albright years are seen as the golden era of the National Park Service, the time when the agency enjoyed its strongest leadership and most coherent sense of purpose, but that very leadership and purpose eventually led to problems.

YELLOWSTONE NATIONAL PARK

Those most closely involved with the Yosemite Grant saw in it a formula for future wildland reservations.[1] Eight years later, in 1872, the act establishing Yellowstone National Park was signed into law by President Ulysses S. Grant. In certain respects the Yosemite and Yellowstone acts were similar, but in significant ways they differed. The National Park Service considers Yellowstone, not Yosemite, as the progenitor of today's national park system, and thus used its enactment as the basis for its 1972 centennial celebrations.[2] The story of Yellowstone's creation is prominent in Park Service and academic history and lore.

The popular story of Yellowstone's establishment is widely recounted as follows. The area had been known for years as Coulter's Hell; the first part of the name came from John Coulter, a member of the Lewis and Clark expedition who later returned to the headwaters of the Missouri in 1806–1808 in search of beaver for the fur trade, and the second part of the name came from the geysers and other "hellish" features in the area. Coulter's reports were supported by information from trappers and prospectors, so the existence of a fantastic place was well known by the time settlement neared the area after the Civil War. An expedition in 1869 confirmed that there were canyons, waterfalls, and geysers in the area and prompted a more serious expedition the following year. In 1870, an expedition of prominent citizens—the Washburne-Langford-Doane expedition—went to the area. At the end of their stay, they camped at the confluence of the Gibbons and Firehole rivers and discussed around the campfire what they should do. Under the public land laws of the time, which encouraged transfer of public land into private ownership, they could have placed claims on the land in hopes of developing it for profit. However, one of the expedition members, Judge Cornelius Hedges, suggested that the area be made a national park, so that all citizens could see these wonders of nature. After their return, members of the expedition lobbied successfully for their idea. In this way Yellowstone National Park became a reality.[3]

This is an appealing story, one that fits well with the aura of democratic idealism that often surrounds the national parks. However, while the public spiritedness of Judge Hedges and his comrades is not doubted, the single-handedness of their accomplishment is. Other factors both prepared the ground for the reservation and spurred it into existence.[4]

A crucial enabling factor in Congress's decision was the existence of the Yosemite Grant. The Yosemite Grant had provided the precedent for reservations of public land for public recreation. There were, however, several important differences between the Yosemite and Yellowstone Park Acts. The Yosemite Grant was of a small area, while the Yellowstone reservation was huge, about two million acres in size. In fact, the reservation was quite different from that which the members of the Washburne-Langford-Doane expedition urged. Their park would have consisted of the major landscape features, the canyons and geysers, each to be surrounded and protected by a few acres of land.[5] The huge size of the actual reservation reflects Congress's intent to protect undiscovered wonders of nature.[6] A second difference between the Yosemite and Yellowstone Acts is found in the unit of government responsible for management. At Yosemite, Congress turned the land over to the state of California, following the familiar pattern of granting federal property to the state governments. At Yellowstone, however, the state of Wyoming had not yet been admitted to the Union, so Congress retained the area under federal government control.[7] This novel action was an important precedent for retaining federal governmental control of park and forest reservations. Significantly, the Yellowstone Act omitted the wording of the Yosemite Act to the effect that the park was to be permanent. While legislators thought it wise to tie California's hands at Yosemite, at Yellowstone Congress did not wish to limit its own options for the future development of a huge and unknown area.[8]

Congress felt free to throw a broad protective blanket over the area, rather than selectively protecting nature's wonders, because it was convinced that the area was useless for any purpose other than tourism.[9] Yellowstone was far removed from commercial activity and transportation to the area was very difficult, with the result that the idea of a park reservation was not strongly challenged by lumber, mining, water power, or other economic interests. Nor did homesteaders seek the land, as it was remote, in Indian territory and not good for agriculture. Hunters and trappers were on the scene, of course, and would continue to be major headaches for the new park's managers, but they were not an effective pressure group.[10]

While no strong economic interests opposed the park, one influential concern supported it. As at Yosemite, railroad interests saw in Yellowstone a source of tourist revenues. The Northern Pacific Railroad promoted establishment of the park, provided the major means of transportation to it, and became the park's first concessionaire. Railroad officials figured tourists could be carried to the park at little additional expense in terms of future track-laying. One of the major points used to sell Congress on the Yellowstone Park idea was that the development, operation, and maintenance of the park would be carried out by the concessionaire and, therefore, Congress would not have to spend money for recreation.[11]

In the language of the 1872 act, Yellowstone was to be "a public park or pleasuring ground for the benefit of the people." What this meant was nature tourism, with luxurious accommodations affording wealthy visitors comfortable opportunities to view the wonders of nature. The railroads would provide the necessary services and turn a profit in the process. Full access to people from all walks of life—Olmsted's democratic idealism realized in parks—may have been implied in the act's language, but it was not really what anyone had in mind. Nor were they thinking in terms of anything like a wilderness experience, with its connotations of immersion in nature. Luxurious hotels, albeit in a rustic style, were erected close to the natural features for which the park was created. These patterns of access and development at Yellowstone came to typify the early western nature parks, and they would prove important in the evolution of national park policy.[12]

Support for railroad-led development of Yellowstone may have come from those who feared that the junky, uncontrolled pattern of development found at Niagara Falls might be repeated. Even at a place so far off the beaten path as Yellowstone—in the years before park establishment, the area was 500 miles from the nearest railroad, and some visitors traveled 820 miles by steamer and 232 miles by coach to reach it— there were enterprising individuals eager to make a living off tourists.[13] Following the Washburne-Langford-Doane expedition, the U.S. government sent one of its trusted explorers to the area to corroborate the stories. When Frederick Hayden arrived at Yellowstone in 1871, he found people preparing to fence off geyser basins.[14]

Thus, as of 1872 we had a small land grant to the state of California in Yosemite and the creation of a huge national park in Yellowstone. These acts set the pattern for an unwritten congressional policy that only worthless lands—lands not wanted for agriculture or commercial development—might qualify as parks.[15] Parks were seen as cost-free, self-financing enterprises. In this era, settlement of the western frontier moved forward rapidly, while elsewhere urbanization and industrialization expanded. The spirit of free-wheeling capitalism was the order of the day, and understanding of the environmental and cultural values of parks was not developed. If, at minimal cost, we could save a few areas that could turn a tourism profit and be held up to Europeans with pride, that's what we needed. At least that appears to have been the sense of the Congress in 1872.

MANAGEMENT OF THE EARLY NATIONAL PARKS

Congress's lack of commitment to providing quality recreation experiences in these newly created parks was evident in their management.[16] At both Yosemite and Yellowstone, the U.S. Cavalry was sent in to offer some protection, but wildlife was destroyed, timber was cut and burned, and the range was overgrazed. In Yosemite, sheep, which John Muir called "hoofed locusts" because of the damage they caused by their grazing, were an especially big problem. In a futile attempt to disrupt grazing operations, troops would evict the sheep on one side of the park and the shepherds on the other. Park supporters complained about the problems for years. Finally, when the army left in 1898 to fight in the Spanish-American War, severe over-grazing accompanied by a drought led to the starvation of many sheep, and this event was a sufficient crisis to provoke Congress into providing some money ($8,000) for protection. In addition to the sheep, campers left litter, trampled fragile areas, and caused wildfires.

The situation in Yellowstone was about the same. The park was not surveyed at the time it was established, so there were no clear boundaries, making protective law enforcement difficult. Poaching and trapping of the park's abundant wildlife were rampant. These problems were in part the result of Secretary of Interior Carl Schurz's decision to permit hunting, trapping, and fishing by recreationists and residents. This regulation was adopted in part because Yellowstone was a huge and remote park, and it was assumed that visitors would need to live off the land. This reasonable provision became a loophole for profit-oriented exploitation. Managers attempting to protect Yellowstone had almost no support. The only penalty for poaching was expulsion from the park, after which the offender would simply turn around and re-enter. On one occasion, park management was ordered by the U.S. attorney general to return confiscated weapons to the poachers from whom they had been taken. Buffalo heads sold illegally for $400 $1,000 in Bozeman, Montana. Attempts to bring some order to this chaos were made by bringing in the Wyoming territorial police. Unfortunately, the law enforcement officers got to keep half the fines resulting from their work and, encouraged by the profit motive, made too many arrests. Among those they nabbed was a member of Congress from Illinois, and soon afterward territorial law enforcement efforts were stopped. The entire management situation was so scandalous that the U.S. Cavalry was finally brought in during the 1880s, and it protected the area reasonably well for several decades.[17]

Insensitivity to the uplifting experience of nature in the parks was not limited to poachers, grazers, and other utilitarian interests. Few of the early park visitors were imbued with the spirit of preservation. At Yellowstone, souvenir-seekers broke off and carried away tons of the rocks around the mineral springs, and they decimated game and fish populations. Visitors at Yosemite amused themselves by tossing rocks, boxes, and other objects off Glacier Point and marveling at the time it took them to reach the valley floor 3,200 feet below. They were even more entertained when the owner of a hotel on Glacier Point threw a live chicken over the edge:

> With an ear-piercing cackle that grew fainter as it fell . . . the poor creature shot downward; now beating the air with ineffectual wings, and now frantically clawing at the very wind . . . thus the hapless fowl shot down, down, down, until it became a mere fluff of feathers no larger than a quail . . . it dwindled to a wren's size . . . disappeared, then again dotted the sight as a pin's point, and then—it was gone!

Any qualms witnesses to this grisly scene may have had were relieved when they learned that the chicken made the trip every day of the tourist season, and when they encountered the old hen working her way home up the trail to Glacier Point.[18]

Yosemite and Yellowstone in the 1870s and 1880s reflected the prevailing attitudes of the times. Although a philosophical foundation existed for the preservation and experience of nature on nature's terms, it would be many years before these would be strongly realized in the national parks. For the time being, the guiding motivations for park preservation were nationalism and business; one of the central criteria for choosing federal park land was the absence of commercial value; the park management that existed was weak; private entrepreneurs were given wide latitude in carrying out profit-oriented actions in the parks; and visitors displayed little inclination to discard the trappings of commercial recreation.

Americans like to take credit for inventing the national parks idea. Creation stories in this vein may carry the suggestion that the meaning of national parks was struck, in final form for all time, from some eternal template. The wisdom of America's forefathers in the parks is cast in the same tones used to argue the perfection of the United States Constitution. However appealing it may be to create a sense of wisdom and continuity in history, the real story has been much messier. The meaning of the Constitution has been determined by years and years of human conflict adjudicated by a changing cast of Supreme Court justices appointed by presidents who themselves mirror the flux of public opinion. In like manner, the meaning of the national parks has been defined over the years through the struggles over what land should be included and how it should be managed, with appeals made by a changing public to a changing agency. The national park experience as it was defined in the late nineteenth and early twentieth centuries has been challenged over the years, and the challenge has become increasingly definitive since the emergence of the environmental movement in the latter part of the twentieth century.

JOHN MUIR

In 1868, 4 years after the Yosemite Grant and 4 years before the Yellowstone Reservation, the man who was to become the leading spokesman for wildland preservation got off a ship in San Francisco and asked the first person he met how to get out of town. Asked where he wanted to go, he answered, "any place that is wild."[19] With his directions in hand and a puzzled passerby in his wake, John Muir walked east from San Francisco toward the Sierra Nevada mountains and a life devoted to exploring, celebrating, and protecting them and other wild places.

Muir was born in Scotland in 1838. As a young man he showed little promise of the sensitivity for nature that marked his mature years. He was a wild, independent child who ran with a gang that delighted in throwing stones at cats, provoking dog fights, shooting at seagulls with homemade guns, and robbing birds' nests. He would return from such adventures to face regular thrashings from his father. Muir's willingness to inflict pain on other creatures reflected the brutality of the adult world toward him. As Stephen Fox, one of Muir's biographers, notes:

> In Dunbar in the 1840s both pedagogy and child rearing relied heavily on corporal punishment. When Muir and his little band of hooligans attacked wildlife and domestic animals, and started fights with other schoolboy gangs, they were only expressing in their own way the prevailing belief in salutary violence. At best the school curriculum offered a grim diet of religious and classical fare, taught by rote and recited by the squirming scholars before a cane-wielding martinet. Even worse than the dull lessons was the invariable penalty for failure. 'The Scotch simply made the discovery that there was a connection between the skin and the memory,' Muir said later. 'The whole educational system was founded on leather.'[20]

Under the directions and thrashings of his father and school, Muir was forced to memorize much of the Bible.[21] His career as a successful writer may owe much to the rhythms of the King James edition thus imprinted on his mind. Although he rebelled from a young age against his dictatorial father, Muir's movement away from religious orthodoxy came much later, as he pursued his scientific and nature studies to their logical conclusion.

Muir's father, a Christian zealot, followed his religious sect and in 1849 brought his family to the Wisconsin frontier. With the same industry and business sense that had made him a successful grocer in Scotland, he established one of the most prosperous farms in the region. No small part of the farm's productivity came from the relentless work of the children: as the neighbors put it, "Old Man Muir works his children like cattle."[22] Six days a week the family worked, often putting in 16- and 17-hour days. The hardest work fell on John. Exemplifying this labor was the well he dug at Hickory Hill, their second farm in Wisconsin. The well had to be dug to a depth of 90 feet, and all but the first 10 feet was hard sandstone that Muir had to chisel out by hand. For months he was lowered in a basket to his day-long work. When the well reached about 80 feet deep, he barely escaped death from "choke damp," excess carbon dioxide that had settled in the bottom of the well during the night. The next day his father sent him down again to work.[23] Years of such treatment left him with the capacity to withstand physical hardship and the mental toughness he would need in his later life as an outdoorsman.

Chipping away in bad air at the bottom of a ninety-foot well, outharvesting grown men in the heat of the summer, squeezing his chilblained feet into frozen boots, being whipped for imaginary derelictions—the boy grew into a man with the internal resources to make a good mountaineer. He developed within himself a hard, stubborn core beyond the reach of any external situation, a knack for separating his spirit from his physical body. Once he nearly drowned in Fountain Lake. He therefore decided to punish himself "as if my body was one thing and my mind another thing." Rowing out to the middle of the lake, he dove for the first time in his life, headfirst, all the way to the bottom. Back at the surface, he shouted "Take that!" and repeated the process four times, getting even with himself for having lost control.[24]

Books provided Muir with a chance to enlarge his world, and he became an avid reader. His father, concerned about the secular influence of the poetry, mathematics, and grammar books John was reading, tried to enforce a nightly curfew, which led to a collision of wills. Weary of the nightly battles, his father gave his son permission to rise early and read in the morning instead. In response, Muir arrived at a schedule of going to bed at 8 in the evening, arising shortly after midnight, and reading until dawn. This arrangement held until winter, when his father forbade the use of heating fuel for such frivolities. Muir handled this obstacle not by staying in bed, as his father wanted, but by working on mechanical inventions, an activity that involved enough bodily movement to keep him reasonably warm.

Muir's powerful mind poured forth ideas for all sorts of mechanical contrivances. Among other gadgets were an alarm-clock bed which stood him on his feet while simultaneously lighting a study lamp on dark winter mornings, and a mechanized study desk which displayed the book to be read open at the proper page and for a predetermined span of time, then replaced that book with the next and repeated the process through his daily curriculum.

Muir's prowess as an inventor helped him escape from the drudgery of the farm. His local reputation led him in 1860 to an agriculture fair in Madison, where he displayed his work. He was acclaimed a genius and received numerous job offers. The job he took did not work out, and he found his way back to Madison, where he entered the University of Wisconsin and rapidly became interested in geology and botany. The two professors who influenced him most were disciples of Emerson, and they introduced him to transcendentalist philosophy. His understanding of the patterns in nature enabled him to reconcile conflicts between the sciences and his religious background, since it was clear to Muir that those patterns were God's handiwork. Although Muir was enmeshed in the nineteenth century's struggle between science and religion, his own growing interest and belief in science never undercut his essential reverence. Whereas Darwin postulated natural selection as the mechanism guiding evolution, Muir believed that all change in nature arose from God's design.[25] Historian Robert Dorman refers to Muir's religious beliefs as "Christian naturalism" while biographer Stephen Fox suggests that "pantheism" might best capture the essence of Muir's nature-oriented religious beliefs.[26]

With the advent of the Civil War, the pacifist Muir fled to Canada, where he wandered in the Ontario bush for half a year before settling down to a factory job. That time in the wilderness, which he described as "botanizing," served to increase his already powerful sense of the importance of nature in his life. In his factory job, his inventions helped double production. Despite his success at the job, Muir longed for intellectual stimulation and companionship. He wrote one of his former professors, Ezra Slocum Carr, and received a letter in return from Carr's wife Jeanne. Thus began a 10-year correspondence that immensely broadened Muir's mind. Jeanne Carr was older than Muir by 13 years, of New England patrician stock, and well-educated. She adopted the role of Muir's tutor, leading him into "music, painting, political reforms, feminism, psychic phenomena, landscape gardening, fiction and poetry, and Asian philosophies."[27] Prophetically, she even reported to him a psychic's prediction that he would end his wanderings in Yosemite.[28]

When the Canadian factory where he worked was destroyed by fire, Muir returned to the United States, meandering west from New York until he landed another factory job in Indiana, in a large, steam-powered plant producing wagon parts. His mechanical inventive talent again was recognized, and he himself began to fear that this skill would compel him to turn away from his preferred life's work of studying nature. A freak accident helped him make his most crucial life's decision. Mending a leather belt late one night in 1867, the sharp file he was using flew from his hand and pierced his eye, blinding it. The other eye soon was blinded, too, from shock. Weak and sick, Muir spent a month in a darkened room recovering his sight and mulling over his life. This near disaster persuaded him to abandon a promising and potentially lucrative career in mechanical engineering and follow his true calling of examining and celebrating nature firsthand. On his first major outing after the accident, he wandered alone from Indiana to the Gulf of Mexico.[29] Had it not been for a case of malaria, he might have carried out his plan to go on to South America and trace the Amazon to its source. Instead, he went to Cuba, caught an orange boat to New York City, and for $40 booked steerage passage to San Francisco and Yosemite, where he provided for his modest needs by working in a sawmill and herding sheep.

In 1871, 3 years after Muir's arrival in California, Ralph Waldo Emerson visited Yosemite. Muir hovered at the edge of the crowd, too shy to introduce himself to the great man. When he heard Emerson was planning to depart in a few days, he left him a note:

> Do not thus drift away with the mob, while the spirits of these rocks and waters hail you after long waiting as their kinsman and persuade you to closer communion . . . I invite you to join me in a month's worship with Nature in the high temples of the great Sierra Crown beyond our holy Yosemite. It will cost you nothing save the time and very little of that for you will be mostly in eternity . . . In the name of a hundred cascades that barbarous visitors never see . . . in the name of all the spirit creatures of these rocks and of this whole spiritual atmosphere do not leave us now. With most cordial regards I am yours in Nature, John Muir.[30]

Had Emerson scrambled around the mountains as Muir wanted, he probably would have been "mostly in eternity," since at the time he visited Muir in Yosemite he was 68 years old and in poor health. The optimistic and enthusiastic Muir was disappointed over Emerson's reluctance to go climbing with him. They did meet and talk, and though Emerson declined Muir's invitation to hike Yosemite's backcountry, he did send the eccentric young man two volumes of his collected essays. Muir read them and filled the margins with questions and arguments, because he found Emerson less than adequate as an interpreter of natural history.

Muir's relationship with Emerson and his own admission that Thoreau's Walden was his favorite book should not be interpreted as indicating that he was a transcendentalist disciple. Muir drew his own, independent conclusions from his extensive immersion in the natural world, and the transcendentalists' major influence on him was in corroborating his own thinking.[31] In fact, Emerson was not nearly wild enough in his love of nature to suit Muir. While Emerson could write that wilderness "is a sublime mistress, but an intolerable wife," Muir at that time appeared ready to dispense with civilization entirely. Muir was amused that Thoreau considered Walden Pond to be wilderness.[32]

In one of his first jobs in the Sierras, Muir had been a shepherd. Ironically, it was the "hoofed locusts" who led him first to Yosemite, and the
discovery of that miraculous place persuaded him once again against going botanizing in South America. Instead, he took a part-time job running a sawmill and continued exploring the Sierras. One of his occupa-
tions at this time was geology. Intuitively, Muir rejected the cataclysmic
theory, current at the time, which held that landscape features such as
those of his beloved Yosemite were the result of geophysical accidents.
The devout Muir, starting from the premise that "the bottom never fell
out of anything God made," adopted the then novel theory of glaciation
and demonstrated its workings with painstaking measurements of the
movements of Yosemite's glaciers. He presented his findings to the
Boston Academy of Sciences, where he became acquainted with some of
the leading scientists of his day. He also published his findings in the influential *New York Tribune* and the California-based *Overland Monthly,*
and those articles started him on his career as a popular writer.[33] With
Jeanne Carr as his mentor, he also continued his study of botany.[34] By
the time of the Yellowstone Reservation in 1872, Muir had attained a
reputation both as a nature writer and as an amateur botanist, in which
capacity he guided several of the most prominent botanists of his day
through the High Sierras.

Having discovered that he could make a living writing, and finding
himself finally lonely in the wilderness, he moved to Oakland and discovered some of the joys of civilization—like French cuisine, fine wine,
and good cigars. His confidant Jeanne Carr, who had moved there with
her husband, soon arranged a marriage for him. It took 6 years of wary
circling before Muir succumbed. With his new wife, Muir entered her
family's orchard business at a prosperous farm 15 miles north of Oakland.
Eventually Muir took over the business and ran it successfully, devoting
himself to it for about eight years.

He had thus been separated from the wilderness for a long time when
an old friend invited him on a trip to the Washington Cascades in 1888.
He had been there before, and on this trip he was disturbed by the advances the lumbermen had made. Encouraged by his wife, who saw him
reinvigorated by the trip, he divested himself of his responsibilities on the
farm and prepared to write again in defense of threatened nature. He had
been repeatedly asked to write articles for the *Century* magazine by editor Robert Underwood Johnson but had turned them down because of his
farming responsibilities and because writing was a slow, painful process

for him. Now, when Johnson arrived entreating him to revive his literary career, he was prepared to accept.

Johnson's faith in Muir's writing ability was well-founded. Muir was a popular and influential preservation spokesman. The perspective on personal hardship Muir gained on his father's farm, combined with his aptitude for seeing God's handiwork in all facets of nature, gave his nature writing a lightheartedness that was immensely appealing to his readers. Where other outdoor enthusiasts wrote of the challenges of overcoming nature in spite of great personal danger from wild animals, harsh weather and treacherous landforms, Muir recounted his adventures as joyful romps in the woods. Rarely do his accounts note any sense of risk. One such exception is in his story of his first ascent of Mount Ritter. There, halfway up a sheer face, he could see no other handholds, and momentarily was frozen with indecision. Then his "other self," took command, he settled down and calmly completed the climb. Rather than a sense of personal achievement, Muir found in the event a sense of universal integration, another demonstration of the "indivisible harmony of the natural world. Nature included no accidents, no dissonance, no absolute separations. Everything, from the man on the mountain down to the smallest speck, was arranged and loved in equal measure by the Creator."[35]

This was the philosophical core of Muir's life. Man is part of nature, not above nature. He broke with the Judeo-Christian tradition of placing man at the center of things. When he was recovering from malaria during his trek to the Gulf of Mexico, he wrote:

> The world we are told was made for man, a presumption that is totally unsupported by the facts. There is a very numerous class of men who are cast into painful fits of astonishment whenever they find anything, living or dead, in all God's universe, which they cannot eat or render in some way what they call useful to themselves.[36]

In his biocentric approach to the world, Muir's philosophy presaged that of the later ecologists, particularly Aldo Leopold, and the environmentalists of the last 30 years. This way of looking at the world differed radically from that of the utilitarian conservationists. The contrast between Muir's philosophy and Gifford Pinchot's could not have been more fundamental. Whereas Muir saw man as but one part of nature, weighted equally with "the smallest transmicroscopic creature," Pinchot believed that "the first duty of the human race is to control the earth it lives upon."[37]

These two strong-willed, moralistic men would work together for some time, but their ultimate break was preordained.

In 1888 Muir and publisher Robert Underwood Johnson went on a camping trip that set the course of the remainder of Muir's life. At Yosemite, they found the valley in a condition far from that becoming a temple of nature. Under the loose and politicized commission appointed by the governor of California, the valley was occupied by tourist enterprises and agriculture; among other evidence of economic uses were fenced pasturage, impoundments for irrigation purposes, and timber harvesting.[38] In the high country surrounding the valley, Muir and Johnson found damage from sheep grazing and illegal logging. With the goal of protecting the watersheds feeding the valley's streams, Johnson suggested launching a campaign for a nature preserve surrounding the state park. It was to be modeled on the Yellowstone Reservation. In trade for two articles from Muir, Johnson would provide editorial support for a forest reservation surrounding Yosemite and lobby his influential connections in Washington. Two years later, in 1890, success was achieved, with the Yosemite National Park "forest reservation."[39] This act was the first national land preserve consciously directed toward wilderness preservation.[40] It moved through Congress despite opposition from lumber, mining, grazing, and hunting interests.[41] The valley itself and the Mariposa Grove, which Muir and Johnson had initially considered lost, were returned to the federal government in 1906, largely through Muir's efforts.[42]

The legislative success at Yosemite in 1890, together with the lingering problems in the valley, prompted Johnson to suggest an organization dedicated to the defense of Yellowstone and Yosemite. When Muir learned that a group of professors at the University of California at Berkeley was planning an alpine outing club, he melded the two initiatives to form the Sierra Club in 1892. He was elected its first president and served until his death in 1914.

Although Muir's life after 1888 was dedicated to wildlands, it was not until 1897 that he spoke forth unambiguously for wilderness. Until then he maintained an uneasy alliance with the utilitarian conservationists and a personal friendship with Gifford Pinchot. It was partly due to Muir's writing that the 1891 Forest Reservation Act was passed, and that act's silence on the preservation/use question reflected the fact that it was serving both purposes. During the years leading to the 1897 Forest Management Act, however, the necessity of choosing between these incompatible alternatives became clearer and clearer.

Muir met Pinchot when the Forestry Commission studying what to do with the reserves was in California. Based on shared interests in the outdoors and fear of uncontrolled exploitation, Muir publicly supported Pinchot until the 1897 Act. Then, with the emphasis on utilization of the reserves' resources clearly articulated in law, Muir recognized that the preservation interests were not being honored and thereafter ceased his public advocacy of scientific forestry.[43]

According to most historians, the break was sealed when Pinchot publicly advocated grazing on the reserves. In a dramatic encounter in a hotel lobby, Muir denounced him, and thereafter his articles were single-mindedly preservationist. Furthermore, he threw his support behind the national parks, since he viewed the national forests as captured by utilitarian interests.[44]

Muir was successful in his park advocacy. One important element in his success was his access to President Theodore Roosevelt.[45] At Roosevelt's request, TR and Muir went camping in the Yosemite area in 1903. Roosevelt, the ultimate advocate of the rugged life, called the experience of sleeping under the stars and waking up covered with snow "the grandest day of my life." The camping trip was instrumental in creating presidential receptivity for the 1906 Yosemite recession (California's return of Yosemite Valley and the Mariposa Grove to the federal government). It was never guaranteed that Roosevelt, as ardent a utilitarian conservationist as Pinchot, would support noneconomic use of the valley. In the case of a similar valley within the national park, Hetch Hetchy, he would come down on the other side.

SCHISM IN THE CONSERVATION MOVEMENT: THE HETCH HETCHY BATTLE

The 1897 break between conservationists and preservationists was capped by a lengthy, bitter struggle over Hetch Hetchy valley in Yosemite National Park. The schism widened in the twentieth century. It is important to understand the Hetch Hetchy controversy both because of its outcome and impacts and because it illustrates basic issues still facing wildland recreation.[46]

The controversy centered around the proposal of the city of San Francisco to dam the Hetch Hetchy Valley, which had been included in Yosemite National Park in the Yosemite Forest Reservation of 1890. San

Francisco was growing rapidly. It sought to accommodate future growth by securing reservoirs that would supply both water and hydroelectric power. As early as 1876 the city had obtained engineering studies of potential reservoir sites, and by 1882 the city had pinpointed Hetch Hetchy as especially promising. Under a federal right-of-way law, the Secretary of the Interior was authorized to grant the city permission to build the reservoir in Hetch Hetchy Valley. In 1900 the mayor of San Francisco applied for permission to dam the valley, but his application was turned down. In 1906 the San Francisco earthquake occurred, together with severe fire, devastating the city and emphasizing the need for water. That same year San Francisco reapplied for permission to dam Hetch Hetchy, and by 1908 the Secretary of the Interior gave his approval to the reservoir proposal.

With that approval, John Muir and the preservationists launched an intense national campaign to block this intrusion into the national park. The specific issue was the threatened loss of a valley comparable in quality to Yosemite valley, and the larger issue was the challenge to the integrity of the national park idea. President Theodore Roosevelt was put on the spot, caught between his love of the rugged outdoors and his belief in using natural resources for public purposes. Roosevelt asked the Army Corps of Engineers to see if there were alternative sites. The Corps reported that there were alternatives, but that the Hetch Hetchy dam would be $20 million cheaper to build and would produce more power. This is an important point to emphasize: the city of San Francisco could have obtained water and power elsewhere, but it would have cost more money. Reluctantly, Roosevelt gave the project his approval.

John Muir and publisher Robert Underwood Johnson led preservation interests opposed to the reservoir, and their cause was greatly strengthened by women of influence, even though they had not received the right to vote. Women leaders of the Sierra Club enlisted the support of the 800,000 member General Federation of Women's Clubs, and together these organizations vociferously opposed San Francisco's proposal.[47] This organized opposition by prominent women's groups marked a break from their long-standing support of Pinchot and the progressive conservationists, as their utilitarian intentions became more evident.[48]

The Preservationists made Hetch Hetchy a symbol of American greed, materialism, and indifference to ethical and aesthetic qualities. In addition to the argument that Hetch Hetchy was part of a national park and should not be given over to special interests, the publicity played strongly to the ideas developed thus far in the parks movement. The dam was depicted as being against the democratic park ideal of rest and healing for the workers. It was pictured as one more piece of evidence creating the worldwide image of America as ignorant of taste and culture, a place where materialistic interests ran roughshod over spiritual values. As in most severe value conflicts, Hetch Hetchy became not simply a choice between alternative uses of a resource, but a choice between good and evil. Muir blasted the proponents of the dam:

> These temple destroyers, devotees of ravaging commercialism, seem to have a perfect contempt for nature, and, instead of lifting their eyes to the God of the Mountains, lift them to the almighty dollar. Dam Hetch Hetchy! As well dam for water tanks the people's cathedrals and churches; for no holier temple has ever been consecrated by the heart of man.[49]

Advocates of the reservoir proposal got into the mudslinging, too. The *San Francisco Chronicle* called the dam opponents "hoggish and mushy aesthetes," and the city's engineer wrote that they were comprised mainly of "short-haired women and long-haired men."[50] More substantially, their case rested firmly on the belief that the human benefits that would flow from the reservoir far outweighed any possible aesthetic losses. One member of Congress who supported the reservoir argued that "there can be no higher form of conservation than to use flood waters for drinking, bathing and other domestic purposes rather than to let them flow idly, unsubdued and unattended into the sea."[51] A senator from Montana scaled the rhetorical heights in pushing for the reservoir against the preservationists who "would rather have the babes of the community suffering anguish and perishing for want of sufficient water than destroy something that they may go once in many years and gaze upon in order to satisfy their aesthetic and exquisite taste for natural beauty."[52]

Among other prominent voices supporting the city of San Francisco in the struggle was that of Gifford Pinchot, recently fired from the Forest Service but still very influential. In fact, Pinchot's position as the leading spokesman of conservation had, if anything, been enhanced by his martyrdom in the Ballinger case.[53] Pinchot was interested in the Hetch Hetchy battle because it represented an opportunity to strike a major blow for public power and against private monopolists. In fact, commercial water companies had been interested in the Hetch Hetchy site, too, and had joined Muir and the preservationists against San Francisco's proposal. While the public power issue did not figure prominently in the debates, it was crucial in behind-the-scenes maneuvering.[54]

The role played in the Hetch Hetchy controversy by William Kent is particularly interesting and revealing of the clash of values involved.[55] Kent was at that time a congressman from California. Having made a fortune in business in Chicago, Kent had returned to his native California where he had become a leading figure in the parks movement. In 1903 he bought several hundred acres of virgin redwood forest just north of San Francisco. In 1907 a water company condemned 47 acres of it for a reservoir. Kent concluded the company was primarily interested in the trees, some of which were 300 feet tall. To thwart the water company, he donated the area to the federal government. It was to be preserved as a national monument under the Antiquities Act of 1906. At Kent's request the area was named Muir Woods.[56]

Kent was expected to be a strong opponent of the Hetch Hetchy reservoir proposal. To the preservationists' surprise and dismay, however, Kent came out strongly in support of the dam. He took this position, despite his love for parks, because he felt even more strongly about the need for public power, and he believed the electricity generated at Hetch Hetchy would provide an important counterbalance to Pacific Gas and Electric's virtual monopoly. As a respected preservationist, Kent's position carried great credibility. Once Kent made up his mind, he did not hold back. In letters to his congressional colleagues, for example, he referred to Muir as "a man entirely without social sense . . . with him it is me and God and the rock where God put it and that is the end of the story." Kent offered his opinion that Muir's solitary wilderness wanderings had not allowed him to develop a sense of social life, and that Muir was "a misinformed nature lover" being used by private waterpower interests.[57] Despite this back-stabbing, though, Kent later helped prepare and introduced the National Park Act, worked with the Save-the-Redwoods League, and added more land to the Muir Woods National Monument. Historian Roderick Nash attributes Kent's inconsistent behavior to the crucible of conflict over Hetch Hetchy; the valley could not be both nature preserve and reservoir, and thus a choice had to be made.

The climactic struggle in Congress was long and heated. As the moment of decision approached, the *San Francisco Examiner* printed a special edition with artist's drawings depicting happy families visiting the reservoir as it would be developed for recreational use, and copies of the newspaper were rushed to the senators. More critical, although less visible factors played a role in the final decision. The Secretary of the Interior was then Franklin Lane, the former City Attorney of San Francisco and a long-time supporter of the reservoir proposal. Furthermore, one source of opposition was silenced when San Francisco worked out a compromise with irrigators in the San Joaquin Valley who were contending with the city for the water.[58]

On December 19, 1913, President Wilson signed the bill authorizing the Hetch Hetchy reservoir. A year later, broken by the struggle, John Muir died. The preservationists had lost the battle, although they would eventually win substantial victories in the war. Their movement was coalesced and politicized by the fight, and they would be far more prepared in the future. Like the Alamo, Hetch Hetchy became the symbol of a defeat in pursuit of a worthy end. As Roderick Nash points out, perhaps the most significant aspect of the Hetch Hetchy controversy was that it happened at all. Had it occurred 50 to 100 years before, there would have been no contest, because popular attitudes did not support the preservation of land for aesthetic and recreational purposes. In Nash's words, "What had formerly been the subject of national celebration (conquering and developing wilderness) was made to appear a national tragedy."[59] Ironically, as historian Frank Graham notes, the public power argument did not prove out:

> The Senate passed the bill in 1913 and Hetch Hetchy was destroyed. Fortunately, perhaps, John Muir did not live to see the dammed waters creep up over those cliffs across which the streams once had fallen like silver scarves. He died the next year. Though the dam was built, World War I and other developments slowed the pace of construction, and when the pipes were opened at last in the 1930s the city had no means of distributing the water and sold out to the Pacific Gas and Electric Company—the very result that Pinchot, Norris, and the other utilitarian conservationists had hoped to avoid by destroying the valley. Today, while nearby Yosemite is visited almost to destruction, Hetch Hetchy, which might have relieved the tourist pressure, is comparatively neglected, its litter of stumps and barren rocks ceaselessly covered and laid bare again as the water rises and falls according to the city's needs.[60]

MUIR'S IMPACT ON THE PRESERVATION MOVEMENT

Historian Robert Dorman credits Muir with institutionalizing preservation in the national policy arena, with taking "environmental concern out of the books and salons of a few learned devotees and into the realm of national policy and politics."[61] In his writing, and later in his political advocacy, Muir appealed strongly to the middle class of the Gilded Age. His popularity arose not only from his communications skills, which were considerable, but more fundamentally because the times were ripe for his message:

> The popularity of Muir and his message, the receptiveness and the very existence of an audience for him, can only be explained with reference to a variety of social and cultural preconditions that had emereged in America by the 1890s. Most fundamentally, between 1860 and 1900 the United States became a more crowded and a more urbanized country. The population grew from 31 million to 75 million, and the percentage of Americans living in urban areas doubled, from only 20 percent in 1860 to 40 percent in 1900. Meanwhile, the nation was expanding across space as well, with twelve new states joining the union during the same period, all of them in the Great Plains and mountain West regions, demonstrating quite palpably the closing frontier announced by Frederick Jackson Turner. But Americans of the day did not need Turner to tell them that an epoch of the national past was coming to an end, that they no longer lived in the primarily rural, small-town, frontier society of Marsh and Thoreau's time. The evidences of a startlingly new world of metropolises, machine wonders, monopolistic corporations, mass production, and mass consumption were everywhere at the turn of the century. Intercontinental and interurban railroad networks shrank time and distance dramatically, as did the telegraph and telephone. The first skyscrapers began to rise above the bridge towers and church steeples of cities like New York and Chicago, while streetcar suburbs sprawled over the countryside. By the 1910s, the automobile—unimaginable in Muir's youth—was to be commonplace. In the city centers, human warrens spread into sub-subdivided old houses and newer ramshackle tenements, filled with wave upon wave of immigrants recently arrived in search of opportunity. Usually they and the native-born found dehumanizing piecework on factory lines, while the luckier or better educated took the new white-collar jobs in business firms and corporate bureaucracies. Those on the shop floor suffered most, and went on strike the most, in the erratic upswings and downturns and cutthroat competition of the period's overheated economy, as often in depression as it was in boom. On more than one occasion (1877, 1886, 1890, 1892, 1896) "industrial revolution" would have seemed all too ominously appropriate a catchphrase for this violent age, peopled as it was by robber barons, strikebreaking thugs, wild-eyed anarchists, farmers in rebellion, Southern lynch mobs, and Indian-pacifying militarists. But by the 1890s many Americans also came to believe in the dream that the industrial economy was holding out to them, the luminous obverse of the vast crudities and misery it created: the dream of abundance. Already they could see it materializing, in the grand big-city department

stores, in the mail-order catalogues, in the new amusement parks, in their own changing wants and needs. The emergence of this modern consumer economy was to be of signal importance to the cause of conservation, especially so with regard to wilderness preservation.[62]

The shift from a "producerist" economy to a "consumerist" economy, in Dorman's analysis, also brought a shift from a view of wilderness as ". . . supply of free firewood, game, and lumber, and an uncleared area of future farmland . . ." to a view of wilderness as a place for ". . . self-fulfillment, play, indulgence, self-expression, and individuality," all made possible through industrialization. "No longer directly dependent on (or at the mercy of) nature, urban Americans were now free to admire and revel in it. Leisure in the great outdoors was becoming part of a good 'quality of life,' a key catchphrase of the new consumer ethos."[63]

To build a national constituency for wilderness and parks, Muir had to "domesticate" it, in Dorman's phrase. His nature writing, filled with evidence of God's beneficence and eschewing mention of the Darwinian struggle for survival, consistently supported Muir's famous description of wilderness as a balm for the harried spirit of the modern age:

> . . . thousands of tired, nerve-shaken, over-civilized people are beginning to find out that going to the mountains is going home; that wildness is a necessity; and that mountain parks and reservations are useful not only as fountains of timber and irrigating rivers, but as fountains of life.[64]

CREATION OF THE NATIONAL PARK SERVICE

Hetch Hetchy brought to a head a growing sense of concern over the national parks. Each had been established by a separate act of Congress, but no concerted action had been taken to coordinate policy and management of the parks. In addition to Yellowstone National Park in 1872 and Yosemite, Sequoia, and General Grant National Parks in 1890, the following national parks had been established by the time of the Hetch Hetchy decision: Mount Rainier (1899), Mackinac Island (1875), Crater Lake (1902), Wind Cave (1903), Sully's Hill (1904), Platt (1906), Mesa Verde (1906), and Glacier (1910).[65] In addition to the parks, there were reservations (Hot Springs in 1832 and Casa Grande in 1889), a national military park (Chickamauga Chattanooga in 1890) and a number of national monuments established by presidential proclamation under the

1906 Antiquities Act. Between 1905 and 1915, moreover, the growing popularity of the national parks had led to a four-fold increase in visitation, from 85,000 to 335,000 visits.[66] As at Yellowstone and Yosemite, the U.S. Cavalry was frequently called upon in a stopgap effort to limit destruction of these parks, but few coherent and positive steps were taken to assure their protection and their production of quality recreation experiences. The Hetch Hetchy case capped lengthy agitation for a protective agency; the message was: "Look what can happen to a national park if there is no agency to look after it."

The context of the times also spurred development of the national parks movement. As described above by Robert Dorman, it was an era of tremendous population growth and urban-industrial development. The census of 1890 had announced the closing of the frontier, and many people in the cities and the East were feeling nostalgic for its romance. It was a time of new towns, new mills and Model Ts. In many parts of the country the landscape was changing rapidly and strikingly from the frontier to the noise and smoke of progress. Cities themselves in many ways were very disagreeable places: crowded, polluted, and politically corrupt.[67] In this context, park areas came to be increasingly valued by the middle and upper classes who viewed parks as places of relief from urban-industrial conditions—the "lungs of the nation."[68]

The "wilderness cult," a phenomenon that arose in the early years of the twentieth century and is described in the next chapter, supported the national parks movement. However, the alliance has been a rocky one, with a long-lasting struggle between those who have sought to increase visitor use and those who have sought to restrict it. The policies of the National Park Service in its formative years did much to drive a wedge between park and wilderness advocates.

Stephen Mather and Horace Albright

In 1913, the same year Hetch Hetchy was consigned to its watery destiny, Secretary of the Interior Franklin Lane brought in an economics professor as his assistant for parks. The professor was soon transferred to the Federal Reserve Board, but his enthusiastic former student, Horace Albright, stayed on. Albright helped Secretary Lane recruit Stephen Mather, a self-made Chicago millionaire who loved wilderness and parks, for the emerging job of organizing a protective agency for the national parks. Mather was targeted for the job when he wrote his old classmate Lane to complain of the way the national parks were being managed. Lane responded to Mather with a challenge: "Dear Steve," he wrote, "If you don't like the way the national parks are being run, come on down to Washington and run them yourself."[69]

Mather accepted the challenge. Like Olmsted, Muir, and Pinchot, Mather was admirably suited to his calling. With excellent political connections, great personal wealth, a high degree of organizational skill, boundless energy, and the persuasive skills of a great salesman, Mather became the embodiment of the national parks in their early years.[70] Mather teamed with Albright to bring dynamic and effective leadership to the National Park Service. Albright was essential to Mather's success. His down-to-earth steadiness complemented Mather's more mercurial personality.[71] Several times Mather suffered nervous breakdowns, and Albright effectively took command of the agency. He went on to serve as the second director of the Park Service and as a leader in the parks movement.

The National Park Service Act of 1916 and NPS Management Regulations

The first priority for Mather and Albright was to secure legal authorization for an agency to manage the national parks.[72] National parks and monuments had been created in separate acts of Congress without clear guiding policy. Some congressional delegations had recognized the pork barrel potential in national parks and had pushed through a number of questionable parks (Platt, Sully's Hill, Wind Cave, and Mackinac Island). If national parks were to be respectable and worthy of future budgetary support, standards of quality had to be established and enforced. In existing parks, too, better and more uniform management was badly needed if the national parks were to be viewed as a system and thus derive the strength that comes with numbers.

Mather and Albright inherited a substantial legacy of momentum for a parks bureau. Bills to authorize a management agency had been introduced in Congress since as early as 1900. Three secretaries of the Interior had urged creation of a bureau. The Sierra Club had taken up the cause in 1910, and National Parks Conferences in 1911 and 1912 had recommended creation of an agency to manage the national parks. Led by Mary Belle King Sherman, the two million member General Federation of Women's Clubs backed the movement as well.[73] Horace McFarland of the American Civic Association persuaded President Taft to speak at the American Civic Association Convention in 1911. Taft came out in support of a parks agency, and in 1912 he sent a special message to Congress requesting their authorization of it. Finally, William Kent introduced a bill, and after a House-Senate conference ironed out differences concerning grazing in the parks, the National Park Service Act of 1916 was passed.

While others played a major role in the passage of the National Park Service Act, Mather and Albright were anything but bystanders. Mather's promotional genius and Albright's dogged determination were crucial in transforming a long-standing idea into political reality.[74] Mather, the paradigmatic American salesman, hired writer Robert Sterling Yard as his publicity director and launched a campaign to inform Americans about their parks and persuade them to vacation there. Part of this campaign was the *National Parks Portfolio,* a series of pamphlets on individual parks, written by Yard. The Department of the Interior mailed the portfolio to hundreds of thousands of individuals on a mailing list assembled by the General Federation of Women's Clubs.[75]

Mather himself worked to build support among influential elites. He employed such promotional schemes as an educational train trip from Chicago to California and a camping trip in the High Sierras of California to acquaint influential legislators, writers, government officials, publishers, and lecturers with existing and prospective national parks. These extended outings also gave Mather and Albright ample opportunity to deliver their sales pitch for the parks. An exceptionally successful businessman, Mather also courted business interests and succeeded in persuading them that the parks would attract "tourist gold." For his part, in addition to his invaluable assistance in Mather's promotional efforts, Albright was responsible for finally persuading the senators and representatives to resolve their differences and complete the legislative effort.

The language of the 1916 act conveys the central concept of parks as "natural museums" intended to preserve remarkable scenic and cultural features and promote their enjoyment by the public. This phrasing is similar to that of the 1864 Yosemite Grant. That resemblance may be explained in part by the fact that Frederick Law Olmsted's son, who had assumed control of his father's landscape architecture firm, helped draft the bill. The purposes of the parks, so stated in the act, were:

> . . . to conserve the scenery and the natural and historic objects and the wild life therein and to provide for the enjoyment of the same in such manner and by such means as will leave them unimpaired for the enjoyment of future generations.[76]

This statement of purpose contains the ambiguity often found in congressional directives. The language of the law reflects the conflicts involved and the interests compromised in reaching an agreement which attempts to balance preservation and use. In the subsequent history of the National Park Service, and particularly in the era of mass visitation following World War II, the use/protection directives of the act have been the perpetual subject of controversy and reinterpretation. Much as combatants in religious issues draw conflicting support from sacred documents, both those who advocate development of visitor accommodations and services and those who feel the national parks must be "de-civilized" have found justification in the 1916 law.

A 1918 letter from Secretary of Interior Lane to Park Service Director Mather, in all likelihood drafted by Mather for Lane's signature, set basic administrative policies:

> First, that the national parks should be maintained in absolutely unimpaired form for the use of future generations as well as those of our time; second, that they are set apart for the use, observation, health, and pleasure of the people; and third, that the national interest must dictate all decisions affecting public or private enterprise in the parks.
>
> Every activity of the Service is subordinate to the duties imposed upon it to faithfully preserve the parks for posterity in essentially their natural state. The commercial use of these reservations, except as specially authorized by law, or such as may be incidental to the accommodation and entertainment of visitors, will not be permitted under any circumstances.
>
> In studying new park projects you should seek to find "scenery of supreme and distinctive quality or some naural feature so extraordinary or unique as to be of national iterest and importance . . .
>
> The national park system as now constituted should not be lowered in standard, dignity, and prestige by the inclusion of areas which express in less than the highest terms the particular class or kind of exhibit which they represent.[77]

These basic policies would be the subject of many controversies. There has been a persistent struggle over which potential parks should be included. Impulses to include new parks as a source of economic stimulus for depressed regions, for example, have been weighed against the eventual diluting of resources for the operation and maintenance of existing parks and the degradation of system standards. For parks included in the system, the major ongoing concern is with the appropriate level of development.

Gaining Permanence for the National Park Service

With an agency and basic policies on paper, Mather and Albright set out to fully establish both.[78] They sought to develop a constituency for the parks, a group of interested supporters that would help them fight off those who might want to mine, log, and otherwise radically change the natural scenic attractions of the parks, and that would secure the Park Service against the predatory intentions of the Forest Service.[79] Mather expressed deep gratitude to the women's organizations that helped sway public opinion in favor of creating the National Park Service, but then proceeded to staff the agency primarily with men, particularly engineers and landscape architects.[80]

Mather and Albright sought to attract both wealthy, well-connected elites and the growing number of less affluent citizens who could visit the parks in their automobiles. To help in building a base of support, Mather sought to develop the railroads' role. If they would build spur lines to the parks and erect fancy hotels, the elites whose support he was courting would come to use them for extended vacations, as Europeans used their mountain resorts. To encourage lengthy stays, Mather promoted development of tennis courts, golf courses, swimming pools and other attractions in the parks.[81] As automobiles gained in popularity with the advent of Henry Ford's Model T, Mather saw the potential of another, larger constituency, and he actively encouraged automobile visitation. Ironic as it may now seem, from the perspective of the recent battles over roadless areas and the Sierra Club's prominent role in wilderness review, John Muir had also lobbied for automobile access.[82]

Some historians and policy analysts are critical of Mather's development program, considering it to be a classic case of empire building. These critics see it as a grand campaign to get people from all walks of life into the parks with little thought for quality.[83] They also refer to roads and other examples of development as evidence that the founders of the national park system did not define "unimpaired" as undeveloped or as strict preservation of natural resources.[84]

There is another view, however, which recognizes that Mather's constituency-building efforts, while setting a facility-development trend that plagues the parks today, were thoughtfully conceived and necessary for the times. The National Park Service in Mather's time was a fledgling agency, and as the histories of the Department of Education and the Bureau of Outdoor Recreation have shown, agency life can be a tenuous thing. Mather's Park Service was challenged by the same western boomer philosophy that bedeviled Pinchot's Forest Service, and for several reasons the challenge to the parks was greater. First, it was harder to establish parks than national forests, since an act of Congress was required. Second, in parks the resources really were "locked-up," while in forests some economic uses were permitted, thus assuaging extractive interests somewhat. Third, unlike the national forests, park management policy had no provision for giving money to local governments in lieu of taxes they would have collected on the lands. Instead of charging park visitors fair market value (and thus defeating their clientele-building program), NPS leadership promoted parks as magnets for tourist money.[85] In this way, early park policy encouraged the development of tourist industry on park borders, and in some parks today—for example, Great Smoky Mountain and Rocky Mountain national parks—this latter-day Niagara Falls atmosphere at the entrances to the park creates major planning and management challenges.

The great irony was that, after Hetch Hetchy, preservationists, realizing that the scenic merit, worthless lands, and national pride arguments alone were insufficient, took a new and more effective line of attack: parks had economic value because of recreation and tourism. Tying together emotional and economic values did more than anything else to further the national park idea and gain political support.[86] This union also did more than anything else to create many challenges the parks face today in terms of visitor impacts.[87]

The National Park Service had to survive bureaucratic threats, as well. Those who cared about parks had little reason to believe their interests would be served if, as Pinchot advocated, the parks were turned over to the Forest Service. Henry Graves, Pinchot's successor and a far more pragmatic administrator, moved strongly to improve his agency's image in outdoor recreation. Graves publicly suggested that some areas of the national forests should be managed for preservation and some for intensive recreation. He hired landscape architects to do recreation planning, authorized leasing of National Forest lands for second homes and group camps, supported the wilderness proposals of Aldo Leopold, and took other steps to demonstrate Forest Service interest in outdoor recreation. In so doing Graves made the Forest Service into more of a "functional competitor" to the Park Service than it had been under Pinchot and thus threatened to absorb the Park Service in the name of managerial efficiency.[88]

However, as policy analyst Ronald Foresta observes, care must be taken not to attribute Mather and Albright's promotional efforts merely to survivalism. Mather, Albright, and their allies shared the ideology of the progressive era, the same ideology that drove Pinchot and Roosevelt, even if the park advocates disagreed with the foresters over the means to the end of human improvement.[89] One of the central beliefs of the progressives was that government should act to secure benefits for the common good. In seeking to improve access to and use of the National Parks, Mather and Albright were sincerely seeking to enhance the general welfare.[90] Under Mather and Albright, too, mass recreation facilities tended to be concentrated at special attractions, while most of the large parks were left largely undeveloped.[91]

Thus, with the Mather-Albright era of the National Park Service, preservationist strength, which had matured in the Hetch Hetchy controversy, helped provide a climate favorable to the establishment of the national parks as a consolidated system. An energetic, politically astute salesman, Stephen Mather, successfully seized the opportunity. With the essential assistance of Horace Albright, Mather worked hard and successfully to expand the system, but without compromising the standards for scenic quality of national significance.

Unfortunately, the focus on scenery led to a system of parks that, well into the twentieth Century, "emphasized only the high, rugged, spectacular landforms of the West; invariably park boundaries conformed to economic rather than ecological dictates." In other words, to be considered as national parks, areas had to be deemed virtually worthless for agricultural or industrial uses.[92] The worthless lands argument also justified designation of Indian lands as national parks:

> . . . the land included in Indian reservations . . . was generally regarded as economically marginal—or next to worthless. As a result, many Indian lands, if nothing else, were prima facie candidates for eventual inclusion in the parks. As the expanding park movement came to be directed by its own powerful bureaucracy, reservation land became all the more attractive. At parks like the Badlands, Glacier, and Mesa Verde, the government claimed that certain Indian lands were more useful in a national park than a reservation. The "worthless lands" rationale proved as popular in negotiating with Indian tribes as it had long been useful in placating business interests when the subject of parks came up on Capitol Hill.[93]

In the process of building political support for the parks, Mather and Albright gave emphasis to tourism to the point that in many cases the resource preservation mandated by the NPS organic act was somewhat lost.[94] The chorus of lamentations about park overdevelopment that came in the 1970s, however, viewed park development from a very different perspective from that which was prevalent in the 1920s and 1930s. Then, parks were new and a national clientele strongly attuned to preservation did not exist. Some early critics of Mather's policies were heard from, to be sure, and they decried the emphasis on park development and mass tourism. But it would not be until the environmental movement of the late 1960s and 1970s that there would be strong popular support for "de-civilizing" the national parks. To survive, the parks had to get from there to here, and an unbending preservationist approach would have made this passage much more dubious.

NOTES

1. Huth, *Nature and the American*, p. 150.
2. Our decision to emphasize the Yosemite Grant as the beginning of the national park system is supported by Runte, *National Parks*, p. 30: "In fact, therefore, if not in name, Yosemite was the first national park."
3. Brockman and Merriam, *Recreational Use of Wild Lands*, pp. 43–44, is the source for the story of the Washburne-Langford-Doane expedition. Although Hedges suggested national park designation, it was explorer Ferdinand Hayden who recommended a bill to Senator Pomeroy of Kansas to declare Yellowstone a national park, and Pomeroy introduced the bill on December 18, 1871 (U.S. Geological Survey, "Ferdinand Vandiveer Hayden and the Founding of Yellowstone National Park"; and Runte, *National Parks*, p. 45).
4. Sellars, *Preserving Nature in the National Parks*, pp. 7–10, questions the altruism of the story, as well, suggesting that the real motive was tourism. Runte, National Parks, agrees.
5. Nash, *Wilderness and the American Mind*, p. 140.
6. Ibid., p. 112.
7. Huth, *Nature and the American*, p. 152.
8. Runte, "Are National Parks Forever?" p. 4.
9. Runte, *National Parks*, Chapter 3.
10. Ise, *Our National Park Policy*, pp. 19–21.
11. Runte, *National Parks*, pp. 44–45.
12. Nash, *Wilderness and the American Mind*, pp. 112–113; Sellars, *Preserving Nature in the National Parks*, pp. 16–22.

13. Ise, *Our National Park Policy,* p. 19, describes travel difficulties in the early parks.

14. Runte, *National Parks,* p. 44.

15. Runte, *National Parks,* is the definitive treatment of the "worthless land hypothesis."

16. Descriptions of early management at Yosemite and Yellowstone are from Ise, *Our National Park Policy.*

17. Burnham, *Indian Country,* pp. 24–25, traces a paradox that unfolded at Yellowstone. The slaughter of buffalo was carried out largely by professional hunters, supported by the railroads, and defended by the government. This decimated the economy of the Plains tribes and justified their placement on reservations. But, while the buffalo were being annihilated, a preservation philosophy emerged. The buffalo hunter, once an American legend and subject of works of art, was now cast as a scourge. The bison would eventually be protected in Yellowstone National Park as a symbol of wilderness, the same wilderness from which the Indians had been removed. In this way, contrasting policies—buffalo slaughter and buffalo protection—were condoned by the federal government and enforced by the U.S. Army within the short span of 25 years.

18. Runte, *National Parks,* pp. 163–164.

19. Nash, *Wilderness and the American Mind,* p. 125.

20. Fox, *John Muir and His Legacy,* p. 29.

21. Nash, *Wilderness and the American Mind,* p. 123.

22. Fox, *John Muir and His Legacy,* p. 32.

23. Teale, *The Wilderness World of John Muir,* pp. 49–50.

24. Fox, *John Muir and His Legacy,* p. 34.

25. Dorman, *A Word for Nature,* pp. 122–129.

26. Ibid., p. 113; Fox, *John Muir and His Legacy,* pp. 358–374, discusses the role of religion in the preservation movement.

27. Fox, *John Muir and His Legacy,* p. 46. Also, see Cohen, *The Pathless Way,* for Carr's influence on Muir.

28. Fox, *John Muir and His Legacy,* p. 49.

29. Muir, *A Thousand Mile Walk to the Gulf.*

30. Fox, *John Muir and His Legacy,* p. 5.

31. Ibid., p. 82.

32. Nash, *Wilderness and the American Mind,* p. 127.

33. Dorman, *A Word for Nature,* p. 124.

34. Kaufman, *National Parks and the Woman's Voice,* p. 7. In her mid-40s, Jeanne Carr camped and completed botanical studies in Yosemite's high country with Muir, artist William Keith, botanist Albert Kellogg, and her son.

35. Fox, *John Muir and His Legacy,* p. 13.

36. Ibid., p. 52.

37. Pinchot, *The Fight for Conservation.*

38. Ise, *Our National Park Policy,* p. 71.

39. Act of October 1, 1890 (26 Stat. 650).

40. Nash, *Wilderness and the American Mind,* p. 132.

41. Ise, *Our National Park Policy,* p. 57.

42. Fox, *John Muir and His Legacy,* pp. 127–128.

43. Dana, *Forest and Range Policy,* pp. 107–109.

44. Nash, *Wilderness and the American Mind,* pp. 133–140. Char Miller, *Gifford Pinchot and the Making of Modern Environmentalism,* pp. 119–125, argues that this familiar account is wrong. He points out that Pinchot and Muir's warm personal relationship continued after the alleged meeting, and he questions whether the meeting ever happened. Miller concludes that writers on both sides of the conservation/preservation struggle have sought to construe history in ways that favor their preferred side by denigrating the most visible figures on the other side. In addition, as Miller notes, Muir and Pinchot were themselves skilled in public relations and adept at portraying opponents' actions unfavorably. As Miller concludes, "What makes this acrimony so intriguing is that the relationship between Muir and Pinchot once was so benign."

45. Evidence of the quality of Muir's relationship with Roosevelt is shown in the way he chided TR about his hunting: "Mr. Roosevelt, when are you going to get beyond the boyishness of killing things?", as found in Nash, *Wilderness and the American Mind,* p. 139. Documentation of TR's sport hunting binges is provided in Morris, *The Rise of Theodore Roosevelt.*

46. This account of the Hetch Hetchy conflict is primarily from Nash, *Wilderness and the American Mind,* pp. 161–181; and Ise, *Our National Park Policy,* pp. 85–96.

47. Merchant, "Women of . . . ," p. 78

48. Merchant, *Major Problems,* p. 58; Kaufman, *National Parks and the Woman's Voice,* pp. 30–32.

49. Fox, *John Muir and His Legacy,* p. 144.

50. Nash, *Wilderness and the American Mind,* p. 169.

51. Ise, *Our National Park Policy,* p. 91.

52. Ibid., pp. 93–94.

53. McGeary, *Gifford Pinchot,* p. 150, notes Pinchot's conscious decision to become a martyr for conservation.

54. Ise, *Our National Park Policy,* pp. 86–89.

55. Nash, *Wilderness and the American Mind,* pp. 172–175.

56. Fox, *John Muir and His Legacy*, p. 135.

57. Nash, *Wilderness and the American Mind*, p. 174. Kaufman, *National Parks and the Woman's Voice*, p. 32, reports that in a message to Pinchot, Kent wrote that the Hetch Hetchy dam was being jeopardized because of a plan "engineered by misinformed nature lovers and power interests who are working through the women's clubs." Words like these represented an attempt by dam proponents to discredit their opposition by labeling them as sentimental, unscientific, and effeminate.

58. Ise, *Our National Park Policy*, p. 93.

59. Nash, *Wilderness and the American Mind*, p. 181.

60. Graham, *The Adirondack Park*, p. 163.

61. Dorman, *A Word for Nature*, p. 105.

62. Ibid., pp. 130–131.

63. Ibid., pp. 131–132.

64. Nash, *Wilderness and the American Mind*, p. 140.

65. Conservation Foundation, *National Parks for a New Generation*, Appendix B; Foresta, *America's National Parks and Their Keepers*, p. 12.

66. Dana, "The Curtain Rises," p. 2.

67. Ibid., p. 2; Fox, *John Muir and His Legacy*, p. 115.

68. Though this became the dominant view of the predominantly white middle and upper classes, it was certainly not the only view. For example, Burnham, *Indian Country*, pp. 15–58, points out that Indians were banned from Yellowstone and run out of Yosemite and many other national parks. They have fought to maintain their property and their rights in Death Valley and other parks for at least 100 years. Clearly, Native Americans did not view national parks as the "lungs of the nation" but as their original homeland.

69. Runte, *National Parks*, p. 101.

70. Shankland, *Steve Mather of the National Parks*; Foresta, *America's National Parks and Their Keepers*, pp. 9–59; Sellars, *Preserving Nature in the National Parks*, Chap. 3.

71. Foresta, *America's National Parks . . .* , p. 9.

72. Ise, *Our National Park Policy*, pp. 185–193.

73. Kaufman, *National Parks and the Woman's Voice*, p. 33.

74. Swain, "The Passage of the National Park Service Act of 1916."

75. Kaufman, *National Parks and the Woman's Voice*, p. 35.

76. Act of August 25, 1916 (39 Stat. 535).

77. Dana, *Forest and Range Policy*, pp. 200–201.

78. Foresta, *America's National Parks and Their Keepers*, p. 21–30.

79. Ibid., pp. 19–21, Gilligan, "The Development of Policy and Administration," p. 48, notes that the Committee on the Organization of Governmental Sci-

entific Work recommended that the national parks be put under Pinchot's control, and wryly observes that the committee was Pinchot's idea, included him as a member, and met in his house.

80. Kaufman, *National Parks and the Woman's Voice,* pp. 33–55, observes that, seeing limited access to the National Park Service at the national level, women focused their energies on expanding the system through work at the local level. Before the 1916 act was passed, state women's federations were involved with nine national park campaigns, including Sequoia, Olympic, and a state park that would become the nucleus of Everglades. After the creation of the Park Service, state federations and other women's organizations were influential in creating Joshua Tree National Monument and Kings Canyon National Park in California, Great Sand Dunes National Monument in Colorado, and a state park that later became Indiana Dunes National Lakeshore.

81. Ise, *Our National Park Policy,* p. 198.

82. Hendee et al., *Wilderness Management,* p. 31.

83. Gilligan, "The Development of Policy and Administration . . . ," p. 155.

84. Sellars, *Preserving Nature in the National Parks,* pp. 45–46.

85. Dana and Fairfax, *Forest and Range Policy,* 2nd ed., pp. 109–111; Sellars, *Preserving Nature in the National Parks,* Chap.3.

86. Runte, *National Parks,* Chapter 5.

87. Sellars, "The Roots of National Parks Management," explains that the wording of the 1916 act was clearly based on public recreation and the maintenance of scenic beauty for public health, both of which are utilitarian concepts. The term "unimpaired" was added to make certain that the national parks would be available for future generations. However, by interpreting "unimpaired" to mean controlled development that would not damage the sublime beauty of national park landscapes for public enjoyment, the founders placed major qualifications on the term.

88. Foresta, *America's National Parks and Their Keepers,* pp. 19–21.

89. Sellars, "The Roots of National Parks Management."

90. Foresta, *America's National Parks . . . ,* pp. 28–29.

91. Ibid., pp. 29–30.

92. Runte, *National Parks,* p. 55.

93. Burnham, *Indian Country . . . ,* p. 26.

94. Sellars, "The Roots of National Parks Management."

CHAPTER 7

ORIGINS OF
WILDERNESS POLICY

The National Wilderness Preservation System consists of 104.7 million acres of federal land in 628 separate units.[1] Four different federal agencies manage this wilderness estate: the National Park Service, Bureau of Land Management, and Fish and Wildlife Service in the U.S. Department of the Interior, and the Forest Service in the U.S. Department of Agriculture.

With 34.8 million acres of designated wilderness under its aegis, the Forest Service is not the leading agency in terms of wilderness real estate. That distinction falls to the Park Service, which is responsible for a total of 44.0 million acres (most of which is in Alaska). Nevertheless, in our presentation of wilderness policy we have chosen to focus on the Forest Service. It was in the Forest Service that the concept of wilderness as we now know it was born, and it was in that agency that the definitive policy battles that have shaped the current system were fought.

A close examination of the history of wilderness policy illustrates many of the key elements of the policy formation process described in the first chapter. In this chapter, we examine some of the key ideas underlying wilderness policy; explain how the competition between the Forest Service and National Park Service contributed to policy development; introduce several "policy entrepreneurs"; consider how broader societal conditions affected the shaping of wilderness policy; and illustrate the truism that the passage of a new law is but one stage in an evolving debate.

IDEAS BEHIND THE WILDERNESS MOVEMENT

The early national park experience has aptly been labeled "nature tourism."[2] Although their spiritual champion, John Muir, encouraged early park visitors to seek firsthand contact with nature, most sought to experience the great outdoors in relative comfort. While living arrangements in the parks followed a rustic theme, it was often a refined rusticity designed to appeal to elites. Excursions were made by foot, wagon, or pack animal to view natural attractions such as waterfalls, geysers, cliffs, and wildlife, but guides handled most of the dirty work, and the visitors could anticipate a good meal, comfortable beds, and pleasant socializing when they returned to the lodge.

While the comfortable approach to nature appealed to many, others sought to meet nature on nature's terms. Increasingly in the closing years of the nineteenth century and the first decades of the twentieth, there emerged what historian Roderick Nash has called the "wilderness cult," a collection of individuals and organizations united by their interest in experiencing untamed nature.[3] The desire for close encounters with real nature was not new in America, as evidenced by Thoreau's writings. What was new, however, was the rapid expansion of this interest among the dominant middle class of the time. Suddenly, it seemed, interest in "roughing it" was everywhere. Hiking and mountaineering participation grew rapidly, outdoor groups blossomed, and magazines featured accounts of wilderness adventures.

Interest in wilderness shared certain common origins with the earlier interest in national parks, but in significant ways the movements differed. As we have seen, the national park idea grew out of a mixture of romantic idealism, anti-urbanism, nationalism, and commercialism, all played out against a growing American awareness of civilization's advances and the loss of natural areas. The wilderness movement encompassed all these elements. However, while commercial interests also worked to support wilderness, the makeup of those interests was different from those that had supported the national parks. The railroads were not a major factor in the growth of wilderness policy, since the very idea of wilderness is rooted in the rejection of social entanglements and landscape modifications, both of which are central features of the large-scale commercial recreation they had encouraged in the national parks. On the other hand, outfitters and guides were present from the beginning, but many were individualists who themselves were as interested in living close to nature as in making a profit.

Nationalism was a strong driving force behind the wilderness movement, as it had been for the earlier parks movement. However, the coloration of the nationalistic spirit associated with parks and wilderness was tellingly different. The early parks owed their establishment in part to the belief that they would demonstrate to skeptical Europeans that we Americans had resources equivalent in cultural value to their castles and cathedrals, and that we were civilized enough to recognize their worth and protect them. Once established, according to theoretician Frederick Law Olmsted, the parks would be important agents of civilization and democracy. With the growth of interest in wilderness, nationalism appeared as a mirror image of the form it took for parks. Rather than proclaiming that we Americans were as civilized and therefore as good as the Europeans, the wilderness cult gloried in the apparent barbarianism of a life close to nature. Primitivism was associated with youthfulness, vigor, masculinity, and the future. America, with its many opportunities for wilderness recreation, was at a great advantage over decadent old Europe.

Many factors underlay the emergence of the wilderness movement's primitivistic nationalism, and one of the most important was the sense of the disappearance of the western American frontier. Following the Civil War, settlement proceeded rapidly westward. By 1890 the U.S. census reported that, since isolated settlements had so penetrated the unsettled area, a "frontier line" could no longer be said to exist. This fact formed the starting point for one of the most influential essays in American history, "The Significance of the Frontier in American History," by Frederick Jackson Turner.[4]

Frederick Jackson Turner and the Frontier Hypothesis

In his essay, presented in 1893, Turner developed his "frontier hypothesis." Turner argued that it was not the founding fathers working out the U.S. Constitution who created and assured the endurance of American democracy, but pioneers on the frontier struggling against adversity.[5] As Curt Meine states in his biography of Aldo Leopold, "He [Turner] distilled his idea down to a memorable sentence: 'The existence of an area of free land, its continuous recession, and the advance of American settlement westward, explain American development.'"[6] As Turner conceived it, the open land of the frontier provided opportunities for the ambitious poor of urban industrial America, and thus gave every person a chance to be personally independent. Such opportunity was prerequisite for democracy. At the same time, it was the frontier, of all parts of the country, that played the leading role in promoting the growth of democratic institutions. The frontier experience nurtured a viable national democracy in a number of ways. It encouraged intermingling of people from different backgrounds (the melting pot idea). The frontier also strengthened the national government against sectionalism by forcing it to provide internal improvements, like railroads and canals, which unified our commerce and culture. In addition, and perhaps most important in Turner's mind, the frontier encouraged the development of individualism. Turner ascribed to the frontier's influence certain characteristic American ways of thinking.

> From the conditions of frontier life came intellectual traits of profound importance. The works of travelers along each frontier from colonial days onward describe certain common traits, and these traits have, while softening down, still persisted as survivals in the place of their origin, even when a higher social organization succeeded. The result is that to the frontier the American intellect owes its striking characteristics. That coarseness and strength combined with acuteness and inquisitiveness; that practical, inventive turn of mind, quick to find expedients; that masterful grasp of material things, lacking in the artistic but powerful to effect great ends; that restless, nervous energy; that dominant individualism, working for good and for evil, and with all that buoyancy and exuberance which comes with freedom — those are traits of the frontier, or traits called out elsewhere because of the existence of the frontier. Since the days when the fleet of Columbus sailed into the waters of the New World, America has been another name for opportunity, and the people of the United States have taken their tone from the incessant expansion which has not only been open but has even been forced upon them.[7]

Turner was to spend the rest of his working life developing the frontier hypothesis. He never found a convincing answer to the dilemma he so persuasively presented: if the frontier was the essential engine of democracy, what was to become of us now that the frontier was gone, as the 1890 census had announced?[8] It was left for later intellectuals, most notably Aldo Leopold, to suggest wilderness reservations as a modern substitute for the pioneer's frontier.

Turner's frontier hypothesis joined other streams of thought to form a major river of anti-urbanism in the first several decades of the twentieth century. Evidences of the interest in nature include the foundation of the Boy Scouts (1910) and Girl Scouts (1912); the fascination with natural history in expository and fictional writing, which included such popular nature-oriented novels as Jack London's *Call of the Wild* (1903) and Edgar Rice Burroughs' *Tarzan of the Apes* (1912); the growth of suburbs and the related "garden city" concept; the country life movement led by Liberty Hyde Bailey of Cornell; expansion of national park visitation, and many other indicators of anti-urbanism in philosophy, architecture, sociology, dance, political science, and other fields.[9]

The nature movement has been interpreted as a nostalgic attempt to recover an idealized past at a time of rapid urban and industrial growth. It has also been linked with fears that the waves of European immigration—the "new immigration," from southern and eastern Europe—would overwhelm the established descendants of earlier immigrants from England and northern Europe. Toughening in the wilderness would encourage "the lost manly virtues" of the pioneers and thus avoid "race suicide." The ideas of Darwin and Spencer were often on the minds of America's gentry. Analogies between themselves and the Romans facing their end at the hands of the barbarians prompted them to consider ways they and their heirs could be toughened.

Thus, for members of the wilderness cult as for Frederick Jackson Turner, untamed nature played the role of vital adversary. Contrast this with the spirit in which John Muir visited nature. The sense of calm and peace flowing through Muir's journals is in striking contrast with the accounts of challenge and achievement that fill the pages of our outdoor adventure magazines. The voice of wilderness adventure comes through clearly in an 1893 Boone and Crockett Club publication.

> Hunting big game in the wilderness is a sport for a vigorous and masterful people . . . (requiring that the hunter be) . . . sound of body and firm of mind, and must possess energy, resolution, manliness, self-reliance, and a capacity for self-help . . . (characteristics) . . . without which no race can do its life work well.[10]

One of the authors of this macho manifesto was the old Rough Rider himself, Theodore Roosevelt. Note the difference in tone and attitude toward nature in the words of John Muir:

> Thousands of tired, nerve-shaken, overcivilized people are beginning to find out that going to the mountains is going home; that wildness is a necessity; and that mountain parks and reservations are useful not only as fountains of timber and irrigating rivers, but as fountains of life.[11]

Where Roosevelt the hunter saw wilderness as a place to develop race-preserving manly virtues, Muir the anti-hunter saw wilderness as a sanctuary where the Creator's handiwork could be experienced. The chief twentieth century prophet of wilderness, Aldo Leopold, began his career as wilderness advocate with attitudes close to Roosevelt's and gradually moved to an intellectual position closer to Muir's.

WILDERNESS AND THE FOREST SERVICE

Wilderness is primarily a Forest Service story. Other federal agencies manage wilderness, and seven states have established their own wilderness systems comprising 2.7 million acres.[12] However, wilderness policy has been hammered out primarily through controversy over national forest lands management. In turn, Forest Service recognition of wilderness as a legitimate land use was prompted largely by challenges from the National Park Service as both agencies attempted to respond to growing popular interest in wildland recreation.

Gifford Pinchot, leader of the Forest Service in its formative years, never fully acknowledged the legitimacy of outdoor recreation as a use of the national forests.[13] To Pinchot, the 1897 Forest Reservation Act was clear: the purpose of the forest reserves was to provide a continuous supply of water and timber. His little "Use Book," the predecessor to today's ponderous Forest Service Manual, did note as an aside, "quite incidentally, also, the National Forests serve a good purpose as playgrounds for the people . . . and their value in this respect is well worth considering."[14] People did use the national forests for hiking, camping, hunting, and other recreational activities, but outdoor recreation was an informal by-product of forest management for tangible economic benefits; recreation was tolerated as long as it didn't get in the way. Nevertheless, the national forests had immense potential for recreation, and pressure for it grew rapidly.

The first official recognition of recreation by the Forest Service came in 1915, when Congress, prompted by Pinchot's successor Henry Graves, authorized the Service to grant permits for second homes and resort hotels.[15] Several factors probably led to this action, including the fundamental Forest Service policy of supporting local economic development and the emerging competition with the national parks. At that time, with Mather's orientation toward elites in the national parks, the Forest Service encouraged the populist image of the national forest as "the people's recreation areas," close-to-home recreation areas for people who couldn't afford the national parks.

Recreational use of the national forests was expanding rapidly and forcing the agency to respond. By 1911 an estimated 3 million people used the forests for recreation.[16] Henry Graves, an astute administrator who was less dogmatic than Pinchot, attempted to respond to the growing demand for outdoor recreation. Graves hired landscape architect Frank Waugh to assess the outdoor recreation potential of the national forests and to make recommendations for Forest Service actions. In his 1918 report, Waugh recommended that the Forest Service protect natural beauty and scenery, make recreation a use of forests equivalent with timber and grazing, and hire a landscape architect to plan for recreational use of the forests.[17] With the Waugh report, the Forest Service had developed the rationale for recreational use of the National Forests.[18]

Between 1916 and 1921 Congress appropriated $33 million for forest road development, particularly to assist in fire protection. As roads were built, the wilderness began to shrink.[19] With victory in World War I came relief from wartime constraints and a surge in nationalistic pride, exemplified by the railroads' "See America First" campaign. Automobile ownership expanded after the war, and recreation use pressures on the national forests (as on the national parks) grew rapidly. From 3 million in 1911, visitation expanded to 11 million by 1924. Chief Forester Graves in 1920 called for the development of a clear recreation policy to meet these emerging demands, and this initiative was carried forward by Graves' successor, Col. William B. Greeley. However, the effort to accommodate recreation on the national forests was blocked by an alliance of Park Service advocates and commodity users who argued that recreation programs on the forests would duplicate park activities and be a misuse of the forests.[20] Opposition came as well from within the Forest Service. Many field managers in the Forest Service were hostile to recreation, in part because of their utilitarian ethic and in part because funds devoted to recreation came at the expense of other management efforts. In some cases foresters attempted to discourage recreationists by concealing trails, failing to post directional signs, and taking other actions to sabotage the growth of recreation.[21]

By the 1920s the Forest Service found itself under pressure from many sides. There was growing recreational use of the forests, despite little encouragement by the agency. The National Park Service was building a great deal of popular support and beginning to seek expansion by obtaining Forest Service lands. Private interests who wanted to develop forest resources for profit were there, as always. In addition, some scientists

were beginning to call for the establishment of preserved areas for purposes of ecological study.[22] Conflicting external demands were mirrored
by debate within the agency. The call for wilderness preservation began
to be clearly articulated in word and deed.

Early Steps Toward Wilderness Policy in the Forest Service

Two Forest Service employees share credit for taking the first steps toward an explicit wilderness policy. Aldo Leopold was a forester stationed
in northern New Mexico, while Arthur Carhart was a landscape architect
whose recreation planning duties carried him to many different forests.
There is controversy among historians as to which of these two men
should be given credit for originating the wilderness preservation concept.[23] Carhart and Leopold discussed their mutual interests in wilderness
during the period when the first specific steps were taken, so it is difficult
to sort out credit. In what follows we will concentrate on Leopold's contribution, since it was most clearly stated, while recognizing that
Carhart's thought and actions may have helped shape Leopold's.

Carhart's plan for Trappers Lake in the Colorado high country is frequently mentioned as the first major step toward a wilderness preservation policy in the Forest Service. In 1919 the Forest Service sent Carhart
as a "recreation engineer" to survey the lake for vacation home development, a policy the Forest Service was then promoting on its lands. Struck
by the natural beauty of the lake, Carhart recommended that vacation
homes be kept a half-mile from the lake and that the whole lake area be
kept open for general public use. In addition, he suggested construction
of "a good large public camp," to be located not on the lakeshore but along
the stream flowing from the lake and therefore out of sight from the lake.
Carhart then carried his proposal through the Forest Service hierarchy to
success.[24] The Denver District Office of the USFS approved Carhart's
proposal to preserve Trapper's Lake proper in its pristine condition without roads or summer homes.[25]

Carhart's Trappers Lake plan was an important step toward wilderness
policy in that it explicitly recognized the negative consequences of recreational development. However, it was far from being a full realization of
the wilderness idea. The primary concern was scenic integrity, not immersion in a primitive natural experience. The expansive size and remoteness from humanity entailed in the wilderness idea were not present
in Carhart's plan for Trappers Lake.

Leopold's 1921 Wilderness Proposal

The first clear and public call for wilderness came in 1921 in Aldo Leopold's *Journal of Forestry* article entitled "The Wilderness and its Place in Forest Recreation Policy."[26] Leopold's article was prompted by a 1918 proposal to build an automobile road on the Gila National Forest in New Mexico where he was then assistant forest supervisor. Since Leopold was a forester and big-game hunter—someone not seen by other foresters as a wild-eyed, nature-loving romantic—his ideas carried weight in the forestry profession. The 1921 article was extremely important. While Leopold did not occupy a position of sufficient power to bring his ideas into reality, his ideas in the 1921 article and elsewhere were transformed into policy through the leadership of Chief Forester William B. Greeley and Assistant Forester L.F. Kneipp.[27]

Leopold began his article by endorsing the general wisdom of Pinchot's "highest use" philosophy of forest management. In Pinchot's shorthand version of utilitarian philosophy, "wise use" was defined as the greatest good for the greatest number over the longest time. According to Leopold, Pinchot's approach had been effective and had allayed fears of the "lock-up" of forest resources. However, Leopold argued, it would be wrong to think of highest use only in terms of "industrial development." For certain forest lands, preservation as wilderness would be the highest use, since it would answer the needs of small groups of people whose concerns might otherwise be ignored. In attending to the interests of wilderness enthusiasts, wilderness preservation would follow the crucial principle of democracy that the rights of minority (not racial or ethnic minorities, but those not in the majority) groups should be protected as far as possible—i.e., avoid the "tyranny of the majority" feared by the founders of the country. In this connection, Leopold clearly identified the emerging conflict between the large number of recreationists wanting facilities and comfort and the small number seeking to rough it in nature. He also suggested that awareness of this issue was growing among both foresters and the sporting public.

In his article, Leopold defined wilderness as "a continuous stretch of country preserved in its natural state, open to lawful hunting and fishing, big enough to absorb a two-week's pack trip, and kept devoid of roads, artificial trails, cottages, or other works of man." He assumed that only a small fraction of the national forests, and not more than one area in each state, would be preserved as wilderness; that only areas not readily or economically developed would be preserved; and that each area would be representative of forest land of a type that would disappear under business-as-usual policies. Since it would be impossible to re-create wilderness once an area had been developed, Leopold argued that a forward-looking policy was needed to identify areas where development should be preempted.

Leopold went on to suggest that a wilderness area be created in the Gila National Forest. He described the area as being nearly 500,000 acres in size, isolated topographically by mountains and box canyons, and—adhering to the "worthless lands" formula in use since Catlin's time—of little value for agriculture. He identified the Gila as the last typical wilderness area remaining in the southwest mountains. Interestingly, he noted that cattle grazed the entire area, but opined that the historical associations of its use as range would actually enhance the wilderness experience.

In concluding his article, Leopold compared the growth of interest in wilderness preservation with the earlier emergence of concern about forest conservation. Both began with vague feelings that the "inexhaustible" resources were headed for destruction if action were not taken, and both grew to recognize that quality was equally as important as quantity.

With the support of local hunters, Leopold's proposal for the Gila won regional Forest Service approval the following year. Later, in 1924, with Greeley's and Kneipp's leadership, the Forest Service offically designated the Gila roadless area. By 1925 there were five such roadless areas in the National Forest System, and several more were under consideration.[28]

Carhart was also making progress at this time, most notably in his efforts to establish a roadless area in the Superior National Forest in Minnesota. Based on reconnaissance trips he had made to the area in 1919 and 1921, Carhart developed a proposal for a lakeland wilderness area. His proposal was approved by the Secretary of Agriculture in 1923 and, supported by later legislation, Carhart's plan provided the basis for today's million-acre Boundary Waters Canoe Area Wilderness.[29]

The Gila and Superior National Forest successes were representative of a growing interest in wilderness preservation within the Forest Service in the early 1920s. While the effectiveness of Carhart's and Leopold's efforts cannot be doubted, other forces were also at play. Most important, perhaps, was the aggressiveness of the Park Service under Stephen Mather's leadership. The Park Service, riding a crest of popularity based on nationalism, popular interest in nature, a rapidly improving road system, the growth of private automobile ownership, and a bullish economy, was bidding to take over Forest Service land with high recreation value. In addition, Mather pressed Congress to cut off Forest Service funds for recreation management.[30] The bitter legacy of Pinchot's zealous utilitarianism could be seen in the support the Sierra Club gave Mather in this effort. As Chief Forester William B. Greeley moved toward wilderness preservation policy, he was responding not only to the imminent threat from the Park Service, but also to the memory of forestry's debacle in the Adirondacks.[31] The first priority for agencies, as it is for individuals, is survival, and that entails building political and budgetary support.[32]

Recognition of the power of the nature movement came with the first National Conference on Outdoor Recreation in 1924. The conference adopted a resolution recognizing recreation as a resource of the national forests. Wilderness, however, had not yet attained the status of a major concern. Although the benefits of outdoor recreation were much discussed, no one mentioned wilderness per se. At the second conference, held in 1926, Leopold spoke. He called wilderness the fundamental recreation resource and urged a national wilderness preservation policy. In that same year Chief Greeley publicly endorsed wilderness. The 1928 National Conference on Outdoor Recreation issued a report on wilderness, which drew heavily from Leopold's thinking, and reported the results of an inventory of roadless areas in the United States.[33]

The assistant chief of the Forest Service, L.F. Kneipp, directed the inventory. Kneipp had been strongly influenced by Leopold, and he understood the rationale for wilderness preservation as well as the difference between wilderness and the comfort-oriented recreation encouraged by the Park Service. The cutoff size for Kneipp's inventory was 230,400 acres (ten townships or 360 square miles). The inventory found 74 areas of this size totaling 55 million acres, approximately a third of the total acreage of the national forests. Recall that Leopold had called for areas of 500,000 acres and had assumed that only a small fraction of national forest land would be designated wilderness. The shrinkage in the size necessary to be considered wilderness would characterize the wilderness struggle down through the years. One reason for this initial official size reduction may have been an effort to preempt land grabs by the Park Service. Most of the national parks established during this time were carved out of the national forests. Thus, if primitive wildlands were identified as Forest Service property and a use with growing political support (i.e., wilderness) was being considered, transfer to the National Park Service might be blocked.

The agitation by Leopold and others, together with the Park Service challenge, resulted in the so-called L-20 Regulations of 1929. These regulations were intended to provide administrative protection for Forest Service wilderness lands. A 1928 draft of the regulations was reviewed in the western districts and was strongly criticized because they "locked up" natural resources needed for the economic development and viability of local communities and because they restricted administrative flexibility. Pinchot's legacy was clear in these responses: resources were to be used; the economic viability of local communities was a primary consideration in land use decisions; and the trained foresters at the scene were the experts who should make those decisions. Pinchot's legacy was also clear in the impact the district-level review had on the regulations. In its early years, the Forest Service was a decentralized agency; the rangers exercised significant decision authority, and since they didn't like them, the draft regulations were substantially softened.[34] Essentially, as finally approved, the L-20 Regulations were little more than a request to the districts to do what they could to preserve undeveloped areas. Lands designated under the L-20 Regulations were officially called "primitive" areas. Special plans had to be prepared for each primitive area, and some land uses (e.g., second home leasing) were forbidden. However, among the activities permitted on primitive areas were virtually all those associated with commercial forest management.[35]

Chief of the Forest Service Greeley, Assistant Chief Kneipp, and Leopold fought for stiffer regulations, but foresters within the agency resisted them because they felt commercial use should be foremost. Resistance also came from foresters eager to develop recreation facilities to compete with the Park Service. Despite their acknowledged weaknesses, however, the L-20 Regulations were a milestone event. They represented the first attempt to establish wilderness as a general classification of land use with specific management guidelines.[36]

ALDO LEOPOLD

In recognition of his sustained effort in writing and speaking on behalf of wilderness, Aldo Leopold is given much of the credit for the pathbreaking L-20 Regulations. However, the work that was involved there was but the beginning of his contribution to wildland recreation and, more broadly, to environmentalism. Leopold was one of the most effective intellectual leaders in the history of American resource management. He combined the logic of a scientist with the ethical and aesthetic sensitivity of a poet. The voluminous and persuasive writings of this hunter who became a philosopher of ecology helped change the mindset of the nation about natural resource use. His own life and the development of his thinking about man and nature demand treatment beyond an accounting of his role in the L-20 Regulations.[37]

Leopold was born in Burlington, Iowa, in 1887. The son of a wealthy and prominent architect-banker-furniture manufacturer, he spent much of his boyhood exploring and absorbing nature firsthand along the Mississippi River. He went to Yale Forestry School, and after graduating with a master's degree in 1909 joined the Forest Service in the Arizona-New Mexico area. By 1912 Leopold was supervisor of the Carson National Forest, which encompassed approximately 1 million acres in northern New Mexico.

In 1913, Leopold fell ill after severe exposure in a flood and blizzard. A country doctor misdiagnosed his illness, and Leopold suffered a near-fatal attack of kidney disease. It took him 18 months to recover, during which time he busied himself reading, thinking, and fishing. When he was well enough to return to the job, he undertook leadership of fish and game work in the Southwestern District. This work was less taxing than that of a forest supervisor, and Leopold accepted it for good reason: a recurrence of his kidney disease might have been precipitated by overexertion and might well have killed him. In addition to being safer, this assignment fit perfectly with his interests as a sportsman, and he attacked his task with great energy.

Perhaps the most interesting aspect of Leopold's work of this time, in light of his later intellectual development, was his vigorous effort to control predators. His self-described program called for producing sufficient game and fish on the "waste lands" of his district to support 20,000 recreationists who would bring $25 million into the region. To do this he had to carry on "a fight on predatory animals."[38] From that early assignment, premised on controlling a specific attribute of nature in order to produce monetary benefits to society, Leopold's perspective on the relationship between humans and nature would be totally transformed in the three and one-half decades before his death. Leopold's essay, "Thinking Like a Mountain," describes his transformation memorably.

In 1915, after Congress recognized the importance of recreation on the national forests in the same act that authorized vacation homesite leasing,

Leopold was assigned leadership for recreation planning in the district. During this work in 1916 and 1917, he became increasingly aware of the ways recreational development harms open, natural land. This recognition helped lead him to his 1921 wilderness proposal.

Following a year away from the Forest Service, Leopold returned in 1919 as assistant forester in charge of operations. He was successful in this administrative position, while still finding time to press his proposal for a Gila wilderness. He also greatly enlarged his understanding of the emerging science of ecology, both through reading and his own keen observation. As early as 1923, his writings showed that he understood the ecological complexity of the Southwest and the ethical dimensions of conservation.[39]

Leopold's achievements as an administrator led in 1924 to his transfer to the Forest Service's Forest Products Laboratory in Madison, Wisconsin. For such an avid outdoorsman as Leopold, this must have been a difficult assignment, but in key ways it was beneficial; it brought him into contact with intellectuals like Frederick Jackson Turner, who lived two houses down the street, and the distance from the Southwest may have provided him with beneficial perspective for his ongoing reflections on his experiences there.[40] He continued his work on wilderness by developing a philosophical justification for its preservation that was based on Frederick Jackson Turner's frontier hypothesis. He argued that wilderness helped maintain quality in American life, and that many of the things most characteristic of American life were the result of our wilderness heritage.

> . . . if we have such a thing as an American culture (and I think we have), its distinguishing marks are a certain vigorous individualism combined with an ability to organize, a certain intellectual curiosity bent to practical ends, a lack of subservience to stiff social forms, and an intolerance of drones, all of which are distinctive characteristics of successful pioneers. These, if anything, are the indigenous part of our Americanism, the qualities that set it apart as a new rather than an imitative contribution to civilization (and therefore) is it not a bit beside the point for us to be so solicitous about preserving (American) institutions without giving so much as a thought to preserving the environment which produced them and which may now be one of our effective means of keeping them alive?[41]

Thus, for Leopold, it was important to preserve wilderness not only as a playground for recreationists but as the birthplace of American culture.

He argued that we have a duty to give future generations the chance to experience personally settings that had shaped our culture. Leopold expressed his personal feelings poetically: "I am glad I shall never be young without wild country to be young in. Of what avail are forty freedoms without a blank spot on the map?"[42]

After four years at his job at the Forest Products Lab, Leopold struck out on his own. With a grant from the Sporting Arms and Ammunition Manufacturers Institute, he undertook a game survey and in the process established himself nationally as an expert on game management.

Leopold's newly won expert status soon brought him into a position of leadership in wildlife policy. He sought, in essence, to develop a new profession based, like forestry, on scientific management. That goal led him, among many other efforts, to write a textbook. *Game Management,* published in 1933, is still in print and still regarded as a basic text. The central thesis of Leopold's text reveals the legacy of the progressive conservation era passed on to Leopold through his forestry training—the belief in the possibility of intelligent control of the environment to produce a sustained yield of human benefits, in this case wild game for hunting. As a corollary to his belief in environmental control, Leopold believed people could also be controlled, and this led him toward the eventual development of philosophical ideas about the human use of nature.

In 1933 Leopold accepted a newly created chaired professorship in game management in the Department of Agricultural Economics at the University of Wisconsin. In creating this new position, an extraordinary event during the Great Depression, the university sought to develop beneficial uses of the badly abused farm lands that had reverted to the state because the owners could not pay the taxes. For the next 15 years Leopold taught and pursued research on wildlife management, gaining recognition as the "father of wildlife management."

Our failures are often our most instructive experiences, and so it was for Leopold during these years. Repeatedly, he and his cadre of graduate students failed in their efforts to control wildlife populations. These failures led them into more basic ecological research. In turn, his growing understanding of ecology revolutionized his whole outlook. One of Leopold's biographers, Susan Flader, identifies three events in 1935 that signaled this fundamental shift in his intellectual framework. First, he joined with others to establish The Wilderness Society. He associated the society with promotion of a new attitude, "an intelligent humility toward man's place in nature." This new attitude included recognition of the place of predators in maintaining healthy ecosystems. At the same time, he shifted his justification of wilderness preservation from the recreational and historical perspective of his 1921 article to an emphasis on ecological and ethical considerations. Second, Leopold acquired a worn-out farm with the long-term goal of restoring the land to health. His lyrical reflections on his experiences at the farm were published, after his death, in his classic *A Sand County Almanac*. Finally, in his only excursion abroad, Leopold toured Germany to view their forestry and wildlife management system. He came away shaken by the aesthetic and ecological costs of the extremely artificial, carefully controlled approach to resource management he saw there.

In the 1940s Leopold exerted enormous energy in intellectual and political pursuits. His understanding of ecology and evolution fused in his concept of the "biotic pyramid," a metaphor he used to express his belief in the tendency for ecological systems to evolve toward greater and greater diversity and, therefore, stability. The complexity he then recognized led to his final rejection of the position where he had begun—that humans could successfully single out and promote useful species by controlling their competitors. The ethical consequences of his new understanding were stated in his most influential essay, "The Land Ethic": "A thing is right when it tends to preserve the integrity, stability and beauty of the biotic community. It is wrong when it tends otherwise."[43]

With "The Land Ethic," Leopold had completed a personal intellectual transformation. From a starting point in the utilitarian mold of Gifford Pinchot, where expert professionals scientifically manipulated particular elements of the biota to produce a heavy and sustained flow of tangible human benefits, Leopold had changed to a position far more similar to that of John Muir and his flashing anger with "Lord Man" and "the gobble gobble school of economics." According to philosopher Max Oelschlaeger, Leopold's life's work emerged from the creative tension between two approaches to ecology: "imperial ecology," which seeks to understand how nature works so as to dominate and control it, and "arcadian ecology," which seeks through intuition and philosophy to understand humanity's relationship with nature and nature's ethical claims on human behavior. In Oelschlaeger's words, "Such a creative tension can only be understood as beneficial; Leopold struggled throughout his life to resolve this psychic split, and the land ethic may be understood at least as part of the upshot."[44]

THE 1930S, AN ERA OF INTENSE AGENCY COMPETITION

The 1930s brought the Great Depression and the start of World War II. These events had a huge impact on all aspects of American life, including resource management.[45] Pressures to develop primitive areas were strong and came from commodity interests, social programs, the war effort, and mass outdoor recreation participation.

One of the pivotal figures of this era was President Franklin Delano Roosevelt. Like his cousin Theodore Roosevelt, FDR was concerned with resource management and believed firmly in the gospel of conservation as "wise use."[46] The overwhelming challenges of the Depression and the Second World War forced FDR's interest to center on the use of natural resources to solve social problems and support the war effort. In fairness, FDR's actions were not entirely one-sided. He personally took a hand in the creation of Olympic National Park, signed the Kings Canyon National Park bill, and proclaimed the Jackson Hole National Monument against intense opposition.[47] On balance, however, resource development was the hallmark of Franklin Roosevelt's administration. In using the national parks and forests to stimulate economic growth, put unemployed people to work and fight the war, FDR pushed resource development to an extreme and generated intensified counteracting pressure for preservation.

Roosevelt created a number of programs to put people to work, the most famous of which was the Civilian Conservation Corps (CCC). The CCC, which was FDR's own creation, existed from 1933 until 1943 when the labor needs and economic activity of wartime rendered it unnecessary. During that decade, the CCC employed approximately 3 million people, and much of their work took place in the national parks and forests. They built roads, campgrounds, trails, bridges, and many other recreation-related facilities, as well as carrying out reforestation, soil conservation and other resource management actions. Few would question the CCC's benefits for its participants, but some — wilderness advocates who saw their sanctuaries disappearing — expressed concerns about the CCC's environmental impacts.

A characteristic feature of government under FDR was intense agency competition. Competition had always been there, of course, but under FDR it became a dominant feature of the resource policy landscape. Roosevelt was a pragmatist faced with severe challenges. His response was to establish overlapping and competing agencies in the hope that their struggle would produce new ideas and approaches. As FDR put it: "There is something to be said . . . for having a little conflict between agencies. A little rivalry is stimulating, you know. It keeps everybody going to prove that he is a better fellow than the next man."[48]

Under FDR, the struggle for power and position between the Park Service and the Forest Service that had been going on for years intensified. One major reason was his appointment of Harold Ickes as Secretary of the Interior. Ickes was an abrasive bureaucratic in-fighter and an ambitious empire-builder; he was also an incorruptible, courageous, and dedicated public servant who worked himself to exhaustion for what he believed in. Ickes sought to bring the Park Service and the Forest Service together in a new Department of Conservation, an idea that had been around for 35 years when Ickes adopted it. Had it not been for his self-defeating personal style, which rubbed everybody wrong, he might have succeeded.[49] Adding to Ickes's self-imposed problems was the lobbying effort Gifford Pinchot launched against him. It was a major effort, which Pinchot carried out at the expense of a good deal of his personal fortune.[50]

Expansion of the National Park Service

Ickes' 12-year battle to gain control of the Forest Service was given a major boost in his first year in office. In 1933 President Roosevelt issued two executive orders that greatly enlarged the National Park Service.

One aspect of these orders transferred control of all Forest Service national monuments to the National Park Service. National monuments are areas established by presidential proclamation under authority of the 1906 Antiquities Act. This act was prompted by the damage being done to southwestern prehistoric Indian sites by pothunters and vandals. It authorized the president to set aside "national monuments" to protect "cultural artifacts and objects of scientific importance." The area encompassed by the proclamation was to be the smallest area necessary to accomplish the desired protection, and management responsibility was to remain with the original federal agency. Despite its apparently narrow purposes, the Antiquities Act has been interpreted broadly and used to give immediate protection to threatened resources while awaiting congressional action.[51]

In addition to the Forest Service lands, which expanded the NPS base of western natural areas, the 1933 executive orders also gave the Park Service control of 50 historical areas, including the Civil War battlefields, and the District of Columbia parks, parkways, and monuments. Instantly, the Park Service thus doubled its acreage and annual visitation.[52]

The 1933 executive orders represented the culmination of Stephen Mather's and Horace Albright's efforts to solidly establish the National Park Service. The great, early western parks, the "Crown Jewels" such as Yosemite, Yellowstone, and Grand Canyon had provided a firm foundation for the agency.[53] These parks had given the Park Service a popular and symbolically important core of land to manage. Nevertheless, Mather and Albright had felt the need to expand and diversify the system, and to serve a broader clientele base, in order to prevent absorption by the Forest Service.[54] As the Forest Service slowly responded to the growing public recreation interest, Mather had attempted to brand the Forest Service as incurably utilitarian and therefore incapable of properly managing lands for non-commodity values. But only so much could be accomplished by this containment strategy. To survive, the Park Service had to expand. Expansion in the West entailed some problems with quality, since there were a limited number of scenically spectacular natural areas. As policy analyst Ronald Foresta has put it, "In a sense, there was no place to go but down."[55]

Therefore, the Park Service sought areas in the eastern part of the country. Most of the population and most of the nation's political power were there, and the Forest Service, under authority of the Weeks Act of 1911 and the Clarke-McNary Act of 1924, was busily acquiring land in the East. Thus, it was a major step forward when the Park Service obtained its first eastern park—Acadia, in Maine—in 1919. With the addition of the very popular Great Smoky Mountains and Shenandoah National Parks in the late 1920s, the Park Service had a solid base in the East.

Acquisition of the historical parks in the 1933 executive orders gave the Park Service a new constituency and a role not easily absorbed by the Forest Service. The District of Columbia properties, now known collectively as the National Capitol Parks, were picked up because somebody had to manage them and the Park Service could do it, and also because it was considered politically wise to carry out good stewardship under the eyes of Congress.[56]

The Forest Service and Wilderness

Despite the ascendancy of the Park Service in resource-based outdoor recreation during this time, progress was made within the Forest Service.

The advocacy for recreation by those within the agency since the 1918 Waugh Report bore fruit in a 1932 Forest Service memorandum that identified outdoor recreation as a major use of the national forests, equal with other uses. Twenty-eight years later, the 1960 Multiple-Use Sustained-Yield Act would legislatively ratify this agency policy.

Within the Forest Service, the debate over wilderness continued, with the position of those advocating wilderness strengthened by the Park Service's strong challenge. Foresters favoring wilderness made their case as follows. First, recreation, research, and preservation are suitable uses of the forests, and wilderness provides people with critically needed opportunities for challenge and contact with nature. Second, wilderness designations would demonstrate to Congress that the Forest Service is adequately sensitive to the scenic and recreational values of the forest, and thus prevent land transfers to the Park Service. Third, the parts of the national forests sought for wilderness would not be used for their other resources for several decades, due to their remoteness and the marginal quality of those resources (e.g., timber), so in the meantime they might as well be protected as wilderness (this was the so-called "bank" idea). In turn, foresters opposed to wilderness based their stance on the following reasons. First, wilderness is not an authorized use of the national forests, which were established for improving long-range timber production and water flow. Second, many people in the country were then out of work, so it was wrong to lock up resources. Third, highlighting the scenic and recreational values of Forest Service properties might actually encourage Congress to transfer them to the Park Service. Finally, as to the bank idea, opponents argued that basic inventory work was needed on these remote lands, particularly with respect to minerals, before they were locked up; and the temporary protection might not turn out to be temporary after all, once the land was designated as wilderness.[57]

The L-20 Regulations of 1929 had not satisfied wilderness advocates. By 1933, 63 primitive areas totaling almost 8.5 million acres had been designated in six western Forest Service regions. However, management plans for these areas left much to be desired in terms of wilderness preservation. A total of 23 primitive area plans called for future logging, and 32 of the plans noted that logging was not called for only because timber was remote or inaccessible at present (with improved technology and better markets, logging might be called for). In 8 areas, in addition to the 23 to be logged, fire protection roads were to be built. All but 5 of the 63 areas were below Leopold's suggested 500,000-acre minimum; 41 were smaller than 100,000 acres; and one was only 5,000 acres. State and private inholdings in 22 of the areas made it likely that roads would be built to reach resorts and summer homes. Finally, some primitive areas, including the Gila, had already been reduced in size for various administrative reasons. In short, the L-20 Regulations as they were initially carried out in the western national forests provided inadequate protection of wilderness. Rather than a long-term commitment to wilderness, the Forest Service was demonstrating its conception of the L-20 Regulations as an interim protective measure for certain lands.[58] Increasingly there was agitation for stronger measures.[59]

The wilderness battle within the Forest Service reached a new plateau at the end of the 1930s with the issuance of the "U-Regulations." These regulations, designed to supplant the L-20 Regulations, were a monument to the efforts of Robert Marshall, after whom today's million-acre Bob Marshall Wilderness area in Montana is named.

ROBERT MARSHALL

Robert Marshall was another of the wealthy elites who shaped the history of wildland recreation policy.[60] Marshall was the son of a prominent New York constitutional lawyer who used his legal talents in defense of the Adirondack Forest Preserve and Central Park. Like many other major figures in the conservation movement—e.g., Theodore Roosevelt, John Muir, Aldo Leopold—Marshall's interest in the outdoors was helped along by a period of illness and confinement. When he was 11 he contracted pneumonia, and while recovering he read a book about Lewis and Clark that captured his imagination. The family had a vacation home on Lower Saranac Lake in the Adirondacks, and Bob Marshall spent 21 summers there absorbing nature. A compulsive achiever, he climbed all 46 of the peaks over 4,000 feet.

Marshall's interest in the outdoors led him to take a masters degree in forestry at Harvard. Later, while working on his doctorate in plant physiology at Johns Hopkins University, Marshall wrote his famous "minority rights" argument for wilderness preservation.[61] In this article, published in *The Scientific Monthly* in 1930, he built on Leopold's work, adding ideas emerging from psychology about the stress of modern life. Marshall began his paper by defining wilderness as:

> . . . a region which contains no permanent inhabitants, possesses no possibility of conveyance by any mechanical means and is sufficiently spacious

that a person in crossing it must have the experience of sleeping out. The dominant attributes of such an area are: first, that it requires anyone who exists in it to depend exclusively on his own effort for survival; and second, that it preserves as nearly as possible the primitive environment. This means that all roads, power transmission and settlements are barred. But trails and temporary shelters, which were common long before the advent of the white race, are entirely permissible.

Prior to the settlement of whites at Jamestown in 1607, Marshall noted, North America was essentially undisturbed wilderness.[62] From that beginning, white civilization launched an accelerating assault on wild nature. By 1930, according to Marshall, there remained only 20 wilderness areas 1 million acres or larger in size, and even these were threatened. Fearing the loss of our cultural anchors with the disappearance of the wilderness, Marshall urged action to protect wild areas. He felt action would be needed within a few years. To make such decisions rationally rather than on the basis of emotion, he wrote the article to clarify the benefits and costs of wilderness preservation.

Marshall argued that wilderness provides physical, mental, and aesthetic benefits. Backpacking and other forms of backcountry travel toughen the adventurer in ways normal surroundings cannot; wilderness exploration satisfies a craving for adventure (a "moral equivalent to war"); it offers a retreat from oppressive civilization; and it has special aesthetic power because, in contrast with art made by humans, wilderness is timeless yet dynamic, vast, and appeals to all our senses.[63]

Having presented arguments in favor of wilderness, Marshall took note of some arguments against it. Not surprisingly, this is a brief section that serves largely as a springboard for his next set of arguments. Marshall's account of the case against wilderness can be summarized succinctly: Without developments to assist fire control, wilderness is threatened by fire; wilderness preservation entails opportunity costs, as the economic benefits of timber, water power, and other uses are foregone; and the majority of the recreating public, who seek comfort in nature, will be excluded.

Noting that these objections often lead preservationists to despair, Marshall launched into a strong rebuttal. He argued that if wilderness is located in mountainous regions, few economic values will be lost—this is the familiar worthless lands argument. If foresters would concentrate on reforesting and upgrading management of the most productive sites, which Marshall claimed were yielding at only 22 percent of capacity, "we could refrain from using three quarters of the timber in the country and still be better off than we are today." Additionally, he suggested, even if we failed to produce enough timber to meet demand, we would be economically better off to import timber than to export recreationists and their dollars. Furthermore, the cost of "a couple of million dollars" annually would be relatively low for the "unassessable preciousness" of wilderness, given that as a nation we spend about $21 billion a year for entertainment. Marshall observed that the "automobilists," those who would develop wilderness for sightseeing, had more miles of highway than they could cover in a lifetime. Finally, taking his lead from Leopold, Marshall suggested that it would be philosophically wrong to deny the rights of a minority (wilderness enthusiasts) in order to satisfy the wants of a majority (automobilists):

> It is of the utmost importance to concede the right of happiness also to people who find their delight in unaccustomed ways. This prerogative is valid even though its exercise may encroach slightly on the fun of the majority, for there is a point where an increase in the joy of the many causes a decrease in the joy of the few all out of proportion to the gain of the former.

To Marshall, the idea that we should open up wilderness to accommodate comfort-oriented mass recreation was "almost as irrational as contending that because more people enjoy bathing than art exhibits therefore we should change our picture galleries into swimming pools."

Marshall concluded his article with a call to arms for wilderness preservationists. Marshall's closing words give a sense of this extraordinary policy entrepreneur:

> To carry out this program it is exigent that all friends of wilderness should unite. If they do not present the urgency of their viewpoint the other side will certainly capture popular support. Then it will only be a few years until the last escape from society will be barricaded. If that day arrives there will be countless souls born to live in strangulation, countless human beings who will be crushed under the artificial edifice raised by man. There is just one hope of repulsing the tyrannical ambition to conquer every niche on the whole earth. That hope is the organization of spirited people who will fight for the freedom of the wilderness.

Following completion of his doctorate, Marshall went to Alaska to study how trees grow under severe conditions. He spent 15 months in a tiny village, and his interpretation of native life added to his faith in the value of wilderness in promoting self-reliance and independence. As biographer Stephen Fox explains:

In a remote settlement of 127 whites, Eskimos, and Indians, two hundred miles from Fairbanks, he found the happiest civilization he had known. Living in the village and befriending the residents—he was called Oomik Polluk, "Big whiskers"—he concluded they were happy because their lives so little resembled those of modern urbanities. They were surrounded by a beautiful landscape. They routinely encountered hazards and adventures, testing their skills and courage. They did interesting and varied work that brought direct benefits, not simply wages. They all felt independent ("I'm my own boss") and were not pushed around by distant, impersonal economic forces. "Most important of all," he concluded, "happiness in the Koyukuk is stimulated by the prevalent philosophy of enjoying life as it passes along. The absence of constant worry about the future and remorse about the past destroys much that tends to make men miserable." He returned to modern life with his distaste for cities confirmed.[64]

While Marshall was a true believer in the value of wilderness, he was not completely unreasonable. He recognized that the choice between wilderness preservation and economic or mass recreational use represented an important and difficult value conflict. He felt that careful planning could answer the difficult social balancing question of whether the benefits from wilderness outweighed the costs.

Many of Marshall's efforts were far ahead of their time but would later bear fruit. In the 1930s, for example, Marshall was advocating legislative protection of wilderness, and the Wilderness Act of 1964 was the eventual product of that idea. In 1937 Marshall and members of the Sierra Club discussed ideas like low-impact camping and wilderness rangers, which are well-accepted elements of wilderness management.[65]

Marshall's greatest contribution came not from his writing but from his tireless efforts within the policy making system. His first important government appointment was as Head of Forestry in the Bureau of Indian Affairs. He got the job through his personal friendship with the Secretary of the Interior. He used his position to set aside 12 roadless areas of over 100,000 acres each, on the grounds that the Indians needed places to escape from white culture and that they could make money guiding tourists.

In 1935 Marshall and a small group of other veteran wilderness advocates—Benton MacKaye of the Appalachian Trail, Ernest Oberholtzer of the Quetico-Superior canoe country, Robert Sterling Yard of the National Park Service, and philosophical leader Aldo Leopold—founded The Wilderness Society.[66] The leadership of The Wilderness Society decided to keep its membership small and strongly committed. Being small and radical gave the society ideological strength but made it difficult to attract financial support. Therefore, Marshall personally financed most of the operational costs. In other ways, too, he ventured his personal fortune in pursuit of his wilderness dream. To assess the damage of the New Deal's road-building programs, he personally paid for an independent inventory of all federal roadless areas.

In 1937 Marshall moved to the Forest Service, as head of the Recreation and Lands Division. This appointment was made possible by his personal friendship with the Chief of the Forest Service and was one of a handful of cases in the history of the Service of lateral entry to a high-level position. To familiarize himself with his new domain, he immediately began a series of personal visits to western primitive areas. He was quite a hiker: By 1937 he had logged 200 day hikes of 30 miles or longer, and on one occasion ticked off 70 miles in one continuous hike. All this was done with equipment that was heavy and primitive by today's standards. Western Forest Service people he met during his 1937–39 inventory described him as "forceful, friendly, energetic, intelligent, enthusiastic, an idealist" and "eccentric, unreasonable, illogical, extreme, (and) a character."[67]

Marshall died in 1939, at the age of 38, of a coronary suffered while riding a pullman train from Washington to New York. Though his collapse two months earlier after a wilderness study trip had given warning of a serious health problem, he had not slowed his pace. His untimely death was a great loss to the preservation community, but his intensive efforts had focused and activated the pressure that had been building for years to provide better protection for wilderness in the Forest Service.

The monument to Marshall's labors was the set of Forest Service rules, published in 1939, known as the U-Regulations. Three categories were established by these regulations:

- U-1 "Wilderness": Over 100,000 acres; Secretary of Agriculture's approval needed for designation or boundary changes; prohibited uses included roads, timber harvesting, motorized transportation, special permit occupancy; permitted uses included established grazing, water storage projects, access to inholdings, and administrative and emergency access as approved by the Chief of the Forest Service
- U-2 "Wild": 5,000–100,000 acres; designated by the Chief Forester; managed as wilderness
- U-3 "Recreation": Roadless areas with timber cutting and other artificial uses allowed away from scenic routes and recreation zones (three tracts consolidated in 1958 into the Boundary Waters Canoe Area were the only areas designated under the U-3 regulation)

The protection provided by the U-Regulations was stronger and more permanent than that provided by the L-20 Regulations. The 76 primitive areas that had been designated under the L-20 regulations of 1929 were not automatically included under the U-Regulations. Each area to be designated as "Wilderness," "Wild," or "Recreation" had to have a new plan with boundary adjustments to eliminate commercially valuable timber, minerals, and private land. To allow for the time this planning would take, L-20 lands were to be managed as U lands until such time as the designation process was completed.[68]

Preservation groups like the Sierra Club and The Wilderness Society hailed the new regulations, not anticipating the difficulties in reclassification that lay ahead. One basic problem was the lack of information on timber values, mineral deposits, and existing mining claims. Another basic problem was Forest Service passive resistance; the fact that the wilderness advocates in the agency had temporarily gained ascendance and pushed through the new regulations did not mean they had finally forged a pro-wilderness consensus within the agency. In the 13 years following issuance of the 1939 U-regulations, only a third of the L-20 primitive areas were reclassified. There were also tendencies for only mountaintop and relatively small areas to be classified as wilderness, and these choices raised questions of wilderness quality. Areas that are small or consist of narrow fingers along ridge tops do not allow visitors to remove themselves from society and immerse themselves in nature to the extent that large, well-blocked areas do.[69]

As the decade of the 1930s closed and the nation prepared to enter the Second World War, the wilderness debate continued to revolve around questions of value and impact. These questions, some of which were first raised in the nineteenth century and most of which remain current at the beginning of the twenty-first century, have no easy answers. They represent fundamental value issues for a pluralistic society, and answers to them come not in the form of grand strokes and final solutions, but as a series of best approximations in the face of inadequate information and competing, shifting social values. One of the ways we as a society deal with these complexities is through agency competition. In this light, the battle between the Forest Service and Park Service was one of the critical elements in the institutional evolution toward wilderness protection in the 1930s. In the words of policy analyst Sally Fairfax:

> It is strange how often we decry in government the same competitive forces that are the essential and revered component of the American free enter-

prise system. Competition, which is seen in business as the appropriate and necessary means of assuring adequate quality and choice among tooth pastes, cars, and universities, is typically reviled in government as confusing, wasteful, and inefficient. The competition between the Park Service and the Forest Service frequently is manifest in partisanship or rooting for the "home team." Occasionally, it is petty and destructive. In the case of recreation policy and wilderness preservation, however, we see a clear instance of creative competition. The Forest Service was motivated in part by the fear of land transfers to develop and implement a far-reaching program in land preservation. The competition between the two agencies resulted, moreover, in a much broader and more inclusive spectrum of recreation activities than would have been available to the American people if one agency had been exclusively in charge.[70]

NOTES

1. National Wilderness Preservation System by Federal Land Management Agency (millions of acres).

Agency	Existing*			Potential in continental U.S. only**
	Alaska	Rest of U.S.	Total	
U.S. Dept. of the Interior				
National Park Service	33.8	10.2	44.0	7
Bureau of Land Management	0	5.2	5.2	26
Fish and Wildlife Service	18.7	2.0	20.7	n/a
U.S. Dept. of Agriculture				
Forest Service	5.8	29.0	34.8	3
Total	58.3	46.4	104.7	36+

*Source: Wilderness Network 2003, *www.wilderness.net/nwps*, accessed 4/24/03.
**Source: Loomis et al. 1999.
n/a = not available

2. Hendee et al., *Wilderness Management*, p. 31.

3. Nash, *Wilderness and the American Mind*, Chapter 9.

4. Turner, "The Significance of the Frontier in American History."

5. In recent years, Turner's interpretation of the history of the American West has been strongly challenged by modern historians—e.g., Patricia Limerick in *The Legacy of Conquest*.

6. Meine, *Aldo Leopold*, p. 13.

7. Turner, "The Significance of the Frontier in American History," pp. 117–118.

8. Smith, *Virgin Land,* pp. 301–303.

9. Nash, *Wilderness and the American Mind,* Chapter 9; Fox, *John Muir and his Legacy,* p. 116.

10. Nash, *Wilderness and the American Mind,* pp. 152–153.

11. Fox, *John Muir and His Legacy,* p. 116.

12. Hendee and Dawson, *Wilderness Management,* Chapter 6.

13. Gilligan, "The Development of Policy and Administration . . . ," Chapter 2.

14. Robinson, *The Forest Service,* p. 120.

15. Foresta, *America's National Parks and Their Keepers,* p. 20.

16. Gilligan "The Development of Policy and Administration . . . ," p. 74.

17. Searle, *Saving Quetico-Superior,* p. 19.

18. Hendee et al., *Wilderness Management,* p. 34.

19. Allin, *The Politics of Wilderness Preservation,* p. 68.

20. Dana and Fairfax, *Forest and Range Policy,* 2nd ed., p. 131.

21. Gilligan, "The Development of Policy and Administration . . . ," Chapter 2.

22. Ibid., Chapter 2.

23. Baldwin, *The Quiet Revolution.*

24. Ibid., Chapter 2.

25. Hendee et al., *Wilderness Management,* p. 34.

26. Leopold, "The Wilderness and Its Place . . ."

27. Gilligan, "The Development of Policy and Administration . . . ," pp. 91–92.

28. Ibid., Chapter 3.

29. For the political history of the Boundary Waters Canoe Area, see: Dana and Fairfax, *Forest and Range Policy,* 2nd ed., p. 133; Hendee et al., *Wilderness Management,* pp. 116–117; Searle, *Saving Quetico-Superior;* and Baldwin, *The Quiet Revolution.*

30. Baldwin, *The Quiet Revolution,* p. 65.

31. Gilligan, "The Development of Policy and Administration . . . ," Chapter 3.

32. For insight on agency survival, see Hartzog, *Battling for the National Parks,* and Clark and McCool, *Staking out the Terrain.*

33. Nash, *Wilderness and the American Mind,* p. 191.

34. Kaufman, *The Forest Ranger,* and Tipple and Wellman, "Herbert Kaufman's Forest Ranger Thirty Years Later."

35. Hendee et al., *Wilderness Management,* p. 35.

36. Dana and Fairfax, *Forest and Range Policy,* 2nd ed., p. 133.

37. Flader, *Thinking Like a Mountain,* and Nash, *Wilderness and the American Mind,* Chapter 11, are the primary sources of our review of Leopold's life. Other material is from Oelschlaeger, *The Idea of Wilderness,* Chapter 7,

Meine, *Aldo Leopold: His Life and Work,* and Leopold's own writing, particularly *A Sand Country Almanac* and *Sketches Here and There.*

38. Flader, *Thinking Like a Mountain,* p. 12.
39. Oelschlaeger, pp. 212–213.
40. Meine, p. 233.
41. Nash, *Wilderness and the American Mind,* p. 188.
42. Ibid., p. 189.
43. Leopold, "The Land Ethic."
44. Oelschlaeger, *The Idea of Wilderness,* pp. 214–215.
45. Dana and Fairfax, *Forest and Range Policy,* 2nd ed., Chapter 6. Dana and Fairfax is the primary source for the material in the rest of this chapter, unless referenced otherwise.
46. Watkins, "The Terrible-Tempered Mr. Ickes."
47. Personal communication, Ben Twight.
48. Watkins, "The Terrible-Tempered Mr. Ickes," p. 108.
49. Ibid.
50. Personal communication, Ben Twight.
51. The Antiquities Act has been used by 14 of the 17 presidents since its passage to protect more than 100 areas, many of which were later converted to national parks (e.g., Grand Canyon, Zion, Acadia, Statue of Liberty). The "holding action" use of the act was most dramatically shown in President Jimmy Carter's action during the Alaska lands debate of the late 1970s. When use and preservation forces had struggled to a stalemate, Carter proclaimed millions of acres of federal lands in Alaska as national monuments, and this indefinite protection helped break the congressional impasse. Beginning with the Grand Staircase-Escalante in southern Utah, President Bill Clinton used the Antiquities Act to create nine national monuments and expand one other. Former president Carter asked Clinton to add the hotly contested Arctic National Wildlife Refuge to his list of national monument proclamations. (The Wilderness Society, "The Antiquities Act," *http://www.wilderness.org/newsroom/pdf/antiquities.pdf,* accessed 6/24/02).
52. Foresta, *America's National Parks and Their Keepers,* pp. 30–40.
53. Rettie, 1995, Chapter 4: "The Crown Jewels" refers to the "large natural area parks in the western United States." Rettie names Yellowstone, Yosemite, and Grand Canyon as crown jewels, then notes ". . . and perhaps others, depending on one's background or perspective."
54. At present, the NPS is attempting to diversify its workforce as well as add more historical and cultural sites that commemorate the contributions of various ethnic groups to American history (see: "Cultural Resources Diversity Initiative," *http://www.cr.nps.gov/crdi/,* accessed 6/24/02).
55. Foresta, *America's National Parks and Their Keepers,* p. 34.

56. Ibid., pp. 39–40.

57. Dana and Fairfax, *Forest and Range Policy,* 2nd ed., pp. 156–157.

58. Hendee et al., *Wilderness Management,* p. 62.

59. Gilligan, "The Development of Policy and Administration . . . ," pp. 132–135.

60. Ibid., Chapter 5; Nash, *Wilderness and the American Mind,* pp. 200–207; Fox, *John Muir and His Legacy,* pp. 206–212; Mitchell, "In Wilderness Was the Preservation of a Smile."

61. Marshall, "The Problem of the Wilderness."

62. MacLeish, *The Day Before America,* and other new scholarship—e.g., Mann, "1491",—show that, 64 years after Marshall expressed conventional wisdom about Native Americans and their use of the land, a far richer picture is emerging.

63. Nonetheless, Cronon, "The Trouble with Wilderness," argues that an over-emphasis on wilderness creates anti-urbanism and the wrong thinking that "the tree in the wilderness is somehow worth more than the tree in the city."

64. Fox, *John Muir and His Legacy,* p. 207.

65. Hendee et al., *Wilderness Management,* p. 37.

66. Fox, "We Want No Straddlers."

67. Gilligan, "The Development of Policy and Administration . . . ," Chapter 5.

68. Hendee et al., *Wilderness Management,* pp. 62–63.

69. Gilligan, "The Development of Policy and Administration . . . ," pp. 217–220.

70. Dana and Fairfax, *Forest and Range Policy,* 2nd ed., p. 158.

CHAPTER 8

WILDERNESS POLICY FROM WORLD WAR II TO THE PRESENT

Wilderness policy development experienced a temporary interlude during the Second World War. The basic alignment of forces driving the evolution of policy did not change, however. Conflicts between economic development and preservation, on the one hand, and between mass and purist recreation, on the other, continued.

Wartime belt-tightening temporarily interrupted the strong upward trend in wildland recreation participation, which had persisted even through the Great Depression.[1] At the same time, the recreation budgets and staffing of the Forest Service, Park Service, and other agencies suffered greatly, and the state of war justified economic development activities in the national forests. After the war, when Americans resumed their avid pursuit of outdoor recreation, the elements were in place for the sort of perceived crisis that precipitates policy change.

Even more than the New Deal programs, the Second World War served as a springboard for economic recovery, taking the country from the pre-war depression years into the economic growth of the 1950s and 1960s. As economists Marion Clawson and Jack Knetsch would explain in the mid-1960s, growing mass recreation participation was driven by an increasing population with greater amounts of leisure time and disposable income and improved means of transportation.[2] Mass recreation was largely on a collision course with the wilderness movement, since the great majority of people who engage in outdoor recreation do not wish to rough it.

In this chapter, we begin by tracing the events leading from the close of World War II, in 1945, to the passage of the Wilderness Act of 1964. Then we review the struggle over reclassification of L-20 "primitive" areas managed by the Forest Service. We conclude with a review of the ongoing debate involving roadless areas and below-cost timber sales.

THE ECHO PARK CONTROVERSY

A controversy which began in 1949 and culminated in 1956 was the next major event leading to the Wilderness Act.[3] The Echo Park dam proposal, a latter-day Hetch Hetchy, provided a symbolic clash which mobilized preservation interests and prepared them to take the offensive in the political struggle. One half century after the Hetch Hetchy battle was joined, and 36 years after it ended, the Bureau of Reclamation proposed a multiple-purpose dam on the Green River at Echo Park in Utah's obscure Dinosaur National Monument. The monument had been established in 1915 under authority of the Antiquities Act to protect dinosaur fossils, and it had been enlarged to over 200,000 acres in 1938. The monument was comprised primarily of over 100 miles of deep, isolated canyons on the Green and Yampa rivers. As such it afforded superb wilderness river-recreation opportunities, while also providing tempting water resource development possibilities in a part of the country low on water and high on dreams of growth.

In the 1940s the Bureau of Reclamation had begun planning the 10 dam, billion-dollar Colorado River Storage project, one element of which was the dam at Echo Park. When the project was publicly announced, preservation groups seized it as a test case. Echo Park was not the place preservationists would most have liked to defend. Poor road access meant that the area was all but unknown to the public. In fact, low recreation visitation lay behind the Department of the Interior's support of the reservoir project.[4] However, achieving their aims at Echo Park might have provided development interests with an important precedent, so it had to serve as a battleground. Wilderness was threatened in many places, including Olympic and Glacier National Parks, the Grand Canyon, King's Canyon in the Sierras, and the Adirondack Preserve. Echo Park would be the site of a struggle influencing the course of history in all these areas and many more.

In 1950, Secretary of the Interior Oscar Chapman gave his approval to the Colorado River Storage Project, and thereby for the inundation of Echo Park. In a familiar pattern, preservation interests took the fight to the public and to Congress. Howard Zahniser of The Wilderness Society and David Brower of the Sierra Club led them. The public relations effort was enormous and was aided by the old alliance with the press; books were produced, a professional movie was made, and articles appeared in *Life, Colliers, Newsweek, Reader's Digest,* the *New York Times* and other influential publications.

This media blitz concentrated many of the preservation ideas that had been developed since the time of Emerson and Thoreau. Leopold's ecological arguments in favor of wilderness as undisturbed baselines played an especially important role; Benton MacKaye referred to Dinosaur and other wilderness areas as a "reservoir of stored experiences in the ways of life before man." Leopold's land ethic was called forth by a writer who noted that in the United States the area of wilderness was already matched by the area under pavement. Zahniser argued, in words reminiscent of Muir and Leopold, that Dinosaur should be protected as wilderness because there people could learn to see themselves as "dependent members of a great community of life" and to experience the humility necessary for human survival.[5]

Several events in 1950 proved crucial to the preservationists' cause. In that year, Interior Secretary Chapman requested and received Park Service Director Drury's resignation. Drury was a leading preservationist, having come to the Park Service from the Save the Redwoods League, and preservationists viewed his ouster as a threat to their interests. Although Chapman's action was apparently unrelated to the Echo Park case, the outcry it elicited led Chapman to release the Bureau of Reclamation report for review by other agencies. The Corps of Engineers, much to everyone's surprise, broke ranks with the coalition supporting the dam and criticized both the engineering and economic aspects of Reclamation's proposal. Perhaps as a result of these events, in the closing days of the Truman administration Secretary of the Interior Chapman's support of the Echo Park Dam weakened.[6]

With the changeover in the presidency from Truman to Eisenhower, the Colorado River Storage Project received new support, a new proposal, and new bills in the House and Senate. During hearings held in 1954, preservationists made Hetch Hetchy a featured exhibit. Speakers questioned the nation's commitment to the sanctity of the National Park System if we continued to permit such economic depredations. Brower displayed dramatic photos of Hetch Hetchy before and after the dam; the post-dam photos were taken when the reservoir was drawn down and showed mud flats and stumps. Despite preservationist efforts, both the House and Senate subcommittees on Irrigation and Reclamation, which were dominated by westerners, reported favorably on the project and the Echo Park dam. However, the publicity effort had its impact in an eleventh hour flood of letters from park lovers. In one month, the House Committee on Interior and Insular Affairs received 53 letters supporting the dam and 4,731 opposing it.[7] These letters forestalled passage of the bill in 1954.

In 1955, the struggle reopened. This time, Brower shifted from emotional ploys and got into the trenches with the engineers. He used the Bureau's own calculations to show that due to the amount of water that would be lost to evaporation, other sites would be preferable. Although the preservationists lost in the Senate, they won in the House where westerners were less dominant. Finally, in 1956, the Colorado River Storage Project was signed into law—without the Echo Park dam. It was the wilderness movement's finest moment, and it produced increased political support and skill in lobbying. As a result of their victory at Echo Park, the preservationists decided to take the offensive in the wilderness policy struggle.

Before we leave Echo Park, several things should be noted. First, an interesting coalition formed to oppose the irrigation and power interests pushing the project. This coalition demonstrates well the cliché that politics makes strange bedfellows, as wilderness interests were joined by the National Park Service,[8] the Corps of Engineers (possibly for reasons arising out of agency rivalry), by southern California water interests seeking water to further their own municipal growth, and by budget-balancing conservatives upset by the idea of subsidizing irrigation with high-cost power and low interest rates. Second, the outcome illustrates the tradeoffs frequently involved in such controversies. To save Echo Park, the preservationists elected not to fight the Glen Canyon reservoir proposal because it was not part of a national park or monument. However, they recognized that Glen Canyon was a place of scenic and recreational value equal to Echo Park. This tragedy (as perceived by the preservationists) was immortalized in one of the Sierra Club's widely circulated picture books, *The Place Nobody Knew,* and served to remind them of the need to be active and vigilant.[9]

PARK SERVICE AND FOREST SERVICE
THREATS TO PRESERVATION

With the end of World War II, visitation to the national parks surged. Many of the facilities in the parks had been built by the Depression-era public works programs using untreated wood, and then allowed to deteriorate during the war years. The person responsible for the condition of the parks during the 1940s, NPS Director Newton B. Drury, was a quiet, conservative person who did not function effectively in the competitive world of Washington bureaucratic politics.[10] Recreation tends to be one of the first things cut in hard times, so Drury's job would have been difficult even for a person who loved the political fray. The condition of parks soon became a national scandal.[11]

In 1951, Conrad Wirth assumed the position of Director of the National Park Service.[12] Like Mather, Wirth was an adept student of Washington politics who knew how to get things done. He worked personally with President Eisenhower and key members of congress to develop support for the National Park Service. Wirth conceived a massive development program called Mission 66. Mission 66 was a reincarnation of the Mather policy of building political support for the parks by encouraging mass visitation. Begun in 1956 and timed to end in 1966 on the Park Service's 50th anniversary, this program successfully translated the crisis in the parks into dollars for roads, trails, visitor centers and other facilities. Mission 66 was targeted at those parks most threatened by economic development.

Wirth's program was and remains controversial. Some say he saved the parks, while others lay at his feet the creation of a tourist atmosphere they consider wholly inappropriate for the National Parks. Interestingly, it was the extensive road-building effort envisioned in Mission 66 that helped kill the Echo Park project; road building promised increased visitation that would justify preservation of the area in its natural condition.[13] Yet, to preservation groups Mission 66 was anathema. As policy analyst Ronald Foresta has explained:

> Wirth's Mission 66 was the essence of those things they detested; it was the sacrifice of preservation to mass use; it was catering to the lowest common denominator of park taste; it was the submergence of the unique qualities of the individual parks under the weight of seemingly interchangeable, undistinguished development plans. If Mission 66 was a cure for that which ailed the System, it was worse than the disease.[14]

Meanwhile, if somewhat belatedly, the Forest Service also responded to recreation pressures. By this time, visitation to the national forests exceeded the more publicized recreational use of the national parks. Many foresters encouraged recreation, which they viewed as compatible with other uses. These foresters sought management funding for recreation but found their requests blocked by park supporters seeking Park Service supremacy in wildland recreation, by commodity interests who did not want to spread Forest Service funding more thinly, and by wilderness interests to whom developed recreation was almost as bad as clearcutting. Eventually, however, the Forest Service countered Mission 66 with its own Operation Outdoors, a 5-year recreation development program with goals more modest and less construction-oriented than the Park Service program. Operation Outdoors created much less of a splash than Mission 66, yet it was successful in reaching its objectives, and on its foundation the Forest Service began to build the major recreation program that exists today.[15]

If wilderness advocates were threatened by the dam builders as at Echo Park, and if they could not trust the Park Service as demonstrated by Mission 66, they had to remain watchful as well of the utilitarian Forest Service. In the growth years of the 1950s, preservationists increasingly came to see the Forest Service's internal wilderness preservation program as inadequate. New commodity markets and new harvesting and minerals extraction technologies brought many areas that had previously been securely primitive into the sphere of economic interests. Pressure from industry led the Forest Service to open up primitive areas that might otherwise have been classified as wilderness under the U-Regulations.

THE DRIVE FOR A WILDERNESS ACT

Echo Park on Park Service land and similar threats on Forest Service land convinced wilderness interests they needed legislative protection. The concept of legislative protection was not a new idea; Bob Marshall, for example, had advocated such congressional action in the 1930s. The call for legislative protection had been further supported by a 1949 Library of Congress report, requested by an Ohio legislator on behalf of Howard Zahniser of The Wilderness Society. The report presented survey findings indicating that the public wanted wilderness protection at least as secure as that afforded the national parks.[16]

In 1955, Howard Zahniser, the executive secretary of The Wilderness Society, spoke to the National Citizen's Planning Conference on Parks and Open Space for the American People. In his speech, Zahniser proposed a "national wilderness preservation system," which would establish new and uniform administrative procedures for wilderness, while retaining management responsibility in the agencies then involved.[17] In the absence of a congressional veto, wilderness areas would be added to the system by executive order. Senator Hubert Humphrey of Minnesota, a state containing the Boundary Waters Canoe Area wilderness, endorsed Zahniser's concept. In 1956, Humphrey introduced the first wilderness bill. In taking congressional leadership for wilderness, Humphrey subjected himself to political pressure from his northern Minnesota constituents who feared the wilderness bill would damage the tourist trade on which they depended.[18]

The Outdoor Recreation Resources Review Commission

During the legislative battle over wilderness, two important related legislative events occurred: the Outdoor Recreation Resources Review Commission, and the Multiple-Use Sustained-Yield Act. In the first of these, Congress established the Outdoor Recreation Resources Review Commission (ORRRC) in 1958. Despite the existence of the Park Service's Mission 66 and the Forest Service's Operation Outdoors, the tide of recreation visitation was overwhelming both agencies. Furthermore, rapid suburban growth raised concern about open space and urban recreation facilities.[19] ORRRC's mission was to chart a long-range course for the provision of outdoor recreation services. It was to do this by taking inventory of recreation resources and projecting recreation demand in light of fundamental economic and demographic conditions. In other words, the commission was to try to figure out what to do about the well-publicized crisis in outdoor recreation that had emerged in the years after World War II. ORRRC was chartered with almost unanimous support; the National Park Service quietly voiced opposition, because it feared being displaced as the lead federal recreation agency.[20]

In 1962, the ORRRC report was published. It has emerged as a watershed event in the history of U.S. natural resource policy. The report was lengthy (27 volumes) and unsurprising in its conclusions that outdoor recreation participation was high and rising, opportunities were located far from where most Americans lived, and funding and coordination of outdoor recreation services were badly needed. The problems ORRRC identified were obvious to all, and addressing them under conditions of a strong and expanding economy was not viewed as involving serious values choices. Outdoor recreation was a "motherhood and apple pie" issue.[21]

Especially germane to this chapter was ORRRC's endorsement of the wilderness bills then being debated in congress. The commission drew on a report from the Wildland Research Center at UC-Berkeley, which predicted that without legislation wilderness would be lost to competing uses.[22]

The Multiple-Use Sustained-Yield Act

While the blue-ribbon ORRRC panel conducted its review, a second significant legislative action occurred with passage of the Multiple-Use Sustained-Yield Act of 1960. Interestingly, Senator Hubert Humphrey also introduced this legislation, like the wilderness bill it was designed in part to counter. The Forest Service wrote this bill and lobbied hard for it, seeking congressional clarification of long-standing agency policy. In the years before World War II, there had been plenty of land for everybody, including commodity interests, mass recreation interests, and wilderness interests. By 1960 the situation had changed: a strong national economy demanded minerals and timber from the national forests; hordes of recreationists sought developed recreation areas, and their demands on the Forest Service were accompanied by continued challenges from the Park Service; and wilderness interests pressed for the preservation of large areas from both developed recreation and commodity interests. The Forest Service, caught in the middle of these conflicting interests, sought legislative endorsement of its well-established balancing act. Congressional familiarity with the concepts of multiple use and sustained yield is shown in the bill's rapid passage with nearly unanimous support.[23]

The political overtones of the Multiple-Use Sustained-Yield Act are evident. For example, the National Park Service attempted to insert language into the bill to the effect that land transfers from the Forest Service to the Park Service would not be affected. In the years between 1902 and 1960 nearly 5 million acres—nearly a third of the total Park Service land—had been transferred from the Forest Service to the Park Service.[24] The act also attempted to placate wilderness interests with the statement that wilderness is "consistent with the purposes of the Act."

As policy analyst Sally Fairfax points out, the Multiple-Use Sustained-Yield Act was an appropriate culmination of the postwar transitions. New

users and pressures were recognized, but in a traditional way, by reaf-
firming the "wise use" conception of conservation dating from the Pinchot era. The act's vague language provides little guidance to management, while being tactically valuable as a slogan in the Forest Service's
struggle to maintain autonomy.[25]

PASSAGE OF THE WILDERNESS ACT

The road from the first wilderness preservation bill in 1956 to the Wilderness Act of 1964 was long and arduous, and passage of the law was
merely one prominent milestone of this still-continuing struggle.[26] The
concept of preserving large areas as wilderness was a uniquely American
contribution to resource policy, so there were few leads to follow. In addition, wilderness preservation ran counter to several very powerful
forces central to American culture. It thwarted resource development for
profit by private entrepreneurs, and it imposed limits on mass recreation
by prohibiting road-building and facility development. In a country that
idealizes private property, entrepreneurial spirit, and the common man,
any proposal to remove large areas of land from economic development,
and to do so on behalf of a small number of people, was destined to be severely challenged. Beyond these resource-related issues, the debate over
wilderness was part of the larger struggle between Congress and the President for supremacy in national policy making. For these reasons it took
9 years, 65 different bills and 18 legislative hearings across the country to
forge a legislative compromise.[27]

Provisions of the First Wilderness Bill

Senator Humphrey's 1956 wilderness bill, the first of four he would even-
tually submit, reflected the strong part preservation groups played in
drafting it.[28] Humphrey's bill would have established a National Wilder-
ness Preservation System. Included in the system would be lands from the
National Forest System, the National Park System, the National Wildlife
Refuge and Game Range System, and Indian reservations. The 37 Forest
Service areas classified as "wilderness," "wild," and "roadless" under the
U-Regulations would have been included in the National Wilderness
Preservation System upon passage of the act. The Forest Service "primi-
tive" areas, classified under the L-20 Regulations, were to be temporarily

included in the wilderness system, pending their review within nine years by the secretary of Agriculture. The secretary's classification recommendations would be put into effect unless Congress objected to them. Altogether, 65 million acres of Forest Service land would have been studied, and an estimated 35–45 million acres might actually have been classified as wilderness. No Department of Interior lands would have been included in the system immediately, but all roadless areas were to be reviewed within 9 years. For lands on Indian reservations, consent of the tribal councils was required. It has been estimated that over 40 million acres of Department of the Interior land might have been added to the National Wilderness Preservation System through this review process.

Not only was its coverage broad, but Humphrey's first bill was a strong preservation document in other ways, too. It imposed severe restrictions on economic development activities on protected lands. Logging, prospecting, mining, farming, road building, and building of structures were forbidden, as were grazing and the use of motorized vehicles. There were several exceptions to prohibited uses, which reflected the history of the wilderness idea; pre-established grazing was permitted (as it had been in Leopold's 1921 proposal), and pre-established motorboat and airplane use was allowed (as it had been in the Boundary Waters Canoe Area Wilderness), but only until these uses could equitably be ended. Taking a page from the 1906 Antiquities Act, which allowed the president to protect federal lands quickly, Humphrey's original bill would have had the wilderness areas designated by executive action, unless Congress vetoed the action within 120 days. Finally, Humphrey's bill called for the creation of a National Wilderness Preservation Council, composed of six citizens and five agency representatives, which was to serve as watchdog for the system.

Senator Humphrey's bill was matched 4 days later by Representative John Saylor's identical House bill. Even as Humphrey and Saylor introduced their bills, they knew there would not be time before the close of the 84th Congress to hold hearings, but they wanted to get the issue before Congress. The following year, 1957, they submitted slightly stronger bills, and the formal wilderness debate was underway.

Lines of Debate

The first strong opposition to the Humphrey-Saylor wilderness bill came from water development interests.[29] All of the Colorado River Basin water development organizations that had been involved in the Echo Park battle testified against the wilderness bill. The California State Department of Water Resources presented the most telling case. The department claimed that the massive California Water Plan, an integrated system of mountain reservoirs and viaducts designed to support the predicted tripling of California's 1957 population, would be jeopardized. Any wilderness bill should permit reservoirs, tunnels, conduits, and other water development projects, they argued, since there were no alternative water storage sites, and since the lakes thus created would actually enhance recreational value and would have minimal visual impact. Preservationists had memory of the enhancement the Hetch Hetchy reservoir had provided that area, and they argued in favor of alternative reservoir sites at elevations below the proposed wilderness areas.

Additional opposition to the Humphrey-Saylor wilderness bill came from the mining, lumber, and livestock industries. The objections of these economic interests were similar, and will be handled together. There were five major arguments against wilderness preservation.[30]

First, opponents claimed the legislation simply was not needed, as there was then and always would be plenty of undeveloped land in the West. The bill's proponents, obviously, felt protection was needed, and they asserted "an increasing population, accompanied by expanding settlement and growing mechanization, is destined to occupy and modify all (unprotected) areas."

Second, opponents suggested that the wilderness protection then provided by law on National Park Service lands and by administrative regulation on Forest Service lands was sufficient. Park Service Director Conrad Wirth, for example, claimed that building roads into remote NPS areas did not harm their wilderness character. Proponents of the bill obviously did not share Wirth's conception of wilderness, leading them to question the value of NPS's legislation for wilderness protection. And, based on their experience with the Forest Service in the case of the Three Sisters Primitive Area in Oregon, where in 1954 the agency announced plans to log a fifth of the 250,000 acres, preservationists argued that more than administrative protection was needed for Forest Service lands.

Third, opponents charged that a wilderness law would lock up resources for the use of a small minority of the people, while local economies based on such extractive activities as logging and lumber manufacturing would suffer, and many Americans who would never visit the protected areas would absorb higher housing costs. The bill's proponents pointed out the "option values" in wilderness preservation, explaining that people derive benefits from knowing that they or their children may be able to visit the areas in the future.

Fourth, opponents tried to make the case that it would be immoral and un-American to deny enterprising individuals the chance of making money and, therefore, of improving the economic well being of all, simply for the aesthetic pleasure of the few. A strong economy was essential to the national defense, and this discussion was taking place at the height of the Cold War of the 1950s. Proponents countered by noting that much wilderness was already protected by law (for example, prospecting and mining were forbidden in the national parks). If wilderness areas did prove to contain resources essential to national survival, then they could be developed at that time; in the meantime, protection as wilderness would have prevented squandering those valuable resources. Proponents also stressed the limited economic impact of wilderness protection (the "worthless lands" argument), noting that it was only because the lands were, in fact, worthless that they were still undeveloped. Proponents went on to note that economic benefits of great value, like clean water, would continue to flow from lands protected under a wilderness act. They challenged the local community economic impact argument by noting that when viability of the local economy depends on one-time extraction of a resource, as in the case of mining, that economy is ultimately doomed, anyway. The bill's proponents reemphasized the experiential and restorative values of wilderness, using the intellectual weapons developed since the time of Thoreau. Finally, they emphasized the scientific values of wilderness. From the time of George Perkins Marsh, scientists had become increasingly aware of the importance of undisturbed ecosystems as baselines against which to assess human impact on the environment. Leopold, in his land ethic, further developed this line of thinking. As he put it: "The first principle of intelligent tinkering is to save all the parts." Other scientists noted that wilderness possessed value in adding to the genetic diversity of plant and animal populations, and that it provided habitat for threatened species.[31]

Finally, opponents argued that the wilderness bill would interfere with the long-standing multiple-use sustained-yield policy of the Forest Service. The Forest Service's sensitivity on this matter was shown when they wrote and lobbied successfully for the Multiple-Use Sustained-Yield Act, as previously described. The wilderness bill's proponents countered by pointing out that multiple use could not logically mean every use on every acre, that it was necessary to think system-wide, and that wilderness was consistent with multiple-use doctrine applied system-wide. In response to the point that administrative flexibility was necessary if a sustained yield of benefits were to flow from the forests, wilderness advocates cited the irreversibility of development in wilderness areas. Preservation preserves future options, while development closes out wilderness as a future option.

Leadership in the Legislative Struggle

Howard Zahniser of The Wilderness Society assumed leadership for the preservationists in the legislative struggle. A scholarly man, Zahniser was the embodiment of the humility about human achievement that Muir and the mature Leopold had voiced. Reflecting on the atomic bomb that ended the Second World War, Zahniser said, "as we constantly become more and more nearly lords of creation, there is nothing so much to be feared as ourselves, yet we know so little about fearsome US."[32] Zahniser quit a secure job in the Department of Agriculture to join The Wilderness Society for half the salary. Zahniser's efforts were instrumental in the eventual passage of the Wilderness Act, yet he did not live to see his work to completion. Having labored for wilderness preservation since the late 1940s, he died four months before the act's passage.

Senator Clinton Anderson of New Mexico and Representative Wayne Aspinall of Colorado provided congressional leadership.[33] Anderson and Aspinall chaired the Interior Committees in their respective chambers, and therefore were in pivotal positions for legislation concerning the federal lands. There were remarkable parallels in their lives: they were born within 6 months of each other; they both attended meetings in 1922 at which the original agreements on the allocation of water from the Colorado River were made; both were first elected to Congress on a pledge to assure their states favorable treatment under the Colorado River allocation agreements; both chaired their committees' Subcommittee on Reclamation before assuming the chair of the full committee; both served on the Joint Committee on Atomic Energy; and both retired from Congress in 1973. In addition, both considered themselves conservationists. Their definitions of conservation, however, were strikingly different. For Aspinall, "wise use" meant utilitarian development of natural resources, and the final compromises made to economic interests in the Wilderness Act are testimony to his dedication in pursuing this end. For Anderson, "wise use" was determined in a national, rather than a regional context, and non-economic resource uses could contribute to the national welfare.

In order for wilderness legislation to be enacted, many intertwining and opposing forces had to be untangled and compromised. In the end, out of a large cast of players, it was Anderson and Aspinall who cut the deal necessary to break the deadlock. They were prompted toward compromise by personal and political considerations. Aspinall faced increasing reelection problems as the Colorado electorate shifted away from the ranchers and other resource-based economic interests he defended toward a more urban and preservation-oriented population. For his part, Anderson saw his health deteriorating and became concerned that he would be unable to see the battle through to completion. Thus, both legislators were inclined to compromise if the appropriate trading materials could be found.

Aspinall provided the key, when he identified a general review and revision of the public land laws as something he cared about. In a 1963 speech, Aspinall unveiled his proposal for a $3\frac{1}{2}$ year study, during which time executive agencies like the Forest Service would suspend major modifications in land use. Aspinall was particularly irritated by Forest Service reclassification efforts, then proceeding under the U-Regulations and over his strenuous objections. When Anderson learned that Aspinall really wanted the land law review, he leaned back in his chair and said, "And I want a wilderness bill!" As a member of the Senate Interior Committee staff observed, "Clint's been waiting for something that Wayne really wants." With trading material thus identified, a compromise on a wilderness bill was possible. Many other pieces of the puzzle still had to be put in place and many other events would occur, including President Kennedy's assassination and Zahniser's death, but the key had been found.

Necessary Compromises

In order to obtain passage of a wilderness act, Anderson, Zahniser, and their colleagues had to make numerous compromises. Legislation has been described as a temporary treaty between competing forces that records the terms of surrender, and the Wilderness Act of 1964 was no exception. Preservationists entered 1956 with high hopes, but much had to be sacrificed in order to make any headway.

The first major point of conflict concerned the uses that would be permitted on official wilderness areas. As the law finally passed, more uses were permitted than the preservationists had originally envisioned, and these would continue to be sources of debate. Established motorboat and airplane uses and established grazing were approved, and there was no indication that they would be prohibited at some future time. Administrative roads and protective measures against fires, insects, and diseases were permitted. With the approval of the president, hydroelectric projects with accompanying powerlines and roads could be built. Commercial activities serving wilderness recreation were permitted, setting the stage for present-day struggles between commercial packing outfits and backpackers and between commercial whitewater guides and private boaters. Finally, mining activity was permitted. Prospecting could be conducted and claims made until midnight December 31, 1983, and mining on patented claims could be carried out after that date under "reasonable" regulations to protect wilderness quality.

The second major topic of debate concerned the procedures that would be followed in designating wilderness areas in the future. Preservationists sought a National Wilderness Preservation Council to monitor progress and advise Congress. The agencies, fearing loss of power, successfully blocked this effort. Preservationists also sought a procedure that would designate areas unless Congress took action to stop designation. Preservationists were defeated on this issue, too, largely due to the efforts of Representative Aspinall who feared the general shift in power away from Congress and toward the executive branch and the "imperial presidency." In its final form, the Wilderness Act requires Congress to take the lead in designating individual wilderness areas. Designation is a long, cumbersome process requiring unremitting effort by proponents and providing many opportunities for opponents to block designation of an area. This designation process, initially seen as a defeat for the preservationists, has been seen by some as advantageous. Stewart Brandborg of The Wilderness Society explained this in 1968:

> The education and leadership training of the public, to the end that it may attend to its own interest, has been greatly aided by the Wilderness Law, particularly those provisions which were inserted by the opponents of the measure, requiring that Congress must act affirmatively on each addition to the National Wilderness Preservation System. This "blocking effort," as we saw it at the time, has turned out to be a great liberating force in the conservation movement. By closing off the channel of accomplishing completion of the Wilderness System substantially on an executive level, where heads of organizations would normally consult and advise on behalf of their members, the Wilderness Law, as it was passed, has opened the way to a far more effective conservation movement, in which people in local areas must be involved in a series of drives for preservation of the wilderness areas *they know*.[34]

The Wilderness Act of 1964

Final compromises in the struggle for wilderness legislation were reached and the bill signed into law in 1964. The purposes of the law were to provide places "for the use and enjoyment of the American people in such manner as will leave them unimpaired for future use and enjoyment *as wilderness*" (emphasis supplied). In addition, the law attempted to differentiate wilderness from the "pleasuring grounds" of the National Park System. In the act, wilderness was defined as follows:

> A wilderness, in contrast with those areas where man and his own works dominate the landscape, is hereby recognized as an area where the earth and its community of life are untrammeled by man, where man himself is a visitor who does not remain. An area of wilderness is further defined to mean in this Act an area of undeveloped Federal land retaining its primeval character and influence, without permanent improvements or human habitation, which is protected and managed so as to preserve its natural conditions and which (1) generally appears to have been affected primarily by the forces of nature, with the imprint of man's work substantially unnoticeable; (2) has outstanding opportunities for solitude or a primitive and unconfined type of recreation; (3) has at least five thousand acres of land or is of sufficient size as to make practicable its preservation and use in an unimpaired condition; and (4) may also contain ecological, geological or other features of scientific, educational, scenic, or historical value.[35]

The Wilderness Act designated 54 areas totaling 9.1 million acres of Forest Service land as "instant" (immediately designated) wilderness. All Forest Service lands designated as wilderness, wild, and recreational under the U-Regulations were included. The Forest Service was directed to review all L-20 primitive lands within 10 years.

Seeds of Continuing Conflict

The Wilderness Act reflected conflicts and compromises that would be the basis of future struggles. First, in specifying that in wilderness areas human impacts would be "substantially unnoticeable," the seeds of the so-called "purity debate" were sown. It has been difficult to reach agreement on the level and type of human traces necessary to disqualify an area as wilderness. The Forest Service generally has fought for a strict definition, hoping to retain more lands under multiple-use management, while preservationists have argued for a more lenient definition in order to expand the wilderness system. The purity question was to become the major issue in the Eastern Wilderness Act of 1975.

Second, in referring to "outstanding opportunities for solitude" the act set the stage for a running battle over the size of wilderness. Those opposing expansion of the wilderness system have argued that large areas are needed for true solitude; therefore, smaller roadless areas should not be included in the wilderness system. Those favoring system expansion have contended that wilderness is a state of mind determined by the expectations of individual users; therefore, "pocket" wilderness can qualify. Another controversy surrounding the solitude clause has concerned establishing limits on the recreational use of popular areas. As wilderness visitation grew in the 1970s and agencies tried to restrict the number and types of users, a witches' brew of administrative, scientific, and political problems developed. An example of the struggle over limiting recreational use is found at the Colorado River in Grand Canyon National Park. Agency use limits were challenged in court, where it was found that the Park Service was legally empowered to regulate use and that its actions were not arbitrary and capricious. However, in 1981 an amendment to the Park Service appropriations bill specified that no part of the funding could be used for river management that limited the amount of commercial or motorized use of the Grand Canyon during the summer season. Thus, where legal objections to use management were defeated, political means were found to defeat agency initiatives.[36]

Third, the required review of the Forest Service's L-20 "primitive areas" proved to be extremely contentious, as described below. In addition to controversy over these administratively designated areas, a major policy struggle arose over consideration of what came to be known as *de facto* wilderness," those Forest Service lands that had not been made accessible through forest road development.

Fourth, in specifying continuance of established grazing and motorboat use, and in permitting prospecting until the end of 1983 and mining on proven claims indefinitely, the Wilderness Act reflected unresolved conflicts over these uses that would continue to be sources of contention. Debate on this issue became especially acrimonious during James Watt's tenure as Secretary of the Interior under President Ronald Reagan.

When Lyndon Johnson signed the Wilderness Act into law in a ceremony in the Rose Garden, preservationists exulted in their triumph. The struggle had been joined near the turn of the century by John Muir, sharpened in the 1920s by Aldo Leopold, pushed administratively by Bob Marshall in the 1930s, and advanced legislatively by Howard Zahniser from the mid-1950s. The Wilderness Act represented the culmination of a long and difficult effort.

Looking back on the Wilderness Act, some have interpreted the 1964 act as representing only limited gains for preservationists: the sense of permanence provided by congressional rather than administrative designation of wilderness areas is somewhat illusory, since laws can always be repealed and administrations can thwart the intent of the law through budget manipulations, personnel restrictions, and other devices. Nevertheless, as policy analyst Sally Fairfax explains, some definite gains had been attained. First, the long struggle had raised popular consciousness about wilderness and built support for its protection. Second, the establishment of a national wilderness system made the defense of any given area somewhat easier, much as the 1916 act had for the national parks. Third, the wilderness program begun administratively in the Forest Service was extended by the Wilderness Act to land management agencies in the Department of Interior, particularly the National Park Service—it ". . . reminds Park Service officials that their business is partially preservation, not simply the mass recreation characterized by scenic highways, visitor centers, observation towers, and curio shops." Finally, certain limitations on mining activities were made; a time limit was placed on mining claims, some restrictions were placed on how mining could be carried out (the land had to be returned to its original condition), and mining patents applied only to the minerals and not to the land.[37]

ROADLESS AREA REVIEW AND EVALUATION (RARE)

In 1971, the Forest Service began the first of its wilderness reviews. The acronym for the review was RARE, for Roadless Area Review and Evaluation.[38] According to the 1964 Wilderness Act, the Forest Service was not required to inventory and evaluate all its roadless areas, but only the 34 primitive areas totaling 5.4 million acres designated under the L-20 Regulations. The Service, however, chose to inventory all its roadless areas out of a conviction that sooner or later wilderness proponents would seek designation of lands with wilderness attributes that are not officially designated (so-called "de facto" wilderness areas). The Forest Service's decision to conduct an expansive review was prompted by court action and presidential pressure.[39] In designing RARE, the Forest Service sought to control what it saw as inevitable.[40]

A special review was used, rather than relying on normal forest planning procedures, because the Forest Service wished to restrict the time roadless areas remained in an uncertain status and to limit the occasions for conflict with preservationists. The RARE inventory included roadless, undeveloped Forest Service areas of 5,000 or more acres that did not adjoin existing wilderness or primitive areas. Areas adjoining wilderness or primitive lands could be smaller than 5,000 acres. The Forest Service identified 1,449 areas on the National Forests totaling 56 million acres. In this way, the decision for a comprehensive review of Forest Service lands expanded by roughly 51 million acres the coverage required by the Wilderness Act of 1964.[41]

The Forest Service designed RARE to prioritize its recommendations for wilderness. The agency sought to evaluate each study area's value as wilderness against its value for commodity production. In addition, the Service sought to disperse the system as widely as possible over the United States, to include as many different ecosystems as possible, and to locate some wilderness areas near urban centers. Each area reviewed under RARE was evaluated according to its gross size, quality (an index based on scenic quality, isolation, and variety of opportunity), effectiveness (gross size multiplied by quality index), and costs (direct costs for study, private land and permit acquisition, maintenance, and opportunity costs including minerals, timber, and water benefits forgone).[42]

Another new law made the RARE review more complex and challenging. In the years since passage of the 1964 Wilderness Act, the growth of the environmental movement had led to the passage of the National Environmental Policy Act (NEPA) of 1970. NEPA required federal agencies to prepare environmental impact statements (EIS) for major federal actions and forced them to invite public comment. The Forest Service's RARE effort qualified as a major federal action, and thus a draft environmental impact statement was prepared and subjected to public review. The 1973 draft EIS recommended that 235 new areas totaling 11 million acres be given early consideration as wilderness. In the most extensive public involvement effort ever undertaken by the federal government, the Forest Service held 300 hearings and received over 50,000 oral and written communications. The result of involving the public in this way was the addition of 61 new areas and the deletion of 22 areas. The revised recommendations were for 274 areas totaling 12.3 million acres, with approximately 44 million acres to be released to other uses.[43]

Wilderness advocates criticized RARE quickly and strongly. They argued that it was too rushed to allow careful public consideration, that it was biased toward recreational use over ecological integrity, that it was overly subjective, that gross size was given too much weight, that the economic analysis was flawed because it is difficult to assign monetary value to wilderness benefits, that large areas in more than one district were treated as smaller units, and that timber values were inflated.[44]

Anticipating disappointment with the results of RARE, the Sierra Club and others had earlier sued in federal court to force the Forest Service to protect all 56 million acres as wilderness until they could be adequately reviewed. The suit was based on the claim that the agency had not followed NEPA procedures and that the inventory and selection procedures in RARE were inadequate for the reasons listed above. The Sierra Club sought protection of all 56 million acres of roadless Forest Service land until an adequate review could be completed. The court granted a preliminary injunction which answered the Sierra Club's request. Negotiations prompted by the injunction led the Forest Service to promise that before any part of the 56 million acres was returned to multiple-use management the agency would conduct an acceptable environmental impact review. This agreement undercut RARE's usefulness, since the Forest Service had committed itself to rereviewing each parcel of land. In short, RARE failed to solve the wilderness allocation issue.[45]

THE EASTERN WILDERNESS ACT

The seeds of the next legislative action, the Eastern Wilderness Act, were sown in RARE. Preservationists criticized the Forest Service for omitting the eastern national forests and the national grasslands from review as wilderness. The Forest Service's position since the 1964 Wilderness Act had been that only a few areas in the East qualified under the act. As of 1973 only four eastern Forest Service areas had been designated as wilderness: the Boundary Waters Canoe Area Wilderness in Minnesota, the Great Gulf in New Hampshire, and Linville Gorge and Shining Rock in North Carolina.[46] In RARE, the Forest Service claimed that since the eastern forest lands had previously been cut, burned, farmed, and otherwise used and occupied, they did not qualify as wilderness—they were not "untrammeled," nor was human presence "substantially unnoticeable." Preservationists countered by arguing that in the East, unlike the arid West, vegetative growth and other natural processes had healed or would soon heal abused land and restore its primeval character.

The Forest Service sought to win preservationist support for its purity stance by suggesting that admission of inferior areas might set precedent and eventually jeopardize pristine areas already in the wilderness system. At the same time, the Service sought to limit the number of acres removed from commodity management, and thereby to retain as much of its historical mission of active land management for economic benefits as possible. Furthermore, the Service feared that if cutover lands in the East were included, so might such lands in the West, and vast acreages of western national forest land could be designated as wilderness. Their concerns were not groundless, since a relaxed definition of wilderness might have led to designation of an estimated 70 million acres, or a third of the National Forest System, as wilderness.[47]

The purity issue and the Forest Service's stance on it led to the Eastern Wilderness Act of 1975, an amendment to the 1964 Wilderness Act. In the Eastern Wilderness Act, Congress designated 16 instant areas (totaling 207,000 acres) and 17 study areas (totaling 125,000 acres) on the national forests in the East. Eastern wilderness areas would be part of the National Wilderness Preservation System, rather than becoming a separate system. With Forest Service support, the idea of a "Wild Area System" was floated, but it was rejected because it would have, in effect, ratified the Forest Service's purity argument against expansion of the National Wilderness Preservation System.[48]

The Eastern Wilderness Act again changed the working definition of wilderness, if not the legal definition. As policy analyst Sally Fairfax points out, the act led to the most realistic definition of wilderness: Wilderness is whatever Congress says it is.[49] Leopold had called for areas that could accommodate a two-week pack trip, and he had proposed an area of 500,000 acres; Marshall's inventory had a 300,000-acre minimum and he later argued for a 100,000-acre minimum; the 1964 law had permitted areas as small as 5,000 acres or smaller if they were "untrammeled by man." The mutability of the size standard was matched by Congress's, flexibility concerning human impact. Many of the eastern lands were in public ownership and available for designation as wilderness precisely because they had been so thoroughly abused as to constitute a threat to the general welfare. Passage of the Eastern Wilderness Act helped give new meaning to the irreversibility argument for wilderness. If lands which were denuded and eroding could, through careful custodianship and the

passage of time, be considered wilderness, the term "practical irreversibility" might be most appropriate. Of course, practicality is in the
eyes of the beholder, and so the question can never be resolved in any final way. It is a values issue, and therefore political means of resolution
are paramount. And, since public values are continually evolving, solutions must be somewhat temporary, not truly final.

NEW FOREST SERVICE LEGISLATION

The Forest Service had been an embattled agency since the mid-1960s. An
expanding population and national economy increased demands for commodity production from the national forests. At the same time, these same
underlying factors supported expansion of outdoor recreation participation
and interest in environmental protection. At the center of these colliding
interests was the Forest Service. Traditionally, the agency had operated under the multiple-use philosophy and had taken the position that professional foresters should decide the mix of benefits flowing from their
forests. At the same time that incompatible interests were seeking to enlarge their shares of the national forest pie, public trust in government in
general, and in the omniscient forester in particular, was rapidly shrinking.

In addition to suffering from the erosion of public trust that came to all
agencies as a result of the Vietnam War, Watergate, and other national
traumas, the Forest Service had been attacked for its use of clearcutting.[50]
Acrimonious controversies over management practices on the Mononge-
hela, Bitterroot, Tongass, and other national forests led eventually to a
lawsuit which charged that the Forest Service was violating its 1897 organic act. The 1897 act contained language that limited timber harvesting
in the forest reserves to "dead, matured or large growth of trees" which
must be "marked and designated" before harvest. The courts found for the
plaintiff, the Izaak Walton League. This decision posed a severe threat to
the timber industry and so forced congressional action.

Repeal of the offending language, a simple and expedient approach,
was not taken because many believed a broader overhaul of Forest Service statutory authority was needed.[51] The National Forest Management
Act of 1976 (NFMA), an amendment to the Forest and Rangelands Renewable Resources Planning Act of 1974 (RPA), was seen as the answer.
RPA, which had grown out of concerns over timber supply, inadequate
and unpredictable agency funding, and environmentalist dissatisfaction

with the Forest Service's commodity orientation, directed the Service to engage in long-range national planning for all renewable natural resources. NFMA, in turn, sought to resolve the intense conflicts over use of the national forests by expanding planning activities at the forest level, as well. The Forest Service struggled to carry out the mandates of the RPA and NFMA, with little additional funding and labor to accomplish massive data-collection and public involvement efforts, while simultaneously trying to accomplish its wilderness reviews.

THE ENDANGERED AMERICAN WILDERNESS ACT

The debate over the Eastern Wilderness Act had forced clarification of the purity issue. Environmentalists had succeeded in expanding the wilderness system to the East and to previously abused lands. Now they sought to expand the system in the West to include roadless areas the Forest Service had excluded in its RARE review.

The Forest Service's RARE failed to identify, even as study areas, a number of areas in the West that were of great interest to preservationists. Frustrated by the agency, they turned again to Congress. The result came to be known as the Endangered American Wilderness Act, aimed at protecting the some 20 areas totaling over 1 million acres from multiple-use management. Tellingly, Assistant Secretary of Agriculture Rupert Cutler recommended enactment of the bill, providing the number of areas was increased. As Craig Allin notes, with Cutler's testimony ". . . the Department of Agriculture, in effect, endorsed legislation to protect portions of the American wilderness from its own constituent bureau, the Forest Service."[52]

RARE II

In 1976 Jimmy Carter was elected president, and the tone of the wilderness policy struggle changed. Presidents Nixon and Ford had allies among commodity interests and, while not antagonistic toward wilderness, they were not avid supporters. Soon after he took office, President Carter delivered an environmental message to Congress in which he called the Wilderness Act a "landmark of American conservation policy" and called for prompt expansion of the system ". . . before the most deserving areas of federal lands are opened to other uses and lost to wilderness forever."[53]

Serving as Carter's Assistant Secretary of Agriculture for Conservation, Research, and Education, Rupert Cutler (formerly with the Wilderness Society), pressed for a new review in the hopes of settling the wilderness designation issue in the Forest Service. Unlike RARE, RARE II was designed to "release" for multiple-use management all lands not considered wilderness or needing further study. Despite advice from the Department of Agriculture's lawyers that a nationwide review would not suffice for an environmental impact statement and that ultimately wilderness land allocation would be done in statewide wilderness bills, Cutler pressed forward with RARE II.

RARE II identified a total of 67 million acres of potential Forest Service Wilderness in 2,919 areas. Recall that RARE had identified 56 million acres in 1,449 areas. The growth in potential wilderness from the RARE I total was largely the result of dropping the size criterion even lower; many areas smaller than 1,000 acres, and some islands as small as 1 acre, were included. At the time of the RARE II inventory, 15.7 million acres had already been officially designated as wilderness, and an additional 3.5 million acres were undergoing congressional review. Thus, adding existing, review, and potential wilderness acreage together made a total of 85 million acres, over half the total acreage in the National Forest System.[54]

Policy analyst Craig Allin observes of RARE II that ". . . both commodity and preservation groups watched the RARE II process unfold with a mixture of hope and concern." Commodity interests hoped that large areas of the National Forest System would be freed from consideration as wilderness, but they feared the Carter administration would cave in to preservationists and recommend large new additions to the wilderness system. For their part, preservationists hoped for new wilderness designations, while fearing that "released" areas would permanently be lost.[55]

Results of RARE II were announced in 1979. The Forest Service recommended that 15.4 million acres, a third of which was in Alaska, be designated wilderness, while 36 million acres—58 percent of the total studied—be non-wilderness and opened to immediate commodity development. Wilderness advocates felt betrayed. The State of California sued the U.S. Department of Agriculture to halt plans for development of a *de facto* wilderness area. The federal judge who heard the case found that RARE II did not provide sufficient site-specific information for a valid environmental impact assessment, and he enjoined all development on all RARE II lands in California. Just as the Department of Agriculture's lawyers had predicted, then, RARE II failed as a nationwide environmental impact study of wilderness designation.

Neither side in the debate wanted the RARE II inventory tied up in endless litigation, and both now focused attention on gaining a legislative resolution. Preservationists sought an area-by-area review process, which they believed would allow them to mobilize grassroots support in relevant congressional districts, while commodity interests pushed for a final decision that would open areas not officially designated as wilderness to multiple use management. In the end, the two sides compromised on a "soft release" approach, in which statewide wilderness bills would be decreed as sufficient environmental impact statements, thus satisfying the NEPA requirements, and non-wilderness lands would be released to multiple-use management during the first cycle of the Forest Service management plans (10 or 15 years), after which they could again be considered as wilderness.[56]

ROADLESS AREA DEBATE CONTINUES

While the state wilderness bills moved through Congress, the Forest Service became entangled in yet another controversy. This time the issue was so-called "below-cost timber sales." In these sales, the costs associated with administering timber sales exceeded the revenues from the timber removed by the loggers.[57] Foresters argued that roads were needed for forest fire protection and would benefit recreationists. They suggested that the major costs of these timber sales, those associated with building logging roads, should not be attributed only to the first harvest those roads enabled, and that the initial investment would pay off in future harvests. Preservationists were concerned that forest road building associated with these economically questionable timber harvests would remove released lands from possible future consideration as wilderness. In other words, they accused the agency of attempting to defeat the "soft release" compromise by managing potential wilderness areas in such a way that they would be removed from consideration as wilderness because of evident human impacts—primarily forest roads.

In 1998, during the Clinton presidency and under a chief who was a wildlife biologist, the Forest Service examined the impacts of road construction on roadless areas. The agency then issued an 18-month suspension of road construction in most roadless areas. In 1999, Clinton directed the Forest Service to undertake a major public involvement effort to explore ways of conserving roadless areas. Based on that dialogue, the agency developed a proposed rule and draft environmental impact statement on roadless area management.[58] The draft EIS received over a million comments, the majority of which were favorable.[59] Accordingly, in 2000 the Clinton administration proposed to protect the remaining 60 million acres of roadless areas in the national forests. These areas would be off-limits to road building but not necessarily other uses.

In the draft environmental impact statement issued by the Forest Service under the Clinton administration, the preferred alternative called for prohibiting most new roads in inventoried roadless areas and allowing only logging that could be accomplished without new roads (for instance, by using helicopters or balloons). The huge (9 million acre) roadless area of the Tongass National Forest in Southeast Alaska, with its immensely valuable timber resources, was exempted. The fate of small areas (under 5,000 acres) was left to the normal, local forest planning process. Preservationists objected to the agency's preferred alternative, arguing against all logging in inventoried roadless areas and advocating full protection of both the Tongass and the small areas. The Society of American Foresters registered its opposition to any nationwide prohibition that would limit the ability of local forest managers to deal with the unique characteristics of the roadless areas. The Society of American Foresters further argued that restricting road-building activity would constrain access to the forests for fire, insect, and disease protection, and that problems arising in roadless areas could spread to adjacent public and private forest lands with disastrous consequences.

There was also disagreement over the economic impacts of the Clinton roadless area proposal. The timber industry noted that less than one-third of lands in the National Forest System are suitable for timber production. According to the industry, environmental regulations have severely reduced the harvest, from 12 billion board feet in 1989 to 3 billion board feet in 1999. Restrictions on timber harvesting on the national forests disproportionately injure smaller logging operations, since they have only limited private lands and must depend on the national forests for their timber supply.[60] Environmentalists contended that changing social and economic conditions are reshaping the values of the national forests. For example, The Wilderness Society pointed out that ". . . less than a decade ago, timber was considered ten times more valuable than wilderness recreation whereas now the value of recreation in wilderness and primitive areas on the national forests exceeds the value of the timber logged." They also argued that prohibiting all logging in inventoried roadless areas, including the Tongass, would reduce the Forest Service's planned timber harvest program by only 7 percent, and the reductions to the total U.S. timber harvest, most of which occurs on state and private lands, would be miniscule.[61] They cited a study by economist John Loomis that concludes: ". . . forest products manufacturing and other resource extractive jobs are a minor, and in most cases, declining part of the economy in states with national forest land."[62] Further, The Wilderness Society presented the analysis of a resource economist—commissioned by TWS—which found that ". . . non-labor income, including investment and retirement income, has become the number one source of earnings in most if not all of the states with national forests," and the service sector is now ". . . the main source of job and earnings growth in most of these states, with much of the greatest growth in high-paying service jobs in fields such as healthcare, engineering and management services . . . [and] . . . people in high-paying service jobs and those who collect non-labor income are attracted to areas with a clean environment and pristine wildlands."[63]

The election of President George W. Bush in 2000 once again shifted the playing field. The administration temporarily halted the Clinton ban on road building in roadless areas, claiming that the issue needs to be restudied and that citizens and organizations need more time to respond to such a far-reaching policy. Given the extensive public involvement in the development of the Clinton ruling, and in light of the positive public response, one can predict that Bush's initiative will be strongly challenged.

Judging from historical trends, and given the clash of values involved, future wilderness designations will likely be made on a case-by-case, state-by-state basis, and they will be hotly contested. One can also predict that other events and trends, such as wildfires and the growth of support for ecosystem management, will strongly influence whatever decisions are reached. The political system provides many ways for various interests to have their say.[64]

NOTES

1. Clawson and Knetsch, *Economics of Outdoor Recreation,* Figure 2, p. 44.
2. Ibid., pp. 93–112.

3. The primary source of the Echo Park conflict is Nash, *Wilderness and the American Mind*, pp. 209–219.

4. Allin, *The Politics of Wilderness Preservation*, p. 91; Foresta, *America's National Parks and Their Keepers*, p. 52.

5. Nash, *Wilderness and the American Mind*, pp. 214–215.

6. Allin, *The Politics of Wilderness Preservation*, pp. 92–93.

7. Ibid., p. 93.

8. However, the Park Service, which had been created in response to Hetch Hetchy, did not play an important role in the Echo Park battle. Director Newton B. Drury allowed the Bureau of Reclamation to survey the reservoir site and did not oppose the plan until 1949, by which time Reclamation had amassed strong support for the dam. The leadership in opposing the dam fell to the preservation interest groups.

9. Nash, *Wilderness and the American Mind*, pp. 228–229.

10. Foresta, *America's National Parks and Their Keepers*, p. 49.

11. Ise, *Our National Park Policy*, pp. 534–540.

12. Primary sources on Conrad Wirth and Mission 66 are Dana and Fairfax, *Forest and Range Policy*, 2nd ed., pp. 191–193, and Foresta, *America's National Parks and Their Keepers*, pp. 52–57.

13. Foresta, p. 54.

14. Ibid., p. 55.

15. Dana and Fairfax, *Forest and Range Policy*, 2nd ed., pp. 193–194.

16. Hendee et al., *Wilderness Management*, p. 63.

17. Another persuasive plea for legislation to preserve wilderness came from James Gilligan, in a speech before the Society of American Foresters in 1954. Basing his conclusions on his doctoral review of the Forest Service's wilderness efforts, the most comprehensive effort to that time, Gilligan called for congressional protection of wilderness lands. Congressional action was needed, he felt, because the status quo was biased in favor of economic development, in the case of the Forest Service, and mass recreation, in the case of the Park Service. A broadly based programmatic response was needed. The Wilderness Society published the full text of Gilligan's speech in a 1955 edition of *The Living Wilderness* and supported its conclusions editorially.

18. Allin, *The Politics of Wilderness Preservation*, pp. 102–105.

19. Foresta, *America's National Parks and Their Keepers*, p. 62.

20. Ibid., pp. 62–63.

21. Dana and Fairfax, *Forest and Range Policy*, 2nd ed., pp. 209–212.

22. Hendee et al., *Wilderness Management*, p. 64.

23. Dana and Fairfax, *Forest and Range Policy*, 2nd ed., pp. 200–205.

24. Ibid., p. 209.

25. Ibid., pp. 200–205.

26. Primary reliance for this account of the Wilderness Act's passage is placed on Allin, *The Politics of Wilderness Preservation,* pp. 102–136. Other sources are Hendee et al., *Wilderness Management,* pp. 64–75, and Dana and Fairfax, *Forest and Range Policy,* 2nd ed., pp. 217–221.

27. Hendee et al., *Wilderness Management,* p. 64.

28. Allin, *The Politics of Wilderness Preservation,* pp. 106–108.

29. Ibid., pp. 108–109.

30. Ibid., pp. 110–116.

31. Hendee et al., *Wilderness Management,* pp. 13–15.

32. Fox, *John Muir and His Legacy,* p. 269.

33. Baker, "The Conservation Congress of Anderson and Aspinall."

34. Roth, The Wilderness Movement and the National Forests, p. 2.

35. 78 Stat. 890. 78 Stat. 891, Sec. 2c.

36. Personal communication, Bo Shelby, Oregon State University.

37. Dana and Fairfax, *Forest and Range Policy,* 2nd ed., pp. 220–221.

38. "Inventoried roadless areas are public lands typically exceeding 5,000 acres that met the minimum criteria for wilderness consideration under the Wilderness Act of 1964. The Forest Service used the most recent inventory available for each national forest and grassland to identify the inventoried roadless areas . . ." The FS used the 1979 Roadless Area Review and Evaluation (RARE II) where a recent inventory was not available" (U.S. Forest Service, "Roadless Area Conservation," *www.roadless.fs.fed.us,* accessed 6/24/02).

39. A lawsuit decided in 1969 brought the first solid protection for areas awaiting reclassification. A proposed timber sale on land bordering the Gore Range-Eagle's Nest Primitive area in Colorado was denied by the U. S. District Court on the grounds that the sale would preempt the president's power of adjusting boundaries under the Wilderness Act. This decision forced the Forest Service to protect areas contiguous to primitive areas pending reclassification as wilderness. However, the case did not settle the questions concerning roadless areas which are not contiguous to established wilderness areas.

40. Allin, *The Politics of Wilderness Preservation,* pp. 159–160; Dana and Fairfax, *Forest and Range Policy,* 2nd ed., p. 300.

41. Hendee et al., *Wilderness Management,* p. 102.

42. Ibid., pp. 102–105.

43. Ibid., p. 104.

44. Ibid., pp. 104–105.

45. Allin, *The Politics of Wilderness Preservation*, p. 161; Dana and Fairfax, *Forest and Range Policy*, 2nd ed., pp. 299–300.

46. Hendee et al., *Wilderness Management*, p. 75.

47. Allin, *The Politics of Wilderness Preservation*, p. 159.

48. Ibid., pp. 186–192.

49. Dana and Fairfax, *Forest and Range Policy*, 2nd ed., pp. 300–301.

50. Ibid., pp. 225–229; Robinson, *The Forest Service*, pp. 75–85.

51. LeMaster, "Decade of Change"; Shands et al., *National Forest Policy*.

52. Allin, *The Politics of Wilderness Preservation*, pp. 192–193.

53. Ibid., p. 162.

54. Dana and Fairfax, *Forest and Range Policy*, 2nd ed., pp. 301–302.

55. Allin, *The Politics of Wilderness Preservation*, pp. 162–163.

56. Ibid., pp. 164–165.

57. Risbrut, "The Real Issue in Below-Cost Sales."

58. U.S. Forest Service, "Roadless Area Conservation Documents," *www.roadless. fs.fed.us/xdocuments.shtml*, accessed 6/24/02.

59. Interpreting the significance of comments is challenging. Many responses are "form letters" generated by advocacy organizations; for example, between July and September 2001, the Forest Service received 726,440 responses, but only 52,000 of them were original, individual responses, while the remainder was classified by the service as "organized responses," defined as five or more letters consisting of identical text submitted by different people. The service treats such organized responses as one response, which raises questions about improperly discounting public input, even though the individuals who submit organized responses may be well-informed, engaged citizens with a stake in the outcome.

60. Wirtz, "Roadless initiative more complex than 'knuckle-dragging loggers vs. spotted owls'."

61. The Wilderness Society, "An Historic Opportunity to Protect Our National Forests," *www.wilderness.org/standbylands/forests/roadless_factsheets.htm* accessed 6/24/02.

62. Loomis and Richardson, "Economic Values of Wilderness in the United States."

63. The Wilderness Society, "State economics fact sheets for roadless area campaign," *http://www.wilderness.org/standbylands/roadless/library_facts.htm*, accessed 6/24/02.

64. Adams, *Renewable Resource Policy*, pp. 170–171.

CHAPTER 9

WILDLAND RECREATION POLICY IN THE URBAN SETTING

In the previous two chapters, we focused attention on the wilderness end of the recreation spectrum. We illustrated developments in wilderness by highlighting the actions of the Forest Service, referencing the National Park Service only as that agency's actions prompted Forest Service responses. Now we want to examine the other end of the wildland recreation spectrum we introduced in the first chapter, by looking at the federal experience with nature-oriented recreation in America's cities. To do so, we will concentrate on the National Park Service's response to the push for urban national parks. Since the Forest Service has also responded to the public interest in nearby, urban-oriented nature, we review their urban programs as well.

EROSION OF NPS SELF-DETERMINATION

The urban parks have been difficult developments for the Park Service. To a large extent, difficulty has come about because these cases represent new policy directions, and birth inevitably involves pain. In addition, however, institutional weaknesses within the Park Service have heightened the agency's problems in coping with new demands. Before presenting the story of the urban national parks, therefore, we will briefly review the forces and events since the 1960s that have diminished the Park Service's ability to control its fate.[1]

The Park Service was established in 1916 with the dual mission of protecting the national parks' natural wonders and accommodating public visitation. In the Mather-Albright years, the Park Service established itself as the preservationist equivalent of Pinchot's Forest Service. In those days, the Park Service was an aggressive agency with a strong sense of mission built on a philosophical base in which parks were seen as important contributors to effective democracy. The Park Service was an agency with a reputation for professionalism and political effectiveness. Under its early leaders, the Park Service encouraged mass recreational use of the parks and expanded the system to include new nature parks, parks in the East, historical and cultural parks, some urban parks (the National Capitol Parks), and leadership in outdoor recreation planning. By these actions the agency served the growing public demand for outdoor recreation and assured its own survival.

A shift in Park Service direction came with Newton Drury's directorship in the early 1940s. Drury, who came to the Service from the Save-the-Redwoods League, represented a break with the dominant orientation toward mass recreation. Drury had been repelled by what he called the "cheap showmanship" used to promote park use, and he viewed the director's role as that of caretaker of the parks' natural wonders. Drury served the parks well during World War II by fending off attempts to exploit park resources in the name of the war effort. After the war, however, with the explosion of visitation, Drury's quiet style placed the Park Service at a disadvantage in the bureaucratic competition for scarce funding. Visitors overran the parks, and conditions quickly came to be described as scandalous.

The 1950s crisis in the parks brought Conrad Wirth to the directorship. Wirth had both Mather's expansionist philosophy and his persuasive skills, and soon the Park Service was embarked on the massive development program called Mission 66. Wirth's program responded to the dominant social values in the country. It was based on a sense of confidence about our ability to anticipate and control the future; it assumed that the primary goal of the Service should be to assure that as many people as possible should be able to visit the parks; and it paid little attention to the character or quality of those visits.

The very features that led Mission 66 to be viewed as a success by the dominant social groups were viewed with alarm by others. Preservationists had always found the prevailing development-oriented philosophy distasteful. Even in the Park Service's golden years, there had been trouble. For example, Robert Sterling Yard, a friend from Mather's journalist days whom Mather had recruited as a publicist, split with him over the issue of building political support by catering to visitor tastes Yard considered "vulgar."[2] Once a distinct minority, preservationists came to have far greater influence in the 1960s and the years that followed, as part of the general growth of environmentalism in the United States.

A key figure in the history of the Park Service at this time was Stuart Udall, Secretary of the Interior under Presidents John Kennedy and Lyndon Johnson. He was an unusually active and visible Secretary of the Interior. Udall had a strong preservationist bent, which was clearly displayed in his 1962 best seller, *The Quiet Crisis*. The book was a damning review of America's misuse of its natural resources, and in this respect it was similar to the reviews of Marsh, Pinchot, and others of the progressive conservationist lineage. Udall attributed the nation's conservation problems to wasteful attitudes and a tendency to define progress solely in material terms. These habits of mind derived from the earlier belief that America's natural resources were inexhaustible. Udall labeled this belief the "Myth of Superabundance." Udall felt that technology could be applied to solve our conservation problems, and he argued for governmental leadership in that effort. His thinking about the efficacy of technology and government fit well with the prevailing thinking in Washington. While technology was essential, Udall felt its increased use should be accompanied by basic changes in our attitudes toward nature. In this, Udall picked up Leopold's ideas about an environmental ethic based on the concept of land stewardship.[3]

Udall also forged a conceptual linkage between traditional areas of conservation concern and the growing urban crisis. Just as we had squandered our abundant natural resources, he argued, so had we allowed human potential to waste in our cities. Problems in both areas could be surmounted through the professional application of technical expertise. By developing parallels between traditional conservation and urban social problems, Udall also suggested that his Department of Interior, and by extension the National Park Service, should play a role in addressing national concerns about social equity and the quality of urban life.

Under Conrad Wirth, however, the National Park Service was out of step with the new thinking Udall represented. The Mission 66 development program seemed, in its traditional obliviousness to urban and social issues, to repudiate the interconnected worldview Udall espoused. The Park Service had already been the focus of the Secretary's displeasure because of Wirth's resistance to the Outdoor Recreation Resources Review Commission of the late 1950s. The National Park Service considered itself, on the strength of the 1936 Park, Parkways, and Recreation Area Study Act among other things, as the lead federal agency in outdoor recreation. The ORRRC's conclusion that "the lack of anything resembling a national recreation policy is at the root of most of the recreation problems of the federal government," and its recommendation that a new lead agency for recreation be established, strongly rebuked past Park Service leadership. The commission also placed its weight behind giving primary attention to urban-oriented outdoor recreation. This urban thrust would help draw the Park Service into the confusing new domain of the urban national parks and national recreation areas. The creation of the Bureau of Outdoor Recreation in 1963 provided Udall with a way of pursuing his objectives in recreation. He was not content with that, however, since Wirth represented the bureaucratic inertia President John F. Kennedy had vowed to attack. Soon, Udall publicly embarrassed Wirth and thereby forced his resignation.

As a result of changes in the support provided by interest groups and elites, and because of changes in Congress and the executive branch, the Park Service suffered losses in political support and autonomy in the years after Wirth. Udall replaced Wirth with George Hartzog. Hartzog's competence, particularly in his relationships with Congress, temporarily masked the severe erosion of Park Service strength.[4]

Environmental interest groups, with their swelling membership and growing influence, came increasingly to view the Park Service as wedded to the Mission 66 philosophy. These groups saw the Park Service, like the other federal land management agencies, as entrenched sources of outmoded initiatives; the professionalism that was the hallmark of the progressive era came to be seen as problematic. The Park Service was part of "the establishment" and subject to confrontational criticism. An informal, self-appointed policy directorate comprised of the Sierra Club, The Wilderness Society, National Parks and Conservation Association, Izaak Walton League, and Friends of the Earth met and adopted policy positions which they then attempted, through Congress, to force on the Park Service.

Beginning in the 1960s, the Park Service also suffered losses in support by elites. In the early years, Mather had drawn on his personal friendships among the nation's business, intellectual, scientific, and communications leaders to form a cadre of elite support. He established the Advisory Board on National Parks, Historic Sites, Buildings and Monuments, whose members were appointed by the Secretary of the Interior upon the Service's recommendation. Under Udall this tradition was broken, and board appointments were given for political reasons to individuals with little personal concern for the parks. Elites who did care about the parks frequently found themselves more in sympathy with the environmentalists, and numerous other worthy causes competed effectively with the Park Service for their support.

Relationships with Congress also changed in ways that reduced agency independence. In the early days, Mather built and enjoyed congressional trust, and Congress did not greatly involve itself in the details of the National Park System. Thus, in effect, the Park Service provided policy guidance for itself. In the 1960s and 1970s, however, a number of structural changes in Congress reduced Park Service autonomy. First, congressional oversight capabilities were enlarged through expansion of member and committee staffs, the General Accounting Office, and the Congressional Research Service. This increased support allowed Congress to pay detailed attention to parks. Second, interest groups, aided by new lobbying laws, became more effective in Congress. Third, congressional reforms weakened the seniority system, and that weakening of authority increased the relative value of distributional goods ("pork barrel") as incentives which congressional leaders could use to encourage member support of important bills. Following the postwar expansion in recreation participation and the decline in the attractiveness of traditional pork-barrel projects such as roads and dams, parks came to be seen as valuable distributional goods. Finally, the increasing independence of the electorate meant that party identification by itself would no longer carry an election, and forced members of Congress to scramble for tangible accomplishments—like parks—in an effort to be reelected.

In the 1970s, congressional initiative for Interior Department affairs shifted from the Senate to the House of Representatives. Congressional reforms had relocated power from the committee to the subcommittee level. This enabled California Representative Philip Burton to press his preservation agenda. As chair of the Parks subcommittee of the House Interior committee, Burton pushed through omnibus park bills[5] in 1978 and 1980. These acts, which greatly expanded Park Service responsibilities, brought into the system a number of new areas that were questionable in terms of the traditional tests of quality and significance. Burton recognized this problem, but he justified system expansion because, like many environmentalists, he was concerned that the trend was always toward economic development rather than preservation.[6] Providing immediate protection for valuable areas justified including inferior areas as necessary to garner political support. The National Park Service, weakened as it was, was unable to fend off proposals for inferior parks. Representative Sidney Yates, who chaired the House Interior Appropriations Committee, countered Burton's expansionism, and funds to carry out authorized acquisitions were not forthcoming.[7] Thus, by the early 1980s, the Park Service had over $1 billion worth of authorized but unfunded acquisitions. This backlog is considered one of the Park Service's most important current problems.[8]

The position of the Park Service within the executive branch deteriorated significantly from the 1960s onward. Before Udall's tenure as Secretary of the Interior, and as a result of strong leadership, the Park Service had considerable stature and independence among its sister agencies. The agency's leaders enjoyed long terms in office and nurtured good relations with Congress, support from outside influentials, and an aura of professionalism. From the 1970s onward, however, weak leadership contributed to the problems the Park Service had with preservation groups, potential elite supporters, and Congress. Beginning with President Nixon, the Service's leadership passed quickly through the hands of an undistinguished series of eight different directors. A number of these directors had no direct experience with the national parks, and several with NPS backgrounds deferred to others for policy leadership. The agendas of these eight directors varied from economic development to environmental protection, mirroring the ebb and flow of national politics.[9]

Park Service leadership was further undercut by two other factors—entrepreneurship by Park Service regional directors and superintendents and strengthened central budgetary control. First, as the Service's central leadership in the 1970s and 1980s became weaker, regional directors and the superintendents of the major parks expanded their traditional independence, and many worked directly with local members of Congress and other sources of political influence. Often this bureaucratic entrepreneurship took place without the knowledge, let alone the blessing, of the Washington office. Secondly, President Nixon expanded his budgetary control by converting the Bureau of the Budget into the more powerful Office of Management and Budget. This shifted some of the control of budgets—and therefore destiny—from the agencies to the White House. From 1970 onward, the Office of Management and Budget has played an important role in setting Park Service directions. Passage of the Government Performance and Results Act of 1993 (GPRA) further strengthened this trend.[10]

While these trends signaled a weakening of NPS's policy leadership, the agency's budgets, often considered a measure of agency strength, were growing. According to political scientists Jeanne Clarke and Daniel McCool, the NPS's budget increased impressively up through 1994 as compared to other natural resource agencies. From 1995 to 2002, the NPS budget rose from $1.43 billion to $2.39 billion, an average annual growth rate of 9.5 percent.[11] How can this apparent inconsistency be interpreted? Clarke and McCool attribute the growth in NPS's budgets to Congress's rediscovery of the agency in the 1980s, "when money for traditional pork barrel projects (e.g., dams and roads) was shrinking, and when, after the collapse of the Soviet Union, even the defense budget started declining." These sweeping changes forced Congress to look for "popular but relatively inexpensive projects to bring home to their districts and states [and] the park barrel was born."[12] So, depending on one's point of view, the agency could be seen as either growing or declining in power. From the standpoint of budgets and park units, the NPS grew in power. But, from the standpoint of self-determination, it has enjoyed less and less control over its budgets and the number and types of units that enter the system.

THE URBAN NATIONAL PARKS

In 1972, President Richard Nixon signed bills authorizing the Gateway National Recreation Area (NRA) in New York City and the Golden Gate NRA in San Francisco. With the creation of these "bookend" urban national parks, commonly referred to collectively as the Gateways, a lengthy period of Park Service drift toward an urban role was completed. The ice was broken for expansion of the urban parks into a major component of Park Service activity. Between 1972 and the present, the Park Service has undertaken urban park responsibilities in the Cleveland/Akron area (Cuyahoga Valley NRA, 1975), the Atlanta area (Chattahoochee River NRA, 1978), the Los Angeles area (Santa Monica Mountains NRA, 1978), the New Orleans area (Jean LaFitte National Historical Park and Recreation Area, 1978) the Lowell, Massachusetts, area (Lowell National Historical Park, 1978) and the Twin Cities, Minnesota, area (Mississippi National River and Recreation Area, 1988). Also, since 1980, 13 national historic parks, sites, or memorials have been established in urban areas (e.g., Martin Luther King NHS in Atlanta, 1980). A new designation, "National Heritage Area," will further add to the NPS's presence in urban and suburban areas.[13]

The urban parks have been a significant addition to the National Park System. The eight parks listed above accounted for approximately 11 percent of the year 2000 visitation to the entire system; the Gateways alone accounted for nearly 8 percent of the system's reported visits.[14] The importance of the urban national parks to the National Park Service is not captured in visitation statistics alone, however. No policy area was the subject of greater debate in the 1970s and '80s.[15] It remains a focal point of debate today. A case history of Gateway National Recreation Area will illustrate the origins of some of the most important issues surrounding the urban national parks.

Gateway National Recreation Area: A Case Study

Gateway National Recreation Area was created from surplus military properties, a wildlife refuge, and several parcels of land transferred to the National Park Service from the city of New York. Together, these holdings add up to 26,000 acres in four separate areas around the New York City harbor. Gateway includes 12 miles of ocean beach and 20 miles of frontage on New York Bay. Seven square miles of upland and thousands of acres of wetlands are encompassed in the four Gateway units. Jamaica Bay provides outstanding waterfowl habitat; once badly polluted, it is now recovering under the protection of federal water pollution control programs. In 2000 Gateway received over 7.9 million recreation visits, which is more than the number of visits for Yosemite and Yellowstone combined. Yet Gateway's potential use is far greater, since over 21 million people live in the New York-northern New Jersey-Long Island Metropolitan Area.

Gateway (together with its sister unit, Golden Gate NRA) was a definite policy breakthrough, but it was not without precedent.[16] Since the 1930s, in fact, the Park Service had been edging toward an urban presence. In the 1930s the Service had taken responsibility for the National Capitol Parks, and over the years NPS had assumed management of a number of historical sites in cities. Also in the 1930s, a Park Service study suggested that the federal government acquire beach areas on the Atlantic and Gulf coasts to provide recreation opportunities for the growing urban populations there (nothing came of this recommendation until the 1960s).

The urban push in the Park Service was tempered in the 1940s and 1950s; during the Second World War and the postwar recreation boom, Drury and Wirth concentrated on existing Park Service areas only.

The 1960s again brought definitive steps toward an urban role for the National Park Service. The decade opened in 1960 with the authorization of Cape Cod National Seashore. This extension of traditional Park Service landscape preservation efforts into populated areas was followed in 1964 by Point Reyes and Fire Island national seashores, in 1965 by the Delaware Water Gap National Recreation Area, and in 1966 by Indiana Dunes National Lakeshore.

In the 1960s, as well, several other policies encouraged greater federal involvement in urban open space and recreation. The Housing Act of 1961 authorized the use of federal funds for purchase of open space areas in cities; the new Bureau of Outdoor Recreation was given specific direction to assist local units of government to provide open space; and the Land and Water Conservation Fund Act of 1965, which we detail in Chapter 11, encouraged states and localities to provide urban open space and recreation opportunities.

By the mid-1960s, urban open space had become "an attractive piece of bureaucratic real estate," in Ronald Foresta's words.[17] If the Park Service moved to assert itself in the urban areas, so the advocates asserted, it could anticipate several positive outcomes, including increased agency funding, a greater sense of relevance to the issues of the day, and expansion to new constituency groups and their political support. There were other, less sanguine voices, however, which noted that the Park Service had its roots in the western nature parks and that moving into urban areas might constitute a break with the agency's sense of identity. One specific aspect of this concern was fear that twin career ladders would develop in the agency, and that the new urban career ladder would be seen as faster and more attractive to ambitious young professionals.[18] Critics also warned that the Park Service would be moving into uncharted areas where unclear selection criteria might jeopardize the system's reputation for quality. In addition, they pointed out, new urban units might harm the quality of management at the existing parks, especially the crown jewels, by bleeding off funding.[19]

While the debate over whether the Park Service should be involved in urban parks developed, the Service continued to drift toward a larger role. The Park Service's "Summer in the Parks" program, started in 1968, was credited with helping keep the nation's capitol quiet following Martin

Luther King's assassination. This success encouraged the Park Service to move further toward an urban presence. Director George Hartzog campaigned for "Parks to the People," and Walter Hickel, President Nixon's Secretary of the Interior, adopted and expanded the idea. In the 1972 Nationwide Outdoor Recreation Plan, Hickel proposed an entire system of urban national parks.[20]

In his proposal, Hickel was striking a responsive chord, but the conservative Nixon administration was alarmed by the prospective costs of the urban park idea and by its intrusiveness into local matters. Hickel's grandiose plan was suppressed, and a compromise sought that would demonstrate the administration's responsiveness at minimal cost and with limited growth in federal governmental presence. The Gateway proposal was ready-made for this purpose.[21]

Since the early 1960s, there had been a proposal to turn the surplus federal properties—airfields and other outdated defense properties—into a state park. Both social and economic elites (including Eleanor Roosevelt) and minority groups supported the concept, but opposition from neighborhoods adjoining the areas and the absence of funding had bogged the idea down. In 1969 Secretary Hickel floated a brief, glossy conceptual plan as a trial balloon, but the rest of the Nixon administration showed no great receptivity. Nevertheless, in 1971 Nixon flew over the area and six months later endorsed the Gateway idea. Paired with the Golden Gate National Recreation Area in San Francisco, the Gateways were legislatively established in 1972.

There are a variety of explanations given for the creation of the Gateways, and understanding them will help explain some of the failures as well as the successes of the urban national parks.[22] To start at the broadest level, the time period during which the urban national parks idea gained momentum was one of strong federal government assertiveness. Building on the excitement of President John Kennedy's "New Frontier," President Lyndon Johnson put together his ambitious "Great Society" programs, which expanded the role of the federal government in many aspects of American life. Our economy was surging ahead, the space program had demonstrated our technical wizardry, and the shocks of Vietnam, Watergate, the energy crisis of the 1980s, and terrorist attacks lay in the unforeseen future. It was assumed that we could apply our money and brainpower to correct longstanding problems.

Urban recreation and open space were two aspects of domestic life in which we sought improvements through federal government action. The

Kerner Commission's report on the black riots in Los Angeles (Watts), Detroit, Cleveland, Newark, and elsewhere made it clear that many Americans were not sharing in our improved standards of living. Among other conditions prompting the rioting, according to the commission report, were inadequate recreation facilities readily accessible to the urban poor. The cities, which traditionally had responsibility for neighborhood recreation, were flirting with bankruptcy. If anything was to be done to provide for a more equitable distribution of recreation opportunities, the federal government would have to do it, or so it was widely assumed.

As to open space, the center of political support lay not with the poor and minorities but with elites associated with the growing environmental movement. Urban sprawl, fostered by a bullish economy, a growing population, cheap gas, and a burgeoning freeway network, raised concern that attractive landscapes would be buried under "little boxes made of ticky-tacky," in the words of a popular song by Pete Seeger that satirized suburban growth.

Gateway brought together the growing national interests in social equity and open space preservation. As always, other interests were at play which assisted in advancing new policy. For example, residents living near some of the units wanted things left as they were. They opposed what they felt would be a troublesome invasion of their neighborhoods if mass recreation use was encouraged. Unfortunately for their interests, it did not appear that maintenance of the status quo would be possible. As part of his Great Society housing program, President Johnson had issued an executive order directing that surplus federal lands in urban areas would be given first consideration for use as public housing for poor people. This threat was crystallized in a housing project idea promoted by New York Governor Nelson Rockefeller and powerful public facilities developer Robert Moses.[23] At that point, Gateway's neighbors decided to accept the park proposal as the "least of possible evils," and to concentrate their efforts on scaling down the plan that would be required by the authorizing law.

In fact, that is how it worked out. Hearings on the plan found strong representation by park neighbors seeking to limit development and control recreational use of the area. Under-represented at the hearings were the urban poor most needing recreation facilities. Thus began a prolonged and pronounced movement away from Gateway's serving mass recreation needs. While persistent local opposition was crucial in Gateway's metamorphosis, there were other important factors as well. First, support for Gateway as originally conceived was weak. Interest groups spoke in favor of the original concept, but without strong support from New York City and Mayor John Lindsay, they were ineffective. New York City had endorsed Gateway as a major facility, probably because it wanted federal help with the parks, whose rundown condition was a particularly visible sign of the city's financial weakness. However, faced with the concerted opposition of Gateway's neighbors, and aware that anything as big as Gateway would disrupt the city's social ecology with unpredictable consequences, the city government's support was tepid.[24]

The second factor in the downscaling of Gateway is found in the internal dynamics of the National Park Service. The familiar tug-of-war between serving people and protecting resources came into play once again, according to policy analyst Foresta. The original plan would have provided recreation opportunities to large numbers of people, but it would also have entailed substantial modification of the landscape and disruption of the local communities. Some in the Park Service, particularly the older planners, favored the large-scale concept for Gateway, while others, particularly the younger planners, favored scaling it down. This internal debate combined with the political realities of agency life — avoid controversy if possible, particularly if there is uncertainty about the degree of support from Washington — to produce a plan for Gateway that was much less oriented toward mass recreation than the original conception.

The Park Service's movement away from serving mass recreation needs is illustrated in comparing the original and the 1979 plans for the Breezy Point Unit.[25] In the 10 years between the original conceptual plan and the 1979 plan, the Park Service abandoned its idea of "wiping the slate clean" and creating a new and major intensive recreation facility. Instead, private inholdings were allowed to continue, obsolete military installations were retained and treated as historic sites, transportation to the area was scaled back, and unrestricted recreation use was supplemented by supervised group activity. In these and many other particulars, the Park Service moved away from the idea of mass recreation that had prompted establishment of the area in the first place. In place of facility development to accommodate the recreation needs of the urban poor, the emphasis shifted to preservation and education. Instead of accommodating 300,000 people on a peak day, as envisioned in the 1969 plan, the Breezy Point unit in the 1979 plan would handle 90,000, about the same visitation the area had before Gateway's creation. Yet, the current Gateway website recommends to visitors the following activities:

swimming, sailing, surfing and fishing; learning about ecosystems and their relationship to city life; touring historic military sites; gardening, photography and poetry readings; opera, symphony, and contemporary music and cultural festivals; organized athletics—soccer, football, baseball, tennis and cricket; bird watching, beach clean-ups and nature walks; camping, cycling and sunset walks.[26]

Clearly, the old ambivalence between preservation and mass use is alive and well in Gateway.

One of the most intractable problems at Gateway has been transportation.[27] Although the park is located in the New York City area, reaching it is difficult for the poor it was originally intended to serve. In fact, had transportation not been so difficult, the areas might long ago have been used for public housing. In 1972, a round-trip from Manhattan to Gateway cost $1.70 per person and took 2–3 hours. Recognizing the impact this would have on the urban poor, the Park Service developed a proposal for ferry service, but this idea was discarded as too costly. Five ferries and three terminals would have cost $55 million to bring 60,000 people to Gateway on a peak visitation day like the Fourth of July. By contrast, readily accessible Coney Island accommodated 850,000 people on a peak day. The *New Yorker* magazine sardonically editorialized that the ferry system would involve spending millions of dollars to divert people from Coney Island to Gateway so that peak-day space at Coney Island would be increased from 10 square feet per person to 12. In addition, the time and aggravation involved in queuing at the ferry terminals would decrease the quality of the visitor's overall experience.[28]

Interest in a transportation system relying primarily on busses arose in the late 1970s, but the opposition of middle class communities through which the busses would have passed defeated the proposal. In addition, the Office of Management and Budget consistently opposed using public funds to provide visitor transportation to urban parks.[29] As of 2003, the NPS still does not provide subsidized transportation to Gateway. Visitors who do not arrive by car generally use the New York City mass transit system, which is run by the Metropolitan Transit Authority (MTA). The average MTA visitor spends about $3.00 in round-trip fares, with substantial discounts (50 percent or more) for seniors, Medicare card holders, small children, and students through grade 12.[30] The Staten Island Ferry is another public transportation option. Despite concerns expressed in the 1970s about cost and inconvenience, the NPS is developing alternative transportation plans, including bicycle and ferry transportation.

Under the most recent plan, a ferry will bring city residents to the beaches of Sandy Hook during the summer months. At $25 round-trip per adult ($12.50 for children under 12), this is not a low-cost alternative, but it makes the beach accessible without a car.[31]

Golden Gate National Recreation Area

Gateway can be viewed in part as political expediency capturing a long-standing idea. Golden Gate NRA also owes its existence in part to political concerns.[32] Originally the brainchild of the Bureau of Outdoor Recreation, Golden Gate NRA was conceived as a way of delivering urban outdoor recreation more efficiently under unified administration. The idea languished until 1969 when Alcatraz Island, the former maximum security federal prison in San Francisco Bay, was occupied by radical members of the American Indian Movement. For Alcatraz, the Indians offered the U.S. Government $24 in glass beads and red cloth as symbolic reprisal for the loss of the continent. When the confrontation ended and the last of the Indians were removed in 1971, Secretary Hickel was instructed to do something with Alcatraz, make it a popular action, and do it fast. He gave the National Park Service two weeks to develop a plan. The Park Service dusted off the old Bureau of Outdoor Recreation idea, added in Alcatraz and labeled it Golden Gate NRA.

Soon, Secretary Hickel became a political liability for the Nixon administration and was replaced. With Hickel gone, the Golden Gate NRA drive floundered for a while, until a citizen's group got behind and pushed it. With that citizen's effort a new element was added—a greenbelt along the Pacific Coast north of San Francisco to Point Reyes National Seashore.[33] While the greenbelt was widely supported as a good idea, it had little to do with meeting the recreation needs of the urban poor.

The Golden Gate NRA proposal was combined with Gateway and presented as a finished set by the Nixon administration. Thematically unified by their location at two of America's great ports, the administration saw them as offerings of concern for the plight of the cities, and not as the first of a system of urban parks.[34] The fact that not all cities had available surplus military property and that the Gateways might, therefore, be a demonstration of the impossible was apparently not a major factor in the decision to put them forward. Their establishment demonstrated what many mayors already knew—that the way to upgrade their parks was to find federal help. Soon many urban national park proposals were put forward,[35] and the questions about national significance that had been brushed over with the Gateways were raised again.[36]

Other Urban National Parks

The urban national parks policy story unfolded further with the authorization of the Cuyahoga Valley NRA in 1974.[37] The primary purpose of this act was to protect the landscape integrity of a pastoral area between Cleveland and Akron, Ohio. The Cuyahoga River as it flows through this area is gently falling, with riverside development of a type and extent appropriate for canoe trips, and with sufficiently high water quality for swimming. The infamous "burning river" part of the Cuyahoga is downstream in heavily industrialized Cleveland, where the river enters Lake Erie. The primary policy significance of the Cuyahoga Valley NRA was that, unlike the Gateways, extensive land acquisition would be needed to complete the project. Cuyahoga Valley NRA was the center of extensive controversy because of the land acquisition issue. It was the last NPS unit that included a large amount of private land—33,000 acres—within the boundaries. Of 33,000 acres, 20,000 have been purchased by the NPS or were donated. More than half of the purchases were made within the first 5 years after designation, and most of the controversy occurred during this period. Public support for Cuyahoga NRA is now strong, albeit with some lingering ill will among a few people and residents of one township that lost 90 percent of its land base.[38]

The 1978 omnibus parks act brought a major expansion to the Park Service's urban presence. The act authorized the Chattahoochee River NRA near Atlanta, the Lowell Historical Park in Lowell, Massachusetts, the Jean LaFitte National Historical Park and Preserve in New Orleans, the Santa Monica Mountains NRA in Los Angeles, and the Pinelands National Reserve in New Jersey. Ten years later, Congress established the Mississippi National River and Recreation Area, which includes 72 miles of the Mississippi River running through the twin cities of Minneapolis and St. Paul, Minnesota. Most significant for our purposes was the extent to which these new parks broke new ground in cooperative intergovernmental land management. The land management tools incorporated in these parks pointed the way toward future expansion of the Park Service in a time when available federal land and funding for land purchases is limited and land acquisition, as a policy tool, is controversial.

The central idea in the new urban parks was that of managing "living landscapes."[39] Federal land acquisition was not possible in these cases. It would simply cost too much and cause too much social disruption to acquire fee simple, or complete ownership of the lands. In some cases, in fact, federal acquisition is viewed as destructive of the very characteristics for which the land is valued, since the prevailing forms of private land use add much to the landscape's flavor. Such is the case at Cape Cod National Seashore, where much of what is special about the landscape is the result of long-standing human settlement. If private use that sustained the Cape's distinctive features could be encouraged while uses that destroyed the landscape integrity could be discouraged, the Park Service could perform a valuable service at an affordable price. Thus evolved the predecessor of the new urban parks. In the so-called "Cape Cod formula" Congress specified that if the local units of government produced zoning regulations acceptable to the Park Service, the Secretary of the Interior's power to condemn private land would be suspended. This "Sword of Damocles" provision was a way to extend federal influence to a function—land use regulation or zoning—that the U.S. Constitution reserved to state and local units of government. Insofar as the federal condemnation threat is credible and the Park Service has enough money to buy out private landowners at court-determined prices, this land use control approach can be effective, as it has been at Cape Cod.[40]

At Santa Monica the formula was somewhat different. There, rather than relying on the threat of condemnation, the federal government has adopted an incentive approach. Using federal front money and technical planning assistance, state and local units of government developed a land use plan incorporating a mixture of acquisition and regulation. The plan created the framework for what the recreation area should be in terms of size and character. Within the non-federal but public part of the NRA, local and state agencies are responsible for land use regulations and developments, but the NPS retains the authority to accept or reject projects that involve federal funds or permits.[41] The federal government has provided some funds to implement the plan, including the fee simple purchase of crucial properties and the purchase of easements.

When Santa Monica Mountains NRA was authorized in 1978, capping a decade of local effort to halt suburbanization of this unusual and complex landscape, the federal government owned just over 2,000 (1.5 percent) of the area's 149,309 acres.[42] Approximately 35,000 people lived in the area's 15,900 private homes, which occupied about 10 percent of the area. An additional 3,000 privately owned parcels totaling 80,000 acres were undeveloped. Since the park's beginning, land costs have risen rapidly, most noticeably in 1978 and 1979 when they climbed at 36 percent per year. Development has slowed somewhat, but market pressures remain strong for expensive home building in this area where celebrities like Ronald Reagan and Bob Hope have homes. In addition to rising land costs, Park Service land acquisition efforts have been hampered periodically by federal policies opposing new land acquisition and nondefense governmental spending. For these reasons, purchase of critical parcels has not reached the stated goal. Nonetheless, 90 percent of the NRA is undeveloped and around 69,000 acres are protected parklands. As of 2001, 23 years after Santa Monica NRA was authorized, the Park Service owned about 22,000 acres, roughly one-third of the land it originally planned to acquire. Over half the total land area—76,000 acres—is in private ownership, and 22 percent consists of four State of California park units (Table 9–1). The complex and diverse land ownership mosaic of Santa Monica Mountains NRA is portrayed in Figure 9–1.

Through the 1980s, Park Service policy tended to favor the use of easements as a less-than-full-fee purchase technique. However, easements are no longer as popular.[43] Instead, the Service now favors partnerships, whereby the NPS provides resources for technical assistance and tries to

Table 9–1. Land Ownership of the Santa Monica Mountains National Recreation Area (Source: Draft 2000 GMP and EIS online at *www.nps.gov/samo/supplans/gmp.htm*)

OWNERSHIP	ACRES	PERCENT OF TOTAL AREA
Private Land	76,017	51.00
State of California Parkland	33,271	22.00
National Park Service	21,832	15.00
Other Los Angeles County Land (non-parkland)	3,258	2.00
Mountain Resources Conservation Authority/ Santa Monica Mountains Conservancy Land	7,392	5.00
Other City of Los Angeles (non-parkland)	2,009	1.35
Miscellaneous Public Land	1,463	0.98
COSCA Open Space	96	0.06
Other Federal Land (non-parkland)	936	0.63
Mountain Restoration Trust	1,292	0.87
Los Angeles County Parkland	968	0.65
City of Los Angeles Parkland	447	0.30
Other State Land (non-parkland)	328	0.22
TOTAL	149,309	100.00

Figure 9-1

Current Park Landownership
Santa Monica Mountains
National Recreation Area (SMNRA)
California
U.S. Dept. of Interior, National Park Service, September 2000
(For the original full-color version of this map, see the 2000 General Management
Plan for SMNRA, available online at www.nps.gov/samo)

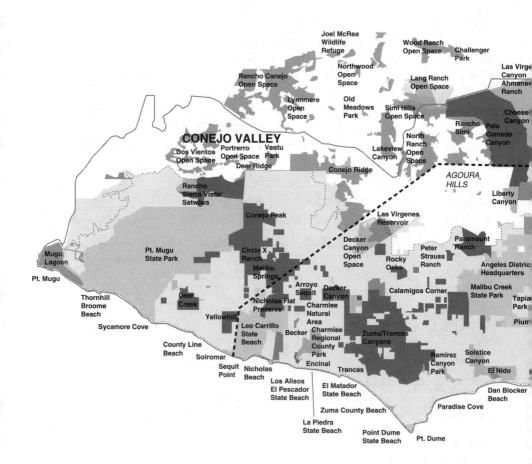

PACIFIC OCEAN

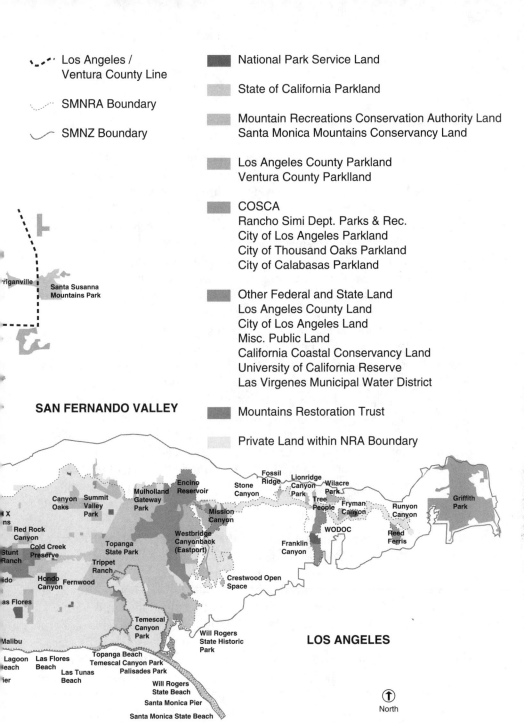

Los Angeles / Ventura County Line

SMNRA Boundary

SMNZ Boundary

National Park Service Land

State of California Parkland

Mountain Recreations Conservation Authority Land
Santa Monica Mountains Conservancy Land

Los Angeles County Parkland
Ventura County Parklland

COSCA
Rancho Simi Dept. Parks & Rec.
City of Los Angeles Parkland
City of Thousand Oaks Parkland
City of Calabasas Parkland

Other Federal and State Land
Los Angeles County Land
City of Los Angeles Land
Misc. Public Land
California Coastal Conservancy Land
University of California Reserve
Las Virgenes Municipal Water District

Mountains Restoration Trust

Private Land within NRA Boundary

SAN FERNANDO VALLEY

riganville

Santa Susanna
Mountains Park

Fossil Ridge
Lionridge Canyon
Wilacre Park
Stone Canyon
Tree People
Fryman Canyon
Runyon Canyon
Griffith Park

Canyon Oaks
Summit Valley Park
Mulholland Gateway Park
Encino Reservoir
Mission Canyon

X ns
Red Rock Canyon
Cold Creek Preserve
Topanga State Park
Westbridge Canyonback (Eastport)
Franklin Canyon
WODOC
Reed Ferris

Stunt Ranch
Trippet Ranch

ido
Hondo Canyon
Fernwood
Crestwood Open Space

as Flores

Malibu

Temescal Canyon Park

Will Rogers State Historic Park

LOS ANGELES

Lagoon
Las Flores Beach
Topanga Beach
Temescal Canyon Park
Las Tunas Beach
Palisades Park

each

ier
Beach

Will Rogers State Beach

Santa Monica Pier

Santa Monica State Beach

North

0   2   4 Miles

control development through regional planning, which involves many entities. Easements are not as popular as they once were because they are often not cost effective; the price of an easement may be as high as 90 percent of the fair market value, yet the property remains in private ownership.[44] Money saved in purchasing an easement may later be absorbed by legal and administrative problems resulting from the nebulous ownership status. The supervision necessitated under an easement leaves the owner with a sense of being watched, and it frequently leads to disputes over exactly what can and cannot be done under the easement. Finally, potential buyers of land with an easement may shy away from the purchase because of a lack of clarity. For these reasons, many managers are not eager to use easements, although they remain useful in selected cases.

For the National Park Service, "partnering" involves working with another management entity or entities under legislative authority that specifically defines the role of the NPS, a federal line item budget appropriation, and a federal management presence that is restricted to supervision and staff support. The NPS provides technical assistance but has limited direct management authority. The NPS can purchase property (buildings, etc.) but must rely on municipalities and communities for matching funds and management. Landowners, local officials, and citizens who share the desire to protect or improve their communities initiate partnerships. Projects are supported through cost sharing, cooperation, and community initiative. The Service's role is to help achieve goals set collectively by the partners.[45]

For example, the boundaries of the Mississippi National River and Recreation Area (MNRRA) include 54,000 acres of river and adjoining land, of which only 43 acres are owned by the NPS. Local interests wanted some sort of protection of this vital corridor, but funds were unavailable for land purchase and the use of eminent domain is highly unpopular. Further complicating the situation, the river corridor runs from rural environments through the center of two major cities (Minneapolis and St. Paul), then to rural settings again. Because of the diversity of landscapes and issues, the NPS developed partnerships with the 30 local governmental units found in the corridor and private organizations interested in the river. NPS personnel assist local governments with critical area plans, funding sources, landscape design, natural resource issues, and geographic information systems. Direct funding and land acquisition are of lower priority at the MNRRA than at Santa Monica. Instead, the NPS relies more on technical assistance and outreach programs to achieve the three goals stated in the legislation that established the MNRRA: "(1) protect, preserve and enhance the significant values of the Mississippi River corridor through the Twin Cities metropolitan area, (2) encourage coordination of federal, state and local programs, and (3) provide a management framework to assist the State of Minnesota and units of local government in the development and implementation of integrated resource management programs and to ensure orderly public and private development in the area."[46]

Santa Monica, Mississippi NRRA, and the other urban parks are variations on the broader theme of the "greenline park," an idea for federal involvement in landscape protection developed in 1975 by planner Charles Little.[47] In this approach, modeled on the English National Parks and the Adirondack Park, critical landscape areas would be designated much as the "blue line" designates the Adirondack park area. In Little's conception, landscape values of the private lands mixed with public lands within the greenline would be protected by a variety of local land use controls supplemented by federal fee and less-than-fee land purchases. In addition to fee simple purchase of critical parcels, a wide variety of less-than-fee purchases of selected development rights would protect certain other areas. Zoning would be used to further control land use without the high costs of land purchase or easements. The whole effort of planning and managing the area would be funded and monitored by the federal government. This is very similar to the partnering approach described above, except that in partnering there is more reliance on self-initiation at the local level and collaborative planning and management.

Through the urban national parks, the National Park Service was brought into regional planning or what Richard Knight and Peter Landres refer to as "stewardship across boundaries."[48] In the view of some observers, these approaches to land use planning and controlling growth represent the future. They point out that the Park Service is still feeling its way into this new territory, yet some notable successes are found.[49] They acknowledge that new levels of managerial sophistication will be demanded, yet they point out cases where it has already been demonstrated.[50] On the other hand, critics view these approaches as inherently unstable and perhaps unworkable. They note that the Park Service, lacking zoning authority, has to rely on persuasion in dealing with local units of government. Local units of government may view the Park Service as an intruder, and they are loath to give up control of the benefits that are to be derived from lands under their jurisdiction. Future conflicts over use of the lands may lead the Park Service to buy out landowners, in which case the parks could become a very expensive burden, or to abandon them, in which case their promised benefits would be unfulfilled.[51] Despite these concerns, the NPS shows little sign of abandoning partnerships and other less-than-fee approaches.

Urban National Parks: Conclusions

The modern urban national parks, much as the early national parks before them, exemplify the groping, evolutionary way in which new policy directions arise. Following years during which a problem is identified, articulated, and elevated in the public consciousness, governmental action is taken which represents a relatively "easy" decision. That action precipitates other related actions, together with debate over whether the apparent new course of action is good. Gradually, adjustments are made. The initial action and later adjustments are strongly shaped by evolving economic and social conditions in the larger society.

It is impossible to assess definitively how successful the urban national parks are, since any such statement is a judgment based on the analyst's perspective. Critics contend that the federal government in general, and the National Park Service in particular, have no business meddling in local affairs. They challenge urban park advocates to demonstrate the national significance of the areas. They decry the unplanned, piecemeal approach Congress has taken in authorizing these parks. They point out that the purposes of the urban national parks have been distorted to emphasize landscape preservation at the cost of mass recreation.[52]

Those of a more positive frame of mind suggest that the urban national parks, flawed as they are, represent the beginnings of a vital new movement in American outdoor recreation policy. Given time and effort, they believe the urban parks can fulfill their promise both for landscape preservation and urban mass recreation. They feel that the Park Service has met the challenge of managing these new parks, and that lessons learned there have generally enriched and improved Park Service management. Forced by the demands of managing the urban parks, the National Park Service has begun to learn about cooperative park management, which entails collaboration and sensitivity to the concerns of private citizens, visitors, and other governmental units and creativity and flexibility in pursuing goals. Urban park supporters note that these new management skills are daily becoming more critical to management of the old, traditional parks and to the process of ecosystem management.[53] Supporters demonstrate that the new parks have not bled funding and staff away from the older parks, and they suggest that, in fact, the new parks may have enlarged the base of political support for the National Park Service to the benefit of the whole system.[54] Finally, it appears that the urban parks have not led to the development of twin career ladders as was feared. Agency tradition continues to draw ambitious and well-qualified people to the traditional parks.

FOREST SERVICE URBAN PROGRAMS

The Forest Service has responded to the growing urbanization of the U.S. population in an understated way. Prompted by influential people like U.S. Representative Sidney Yates from Chicago, who chaired the House Appropriations Subcommittee for Interior and Related Agencies for several decades, the Forest Service has developed an urban perspective in a number of its natural resource programs. Although it has not taken the high-profile route followed by the Park Service in urban areas, the Forest Service's urban and community forestry initiatives have helped create and maintain quality natural environments in urban areas in which many people recreate.

Some of the same forces that led the National Park Service toward its urban initiatives also prompted Forest Service actions. However, the Forest Service has taken a fundamentally different approach to establishing an urban presence and constituency. Unlike NPS, which in the early days of the urban national parks sought full control over land use through land transfers, full fee purchases, and eminent domain, the Forest Service did not seek to acquire forested lands in urban areas.[55] Instead, the Forest Service embarked on an aggressive research, technical assistance, and outreach approach to help metropolitan areas maintain and restore the health of urban ecosystems. In so doing, the FS helps urban entities manage, sustain, or restore trees, forests, and open spaces, many of which are used for outdoor recreation.

In addition, due to urbanization and suburban sprawl, some national forest recreation areas are no longer as remote from dense human populations as they used to be. They have become de facto "urban national forests."[56] Recognizing the impacts on these forests of mass recreation demands by nearby urban and suburban residents, the Forest Service is redesigning its outdoor recreation facilities and revising its management strategies to serve an increasingly numerous and diverse clientele in the "urban-wildland interface."[57]

Addressing the Eighth Urban Forestry Conference held in Atlanta in 1997, Forest Service Chief Michael Dombeck remarked:

> "Eighty percent of Americans live in towns and cities. These people are a critical support base for conservation in America. These are the people who very clearly understand how human impacts on the land affect environmental services such as clean air and water and their families' quality of life. In fact, these are the people whose elected officials will help to determine the future of the national forest system itself. The Forest Service **must** be a leader in promoting urban forestry and conservation. And in fact, our commitment to urban resources stewardship is greater today than ever before."

Dombeck's comments clearly portray continuing support for a Forest Service policy of urban forestry research and assistance. His remarks build upon a Forest Service urban agenda that has its roots in the early 1970s.

During the same year that the Gateway and Golden Gate National Recreation Areas heralded the Park Service's commitment to an urban policy agenda (1972), the Cooperative Forest Management Act of 1950 was amended to give the U.S. Department of Agriculture responsibility for developing an urban forestry technical assistance thrust, known as the Urban and Community Forestry Program (UCFP).[58] Two years later, the national convention of the Society of American Foresters, entitled "Forestry Issues in Urban America," was devoted to identifying policy, research, and technical assistance opportunities and issues in America's cities. Subsequent Forest Service programmatic initiatives and research support were aimed at meeting these and other urban and community forestry needs. For example, the America the Beautiful National Tree Planting Initiative (ATB) was enacted as part of the 1990 farm bill during the first Bush administration. This initiative was designed to help George H.W. Bush achieve a campaign promise to plant 1 billion trees.[59] In addition to a rural forest landowner technical assistance program, ATB authorized additional funding for the Urban and Community Forestry Assistance Program to provide technical assistance, education, and cooperation with communities and organizations.[60]

Forest Service-funded research has provided evidence for the role that urban forests play in improving environmental quality by moderating temperatures, lowering energy use in buildings, absorbing carbon dioxide, reducing noise levels, enhancing air quality, and slowing rainfall runoff and flooding.[61] Outdoor recreation has also been a key focal point of urban forestry research, particularly in the areas of environmental impacts and human benefits of parks, open space, and forest lands.[62] In addition, the FS has been a leader, over the past 25 years, in funding research on:

- Minority groups and diversity in outdoor recreation, mostly in the urban context[63]
- Perceptions and preferences of urban forest users and effects of such settings on psychological well-being[64]
- Public participation in urban forestry[65]
- Community benefits of urban forestry[66]
- Building sustainable urban forestry programs[67]

A recent Forest Service assessment of urban forests highlights the need for additional research to understand human impacts and benefits pertaining to urban forests.[68]

Throughout the 1990s, the Forest Service continued its commitment to urban and community forestry programs, and there is no indication in the new century that funding for these programs will subside. The Forest Service's current strategic plan provides evidence of the agency's commitment to urban forestry.[69] Goal 2 of the plan is called "multiple benefits to people" which means "to provide a variety of uses, values, products and services for present and future generations by managing within the capability of sustainable ecosystems." One of five objectives for achieving this goal states that the FS will improve delivery of services to urban communities.

Highlighting the importance of this objective, the plan notes the following trends:[70]

Since 1970, 86 percent of the total U.S. population growth has taken place in the suburban areas. This movement has led to an accelerating decrease in forest cover in urban and suburban areas in many parts of the country.

One of every seven Americans lives within a 2-hour drive of a national forest, contributing to an annual use of about 82 million visitor days. This number has been increasing over the last several years, with increasing environmental and physical impacts to the national forest lands and facilities as appropriated funds continue to decrease.

To meet the objective of improving services to urban communities, the plan recommends the following five strategies:[71]

1. "Assist State forestry agencies, local governments, and cooperators in protecting and increasing forest cover and green space in urban communities."
2. "Research the relationships between urbanization and forest cover and green space to develop tools and techniques for improving livability."
3. "Support and participate with partners to provide educational opportunities for maintaining and increasing forest cover and green space in selected urban communities."
4. "Build cooperative relationships with communities close to national forests to facilitate management and public support for natural resource management."
5. "Increase assistance to selected cities and communities to improve livability."

The milestone for this objective is "a 5 percent increase in green space within selected urban areas" by 2006.[72] Since the purpose of the strategic plan is to guide future agency actions, this objective and the milestone represent a commitment to the urban agenda.[73]

The Urban and Community Forestry Program (UCFP) is one vehicle for meeting the strategic plan's objective of improving FS service to urban communities. The UCFP falls under the administration of the FS State and Private Forestry Division, but has its own budget line item and legislative authority to provide local communities with technical assistance and funding.[74] Each Forest Service region engages in different activities to meet the goals of UCFP. In the northeastern region, for example, where 92 percent of the forest lands are non-federal, $11.3 million of State and Private Forestry's $67.1 million FY '99 budget went to Urban and Community Forestry Programs.[75] The money was also used to support Urban Resources Partnerships (URPs) in Chicago, New York City, East St. Louis, Philadelphia, Boston, and Buffalo.[76]

The UCFP has enhanced opportunities for outdoor recreation in urban areas, but it is not the only Forest Service program to do so. There are many Forest Service programs that help landowners in urban areas and on the urban/wildland interface.[77] For example, in Chicago the Forest Service has joined the Illinois Department of Natural Resources, the U.S. Environmental Protection Agency and the Grand Victoria Foundation to support a program called "Chicago Wilderness." Chicago Wilderness is a partnership of 92 public and private organizations that are attempting to protect, restore, and manage the protected biological communities in the crescent-shaped area from southeastern Wisconsin to the six-county Chicago region and into northwestern Indiana.[78] "Chicago Wilderness" is significant both because this region contains a high concentration of globally significant natural communities and because of the extent of the partnership. Thousands of volunteers and member organizations do most of the work, applying for project funding through the Chicago Region Biodiversity Council. In partnerships of this kind, the Forest Service is moving a great distance from the sovereignty it enjoyed on the early national forests.

Another example, which involves interagency cooperation and the stretching of federal dollars, is the Chicago Rivers Demonstration Project, a series of river enhancement projects on rivers in the Chicago areas.[79] Various public and private organizations are collaborating in an attempt to restore degraded waterways via community-based projects. The partners include the Forest Service, Corps of Engineers, National Park Service, U.S. Fish & Wildlife Service, Friends of the Chicago River, and the Metropolitan Water Reclamation District of Greater Chicago. Projects include wetlands and prairie restoration; restoration of historical structures; trail, park, and open space development and preservation; clean-ups; and other community-driven activities. The Forest Service role is technical assistance plus some cost sharing in these projects. The lead agency is the National Park Service through its Rivers, Trails, and Conservation Assistance program.

CONCLUSIONS

Taken together, the urban national parks and urban forestry programs represent relatively current policy changes in the Park Service and the Forest Service. Both agencies have been moving for some time now in new directions as the result of a major societal change, urbanization. As they did with the challenge presented by the demand for wilderness, the Park Service and the Forest Service have found ways to adjust to changing social values and conditions. And both agencies find their policy frontiers increasingly set in the context of management at both ends of the spectrum.

NOTES

1. This section is based on Foresta, *America's National Parks and Their Keepers,* pp. 9–91. Except as otherwise referenced, Foresta is the source of information on NPS agency history as regards urban national parks. Foresta, Hartzog, *Battling for the National Parks* and Freemuth (1989), "National Parks: Political versus Professional Determinants of Policy," agree that NPS's ability to determine its own fate eroded in the 1960s through the early 1990s. Freemuth (p. 284) goes one step further by contending that the NPS has always been a "responsive agency" as opposed to an autonomously expert one, meaning that national park policy has always been and will continue to be made in the political arena. As further evidence, Sellars (*Preserving Nature in the National Parks*) laments the absence of NPS self-determination or political will in using more of a scientific basis for its resource management decisions.

2. Cahn, "Horace Albright Remembers the Origins"; Conservation Foundation, *National Parks for a New Generation,* p. 302.

3. Udall, *The Quiet Crisis;* Foresta, *America's National Parks and Their Keepers,* pp. 65–66.

4. McPhee, "Ranger."

5. An "omnibus" bill is a package of many, often unrelated, proposals in a single, large piece of legislation, such as tax, education, and appropriations bills; a parks omnibus bill, such as the one referred to here, establishes a large number of parks and/or park programs, not just one.

6. See David Brower's views as portrayed in McPhee's "Encounters with the Archdruid."

7. However, later in this chapter, Yates is credited with providing much of the support needed to fund certain urban forestry initiatives.

8. Conservation Foundation, *National Parks for a New Generation,* pp. 243–250. However, with acquisitions of new parklands throughout the 1990s and the Clinton administration's use of the Antiquities Act of 1906 to set aside a number of new national monuments, the unfunded acquisitions backlog no longer appears to be one of the NPS's most important current problems. The NPS's 2001–2005 Strategic Plan makes no reference to unfunded acquisitions as being a problem. In fact, there is no reference to acquisition of new parkland at all (*www.nps.gov*). Instead, the strategic plan emphasizes partnering and the use of "less-than-full-fee" techniques in order to "expand" the system, not necessarily outright acquisition. The focus seems to have switched to the backlog of unfunded maintenance and repair as a major current issue (USGAO. 2001. "Major Management Challenges and Program Risks: Department of the Interior." USGAO Performance and Accountability Series, GAO-01-249. Washington, DC: USGAO). In addition, the author of "Private lands, public challenge: NPS continues its push to buy private land

to protect parks" notes that the NPS has identified more than 1.7 million acres of private inholdings it wants to purchase at a cost of $1.4 billion (National Parks Magazine, Sept.-Oct., 2000). The use of condemnation or the outright purchase of new park lands does not appear to be a current trend.

9. Nixon replaced George Hartzog with Ronald Walker. Walker, a White House aide with no background for the director's job, was selected more for his loyalty to the president than for his competence. Walker's inexperience led assistant Secretary of the Interior Nathaniel Reed to undertake more and more of the director's responsibilities. Partially as a result of his handling of the Yosemite plan, Walker was replaced by long-time Park Service employee Gary Everhardt. Everhardt seemed out of place in Washington, and he did not provide the Service with strong guidance. President Carter replaced Everhardt with William Whalen, but his role was largely limited to carrying out daily duties, and policy leadership was handled by the environmentalist Secretary of the Interior Cecil Andrus. Under President Reagan, attention focused on Secretary of the Interior James Watt and his campaign to encourage park development, while trusted veteran Russell Dickinson moved up from the ranks to manage the Park Service's daily affairs. In 1985, Dickinson was succeeded by William Penn Mott, who attempted to return the Park Service to the expansionist posture of Mather and Wirth (Barry Mackintosh, "Directors of the National Park Service," *www.di.nps.gov/ history/direct.htm;* Butler, *Prophet of the Parks: The Story of William Penn Mott, Jr.*). In 1989, the first Bush administration replaced Mott with James Ridenour, who was less willing than his immediate predecessor to accept system additions driven by local economic development interests. In 1993, President Clinton replaced Ridenour with Roger Kennedy. Kennedy had a diverse background in banking, television, historical writing, and museum administration. Before being appointed to the NPS, he was director of the Smithsonian Institution's Museum of American History, and he worked to expand NPS educational programs. In 1997, at the end of Clinton's first term, Kennedy resigned and was replaced by Robert Stanton. Stanton was the first NPS careerist since Dickinson. He began as a seasonal ranger at Grand Teton in 1962, served the NPS as ranger, superintendent, deputy regional director, assistant director, and regional director of the National Capital Region. As NPS's first African-American director, Stanton took a keen interest in increasing the diversity of the staff and public programs to better serve minority populations. He pushed hard for creation of new historical and cultural NPS units that tell the history of minorities in the America, like Little Rock Central High School NHS, the Tuskegee Airmen NHS, and the proposed National Underground Railroad Network to Freedom. The current NPS director, Frances Mainella, is a Bush appointee who also possesses a parks and recreation background, having formerly taught physical education and directed the Florida Department of State Parks. She is seen as a centrist, one who tries to balance pressures to protect parks from commercial development and making them more accessible.

10. All federal agencies are required to have strategic plans because of the Government Performance and Results Act (GPRA) of 1993. Enacted during first year of the Clinton Administration (part of Vice President Al Gore's "Reinventing Government" program), GPRA requires that agencies establish standards measuring their performance and effectiveness. The first round of strategic plans was submitted to Congress and OMB in 1997. Since they are to be updated every 3 years, the 2000 plans are now being released. The significance to the policy process and to the point about the increase in centralized control is that OMB and Congress are using these plans to guide budget decisions. The agencies are relying on these plans as well. For example, the new NPS strategic plan clearly states that "The Director, Deputy Directors, each Regional Director and Associate Director will allocate sufficient resources (staff, funds, etc.) to meet the NPS goals servicewide." So the goals in the strategic plans ostensibly carry a lot of weight. To develop goals, the NPS, at least, relies heavily on the findings in the GAO reports. Each park has to develop its own strategic plan and annual performance plan, which tailor or adapt the servicewide goals to align with their own missions. Park superintendents are evaluated in terms of hiring, firing, and promotion decisions based on their park's annual performance reports.

11. However, the rate of growth has slowed in the last three budget cycles. "Ten Year Budget History of the NPS," accessed online at *http://165.83.219.72/budget2/index.cfm,* 5/10/02; the FY 2003 President's Budget Request for the NPS is $2.422 billion.

12. Clarke and McCool, *Staking out the Terrain: Power and Performance among Natural Resource Agencies,* p. 195.

13. For the definition of a National Heritage Area and examples, see: *http://www.ncrc.nps.gov,* *http://www.cofc.edu/heritage/index.html* and *http://www.ohioeriecanal.org/nationalheritage.html* (accessed 5/21/02).

14. Visitation data accessed online, 6/1/01, from http://www2.nature.nps.gov/npstats and via personal communications with Butch Street, NPS, Lakewood, CO.

15. Foresta, *America's National Parks and Their Keepers,* p. 169.

16. Ibid., pp. 169–173.

17. Ibid., p. 173.

18. Sharpe, "The National Parks and Young America."

19. Foresta, pp. 175–176.

20. Ibid., pp. 177–179.

21. Ibid., pp. 180–181.

22. In addition to Foresta's analysis of Gateway, see Smith, "The Gateways"; Conservation Foundation, *National Parks for a New Generation;* and Mitchell, "The Regreening of Urban America."

23. Caro, *The Power Broker,* is a fascinating account of Robert Moses's career.

24. Foresta, pp. 192–196, 202–205.

25. Ibid., pp. 205–212.

26. "Gateway National Recreation Area Recreation Activities," *www.nps.gov/ gate/pphtml/activities.html,* accessed 5/05/03.

27. This is still the case. According to the Great Outdoor Recreation Page (*www.gorp.com,* accessed January 2001), access to Gateway's units is still via mass transit, with a number of connections involving subways and busses, or via automobile.

28. Smith, "The Gateways," pp. 226–227.

29. Recent transportation projects at Yosemite, Grand Canyon, and Zion seem to indicate a modification in OMB policy. In these cases, the NPS has paid or will pay to build parking lots outside the park and then facilitate the formation of a regional transportation authority or subcontract with private companies to provide bus transportation. It's not clear if any of this will be "subsidized," but Congress is at least funding the concept of reducing traffic volume.

30. Personal communications, Brian Feeney, Public Affairs Office, Gateway NRA, 6/1/01; also online at the Metropolitan Transportation Authority's home page, *http://www.mta.nyc.ny.us/libus/index.html,* accessed 6/1/01.

31. Personal communications, Brian Feeney, Public Affairs Office, Gateway NRA, 6/1/01. Mr. Feeney also noted plans to start daily ferry service between the Rockaway Peninsula and Manhattan, which would make it easier for people to visit a national park site in New York City without a car.

32. Smith, "The Gateways," pp. 228–234.

33. The total park area is about 74,000 acres (30,600 acres are federal; 43,100 acres are non-federal) with approximately 28 miles of coastline. GGNRA includes Alcatraz Island, Fort Point National Historic Site, Muir Woods National Monument and the Presidio of San Francisco, *www.nps.gov/goga/index.htm,* updated 1/23/01. The Presidio became part of GGNRA in 1994 and since 1998 it has been managed by the NPS and the Presidio Trust. The trust is a special public-private governmental agency charged with managing most of the buildings and making the park financially self-sufficient by 2013.

34. Foresta, p. 180.

35. Duddleson, "National Parks Are Beset by Policy Problems."

36. The National Park Service continues to offer a variety of grants-in-aid and technical assistance programs to assist communities, cities, and other units of government acquire, develop, and protect lands and waters for recreation and other uses. See "Federal Lands to Parks," "Land and Water Conservation Fund," "Hydropower Recreation Assistance," "Rivers, Trails and Conservation Assistance," and "Urban Park and Recreation Recovery" programs, all of which are described on *http://www.ncrc.nps.gov/,* the NPS's National Center for Recreation and Conservation website, accessed 5/22/02.

37. Conservation Foundation, pp. 61–63, is the primary source for much of this information on urban national parks other than the Gateways.

38. Personal communications, John Debo, Superintendent, Cuyahoga Valley NRA, 2/16/01.

39. Conservation Foundation, pp. 258–269.

40. However, recent court rulings related to "takings," may be casting some doubt on the use of federal regulation or zoning. The current trend toward partnering (discussed later in this chapter), is an attempt to avoid both the ill-will associated with the use of eminent domain and the takings charges that may result from regulation or zoning.

41. The source of this information is the *Santa Monica Mountains NRA General Management Plan and Environmental Impact Statement, 2000.* The 1998 Land Protection Plan (LPP), used to develop the 2000 GMP/EIS, uses GIS software and data to identify significant natural, cultural, and recreational re-source parcels. Each parcel is assigned a score and hence a rank order, which the NPS uses to prioritize future land acquisition efforts, via direct purchase, land transfers, or land exchanges. The NPS also uses the LPP to assess al-ternative approaches to resource protection, such as conservation easements, land exchanges, and habitat conservation plans.

42. Conservation Foundation, pp. 291–332.

43. At first glance, the numbers do not seem to support such a claim. Accord-ing to the Park Service's Land Resource Office in Washington, DC, the NPS had easements on 252,000 acres as of December, 2000. These include scenic, conservation, and right-of-way easements. This is nearly a 400% in-crease over the 1980 figure of 64,500 acres in easements. Nonetheless, 122,000 of the 252,000 acres in easements are in one park—Badlands. Fur-thermore, the proportion of NPS land in easements compared to the total amount of NPS acreage has not changed that much—0.1% in 1980 to 0.3% in 2000.

44. Personal communications, Barbara Nelson-Jameson, NPS Great Lakes Re-gion—Rivers, Trails and Conservation Assistance Coordinator, 2/14/01; and John Debo, Superintendent, Cuyahoga Valley NRA, 2/16/01.

45. See *http://ncrs.fs.fed.us/epubs/chicagoriver/pdf/illmich.pdf* for an example of a partnership in Chicago. The new designation of "National Heritage Area" is another example. Money is appropriated by Congress and placed in NPS's budget as a "pass through" to local units of government. Goals are then negotiated and carried out by the partners. According to Barbara Nel-son-Jameson, NPS Great Lakes Region—Rivers, Trails and Conservation Assistance Coordinator (personal communications, 2/14/01), Denny Galvin, Deputy Director of the NPS is credited with the national heritage area con-cept. She also noted that there is a big debate about these heritage areas be-cause, though the Bush administration is pushing for them, there are no cri-teria for selection, thus making these areas prone to "park barreling."

46. "Significance of the Mississippi National River and Recreation Area" (www.nps.gov/miss/mnrra/natsig.html) , revised 11/13/98.

47. Little, *Greenline Parks* and *Greenways for America.*

48. Knight and Landres, *Stewardship Across Boundaries.*

49. These units are even promoted by tourism organizations as part of a destination package of attractions—e.g., Santa Monica was recently touted in an L.A. newspaper article as being the backbone of an ecotourism experience in L.A.! (MSNBC online article by Miguel Llanos, 2001: "Eco-tourism in Los Angeles? Santa Monican Mountains and electric rental car make it so".)

50. Conservation Foundation, Chapter 6. Also, Knight and Landres, *Stewardship Across Boundaries.*

51. Foresta, pp. 255–259.

52. Smith, "The Gateways"; Mitchell, "The Regreening of Urban America"; Frome, *Regreening the National Parks.*

53. For discussions of these new skills and case studies of their applications, see: Chapters 9 and 10 in Berry and Gordon (Eds.), *Environmental Leadership;* McNeely (Ed.), *Expanding Partnerships in Conservation;* Chapters 8 through 14 in Knight and Landres (Eds.), *Stewardship across Boundaries;* and Wondolleck, *Public Lands Conflict and Resolution: Managing National Forest Disputes.*

54. Conservation Foundation, *National Parks for a New Generation.* After being critical of the urban parks, Foresta offers some encouragement in his conclusions.

55. There are always exceptions. For example, In Region 9, the FS acquired an area now called the Midewin National Tallgrass Prairie, located about 2 miles west of Chicago near Joliet on the site of the former Joliet ammunition factory. This provides recreation and education opportunities for urban residents.

56. See *www.fs.fed.us/recreation/permits/urban,* updated 10/95.

57. Chavez, "Managing outdoor recreation in California: visitor contact studies 1989–1998," and Gobster, "Managing urban and high-use recreation settings . . ."

58. Deneke, "Technical assistance, education, and research programs in urban forestry," p. 468. The author makes it clear, however, that funding to implement the Urban and Community Forestry Program was not authorized until Fiscal Year 1978.

59. Cubbage et al., *Forest Resource Policy,* p. 475, note other reasons for the passage of the bill as well and a variety of sources of support including Congress and environmentalists who wanted to do something about threats to climate change. The American Forestry Association and National Association of State Foresters also supported the bill because they wanted to revive federal private forestry programs.

60. Toward the end of the Clinton administration, the Secretary of Agriculture proposed including UCFP as part of the Land and Water Conservation Fund legislation being considered, as a way of assuring a reliable annual budget for urban forestry programs. This inclusion did not happen under the Bush administration; however, recent (2002) Farm Bill increases, which include increases in funding for the UCFP program, indicate continual executive support for urban and community forestry technical assistance programs.

61. Heisler et al., "Energy savings with trees"; McPherson et al., "Chicago's urban forest ecosystem"; and Nowak et al., "Modeling the effects of urban vegetation on air pollution" as cited in Dwyer, et al., *Connecting people with Ecosystems in the 21st Century: An Assessment of our Nation's Urban Forests,* p. 2.

62. For example, see USDA Forest Service General Technical Report NE-13 (1975), "Municipal Watershed Management Symposium Proceedings," and Rowntree and Wolfe (1979), "Abstracts of urban forestry research in progress."

63. Personal communications, John Dwyer, Project Leader—Managing Forest Environments for Urban Populations, USDA Forest Service, North Central Forest Experiment Station, Chicago. Also see Chavez, "Managing outdoor recreation in California: visitor contact studies 1989–1998" and Gobster, "Managing urban and high-use recreation settings. . ."

64. For summaries and applications of this research, see Kaplan and Kaplan (1989, 1998), Schroeder (1989, 1990), and Schroeder and Ruffolo (1996).

65. Gobster, "Managing urban and high-use recreation . . ."

66. Ibid.

67. Tipple et al., "Urban forestry administration in the Netherlands"; Tipple and Wellman, "The living infrastructure . . ."; Wellman and Tipple, "Working with the community . . ." and "Governance in the wildland-urban interface."

68. Dwyer, et al., *Connecting people with ecosystems in the 21st Century: An assessment of our nation's urban forests.*

69. USDA Forest Service Strategic Plan (2000 Revision), online at *www.fs.fed.us/plan.*

70. For additional information, see Dwyer et al., *Connecting people with ecosystems in the 21st Century: An assessment of our nation's urban forests.* In this extensive report, the authors assess the degree of urbanization and urban tree cover in the U.S. and causes of changes over time. They then make suggestions about future forest management in urban areas that will improve environmental quality and human health.

71. Ibid., p. 26.

72. Ibid., p. 26.

73. As a policy document, the strategic plan not only guides actions and investments, but also sets milestones for evaluating progress toward the goals. As

required by the Government Performance and Results Act of 1993 (GPRA), annual performance plans will address specific management actions and investments needed to make progress toward meeting the goals and objectives of an agency's strategic plan. Annual performance plans reflect local needs identified in resource management plans for national forests and grasslands; they also reflect plans for research and assistance to tribal governments, states and communities. Subsequently, annual budget proposals seek the funding needed to carry out the agency actions and investments described in various plans. The significance to the policy process is that OMB and Congress use these plans to guide budgetary decisions.

74. Personal communications, Ed Dickerhoof, Economist, USDA Forest Service, Research & Development, Washington, DC, 2/8/01 and 5/29/2002. The UCFP budget was $35.6 million of the total $251 million for all of the State and Private Forestry division for FY 2001; $36 million in FY 2002; $36.6 million is the President's budget request for FY 2003.

75. This $11.3 million was used in a variety of ways. For example, it was used to assist New York City and Chicago locate and replace thousands of trees infested with Asian longhorned beetle, an introduced pest that kills hardwoods.

76. *http://www.fs.fed.us/spf/coop/ucf_general.htm* updated 1/29/02, accessed 5/20/02. The URP in Chicago is a partnership of seven federal agencies formed to work in communities to develop natural resources projects with local governments and non-profit organizations. The idea is to provide some initial seed money and facilitate the process of forming community coalitions which then obtain substantial funding from sources outside the URP (*www.hud.gov/local/chi/chiurp1.html*, updated 2/4/00, accessed 1/22/01).

77. Personal communications, John Dwyer and Paul Gobster, USDA Forest Service, North Central Forest Experiment Station, Chicago, 02/02/01.

78. The significance is that the Chicago region is one of only a few metropolitan areas in the world that contains a high concentration of globally significant natural communities. Thousands of volunteers and member organizations do most of the work. Member organizations apply for project funding to the Chicago Region Biodiversity Council, which directs the Chicago Wilderness initiative and its programs (*www.chiwild.org* accessed 5/22/02).

79. Gobster and Westphal (Eds.), *People and the River: Perception and Use of Chicago Waterways for Recreation. http://ncrs.fs.fed.us/epubs/chicagoriver/ index.html* (updated 8/3/01, accessed 5/22/02). 1998. (Chicago Rivers Demonstration Project Report, 192 p.) Milwaukee: WI: U.S. Department of the Interior, Park Service, Rivers, Trails and Conservation Assistance Program (*www.ncrs.nps.gov*)

CHAPTER 10

MANAGEMENT: TODAY'S POLICY FRONTIER

The history of this country's wildland recreation policies is replete with
difficult allocation and management issues. From the beginning, Americans have struggled to reach collective decisions about how the national
welfare would best be served in questions about damming or not
damming the Colorado River, cutting or not cutting the redwoods, allowing or not allowing suburban development of the Cuyahoga River Valley,
and a host of other controversies. In the process of choosing between economic development and preservation, Americans and their institutions
have created a huge and varied wildland recreation estate, which extends
from the remotest reaches of Alaska to the core of our most populous
cities. At the same time, and interwoven with the allocation issue, Americans have wrestled with questions about the kinds and amounts of recreational use that are most appropriate for the areas they have set aside. Interests which may have come together to protect a forest from logging
have found themselves at odds in discussions about whether mass or
purist recreation should be encouraged in the area thus preserved.

In 2000, we made the transition from a Democratic to a Republican administration. Under the Democratic Clinton administration, the size of the
U.S. wildland recreation estate was significantly increased. For example, in
1994, the California Desert Protection Act added 7.58 million acres to the
National Wilderness Preservation System (NWPS). In 2000, Congress bol-
stered the size of the NWPS by an additional million acres. By executive

order, Clinton established 11 new national monuments in 2000 and expanded 2 others, thereby adding more protection to about 5 million acres of federal land, mostly in Bureau of Land Management areas.[1] The Republican Bush administration, on the other hand, has indicated less interest in expanding wildland recreation areas.[2] Instead, they increased funding for maintenance of park facilities. They are also attempting to delay or weaken the Clinton administration's ban on road building and logging in FS roadless areas and are pushing to open portions of the federal estate for oil and gas exploration. Allocation issues continue to arise, but most of the focus now is on the management of established wildland recreation resources. A new cycle of policy-making has begun, as old concerns about appropriate use that were overshadowed by land allocation issues once again command our attention.

To say that our attention is shifting from allocation to management is not to assert that allocation issues have disappeared or may disappear in the future. It might be thought that we will finally decide, at some point in the future, which lands are worth saving for recreation and which should be dedicated to other uses. But this line of thinking fails to recognize that wildland recreation resources are created by our evolving culture.[3] As the Conservation Foundation phrased the idea in a report on the national parks:

> Searchers for completeness seem to assume that park sites are in finite supply and that the task is to select the best ones for inclusion in the national system. Lesser sites—those not of "outstanding national significance"—are viewed as more appropriate for state, local or private parks. This kind of attitude is misconceived, however, overlooking the fact that parks are not simply found but are created for a variety of purposes. It is from this perspective of creativity that the park system carries a message not only about quality resources but also about the evolving values of the country that has preserved and managed these resources in ways sensitive to its people's changing demands and aspirations as well as to the needs of the places themselves.[4]

This quotation is an elaboration of Zimmerman's statement cited in our first chapter: "Resources are not, they become." Because our society is continually changing, wildland recreation allocation issues will be quiescent only temporarily. And they are not altogether quiet, at that. The National Parks Conservation Association is urging the expansion of 5 existing parks and the creation of 10 new park sites, including the Loess Hills of western Iowa, Bioluminescent Bay in Puerto Rico, the Gaviota Coast of California, and the Sonoran Desert in Arizona. These calls for action are not mere rhetoric, but live issues in the ongoing policy discussion. For example, conservation organizations lobbied successfully for the creation of the 11,000-acre Tallgrass Prairie National Preserve (Kansas) in 1996. In 2000, Congress authorized the expansion of Great Sand Dunes National Monument and Preserve in Colorado by 100,000 acres and added 661,000 acres to Craters of the Moon National Monument in Idaho.[5]

Nevertheless, for the immediate future it appears that the policy discussion for wildland recreation will center on management issues. As we will see, many of the current issues represent old concerns in new guises. Our solutions to the new issues, like our solutions to the old, will be forced by circumstance, conditioned by larger social forces, and temporary.

This and the next chapter focus on the relationships between policy and management. In this chapter, we revisit Yosemite National Park to examine some of the most fundamental management issues: Should we emphasize preservation or use? Which uses are appropriate? Which are not? We close this chapter with a review of other critical management issues facing wildland recreation managers in the twenty-first century. In Chapter 11, we look more closely at some of the realities managers face in their attempts to implement policies and some of the policy tools they use in carrying out their missions.

CURRENT ISSUES IN WILDLAND
RECREATION MANAGEMENT

Many wildland recreation management issues are now in various stages of resolution. In this section, we discuss in detail one case that represents the omnipresent preservation versus use debate. We then quickly review other current policy issues that make the manager's job dynamic and challenging. This review of management issues is not intended to provide exhaustive or systematic coverage for the National Park System, the Forest Service, or the National Wilderness Preservation System, and it includes little on wildland recreation management issues facing other federal agencies and state and local governments. Nevertheless, the review will provide a reasonably representative summary of important contemporary concerns.

As the national park historian, Alfred Runte, points out, "one man's civilization can just as easily be another's wilderness."[6] Runte was referring to the age-old preservation versus use debate that has forged much of our wildland recreation policy, including the policies for urban natural areas. A classic case of this debate, the Yosemite Valley Plan, is presented below. Runte continues:

> More than a century after the inspiration of the national park idea the issue remains: at what point is conservation in fact sacrificed for the sake of novelty and convenient access? Conceivably, a definitive answer may never be possible.[7]

We are not so much concerned with finding definitive answers as we are in understanding the policy process and how it affects, and is affected by, management. As such, the Yosemite Valley Plan is a milestone of sorts. In the plan, the Park Service tries to clarify the limits to the novelty and convenient access that Runte refers to. The plan is a compromise among competing factions of park interests. It is not a definitive answer but a work-in-progress. It demonstrates that the old adage, "persistence pays," can be used to describe the policy process. The plan is a policy statement that park planners and managers must implement. Implementation will require additional Congressional appropriations, further dialogue with competing interests, and the inevitable challenges, both legal and non-legal, to the decisions that the planners and managers make. Such is the nature of the policy process itself, which we described in Chapter 2. Because of its role in implementation, management is integral to the policy process (Figure 2–2). Management provides "ground-truthing" for policy. In the detailed process of putting policy into practice, we are bound to learn things that may force adjustments in current policies or lead to future policy changes. Good managers are well aware of their critical role in the larger policy process, and they look for opportunities to shape how policies are implemented so as to contribute to larger goals.

YOSEMITE REVISITED

In the Mather-Albright era, the National Park Service established a general management policy that was consistent with the country's dominant social values and therefore was successful. The Mather-Albright policy, which emphasized the development of facilities and services to encourage mass visitation and build political support, was itself the product of conflict and compromise, of course, as are all policies. John Muir, for example, supported the idea of allowing automobiles in the parks. At the same time, Muir must have had doubts about the spiritual value of the convenient recreation behavior automobiles would foster. This is how Muir described the people he guided around Yosemite in 1870:

> All sorts of human stuff is being poured into our valley this year . . . and the blank, fleshly apathy with which most of it comes in contact with the rock and water spirits of the place is most amazing . . . They climb sprawlingly to their saddles like overgrown frogs pulling themselves up a stream-bank through the bent sedges, ride up the valley with about as much emotion as the horses they ride upon . . . and long for the safety and neatness of their proper homes.[8]

If John of the Mountains later swallowed his outrage because he saw in automobile visitation a way to assure the parks' survival, others were less circumspect. In 1912 James Bryce, the British ambassador to the United States, addressed the American Civic Association on the subject of nature and civilization in this country. He suggested that America was tending toward the condition found in Europe, where an increasing and more civilized population sought greater contact with nature, while at the same time the pristine nature people sought was diminished by civilization. Bryce warned that the scenic resources in America could no longer be considered inexhaustible, and he spoke specifically about automobile access to Yosemite.

> There are plenty of roads for the lovers of speed and noise without intruding on these few places where the wood nymphs and the water nymphs ought to be allowed to have the landscape to themselves . . . if Adam had known what harm the serpent was going to work, he would have tried to prevent him from finding lodgement in Eden; and if you were to realize what the result of the automobile will be in that wonderful, that incomparable valley, you will keep it out.[9]

Just as Mather's successful formula for mass recreational use of the parks reached its apogee in Mission 66, fundamental social changes helped set the stage for its repudiation. Preservationist voices, which had always existed but were drowned out in the general consensus, rose to the fore as the consensus unraveled and new environmental knowledge won converts to the preservationist side.

The recent planning history of Yosemite National Park provides an excellent illustration of this transition to new policy. Yosemite is the place where the national park idea was born, and it remains one of the most important national parks in terms of its symbolism to the public and its centrality to the Park Service's mission. To a considerable extent, "As Yosemite goes, so goes the National Park System," and in fact the recent developments there are representative of trends throughout the national parks.[10]

History of the Yosemite Plan

By the early 1970s, the cycle of facility development leading to increased visitation, which in turn prompts more facility development, had pushed Yosemite to the crisis point.[11] Preservationists had become increasingly concerned about the sheer numbers of people visiting the park. Between 1954 and 1967 annual visitation had doubled, rising from 1 million to 2 million visits. Preservationists were also pointed in their criticism about the amount and types of development in the park. As of 1976 Yosemite Valley alone had 1,498 lodging units, along with:

> 3 restaurants; 2 cafeterias; 1 hotel dining room; 4 sandwich centers; 1 seven lift garage; 2 service stations with a total of 15 pumps; 7 gift shops; 2 grocery stores; 1 delicatessen, 1 bank; 1 skating rink; 3 swimming pools; 1 pitch-and-putt golf course; 2 tennis courts; 33 kennels; 114 horse and mule stalls; 1 barber shop; 1 beauty shop; and 13 facilities for the sale of liquor.[12]

Then in 1970, the first "riot" in a national park placed Yosemite's problems under national scrutiny and lent a sense of urgency to master planning efforts that had been underway since 1968.[13] The riot, which consisted of a July 4 confrontation between Park Service rangers and a group of "flower children," was provoked by the hippies' refusal to remove themselves from a meadow where they had congregated to sing, get high, and try to offend "straight" visitors and their protectors, the Park Service rangers.[14] It was a classic counterculture confrontation with the establishment, a set piece common to the times. Uncommon, however, was its location in a national park. National parks had always been viewed as special places, sanctuaries set apart from society and its troubles.[15]

If there was but limited sympathy for the people who provoked the conflict, there was recognition of the legitimacy of some of their complaints. Wasn't their approach to Yosemite at least as much in keeping with the spirit of the place as that of the middleclass visitors in their RVs?

By 1971 the Park Service had pulled together a conceptual master plan for Yosemite. For Yosemite Valley, the 1-by-7 mile focus of most of the problems, the conceptual plan called for complete elimination of private

automobiles, the establishment of a mass-transit system, and the relocation of certain buildings to El Portal at the western entrance to the valley.[16] As this concept moved through the review process, however, events
unfolded which set off a new round of planning that was not completed
until 1980.

The trouble began in 1973, when MCA (formerly Music Corporation
of America), an entertainment conglomerate based in Hollywood, entered
the picture. MCA purchased the major concessionaire in the park,
Yosemite Park & Curry Co., for $7.2 million. Concessions are usually
for-profit enterprises offering goods and services (lodging, food, sou-
venirs, tours, etc.) to park visitors on a contractual basis. Their history can
be traced back to the Yellowstone Park Act of 1872, in which Congress
deliberately permitted business operations in the park. By law, Congress
decreed that the minor amounts that it allocated to protect and improve
Yellowstone ($10,000–$20,000) should be substantially augmented by
concession revenues.[17] Ten years after Yellowstone's establishment, the
Northern Pacific Railroad, seeing the profit opportunity, created the Yellowstone Park Association, which built hotels and dominated transportation between the park and the train.[18]

With estimated annual gross receipts of more than $56 million in 1983,
Yosemite Park & Curry Co. was the largest concessionaire in the National
Park System. In 1974, columnist Jack Anderson broke the story that MCA
had covertly influenced the new Park Service plan then being developed.
Instead of reduced development, as the original Park Service concept had
called for, the revised plan would have permitted more development in the
park. Concessionaire lodging was to remain in the Valley instead of being
relocated to El Portal, the ban on private automobiles was to be postponed,
and a restaurant and gift shop were to be built at Glacier Point, about 250
yards from the edge of the Valley. These changes in the plan would have
significantly enhanced the concessionaire's prospects for profit.

In addition to influencing the plan, MCA did several other things that
raised alarm. Yosemite Park was used in the filming of a short-lived television series, and as part of the production some of the park's rocks were
painted to make them more photogenic. The idea of painting Yosemite's
rocks—the very granite that prompted John Muir's rhapsodic prose and
Ansel Adams' photographic art—was a symbolic slap in the preservationists' face. MCA also floated the idea of an aerial tram from the Valley to the new restaurant/gift shop at Glacier Point, and although this idea
was not incorporated in the plan, it raised preservationists' hackles still

further. Finally, MCA sought to drum up convention business by advertising the park's accommodations in terms such as the following: "This isn't no-man's land. Or primitive wilderness. This is civilization."[19]

Preservationists, who had always been troubled by development at the park, could be counted on to howl in anger at these developments, and howl they did. When it was revealed that NPS Director Ronald Walker had insisted that MCA review the Park Service plan, that he had made arrangements for western NPS superintendents to be guests of MCA's subsidiary, Universal Studios in Hollywood, and that President Nixon's reelection campaign had received secret contributions totaling $183,000 from two MCA executives, the pressure to stop the plan and begin again became overwhelming. With congressional hearings in the offing, Assistant Secretary of the Interior Nathaniel Reed rejected the NPS plan and ordered the agency to start over.[20] In taking this action, Reed observed that the plan appeared "to have been written by the concessionaire."

The MCA-influenced plan for Yosemite was stopped for both substantive and procedural reasons. Substantively, the plan crossed the ill-defined but real border between reasonable concession activity and crass commercialism. Yosemite is a sufficiently important American symbol and the attempt to use it for commercial gain was bold enough that it became an excellent test case in the longstanding debate over preservation versus use. Procedurally, too, the plan provided an excellent opportunity to open up traditional Park Service decision-making. The political climate for this was favorable. Following years of national agony in the Vietnam War, during which the failures of closed governmental planning were repeatedly revealed, came Watergate. The Watergate scandal further weakened trust in government and added fire to the drive for greater public involvement in planning.[21]

In an effort to overcome public suspicions that it was in collusion with the concessionaire, the Park Service's planning process at Yosemite was a model of openness, and it set the tone for planning in the entire agency. The Yosemite planning team held 48 informal public workshops attended by more than 6,000 people. Most of Yosemite visitation was from California (70 percent in 1975), and therefore the public involvement effort within the state was extensive. In addition, since Yosemite is a nationally important scenic resource, there were workshops in seven other locations across the United States. Yosemite Park workbooks, reflecting ideas and opinions voiced at the workshops and designed to elicit citizen views on the direction park management should take, were completed by 20,700 people. A mailing list of more than 60,000 names was compiled, and those on the list were kept informed of the plan's progress through a newsletter.

In addition to reaching out to citizens outside the park, the planning team in 1975 conducted a survey of park visitors.[22] Yosemite visitors tended to be well-educated; 70 percent of those surveyed had attended college and a third had done graduate work. Visitors also tended to have extended association with the park; the average visit lasted three and one-half days, and more than a third of the visitors were visiting Yosemite for at least the fourth time. These facts of education and familiarity proved that Yosemite had a substantial body of concerned and articulate patrons interested in decisions about park management.

The 1975 survey asked visitors to comment on problems they felt existed in the park. The major complaint of the visitors surveyed in 1975 was crowding in the Valley, yet they did not endorse a wholesale cutback on private automobile use of the park. Visitors also were asked to identify activities and services they favored. Something less than a "wilderness ethic" emerged from their responses. Seventy percent of park visitors wanted grocery stores, gas and oil service, bike rentals, and public transportation; 50 percent wanted short-order food, restaurants, stables, medical and dental services, churches, laundries, a mountain climbing school, gift shops, and sporting goods stores; and 35 percent wanted entertainment, alcoholic beverages, car rental, and beauty/barber shops.[23]

Visitors' expressed preferences for a slight decivilizing of the status quo had to be balanced against the preferences expressed by other individuals and groups. In addition, public preferences had to be reconciled with the Park Service's own judgment of appropriate management strategies based on its sense of mission and knowledge of the resources for which it is responsible. The end product of these many sources of information is the General Management Plan (GMP). The first GMP was developed in 1980, and it was revised and updated in 2000. Politics has been defined as the art of the possible, and wildland recreation planning, although it involves technical skills, is ultimately a political enterprise. From the many value judgments about what a national treasure like Yosemite should be—covering the entire spectrum from a pristine nature shrine to an amusement park that happens to be located in an attractive natural setting—a workable compromise must be forged. The 1980 plan, described next, was an extension of the policy process behind it, and, like those policies, it was a temporary compromise between conflicting visions.

Highlights of the 1980 Yosemite Plan

Commentators have described the central thrust of the new General Management Plan as an attempt to "decivilize" Yosemite. As with any such one-word description, interpretation is required. The plan did not call for removal of all or even most of the trappings of civilization that had accumulated in the park over the years. Just as huge oil tankers require many miles to change direction, a great national institution like Yosemite National Park cannot have its course radically and instantaneously altered. What the 1980 General Management Plan proposed, therefore, was a set of actions that extended the change of direction begun by the Park Service in the 1970s toward a less crowded, less artificial park.

A briefing statement issued by the Park Service in 1984 summarized the major actions in the plan:

- Designation of 90 percent of the park's three-quarter million acres as wilderness, forever free from development
- Removal from Yosemite Valley of substandard National Park Service and concessionaire staff housing and relocation of warehouses, maintenance, and storage buildings, administrative offices, and other nonessential facilities outside the park to El Portal
- Reduction of concessionaire-operated lodging facilities in the park by 10 percent, including a 17 percent reduction of overnight facilities in Yosemite Valley
- Reduction in use of private vehicles in Yosemite Valley as alternate transportation options are expanded with a long-range goal to eliminate vehicles from Yosemite Valley
- Identification and enforcement of specific carrying capacities within the park for both day use and overnight occupancy
- Improvement and expansion of information, interpretive, and reservation services[24]

As a symbolic gesture of what was to be, Yosemite superintendent Bob Binnewies moved out of the Valley and into El Portal, the first and only Yosemite superintendent to do so. His action was a clear signal that significant changes needed to be made.[25]

1980 and 2000 Yosemite Plans Compared

The 1980 General Management Plan (GMP) and the 2000 Yosemite Valley Plan (YVP) are different in geographic scale. While the 1980 GMP addresses parkwide issues, the 2000 YVP emphasizes issues in Yosemite Valley. The 2000 plan amends but does not replace the 1980 plan; the 2000 plan for the valley provides more details on how to implement the actions and goals of the 1980 General Management Plan.[26]

Some of the actions recommended in the 1980 plan were implemented, while others were not.[27] Perhaps the most visible changes involve vehicle parking. Shortly after the 1980 plan was released, the large parking area in front of the village mall and visitor center was eliminated and replaced with a pedestrian mall. This was done to improve pedestrian circulation and to provide space for shuttle bus transfers (see Figure 10–1, Yosemite Village area).

From the 1980s to the early 1990s, the Park Service moved some housing, buildings, and functions out of the valley. Certain administrative functions were moved to El Portal, but it was the movement of the entire Yosemite maintenance function to El Portal that was the most profound and costly (approximately $50 million).[28] The relocation of the administrative and maintenance functions had the added benefit that employees could avoid commuting to the Valley, thereby enabling them to live outside Yosemite in their own housing. The NPS built some government-owned housing for employees in El Portal, but many employees also live in rented or purchased housing in local communities, a local economic benefit not realized when all employees lived in the valley.[29]

Finally, the number of concessionaire-operated lodging facilities in the park was reduced. In the 1990s, following a series of sales and exchanges, the NPS entered into a contract with Yosemite Concession Services to provide lodging and other services. Under the terms of this contract, the number of overnight accommodations has been reduced beyond the reduction originally called for in the 1980 plan.[30]

However, some key recommendations pertaining to Yosemite Valley were not implemented in the two decades following the 1980 General Management Plan. Except for some concessionaire-operated lodging accommodations, neither commercial establishments nor vehicular traffic were reduced. Comparison of the 1980 and 2000 valley plans reveals nearly identical road and shuttlebus systems. Despite constant pressure from the National Park and Conservation Association, environmental groups and the National Park Service itself to reduce the level of development and traffic, there are still traffic jams in the peak of the summer season in Yosemite Valley. Nonetheless, efforts to reduce congestion are underway. In addition to replacing a parking lot with a pedestrian mall, as

Figure 10-1

Yosemite Valley
Development Concept – 1980
Yosemite National Park
U.S. Dept. of Interior, National Park Service
(For the original full-color version of this map, see the 1980 General Management
Plan for Yosemite National Park, available online at www.nps.gov/yose)

 Use Limited to Automobile Carrying Capacity

Shuttle Only

YOSEMITE LODGE
- retain 364 units
- remove 117 units from the floodplain
- reduce commercial services
- redesign gas station

SUNNYSIDE CAMPGROUND
- retain 38 sites

INDIAN CULTURAL CENTER
- restroom

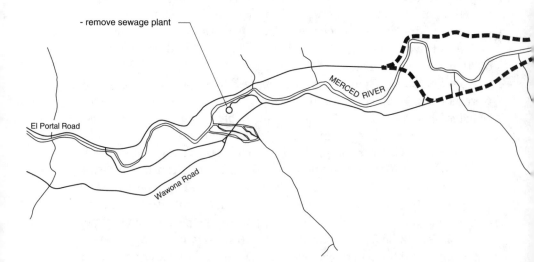

- remove sewage plant

MERCED RIVER

El Portal Road

Wawona Road

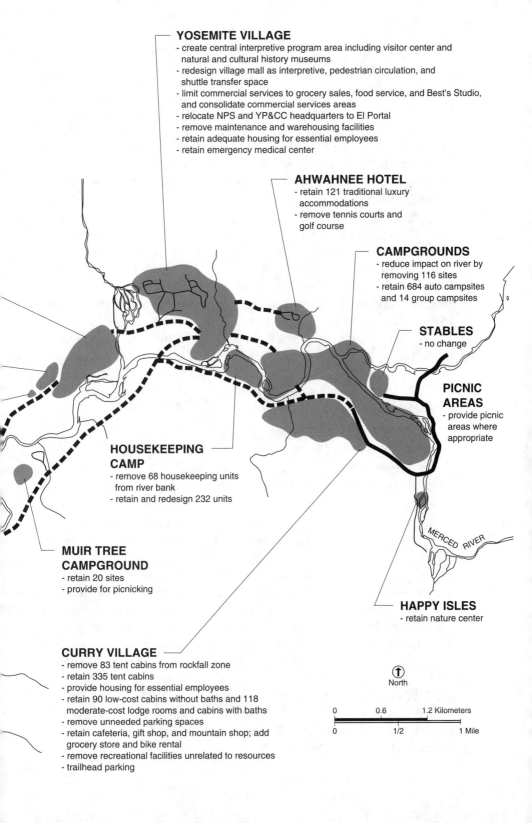

YOSEMITE VILLAGE
- create central interpretive program area including visitor center and natural and cultural history museums
- redesign village mall as interpretive, pedestrian circulation, and shuttle transfer space
- limit commercial services to grocery sales, food service, and Best's Studio, and consolidate commercial services areas
- relocate NPS and YP&CC headquarters to El Portal
- remove maintenance and warehousing facilities
- retain adequate housing for essential employees
- retain emergency medical center

AHWAHNEE HOTEL
- retain 121 traditional luxury accommodations
- remove tennis courts and golf course

CAMPGROUNDS
- reduce impact on river by removing 116 sites
- retain 684 auto campsites and 14 group campsites

STABLES
- no change

PICNIC AREAS
- provide picnic areas where appropriate

HOUSEKEEPING CAMP
- remove 68 housekeeping units from river bank
- retain and redesign 232 units

MUIR TREE CAMPGROUND
- retain 20 sites
- provide for picnicking

HAPPY ISLES
- retain nature center

CURRY VILLAGE
- remove 83 tent cabins from rockfall zone
- retain 335 tent cabins
- provide housing for essential employees
- retain 90 low-cost cabins without baths and 118 moderate-cost lodge rooms and cabins with baths
- remove unneeded parking spaces
- retain cafeteria, gift shop, and mountain shop; add grocery store and bike rental
- remove recreational facilities unrelated to resources
- trailhead parking

MERCED RIVER

North

| 0 | 0.6 | 1.2 Kilometers |

| 0 | 1/2 | 1 Mile |

noted above, numerous maintenance and administrative structures have been relocated outside the valley, and campsites have been relocated. Expansions to walk-in campgrounds are imminent.[31] As evidence of the intent to reduce vehicular congestion, paved bikeway and foot trails are called for in the 2000 plan; they are not mentioned in the 1980 plan.

The recent planning efforts took on more urgency following the flood of 1997, one of the greatest floods in the park's history.[32] The flood damaged the El Portal road and the three other main routes leading into the park. It also harmed water, sewage, and power systems, campsites, and lodging units and employee housing. Thus, the flood provided the planning team the opportunity to rethink the appropriate number and location of campsites, roads, and other facilities in the valley. One specific upshot from the flood will be an increase in the amount of river corridor restored to its natural function.[33]

The 2000 YVP clearly attempts to address the actions not accomplished since 1980. In so doing, it follows the five broad "de-civilizing" goals of the 1980 GMP:

- Reclaim priceless natural beauty
- Reduce traffic congestion
- Allow natural processes to prevail
- Reduce crowding
- Promote visitor understanding and enjoyment

As was true for the 1980 plan, the 2000 plan for Yosemite Valley featured extensive public participation. The Park Service released a draft of the plan in March 2000 and convened a series of public workshops. Planners also made the draft plan available for comment on the internet. During the 4-month comment period, park planners received and analyzed over 10,000 comments. Based on the concerns raised during the comment period, the NPS made changes. For example, critics of the draft plan did not like its apparent preference for "upper-end tourism."[34] The draft called for decreasing the number of inexpensive tent and housekeeping cabins and adding 40 rooms to the Yosemite lodge. The final plan recommends increasing the number of housekeeping cabins from 52 to 100 and tent cabins from 150 to 174. Campsites are to be increased from 465 to 500. The NPS recommends decreasing the number of rooms at the Yosemite Lodge from 386 to 251.

In a speech delivered in the Yosemite Valley in November 2000, Secretary of the Interior Bruce Babbitt released the final plan. A "no action" period followed, allowing citizens to consider and comment on the final plan. The Pacific Southwest Regional Director of the NPS, John Reynolds, then signed the final Yosemite Valley Plan and, in so doing, selected the preferred alternative (Alternative 2 of the five alternatives). Following the broad goals of the 1980 GMP, the preferred alternative will remove development from along the Merced River and move facilities out of the Yosemite Valley.[35] Over 250 actions are recommended, including:

- Eliminating a proposed parking site near El Capitan
- Expanding the shuttle bus system for all visitors
- Proposing 2,040 parking spaces for day visitors, only 550 of which will be in the Valley (during the busiest seasons, day visitors would use an out-of-valley parking lot and take a shuttle bus)
- Removing some historic Merced River bridges
- Moving some of the facilities of Yosemite Concession Services (stables, administrative offices, and garage) out of the Valley
- Moving housing for hundreds of NPS employees out of the park

The NPS does not have the authority to create a regional transportation system (outside park boundaries). Instead, park staff intends to work cooperatively with surrounding communities, the State of California, and the U.S. Department of Transportation to create a regional transportation system, as called for in the 1980 GMP.[36]

Secretary Babbitt confirmed that the new plan continues to favor nature a little more than people:

> I believe at the heart of this restoration is a recognition that it's our obligation to invite visitors away from their automobiles, and in the process of doing that to restore the peace and quiet of this valley.[37]

Authorities of the National Park Service signed the Final Environmental Impact Statement for the 2000 Yosemite Valley Plan on December 29, 2000. The signing marked the end of the planning process. However, it did not mark the end of public participation. Contrary to typical processes, public participation will continue throughout the design and implementation phases. Some projects began in 2001, but the full plan will take 10–15 years to implement.[38] The NPS has available $180 million to begin implementing the final plan, but an additional $442 million in congressional appropriations will be required to fully implement all the plan's recommendations.

Conclusions about Yosemite

The 25-year planning process at Yosemite exemplifies the policy process described in Chapter 2. It also shows how pivotal the agency is in that process. For the 2000 Yosemite Valley Plan, for example, not only did NPS staff have to incorporate the views of diverse publics and comply with 28 laws, regulations, and executive orders (see the appendix), but they had to exercise their expertise and find ways to express their core professional values. During the next 25 years and more, Yosemite management staff will continue to carry out its function in the policy process by forming partnerships, making the case for necessary funds, implementing the plan's recommendations after consultation with various publics, and modifying the plan in response to changes in the physical environment and the social climate.

The 2000 Yosemite Valley Plan demonstrates the length of time it can take to implement policy and the importance of persistence in achieving a vision. The NPS conducted a study several years ago about what happens throughout the system after general management plans are approved. In general, a third of the recommendations are implemented within 10 years, a third are programmed to be done and awaiting full implementation within another 10 years, and a third are deemed to be no longer appropriate or a priority.[39] That is, something happens either administratively, politically, technologically, or scientifically to render the last third invalid. "So, if the first two-thirds is a 20-plus year program, then after that it is usually time to redo the plans anyway . . . the process really does work."[40] And, consistent with a planning process that involves many people with diverse values, developers have criticized the plan for restricting access to a public place while environmentalists have argued that it did not go far enough to protect Yosemite. The age-old debate shows little sign of diminishing.

The Yosemite case illustrates venerable policy questions about how we try to satisfy conflicting human demands for scarce resources. We now turn our attention to other broad policy questions that affect how managers carry out their missions. These broad policy questions stem from documented threats to the parks—both internal and external—some of which are due the same pressures that caused Yosemite to pursue its de-

civilization strategies. In the paragraphs that follow, we will again observe the critical role that managers play in responding to changing social
values and reconciling competing interests.

MANAGEMENT ISSUES INVOLVING EXTERNAL THREATS

In 1980 the National Park Service, in response to a congressional request,
published a report on the threats facing the National Park System.[41] Based
on a survey of Park Service superintendents, natural and cultural resource
managers, scientists, and planners, the report identified 73 distinct categories of threats to park resources, values, and visitor experiences. In all,
4,300 individual threats were identified system-wide. Over half the total
reported threats were attributed to sources beyond park boundaries. Problems were found to be concentrated in the larger parks (the 63 natural areas of over 30,000 acres), and particularly in the most sensitive of these,
the 12 biosphere preserves.[42] The report suggested that this imbalance
may be the result of insufficient reporting at smaller, less carefully
watched parks, and that, therefore, the general picture may be even more
serious than it seemed. A survey of NPS superintendents conducted by
the U.S. General Accounting Office in 1994 and 1996 confirmed this sus-
picion. The surveys found that many parks contained resources that had
been negatively impacted by external and internal activities and that these
impacts were likely to grow.[43]

In the early days, the parks were protected by their remoteness. Now,
adjoining civilization threatens the parks in many different ways.[44] Many
of these same threats challenge national forest and wilderness managers
as well. They have become key policy issues affecting decisions about
how to best manage the wildland recreation estate and associated natural
resources.

Air Pollution

Air pollution problems, especially in the parks of the arid Southwest, attracted a great deal of attention in the 1980s. Today the list of parks where
visibility is a concern has expanded from coast to coast.[45] At Grand
Canyon, Sequoia, Canyonlands, Arches, Mount Rainier, Acadia, Shenandoah, Great Smoky Mountains, and Big Bend, average visibility has declined in recent years. Scientists report that visibility once averaged 90

miles in Eastern parks and 140 miles in Western parks, but those averages have slipped to 18–40 miles and 35–90 miles, respectively. At Grand Canyon, where the sense of spaciousness is so important to the visitor's experience, the natural 200-mile visibility range is reduced on some days to 20–50 miles, thus obliterating the view of the opposite rim. In 1999, the Izaak Walton League noted that:

> National park ozone monitors recorded 209 days where the air violated the federal 8-hour ozone smog health standard, and many parks recorded higher concentrations of ozone smog than our densely populated metropolitan areas. This summer, Great Smoky Mountains National Park recorded 52 days where the air pollution levels violated the federal health standard, therefore making the air unhealthy to breathe on one out of every three summer days. In 1998, Shenandoah National Park recorded higher concentrations of ozone than any city in the Southeast except Atlanta, Ga., and Charlotte, N.C.[46]

Many sources of this air pollution have been implicated, but the largest sources are a) the older coal-burning power plants that are exempted from meeting Clean Air Act standards, b) vehicle exhaust, and c) pollution drifting from smelters and refineries.[47] Of perhaps even greater concern than the visible ozone haze in the parks is the invisible acid rain and toxic mercury pollution threatening many areas. As a means of combating the most serious source of park air pollution—haze-causing emissions from older, large power plants and other industrial facilities—the EPA published national park visibility guidelines in the federal register on July 20, 2001.[48] Known as the BART rule (Best Available Retrofit Technology), this proposed amendment to the Clean Air Act guides states and tribal air quality agencies in deciding which plants must install air pollution controls and the appropriate types of controls to install.

Energy Development

Politics and economic conditions cause flux in the nature and urgency of external threats. Nowhere can the influence of these forces be more vividly seen than in the case of energy development. Threats to the parks from mining and oil/gas exploration have increased in recent years as we have sought to develop domestic energy sources and strategic minerals that would reduce our dependence on foreign sources. Under President Carter, Secretary of the Interior Cecil Andrus halted strip mining proposed for the Alton coal field just 4 miles from Bryce National Park. Andrus based his ruling on the Clean Air Act, which requires preservation of scenic vistas, located outside of parks, which are important to visitor experiences within the parks. In Secretary Andrus's judgment, strip-mining near Bryce would have significantly harmed scenic vistas seen from the park. Under President Reagan, with his emphasis on national security and economic growth, Secretary James Watt refused to list such "integral vistas," attempted in the courts to reverse Andrus's ruling, and sought changes in the Clean Air Act to permit such mining. Noting that "Yellowstone is more precious than gold," the Clinton administration reached an agreement in 1999 with the Crown Butte Mining company to halt construction of the proposed New World Mine. Fearing that the acid-generating tailings from the underground gold, silver, and copper mine would negatively affect Yellowstone's water quality, wetlands, and wildlife, the federal government worked out a deal with Crown Butte for the purchase of their properties and interests in the New World Mining District. Urged forward by the Bush administration's proposed energy policy, energy shortages in California, and rising gasoline prices, Secretary of the Interior Gayle Norton supported the president's controversial plan for oil exploration in the Arctic National Wildlife Refuge. In the 107th Congress, the House supported the President's proposal, which was subsequently defeated by the Senate on two separate occasions (April 2002 and March 2003).[49] Along with the first negative vote on the president's proposal in 2002, the Senate voted to support a law that would prohibit oil and gas drilling in all national monuments.

Even Yellowstone's famed geysers have been threatened by applications for geothermal development leases in Known Geothermal Resource Areas (KGRAs) outside the park, such as the Island Park KGRA west of the park, and the Corwin Springs KGRA north of the park near LaDuke Hot Springs. Little is known about the subsurface connections between the Known Geothermal Resource Areas and Yellowstone, but fear of the potential harm to park geysers is heightened by knowledge that Yellowstone's thermal resources lie in what the experts consider to be the only undisturbed geyser basins left worldwide. Furthermore, more than 75 percent of the world's geysers, including the world's largest, are contained in seven major basins in Yellowstone.[50]

The aftermath of another, earlier effort to achieve energy independence threatened Canyonlands National Park in Utah. In the early 1980s, the Department of Energy, seeking disposal sites for radioactive wastes—which nobody wants—selected a site about 1 mile from the park as a possible alternative. In addition to fears related to radioactivity, opponents of the selection objected to a 30-mile railroad, to be built as part of the project, which could have been seen and heard from inside the park. In 2002, and with many expressing renewed enthusiasm for nuclear power, the U.S. Department of Energy, with support from the Bush administration, identified the Yucca Mountain site, 100 miles northwest of Las Vegas, Nevada, as a permanent repository for its nuclear wastes. Since the state of Nevada has sued the federal government in an attempt to halt the project, the location of America's nuclear waste storage is still uncertain.

In all these cases, despite the devil-baiting rhetoric that fills the air, we are faced with choices between goods, rather than between good and evil. The oil embargo of the 1970s and recent brown-outs and rolling black-outs in California are dramatic lessons in our national education about the importance of self-sufficiency and the perils of over-consumption. As the Persian Gulf War demonstrated, the world is so full of hostility and supply lines are so readily interrupted that we would be foolish to rely too heavily on foreign sources of critical resources. Most people may agree with this general sentiment, but when it comes to deciding how much we are willing to pay for such security in the form of damaged park resources, consensus dissolves and we are left hurling insults and nonnegotiable demands at each other across a widening free-fire zone.[51]

Water Development

External threats to the parks that are justified by appeals to national security are possibly the most dramatic instances of the venerable preservation/development conflict, but other threats are equally significant. One of the most familiar external threats to the parks is found at Everglades National Park.[52] Water development projects built since 1890 north of the park have controlled flooding, thus permitting the use of former wetlands for housing and agriculture. However, these engineering accomplishments have also interrupted the southward flow of water that is the lifeblood of this unique natural area. Ecologists have for years warned of the massive ecological disruptions the water diversions are causing. Populations of some wading bird species are reported to have been reduced by 90 percent in the last half-century. Fish populations in the Kissimmee River basin and in Florida Bay have been markedly reduced.

Now, Florida and the federal government have begun a long-term effort to "decivilize" South Florida water resources. Starting in 1985, three new dams on the Kissimmee River directed water back into the old, twisting river channel, and thus began the process of restoring more natural water levels and associated wetlands. In addition, the South Florida Water Management District restored natural water levels on a 60,000-acre tract of the Everglades that had been overdrained. However, the most dramatic and comprehensive set of actions to restore natural water flows to the "Sea of Grass" has just begun. Near the end of his second term of office, President Clinton signed the Water Resources Development Act of 2000, a strongly bipartisan law, which was also endorsed by Florida Governor, Jeb Bush.[53] This act authorized $1.4 billion for specific federal-state cooperative restoration projects. The total cost of the project, to be authorized in future acts, will be approximately $8 billion. The U.S. Army Corps of Engineers will lead the project, which will take 30 years and involve removal of manmade structures that have obstructed natural water flows, construction of facilities to recycle wastewater, and storage areas to hold freshwater that now flows unused into the ocean. Clinton's Secretary of Interior, Bruce Babbitt, called it "the largest environmental restoration project ever."

Florida's dramatic action can be attributed to other factors in addition to growing ecological awareness. Although agriculture remains one of the dominant economic activities in South Florida, growing tourism and a burgeoning permanent population have forced reconsideration of historic land use patterns. South Florida's future depends heavily on the freshwater available in the Biscayne Aquifer, and as surface drainage has proceeded, increasing concern has arisen over the aquifer's recharge system. In addition to concerns about fresh water, there is growing realization that the quality of the natural environment is important to Florida's future attractiveness for both tourism and permanent economic development.

Wildlife

As at Everglades, many of the threats to park and wilderness areas involve wildlife. Nowhere is the issue more starkly portrayed than in the case of Yellowstone's grizzlies.[54] Abundant wildlife, and the presence of large animals like elk, bison, and bear, were important factors in Yellowstone's establishment in 1872. The grizzly bear is arguably the most important symbol of America's wildlands. Yet grizzly management has been greatly troubled for decades. One particular source of difficulty stems from the fact that Yellowstone National Park's boundaries do not conform to the bears' natural range, or to their range as altered by human activity within the park.[5]

In 1962, following intensive public outcry over Park Service efforts to reduce the Yellowstone elk population, Secretary of the Interior Stuart Udall established a committee to evaluate the overall game-management program of the National Park Service. Chairing the committee was Professor of Zoology Starker Leopold, Aldo Leopold's son. The Leopold report, issued in 1963, recommended a policy goal of creating "a reasonable illusion of primitive America." According to park historian Richard Sellars, the Leopold report did not focus in detail on bear management, thus leaving it open-ended as to the better approach: manipulation or natural regulation.[56] Internationally recognized wildlife researchers John and Frank Craighead argued for a gradual closing of the dumps, but prompted by grizzlies' killing two women in Glacier in 1967, the superintendent opted for a quick closure, thinking visitors would be safer that way. The rapid closure was a prime example, according to Sellars, of how the NPS made a key management decision in contradiction to prevailing scientific opinion and with little scientific evidence of its own. The decision also exemplifies why we argue (Chapter 2) that knowledge of the policy process is critical. The Department of the Interior and the National Park Service adopted the recommendation as policy, and bear-feeding programs that had been in place since 1897 were stopped.[57] As food provided by humans was removed, hungry bears wandered outside park boundaries in search of food. In some cases these far-ranging animals turned up 75 miles from the park. Where bears moving beyond the park boundaries once found wild areas, they now found civilization and trouble. Ranchers, shepherds, hunters, and poachers killed the bears. The Craigheads estimated that since the garbage dumps were closed, the number of grizzlies killed outside park boundaries rose to two and one-half times its previous level.[58]

As in so many of the natural resource management problems, the lack of decisive scientific information increased delay and controversy over Yellowstone bear management.[59] Opponents of the anti-feeding policy claimed that it decimated the bear population and forced bears to search for food and, in the process, to find trouble. Scientists learned that, after the sudden closures, the size of bear home ranges increased, while body size, reproductive rates, and average litter size decreased.[60] Supporters of the policy contended that it worked and that a natural grizzly population would be reached. Even with the numbers that were slain, the grizzlies survived but the margin of error was so small that by 1975, the grizzly bear was listed as a threatened species pursuant to the Endangered Species Act. Referring to grizzly bear policy in the early '70s, Sellars concludes:

> In the push toward natural regulation and in a concern for safety, the Park Service had been in a sudden hurry with grizzly bear management. It seemed compelled to change a feeding policy that had existed for nearly a century, during which time it had had ample opportunity to conduct its own research on the bears but had neglected to do so.[61]

In 1973, the Interagency Grizzly Bear Study Team was created to conduct research needed by various agencies for immediate and long-term management of the grizzly bears in the Greater Yellowstone Area.[62] The study team included biologists from the Park Service, the U.S. Fish and Wildlife Service, the U.S. Forest Service, and the state governments of Wyoming, Idaho, and Montana. The team evaluated the bears' critical habitat, which included expansive tracts of land outside the boundaries and Yellowstone National Park, and developed a "recovery plan." Despite early losses in the 1980s,[63] the grizzly bear population in the Greater Yellowstone Ecosystem is now estimated to be anywhere from 300 to 600.[64] While removing the bear from the threatened list appears to be several years away, the study team is preparing a conservation strategy that will guide management of grizzlies when they are de-listed.[65] Thus, the assumption is that grizzly bear recovery is imminent.

> . . . the Craighead studies and the grizzly bear controversy helped spawn a coordinated approach to management of this species by federal and state agencies.[66]

In the case of the Yellowstone grizzlies, coordinated management coupled with a good deal of persistence seems to have paid off.

MANAGEMENT ISSUES INVOLVING INTERNAL THREATS

At the same time wildland recreation managers attempt to counter external threats to their lands, they must respond to internal threats—as suggested by the catch-phrase, "we are loving our parks [and wilderness areas] to death." There is ample evidence that wildland resources and the recreation experiences they provide are changing as a result of increasing visitation. However, moving from that statement to the simple conclusion that there are too many people is fraught with difficult policy questions.[67]

Responses to Use Pressures

Wildland recreation participation has grown rapidly in the past, and it continues to grow. Overall, recreational use of federal park and forest lands rose at a rate of nearly 10 percent per year in the years between 1910 and 1960. Except for drops during World War II, which affected both agencies, and reduced use of the national parks during the oil crises of the 1970s, the overall growth in national park and forest recreation has been strong and remarkably constant.[68]

Management personnel and budgets have not kept pace with visitation. Not only have the agencies had to accommodate more recreation visitors, but also they have been given new responsibilities. The National Park System was greatly expanded in the 1970s omnibus park acts and with numerous additions since then, and the Forest Service was directed to lead a nationwide renewable resource planning effort. Thus, neither agency has been well positioned to respond to the growing recreational use of their lands.

Any human use changes wildland areas in some way. The difficulty lies in defining exactly how much change is acceptable. The recent combination of increased visitation and stable or shrinking managerial resources has brought changes many now consider unacceptable. On the positive side, it has forced innovations and collaboration. For example, natural resource institutions are increasing the supply of accessible natural areas near where people live by restoring wetlands and other areas that have been inaccessible for some time due to pollution.[69] Often these areas have multiple owners, thus demanding the creation of partnerships. Some of these areas, for example the area surrounding Chicago (described as the "Chicago Wilderness" in Chapter 9), will be quite large when they are completely restored. However, given recent budget cuts and an uncertain economy, one nagging question remains: are wildland recreation management problems perceived to be serious enough to warrant measures to provide more funding and efforts to enhance the professional status of wildland recreation management? The funding issue will be taken up in detail in the following chapter and professionalism will be addressed in the concluding chapter. For now, we want to focus on some of the more pressing internal challenges that wildland recreation managers face.

In examining the internal challenges, it must be borne in mind that the definitions of "impact" and "threat" vary a great deal socio-culturally and according to management objectives. Since naturalness is a continuum,[70] what constitutes a threat—and the appropriate management responses—will vary from one end of the continuum to the other.[71] Furthermore, the impacts of recreation use should be evaluated in relation to other types of impacts. For example, in wilderness areas, the authors of a well-known text point out that far greater threats to the ecological functioning of the wilderness come from acid rain, fire suppression, and livestock grazing than from recreational use.[72]

There are hundreds of particular management issues that are internal to park and wilderness areas. Broadly speaking, there are management issues pertaining to resources and to visitors' experiences. Resource-related issues can be broken down into those involving natural and cultural resources. A definitive discussion of each category of internal issues is beyond the scope of this book, but a few examples will illustrate them.[73] Some of these issues, though not all, result from increasing visitation. Most, though certainly not all, could be solved if there were enough information, funds, labor and—most importantly—consensus on management objectives.

Damage to Vegetation and Soils

Soil condition and vegetative health are interrelated. Direct vegetation impacts include abrasion, breakage, loss of species diversity, and loss of vegetative cover. Soil impacts caused by recreational use include loss of leaf litter and humus layers, compaction, increased surface water runoff, and erosion.[74] These impacts, in turn, affect the health and composition of the remaining vegetation.

The extent of these impacts depends on many factors, including type of recreation activity, slope, and soil type. For example, camping and picnicking in areas with fine-textured soils and soils with low organic matter create the most soil compaction. Soil compaction, in turn, places stress on vegetation as the flow of air and water and the movement of nutrients to plants' roots are reduced.[75] Many wildland recreation areas are on land that was passed over for agriculture. These areas often have thin and infertile soils that cannot tolerate much use without loss of vegetative cover. Researchers in the Eagle Cap Wilderness (Oregon) have estimated that as much as 90 percent of the ground cover, up to 2000 square feet, was destroyed in the typical campsite; half the site, the area immediately around the fire ring, was completely devoid of vegetation.[76] Numerous studies confirm that even on lightly used sites in fragile areas, loss of vegetation cover can be nearly as great as the loss on heavily used sites.[77] In some extreme environments, such as those found above timberline in Rocky Mountain National Park, even occasional walking causes lasting damage to alpine vegetation. Unstable barrier islands depend on the binding power of dune grass root systems, and these are quickly destroyed by pedestrian or vehicular use.

Some plants are more resistant to trampling than others primarily due to two factors: (a) reduced competition as the less-trample resistant species die out quickly in heavily used areas, and (b) favorable changes in microclimate (e.g., more light penetration). Thus, it is possible to see a decrease followed by an increase in ground cover as a result of recreation use, but this increase is usually also accompanied by a decline in species diversity. In campsites in Pennsylvania, as human disturbance increased, trampling-sensitive native species decreased while non-native species that were trampling-resistant increased. A plant community developed with a different composition than originally existed. And, even with the increase in trampling-resistant species, the total amount of cover remained reduced by almost one-third.[78]

Wildlife

Wildlife populations in park and wilderness areas are often adversely affected by recreational use.[79] One of the most dramatic cases, once again, is that of the grizzly bears.[80] In the long run unlimited numbers of people and bears cannot coexist in the same territory. If we want to maintain grizzly populations, human use of grizzly territory must be restricted.[81] This includes closure of roads and restrictions on new road construction. Such constraint on human activity is not widely popular.

Wildlife, particularly non-native species, is sometimes the direct cause of the impact. In Grand Canyon National Park, wild burros descended from prospectors' pack animals have for years damaged the natural environment. Early Park Service efforts to eradicate the burros led to a major political and legal battle with animal rights advocates.[82] In Great Smoky Mountains National Park, feral pig populations have caused environmental problems and tied the Park Service into controversy over methods of controlling them. In the same park and in Yellowstone, introduced species of fish have replaced or are threatening native species in streams and lakes.[83] Managers have implemented various methods for addressing these wildlife-related threats, such as the eradication of non-native species of fish, but often mitigation has been limited primarily to studying the problem while insufficient funding and staffing hamper complete resolution of the threat.[84]

Exotics are not confined to wildlife. Non-native plant species have also invaded many wildland recreation areas. Depending on management objectives, such species may be more resistant to trampling than native species, and thus encouraged or left to take their own course. In other cases, agencies and organizations devote tremendous resources annually to the eradication of exotic plants. Common sources of exotic plants where horseback use is prevalent are seeds—in horse manure or feed or stuck to horses' bodies.[85] In other areas, ornamentals planted by homeowners (e.g., purple loosestrife) or fencerows created by farmers (e.g., European buckthorn) have spread on their own or due to birds' droppings.

Cultural Resources

Cultural resources are also changed by recreation visitation. One of the most poignant cases involves the ancient Indian cultural remnants in the Southwest. There, while Mesa Verde and other areas are protected by the National Park Service, Indian dwellings, artwork, and artifacts on nearby public domain land have been looted and vandalized. The Bureau of Land Management is simply spread too thin to stop much of this destruction.[86] Even at Mesa Verde, the Park Service is challenged to retain a degree of historical authenticity while encouraging over 630,000 visitors each year to develop a sense of the ancient Anasazi culture through close contact with their traces.

Furthermore, the American Indian Religious Freedom Act directs agencies to protect the "inherent and constitutional right" of indigenous peoples to exercise their traditional religions. This law mandates that agencies go beyond protecting artifacts, burial sites, and ancient villages to allowing Native Americans to carry out religious activities in parks, forests, and wilderness areas. For example, the Sioux Indians consider the dramatic mountain peak in Devil's Tower National Monument to be a sacred site, thus making current mountain climbing activities inappropriate. The mountain climbers disagree and National Park managers face the difficult task of trying to appease both sides.[87] The irony is that much of the land that Indians want access to or would like to see protected formerly was the land that sustained them.[88] Much of this land is managed by federal agencies (Forest Service, Park Service, Bureau of Reclamation,

Army Corps of Engineers). In forgoing their rights to occupy these lands, native tribes signed treaties and other agreements guaranteeing that their former landscapes would be managed in trust for them by the federal government. In the case of protecting cultural resources, the tribes are being more assertive in holding the government to its obligations.

Threats to Visitor Experiences

At the same time that increasing wildland recreation participation harms natural and cultural resources, it also leads to crowding and conflicts between recreationists. An intractable question facing park and wilderness managers is "how many visitors is too many?"[89] Managers of all kinds of areas ask the question, but it has been of especially great concern to wilderness managers. The Wilderness Act states that wilderness should provide "outstanding opportunities for solitude," but there is a wide gulf between that phrase and a decision to allow only a specific number of people into an area. A considerable body of research has addressed the question of visitor preferences.[90] One goal has been to find out from the visitors what they see as the limits of human contact. Unfortunately for those seeking neat, technically clean answers, visitors vary in their tolerances for encountering others, and if sample surveys are confined to users, those who have abandoned areas they think are too crowded may not be heard from.[91]

The sheer number of visitors is one source of people problems, but not the only source. Even more troublesome, possibly, are incompatible uses. Conflicts between mechanized and nonmechanized forms of recreation — motorboating vs. canoeing, snowmobiling vs. cross-country skiing, trail biking vs. hiking — are traditional and well-documented sources of wildland recreation management headaches. Well-known though they may be, they are not the only incompatibilities found in the great outdoors. Canoeists and scuba divers annoy anglers, hikers dislike following horse pack trains, solo campers and small groups do not enjoy meeting large groups, skilled waterfowl hunters avoid skyblasters, snowboarders clash with downhill skiers, mountain bikers compete with hikers and horseback users, and in-line skaters and skateboarders irritate walkers, runners, and bikers. This list could be extended to great length without changing the basic message: people seek different things in wildland areas, and they vary in their definitions of acceptable behavior on the part of other recreationists. Our parks and wilderness areas are cultural creations in the first place,[92] and conflicts between recreationists using them represent an extension of the process of deciding what they are and should be.

Inholdings

Just as parks and wildernesses are threatened by activities on adjoining lands, so are they threatened by inholdings. Inholdings are an especially serious concern in the National Park System. Many national parks and forests include within their boundaries land owned by private individuals, corporations, and units of government other than the Park Service. While this is the norm in the new greenline parks, inholdings are also widespread in the large, old nature parks. Under Mather, Park Service policy called for purchase of inholdings as rapidly as possible. With the shift in new park creation from setting aside parcels of federal land to acquiring private land, more varied methods were employed to control undesirable land uses within park boundaries, but this new policy applied only to parks acquired after 1959. Earlier parks were still supposed to purchase inholdings as funding permitted or to accept donations. In 1979 a new Park Service policy specified that inholdings in pre-1959 parks were to be acquired only from willing sellers, unless condemnation was necessary to thwart incompatible use. A combination of increased political strength on the part of inholders (who now have their own national lobbying organization) and inadequate congressional authorizations for land acquisition have led to the present backlog of 1.7 million acres of private land at an estimated cost of $1.4 billion.[93] There are a number of concerns associated with this huge backlog. Two of the most important are the uncertainty of many inholders, who expect to be bought out, and the accelerating costs of the land. In *Battling for the National Parks,* former director George Hartzog reminds us that President Reagan refused to request appropriations from the Land and Water Conservation Fund to purchase these inholdings. For this reason, Hartzog notes that there is no current estimate of the cost, but that it may have exceeded $2 billion in 1988.

CONCLUSIONS

Examples such as the decivilizing efforts at Yosemite, guidelines aimed at reducing air pollution and increasing visibility at Grand Canyon and Great Smoky Mountains, restoration of the Everglades, grizzly bear recovery, and restricting visitor behaviors to control recreation impacts are evidence that progress has been and continues to be made to reduce both external and internal threats. Although it may not seem so at the time, persistence, a long-range vision, and an understanding of how the policy process works can pay big dividends in the end. The process of forging new policy is messy and fraught with challenges and delays, but it is necessary in order to achieve the elusive consensus about the appropriate uses (or non-uses) of our wildland recreation estate.

Management plays a pivotal role in this process. Managers determine the nature and the extent of the outcomes of broader policies and rules that are handed down to them. They make their own policies and they attempt to implement plans in the social and political contexts of the times. Their decisions are not cast in stone. Social, political, and cultural contexts change and have profound influence on the decisions that managers make even though many of the issues remain the same. Unhappy parties sue and threaten to sue and the courts overturn, clarify, or revise management decisions. Policies change and managers again attempt to implement them. The cycle that we outlined in Chapter 2 continues. What is new is that managers are being increasingly brought under public scrutiny, required or self-motivated to broaden the public discourse to include underrepresented groups, and forced or self-motivated to forge partnerships with diverse organizations in order to make up for shortfalls in appropriated funds and garner a broad base of public support. We illustrate how managers are going about these tasks in the next chapter with a number of true stories and updates on some of the well-known frameworks and tools that managers use to implement policies.

In lieu of legal remedies, managers of wildland recreation resources have tended to rely on less-than-full-fee options and collaborative approaches to minimize the impact of external threats on park resources. Collaboration has its own set of drawbacks, which we will discuss in the closing chapter, but for now it is sufficient to point out that regardless of which approach is used (legal or collaborative), a key component is now often inadequate. Managers know far less than they need to know about the ecological and social impacts adjoining activities have on their park, forest, and wilderness areas. Recent advances in Geographic Information Systems have helped managers, organizations, and individuals organize what knowledge they have and visualize some of these impacts. Nonetheless, research has been severely underfunded, particularly in the National Park Service, with the result that decisions must often be made on the basis of weak scientific information.[94] Of the over 4,000 specific threats identified in the Service's 1980 report, 75 percent lacked sufficient documentation to support action. Nor is this situation likely to improve under prevailing thinking as only a tiny fraction of the Service's budget is allocated to research.

NOTES

1. Wilderness Society, "Year 2000: The Best for Land Protection in 20 Years," 21 pp. (www.wilderness.org).
2. Nonetheless, the Bush administration's FY 2003 budget includes an increase to the Land and Water Conservation Fund, which is designated for park and open space acquisition and development at all levels of government (see discussion in next chapter). The Bush administration seems to prefer this method of acquisition, which involves a lengthy application and review process, as opposed to acquisition by Presidential decree.
3. Cronon, *Uncommon Ground: Toward Reinventing Nature.*
4. Conservation Foundation, *National Parks for a New Generation,* p. 241.
5. National Parks Conservation Association, "National Parks: The Next Generation," *National Parks Magazine,* Sept./Oct. 2000 online at *www.npca.org/magazine* and "Parks in the 21st Century Initiative" online at *http://www.npca.org/explore_the_parks/new_parks/* (accessed 6/13/02).
6. Runte, *National Parks: The American Experience,* p. 178.
7. Ibid., pp. 178–179.
8. Fox, *John Muir and His Legacy,* p. 14.
9. Runte, *National Parks: The American Experience,* pp. 158–159.
10. Foresta, *America's National Parks and Their Keepers;* Conservation Foundation, *National Parks for a New Generation;* Runte, *National Parks: The American Experience.*
11. Duddleson, "National Parks are Beset by Policy Problems"; Sellars, *Preserving Nature in the National Parks,* p. 208; Runte, *National Parks,* pp. 176–177.
12. Conservation Foundation, *National Parks for a New Generation,* p. 173.
13. National Park Service, "Yosemite National Park: History and Summary," p. 1.
14. Hope, "Hassles in the park."
15. Avoidance of societal conflict is not necessarily the norm in the National Park Service; in fact, conflict is sometimes encouraged. For example, park staff at Little Bighorn National Monument (Montana) facilitates the confrontation

between White and Native American cultures by welcoming sit-ins by Native American activists and by hiring Native American interpreters that offer visitors a less than flattering perspective of General George Armstrong Custer. The name change from Custer Battlefield National Monument to Little Bighorn National Monument was itself controversial and angered Custer buffs. In an interview, a historian at Little Bighorn said that it was the National Park Service's duty to foster cross-cultural learning by providing all sides of the story of Custer's last stand.

16. National Park Service, "Yosemite National Park: History and Summary," pp. 1–2.

17. Yellowstone Act of 1872 as described in Ise, *Our National Park Policy,* pp. 18–19, 29 and Quinn, "Recreation service enterprises on public lands," pp. 11–12.

18. Shankland, *Steve Mather of the National Parks,* p. 117.

19. Everhart, *The National Park Service,* pp. 114–115.

20. Duddleson, "National Parks are Beset by Policy Problems," pp. 12–14.

21. Personal communication with Destry Jarvis, formerly with the National Parks Conservation Association and now with the National Park Service.

22. Information on the visitor survey was supplied by Yosemite National Park.

23. While it is important that the Park Service know something of Yosemite visitors' preferences, it cannot base future planning entirely on them. As a general rule, people like the familiar; a prominent social psychologist, Robert Zajonc, once expressed this idea by rephrasing the well known saying "familiarity breeds contempt" to read "familiarity breeds content." If this saying is true at Yosemite, these visitors may only represent the status quo and not those who had already been displaced to more secluded parts of the park or different places altogether.

24. National Park Service, "Briefing Statement."

25. We are indebted to John Reynolds, NPS regional director of the Pacific Southwest Region, for this insight as well as information pertaining to the events that transpired between the 1980 Yosemite Plan and the present. Mr. Reynolds was Yosemite Plan team captain from 1975 to 1979 and has held numerous administrative and planning positions since, including Deputy Director of the NPS.

26. Final Yosemite Valley Plan and Supplemental Environmental Impact Statement, online at *www.nps.gov/yose/planning/yvp/seis/vol_1a/chapter_1.html,* accessed 6/13/02.

27. Personal communications, John Reynolds, May 2001.

28. Personal communications with John Reynolds; according to Mr. Reynolds, this figure jumps to $150 million if one includes all the sewer, water, and electrical enhancements made in the Valley and in El Portal (a) to prepare for the movement of the administrative and maintenance functions, (b) to

make the necessary infrastructure repairs needed to maintain some facilities in the valley, and (c) to increase energy efficiency.

29. Ibid.

30. Ibid. In the early 1990s, the main Yosemite concessionaire for many years, Music Corporation of America, was sold to the Japanese company, Matsushta, which in turn donated the concession to the National Park Foundation. The National Park Foundation is a congressionally chartered nonprofit foundation created for the purpose of raising private or other non-appropriated funds for the NPS. Since the National Park Foundation is not chartered to operate as a concessionaire, this donation provided the NPS the opportunity to negotiate a new contract for concession services. The new contract with Yosemite Concession Services reduces the number of concession-operated lodging units in the valley.

31. NPS, "List of projects for June 2002 open house," online at *www.nps.gov.yose/planning/openhouse/projects.htm*, accessed 6/12/02.

32. Final Yosemite Valley Plan and Supplemental Environmental Impact Statement, online at *www.nps.gov/yose/planning/yvp/seis/vol_1a/chapter_1.html*, accessed 6/13/02.

33. Personal communications with John Reynolds.

34. Eric Brazil, San Francisco Examiner, Nov. 15, 2000, "Babbitt unveils final Yosemite plan."

35. Yosemite National Park planning documents, online at *www.nps.gov/yose/planning/yvp/*, accessed 6/13/02.

36. There is already a precedent for such a system. To alleviate the problems associated with vehicular traffic in the park, the town of Springdale, Utah, recently implemented a shuttle bus transportation system for Zion National Park. The system uses environmentally friendly propane-powered busses to transport visitors from the town or from Zion's visitor center to the heretofore congested and polluted Zion Canyon (2/14/01 — "Utah town receives national park conservation award"; accessed online 2/16/01, *www.us-newswire.com/topnews/Current_Releases*).

37. Secretary of Interior Babbitt, *www.CNN.com*, Nov. 15, 2000.

38. "Record of Decision Signed for Final Yosemite Valley Plan", *www.nps.gov/yose/news_01/fyvp0102.thm*, accessed 1/16/01.

39. Email from John Reynolds, dated May 29, 2001.

40. Ibid.

41. National Park Service, "State of the Parks."

42. Biosphere reserves are dedicated to long-term ecological monitoring under the United Nations Education, Scientific and Cultural Organization's Man and the Biosphere Program.

43. U.S. General Accounting Office, "Activities outside park borders have caused damage to resources and will likely cause more" (1994); "Activities

within park borders have caused damage to resources" (1996); "Park Service needs better information to preserve and protect resources" (1997). For an insightful, readable review of the wide range of threats to Great Smoky Mountains National Park, one of the most diverse biological reserves and one of the most endangered, see Margaret Brown's *The Wild East: A Biography of the Great Smoky Mountains,* 2000, Gainesville, FL: University Press of Florida.

44. Burton, "Clear and Present Dangers." Representative Burton requested the Park Service survey and based the article on the NPS findings.

45. U.S. Environmental Protection Agency. "Whitman signs proposal to improve visibility in national parks," Press Release, June 22, 2001; Daniel B. Wood. "As visitors flock to parks, pollution comes with them." Accessed online at *www.csmonitor.com/durable/2001/07/06/p4s1.htm.*

46. Izaak Walton League, "Air Pollution in Our Parks: 1999", *http://www.iwla.org/reports/parktext.html;* accessed 7/9/01.

47. Ibid.; Wood, "As visitors flock to parks, pollution comes with them."

48. U.S. Environmental Protection Agency, "Whitman signs proposal to improve visibility in national parks," Press Release, June 22, 2001; U.S. Newswire, "BART Guidelines Published; NPCA Calls for Strong Rule to Protect Air in National Parks," *www.usnewswire.com/topnews/Current_Releases/0720–124.html,* accessed 7/23/01. A 60-day public comment period on the new ruling ensued.

49. The second negative vote in March of 2003 was a bit surprising given that (a) due to the interim Congressional elections in 2002, the Senate majority switched from Democrat to Republican, (b) instead of a separate proposal, the Bush administration attached the ANWR oil exploration proposal to the FY 2004 budget resolution (the Senate vote was to strike the language from the 2004 budget bill), and (c) this vote occurred on March 19, one day before the U.S. entered its second war with Iraq. It appears that for now at least, there is substantial bipartisan rejection of plans to explore for oil in the ANWR.

50. Yellowstone National Park, "Geothermal Resources," *www.nps.gov/yell/nature/geothermal/ycr,* accessed 7/20/01.

51. Susskind and Weinstein, "Towards a Theory of Environmental Dispute Resolution."

52. Graham, "Erasing Man's Mark in the Everglades."

53. U.S. Army Corps of Engineers and South Florida Water Management District, "Water Resources Development Act of 2000," *www.evergladesplan.org/wrda2000,* accessed 7/20/01.

54. Chase, "The Last Bears of Yellowstone"; Chase, *Playing God in Yellowstone;* The reintroduction of the gray wolf into Yellowstone National Park is also a precedent-setting restoration story. As of the summer of 2001, there were about 165 wolves inhabiting the Greater Yellowstone region, the result

of the release of 14 and 16 wolves in 1995 and 1996 respectively into Yellowstone National Park. There are 12–13 packs, 8 of which inhabit areas within park boundaries. For background see: Bangs and Fritts, "Reintroducing the gray wolf to central Idaho and Yellowstone National Park," and Fischer, *Wolf Wars;* For current information, see *www.yellowstonepark.com/news/wolves* and *www.wolftracker.com.*

55. The essential problem is that due to development around the parks, many now exist essentially as islands too small to support populations of the animals they were created to protect. Good support is found in Gleick, "National Parks Becoming Morgues for Many Mammals"; Foreman, "Islands of Doom"; and Zube, "No Park is an Island." For discussions of human influences on wildlife within park boundaries, see Knight and Gutzwiller, *Wildlife and Recreationists: Coexistence through Management and Research;* Hammitt and Cole, *Wildland Recreation: Ecology and Management;* and Sellars, *Preserving Nature in the National Parks.*

56. Sellars, *Preserving Nature in the National Parks,* p. 250.

57. Ise, *Our National Park Policy,* p. 26.

58. At the time of the closure of the dumps, the Craigheads estimated that the grizzly population in Yellowstone was less than 200. During the first 2 years after closure, about 88 grizzlies were killed in or near Yellowstone, mostly because of human safety.

59. Sellars, *Preserving Nature in the National Parks,* pp. 249–253.

60. Despain, D., Houston, D., Meagher, M., and Schullery, P. 1986. *Wildlife in Transition: Man and Nature on Yellowstone's Northern Range.* Boulder, CO: Roberts Rinehart.

61. Sellars, *Preserving Nature in the National Parks,* p. 253; however, for a different perspective on the Interagency Grizzly Bear Study Team and the propensity of the NPS to select only scientific findings that support its position while ignoring or suppressing contradictory evidence, see Wagner et al., *Wildlife Policies in the U.S. National Parks,* pp. 102–103.

62. Further information about the IGBST's research can be found at http://www.mesc.usgs.gov/yellowstone/IGBST-home.htm.

63. According to Wagner et al., *Wildlife Policies in the U.S. National Parks* (pp. 65–66), the grizzly population had declined in 1980 by more than 40 percent, and throughout the 1980s and early 1990s, the grizzly bear population appeared to stabilize (neither decreased nor increased).

64. Glover and Johnson, "Grizzlies had excellent 1996, and this year looks like it may even be better," *www.yellowstonepark.com/this_issue/grizzlies.html,* accessed 7/21/01; Craighead Environmental Research Institute, "North American Grizzly Population Sizes," *www.grizzlybear.org/grizpop.htm,* accessed 7/21/01.

65. U.S. Forest Service, *www.fs.fed.us/r1/wildlife/igbc/Griz_Tracks/Tracks.htm#yes,* accessed 7/21/01.

66. Sellars, *Preserving Nature in the National Parks,* p. 253.

67. More, "The Parks are Being Loved to Death and Other Frauds and Deceits in Recreation Management," argues that the notion that our parks are being loved to death is a myth. Others disagree and their rejoinders and attempted clarifications of More's assertions take up most of the entire Volume 34, Number 1, 2002 issue of the *Journal of Leisure Research.*

68. Clawson, *The Federal Lands Revisited,* pp. 100–103; Cordell, *Outdoor Recreation in American Life;* Cordell and Super, "Trends in Americans' Outdoor Recreation."

69. See Gobster and Hull (eds.), *Restoring Nature,* for recent examples.

70. Brunson, "Managing naturalness as a continuum . . ."; Cronon, "Getting back to the wrong nature."

71. For example, Hendee et al. (*Wilderness Management,* p. 426) note that in wilderness management, the key is to try to render "the imprint of man's work substantially unnoticeable, which implies tolerating some recreation impact, but to prevent the type of damage that disrupts the functioning of entire ecosystems over relatively large areas, especially those that contain rare species and associations among species." Irreversible impacts are most undesirable. However, at the more urban end of the wildland recreation spectrum, the emphasis is not as much on ecosystem integrity (though this is also in a state of flux — e.g., see Gobster and Hull, *Restoring Nature*), but on minimizing the impacts that recreational use has on vegetation, soils, water pollution, litter, etc. And, the attempt is not to try to make human impacts inconspicuous, but to "harden" sites so that they can handle larger numbers of recreational users and simultaneously sustain groundcover, trees, and whatever wildlife remains.

72. Hendee et al., *Wilderness Management,* p. 426

73. Interested readers should refer to Sharpe, Odegard, and Sharpe, *Park Management;* Hammitt and Cole, *Wildland Recreation: Ecology and Management;* Knight and Gutzwiller, *Wildlife and Recreationists;* and Manning, *Studies in Outdoor Recreation,* for detailed discussion on other internal threats. Specific to national parks, see GAO Report GAO/RCED-96-02, "Activities within park borders have caused damage to resources."

74. Hammitt and Cole, *Wildland Recreation Ecology and Management,* pp. 35–52.; Hendee et al., *Wilderness Management,* 2nd edition, pp. 426–439.

75. Hammitt and Cole, p. 44.

76. Hendee et al., 2nd edition, p. 437.

77. Hammitt and Cole, p. 62.

78. Ibid., pp. 63–65.

79. Hendee et al., *Wilderness Management,* note that with but three exceptions, recreation use generally has not disrupted the integrity of large wilderness ecosystems. One of these exceptions is the disturbance of wildlife due to habitat destruction and harassment (p. 426).

80. Also see Knight and Gutzwiller, *Wildlife and Recreationists,* for other dramatic examples, such as Florida manatee deaths and injuries due to recreational boating.

81. Allin, *The Politics of Wilderness Preservation,* pp. 102–104.

82. Ibid., p. 105.

83. The same has been observed in wilderness areas; see Hendee et al., *Wilderness Management,* p. 426.

84. GAO Report GAO/RCED-96-02, "Activities within park borders have caused damage to resources," p. 19.

85. Hammitt and Cole, *Wildland Recreation Ecology and Management,* p. 185.

86. Foresta, *America's National Parks and Their Keepers,* p. 62.

87. Personal interview, Deborah Bird, Superintendent, Devil's Tower National Monument, June 24, 1993.

88. Rudzitis, *Wilderness and the Changing American West,* p. 66; Burnham, *Indian Country, God's Country,* pp. 9–58.

89. We address the issue of defining carrying capacity at great length in the next chapter.

90. See Manning, *Studies in Outdoor Recreation,* 2nd edition, for a thorough and recent summary.

91. Manning, *Studies in Outdoor Recreation,* pp. 95–97, cites studies that both confirm and disconfirm this "displacement" hypothesis. Depending on the circumstance, those who feel crowded may engage in other behaviors, such as intrasite or temporal displacement, in lieu of abandoning their favorite area altogether.

92. Cronon, *Uncommon Ground: Toward Reinventing Nature,* provides ample examples and support for this important premise.

93. National Parks Conservation Association, "Private lands, public challenge: NPS continues its push to buy private land to protect parks."

94. This is the main theme of Sellars's book, *Preserving Nature in the National Parks,* and a conclusion reached by Wagner et al., *Wildlife Policies in the U.S. National Parks.*

CHAPTER 11

MANAGEMENT: REALITIES OF POLICY IMPLEMENTATION

Public wildland recreation managers are an integral component of the policy system. Managers implement the policies crafted by the interplay of legislative, executive, and judicial decisions. Managers are expected to translate these policies into actions that affect the resources and the publics interested in those resources. They must implement specific policy directives, assure compliance with others, and help craft new policies. Policy directives are frequently—and appropriately—somewhat vague, and managers must fine-tune them to meet local conditions. All the while, they must communicate effectively with other agencies and with various publics, since misinformation can throw the best laid plans into turmoil. And, as they identify problems with the policy, they need to provide feedback to agency leadership so that improvements can be made.

The give-and-take of the policy process is vital to democracy. It makes the manager's job frustrating at times, but also dynamic and interesting. Depending on one's perspective, the job of policy implementation can be energizing, rewarding, demanding, overwhelming, humbling, or stifling. At different times and in different situations, it is all these things. But the really good managers have a sound philosophy about their role in the provision of public goods and safeguarding the nation's biological and cultural heritage. They understand their role in the policy process and how to use the process to achieve shared visions regarding the future of wildland recreation resources.

POLICY-MANAGEMENT INTERACTIONS

In a 1986 *Journal of Forestry* article, Gerald Allen and Ernest Gould provided a helpful discussion of the kinds of problems facing forest managers.[1] The points they raised apply well to wildland recreation management. Allen and Gould explain that traditional forestry is comfortable handling complex problems like designing an optimal approach to harvesting the timber on a forest. However, the most serious problems are not such complex problems, but "wicked" ones. Wicked problems have no single correct formulation, only more or less useful ones; they tend to be unique, so there is little chance for trial-and-error learning; there is no stopping point at which we know that all possible solutions have been tried; and they involve high stakes with little room for managerial error.

Attacking wicked problems with traditional problem-solving approaches often leads to trouble. Instead, wicked problems must be approached innovatively and on a case-by-case basis. Allen and Gould's concluding comment is particularly germane for this discussion of wildland recreation management.

> People are the key—People are what make problems wicked, and people
> are the ones who can solve them. Emphasis on people within the organiza-
> tion and on external customers is the central element when wicked prob-
> lems are successfully handled.[2]

In Chapter 10, we broadly outlined some of the traditional management debates and focused attention on the Park Service's plans for Yosemite National Park. Now we turn to four policy-management vignettes that illustrate some of the challenges natural resource managers face as they address wicked problems by attempting to implement specific policies.[3] These site-specific cases are not the glamorous ones that receive wide attention in the media and academic literature. Instead, they illustrate how policy and management interact at the field level. They involve both internal and external threats, and they show how overarching policy directives influence particular decisions. They also reveal the rewards, frustrations, and complexities of today's wildland recreation manager's job, and they highlight the management skills and methods needed for successful policy implementation. We refer to the vignettes in later sections of this chapter where we discuss the tools and decision frameworks that professionals use to address policy-management issues. Specifically, after the four vignettes, our attention turns to carrying capacity, benefits-based management, funding, public participation, and collaborative management.

Vignette No. 1: Recreation, Endangered Species and Forest Planning—The Effects of Ecosystem Thinking

In our first vignette, an environmental organization forced the Forest Service to consult with the Fish and Wildlife Service on the existing planning direction and ongoing activities in four southern California forests. The areas in question have great value under traditional recreation management thinking: they are attractive, water-oriented areas located close to major population areas, and they are very popular. To achieve its aims, the environmental group used technology, scientific data, a macro-policy (the Endangered Species Act), and a lawsuit and ensuing out-of-court settlement. Reconsideration of the impacts of recreation development and other management activities on 63 threatened and endangered species resulted in the closure of some campgrounds, trails, and roads. The southern California national forests are now revising the forest plans. Guiding plan updates will be the Southern California Mountains and Foothills Assessment[4] and consultation with the Fish and Wildlife Service.[5] As a result of the environmental group's efforts, recreation development and use of certain highly attractive areas of the southern California national forests will now be restricted. In addition, there is a prohibition on range, mining, road construction, land exchanges, and fire management activities until forest plans are in compliance with the Endangered Species Act.

How did this come to be, and what does this incident tell us about policy and management? From their establishment in the early 1900s through the 1960s, federal land management agencies, seeking to meet rising demands for outdoor recreation, developed an extensive system of recreation areas and facilities. The emphasis then was locating sites with good access to scenery, roads, and water. Expansion of urban populations increased both demand and development. Starting around 1970, the environmental movement brought a new set of values into the mix, and these values are now resulting in calls to remove or restrict recreation development in ecologically sensitive areas. Ecosystem management, as a concept and in practice, is still poorly understood, but it is influencing policies that affect wildland recreation. Ecosystem management has forced the agencies to manage along ecological as well as political or administrative boundaries. As they attempt to do so, a more diverse set of human values than ever before is brought into consideration. No longer are commodity production and outputs (e.g., visitor services) the primary objectives. Ecosystem management requires a switch in focus to long-term maintenance of ecosystem productivity and resilience within a framework of socially defined goals and objectives.[6]

Since Gifford Pinchot's time, the Forest Service has always considered planning to be necessary for good management[7]. The Forest and Rangeland Renewable Resources Planning Act (RPA) of 1974 and the National Forest Management Act (NFMA) of 1976 establish guidelines and rules pertaining to U.S. forest planning. Congress passed both acts in response to public protests of the 1960s and '70s regarding federal forest management—in particular, clearcutting. These two acts institutionalized a rational-comprehensive planning process for the Forest Service. Through this process, each National Forest assesses its resources and analyzes alternatives for allocating these resources to competing demands (see policy-management vignette number 4 below for an example). As policy tools, both RPA and NFMA are inherently political in that forest plan recommendations are the result of long, detailed, and oftentimes controversial interactions between interest groups, the president's administration, and Forest Service objectives. In addition, national interests may compete with local interests.

Layered on top of the procedural and analytical requirements of RPA and NFMA are restrictions resulting from the influence of the environmental movement. Two pieces of environmental legislation in particular have major impacts of forest planning: the National Environmental Policy Act (NEPA) of 1969 and the Endangered Species Act of 1973. NEPA requires that all federal agencies formally demonstrate that they have examined the environmental consequences of alternative management actions. For the Forest Service, NEPA requires that environmental impact statements must accompany all forest plans. NEPA also requires agencies to obtain and consider comments from persons or organizations that may be affected by agency actions.

A second macro-policy, the Endangered Species Act (ESA), requires that forest plans include provisions for conserving the ecosystems upon which endangered and threatened species depend for survival. The mountains and foothills of southern California constitute the long, narrow band of mountain ranges (6.1 million acres) that parallels the Pacific coastline from Monterey County to the Mexican border. It includes portions of Yosemite and other national parks and 3.5 million acres of national forest land in four national forests: Angeles, Cleveland, Los Padres, and San Bernardino. In this largely Mediterranean climate, most people want to recreate in shaded areas near low elevation streams (i.e., in riparian and aquatic habitats), which also support a large number of imperiled species. The Forest Service is finding it increasingly difficult to meet the demand for recreation while also protecting these habitats.

To comply with the Endangered Species Act, the Forest Service, through its land management planning process (NFMA requirements), is required to consult with the U.S. Fish and Wildlife Service (FWS) whenever a management strategy or program might affect threatened or endangered species. The FWS issues a biological opinion regarding proposed actions, and the opinion becomes part of the direction in the forest plan. However, in the case in question, which originated in the 1980s, the FWS declined to enter into consultation with the Forest Service. The FWS thought the plan was too broad-scale and not site-specific enough to issue a biological opinion. FWS interpreted its obligation as consultation only on site-specific projects.

To overcome this agency impasse, an environmental organization, the Center for Biodiversity, filed a lawsuit against the four national forests for harming 63 threatened and endangered species and not consulting with the U.S. Fish and Wildlife Service in the development of its forest management plans. The lawsuit was successful, and the four national forests must now revise their plans. Maintaining habitat for threatened and endangered species will be a guiding objective for the revisions.

According to Therese O'Rourke, team leader of the plan revision process, revision of the forest plans will require extensive public involvement efforts in which citizens will be asked to suggest alternatives that allow for certain recreation uses while protecting the California red-legged frog and other species. This will be a challenge in an area that has 24 million people who speak over 100 different languages. To meet the challenge, the Forest Service hopes to use a variety of techniques: public workshops in child-friendly places, focus groups, surveys, websites, and multilingual interpretation using retired Peace Corps volunteers. O'Rourke says, "The FS will go to the public, instead of the reverse." When asked how she, as a manager, copes with such a complex challenge, she replied, "It's a big dinosaur; we just take it one bite at a time."

Another upshot of a related lawsuit was that the U.S. Fish and Wildlife Service, following a federal court order, issued a proposed rule to designate 5.4 million acres of the mountains and foothills ecosystem of southern

California as critical habitat for the threatened California red-legged frog, listed under the ESA in 1996.[8] Since the frog's habitat is largely in riparian and aquatic areas, this rule would give even more weight to protection over conflicting recreation uses and developments, such as roads and trails.

Two managers intimately involved with this case have some final messages for current and future managers and policy-makers. First, the process of developing plans, coordinating with other agencies, implementing public participation activities, conducting assessments, responding to court orders, and revising plans is costly, in both time and money. The managers we talked to wonder whether policy changes are needed to streamline the process. For example, policies regarding when agencies must enter into consultation with FWS concerning endangered species could beneficially be clarified. Likewise, they thought FWS should be better funded to do one of its important tasks—consult with the other agencies and issue biological opinions. While clearer policies and more money would help, Therese O'Rourke feels that agency commitment to work together in serving the public is also needed:

> Streamlining procedures and having a positive relationship among the local agency offices will also assist in better consultations. This doesn't necessarily take more money or time, but it does take a commitment on the part of both agencies to work things out. Recently a Memorandum of Agreement was signed in Washington DC by the Forest Service, Fish and Wildlife Service and the National Marine Fisheries Service to streamline consultations. It's about relationships and building the base working relationship with the regulatory agencies. Without it, the consultations can be contentious, costly and time-consuming.

Raina Fulton (Recreation Officer, Angeles National Forest) adds that managers have a set of priorities for the year, based on public involvement and planning processes, but these priorities can quickly be reshuffled in the face of a lawsuit. The money and staff needed to meet the requirements of all macro-policies all the time do not exist. So, managers must balance public demands with the threat of legal action at certain "pressure points," and the two are not necessarily the same. Faced with this dilemma, managers are sometimes forced to put out legal fires rather than following the forest management plan. Understanding how the policy process plays out in area management may enable those involved to address conflicts when they are emerging rather than when they are full-blown, and it may reduce the frustration that comes when plan implementation is temporarily thwarted or permanently derailed. Managers must develop the best plans and policies possible, anticipating as many challenges as they can, but then be flexible and adaptable.

This case also illustrates that public resource managers cannot assume that their efforts to provide recreation opportunities will be well received. Even in the days of Mission 66 and Operation Outdoors, recreation development was challenged. Now, however, opponents of traditional facility development have many more weapons at their disposal. Ecosystem management and the ever-present threat of litigation are forcing managers to work with the public to develop management goals and plans that focus more on ecosystem resilience and impacts on human communities and less on production of commodities and visitor days of recreation.

Vignette No. 2: Americans with Disabilities Act and Recreation Facilities Design

Our second vignette involves the redesign of a heavily used picnic area in the San Bernardino National Forest (California) to include Americans with Disabilities Act (ADA) standards.[9] According to Janna Larson, Landscape Architect and Recreation Planner with the San Bernardino National Forest, federal land managers are committed to meeting the requirements of this act but are running into a number of challenges.

First, ADA is clear and specific for indoor facilities, but vague when it comes to outdoor recreation, especially in less-developed, nature-oriented areas. Because of ADA's vagueness, the agencies often must develop their own standards in trying to improve accessibility. Managers and designers do their best, but they need clearer guidelines that match Recreation Opportunity Spectrum (ROS) guidelines for "easy," "moderate," and "difficult" access categories.[10]

Second, many of the recreation sites on the San Bernardino National Forest have slopes of 5–20 percent, and they are in riparian zones where recreationists want access to the streams that are close to the picnic facilities. It is very difficult, if not impossible, to convert these slopes into the more appropriate 3–5 percent grade necessary to meet ADA requirements. Even when it is possible, tying the grade into the existing landscapes in a natural way is challenging. In addition, these particular riparian areas are dynamic, and depending on the amount of winter rainfall, the channel can shift dramatically, making it difficult to develop permanent hard surface access trails. The shifting channels easily erode trails or leave trails that lead nowhere. Re-doing the trails every year is an expensive undertaking.

Third, it is unclear what type of disability the site is being designed for. The writers of the ADA standards tended to focus on wheelchair accessibility. Standards for persons with visual and other impairments are not as clear or detailed.

Fourth, it is not easy to find sufficient funding to upgrade sites like these. By law, an accessibility analysis must be performed for each site. Typically, the forest landscape architect or engineer evaluates each site for its degree of conformity to a list of accessibility standards and prepares a plan for redesigning the site to meet these standards. Site reconstruction then proceeds. These efforts are necessary and useful but costly and must be made a priority in the annual capital improvements budgeting process. In 1999, it cost $20,000 just to harden the surface of a one-quarter-mile interpretive trail, a section of which had been designed to include "easy" and "moderate" access grades.

Fifth, in seeking ADA compliance for recreation facilities throughout the forest, a major design goal is to avoid segregating persons with disabilities from others. A typical response to meeting ADA requirements has been to develop one or two "easy access" sites at a particular location and conclude that the agency has done its job to improve accessibility. San Bernardino Forest staff wanted to avoid this segregationist approach. Their intent was to redesign facilities so that everyone, regardless of ability, could access and use them. For example, in the picnic area in question, the forest landscape architect identified flatter terrain and completely redesigned the entire area so that each site is universally accessible. Even with the new design, however, accessibility to the water is still an issue. Persons in wheelchairs still cannot move to the edge of the water. Some areas are so rocky and steep that making them easily accessible would entail the type of landscape alterations that would impact the naturalness of the area. Even if these alterations were made so that they blended in, they may not last in the face of erosion caused by floods, fluctuating water levels and currents.

Macro-policies like the ADA are written to be broad and somewhat vague to cover a variety of situations. Implementing the policy on the ground requires creativity and flexibility on the part of the professional design staff and management. Implementation also requires consultation with representatives of the clientele group that will be affected by various redesign alternatives. Lastly, implementation requires money. ADA compliance must be a visible priority in the annual budgeting process. The budget is a powerful policy document.

Vignette No. 3: Incorporating Native American Treaty Rights

Our third vignette is really a collection of cases illustrating the growing number of conflicts arising from attempts to honor Native American rights. Cases like these have multiplied as Native Americans have pressed successfully for recognition of historical treaty rights long pushed aside.[11]

- On the Coronado National Forest in southeastern Arizona, Mt. Graham is a sacred site to the Apaches. For many years, Mt. Graham has been closed to the public because the University of Arizona and the Vatican have large sites where they have built observatories. The Apache have protested by holding sacred runs up the mountain without obtaining FS permits. This civil rights issue has been joined by an environmental issue—concern about the impacts of the planned observatories on the endangered Mt. Graham Red Squirrel—forming a coalition that strengthens both parties. Forest Service managers are inevitably drawn into this conflict.

- On the Coconino National Forest in Arizona, Cellular One was granted permission to build a communication tower on San Franscisco Peaks. The Peaks are of cultural and religious importance to a number of tribes in the Southwest, and Native American activists are trying to have it set aside as a "Traditional Cultural Property" under the National Historic Preservation Act. The Center for Biodiversity, Sierra Club Grand Canyon Chapter, and members of the Navajo, Hualapai, and Hopi Indian tribes appealed the decision. Not only is it a religious site, but the environmental groups are concerned about the exponential growth of communications towers and increasing bird mortality—apparently the nocturnal migrants die either from flying into the towers or from becoming disoriented by their lighting.

- At Death Valley National Park in California, the Park Service, corporate concessionaires, and tourists had, over the years, nearly driven the Timbisha Shoshones from their aboriginal home. Following years of heated debate, President Clinton signed legislation that granted the Timbisha Shoshone Indians ownership of their own reservation (314 acres) within Death Valley National Park.[12] This is an important precedent because it is the first time indigenous people in the United States have been granted treaty lands in a national park.[13] The tribe will be allowed to operate a motel, tribal museum, and administrative center on the reservation. In addition to the reservation, a large region within the park will be co-managed by NPS and the tribe and will allow traditional uses, such as "seasonal camping, gathering of pinyon nuts and other plants for medicinal purposes, but not the taking of wildlife within the Park".[14] Furthermore, the tribe became owners in trust of 7,200 acres of land administered by the BLM outside of Death Valley (not all in the same parcel). This law may affect many of the crown jewel national parks, because almost all have historical relationships with Native Americans. At Olympic National Park in Washington, and in Alaska, Wyoming, Arizona, and elsewhere, tribes are seeking rights to co-manage resources, ban or restrict certain non-Indian recreational uses on sacred sites, and to perform ceremonial gatherings of plants and hunting of animals. Tribes in some of parks, as already is the case in Little Bighorn, may also be allowed to provide their own interpretive programs, with a different perspective about who was there first and how they were treated by the white culture.

Vignette No. 4: Wilderness Recreation, Carrying Capacity and Public Participation

This vignette involves the Hoosier National Forest in southern Indiana, specifically the 13,000-acre Charles C. Deam Wilderness. Horseback use had been common in the wilderness for many years. Trail-related conflicts with other recreationists were frequent. Impacts on trails and vegetation were also regularly observed. The density of uncontrolled, *user-made* trails was 5.4 miles per square mile of land, which is comparable to the density of *officially designated* trails in Central Park in New York City. Only 4 percent of Indiana is in public land, so every trail decision is hotly contested. By design, the Forest Management Plan for Hoosier calls for a designated trail system and the protection of wilderness values, but the plan leaves the on-the-ground details to be developed through scientific analysis and grassroots decision-making processes. The Forest Service staff decided to implement a Limits of Acceptable Change (LAC) planning process to bring all the user groups together and provide the detail needed to implement the plan.

Later in this chapter, we describe LAC. For now it is necessary only to point out that to implement the social component of the LAC, the Forest Service formed a citizen's task force comprised of spokespersons from various organizations and user groups. The task force met every 2 weeks for nearly 2 years. Meetings were often contentious. Nonetheless, consensus was finally achieved and the Forest Service was able to implement several changes that deviated from traditional management practices. In one case involving designated horse trails, the restriction agreed upon by the task force—which included horse user groups—was even more stringent than an earlier Forest Service proposal. The more liberal restrictions on horse use proposed by the Forest Service had brought forth a flurry of challenges and protests. The more restrictive policy agreed upon by the task force was accepted and has so far gone unchallenged.

Les Wadzinski, Recreation Program Manager for the Hoosier National Forest, stated that the reason the task force worked was that it was composed of persons who were willing to compromise. Otherwise, there is no guarantee of success, so such a procedure carries some risk. He recommends it as a "last resort management technique" because of the exhaustive effort to make it successful. The outcome was generally positive. Some groups were happy with the changes; some were not. Environmental impacts have decreased, but each user group continues to lobby for more trails. Thus, this case illustrates the evolutionary nature of policy.

As this vignette shows, macro-policies like the Wilderness Act of 1964 set guidelines as to appropriate uses, but they still leave considerable discretion to managers. In the case of the Deam Wilderness, managers needed to decide on specific trail locations, lengths, and use limits. They took it upon themselves to facilitate an extensive public participation process to develop the required standards. Without this initiative on the part of management, the decision about how to allocate use in the Charles Deam Wilderness might well have been made in the courtroom. The 2-year process was costly, but the Hoosier NF's management plan, which was amended as a result of recommendations made by the task force, was successfully implemented.[15]

MANAGEMENT FRAMEWORKS AND PROCESSES

Over the years, management agencies have developed frameworks to help them cope with the pulling and tugging they inevitably face in trying to implement policy. These frameworks express broad social values embedded in policy and agency practice, and they help managers explain their actions to those who are interested. They serve as a point of departure for specific decisions, helping managers limit the range of options they must consider to a manageable set, make credible decisions, and resolve conflicts between interest groups.

In this section, we review a number of frameworks that have emerged over the years for wildland recreation. Each of these is complex and constantly evolving as lessons are learned in the course of using it, and each has an extensive literature. Our purpose here is not to provide detailed description and analysis of these frameworks, but simply to illustrate how they originated and function in addressing policy issues encountered in wildland recreation management.

The Recreation Opportunity Spectrum (ROS) and Limits of Acceptable Change (LAC) planning processes assist managers in identifying actions that are appropriate for achieving a broad range of benefits while minimizing human impacts on fragile natural resources. Benefits-Based Management (BBM) guides decision-making by asking managers to focus not on the recreation activities themselves but on the individual and societal outcomes of wildland recreation.

All three management frameworks are relatively new and still being modified.[16] A criticism of all three systems is that thus far most applications have focused on recreation. Attempts at integrating BBM, ROS, and LAC with other agency planning systems have been minimal. Therefore, recreation values have not been fully integrated into policy and management decisions involving other resources, such as scenery or wildlife habitat.[17] Even if such integration occurs, wildland recreation decisions will continue to be influenced by the budgetary roller coaster, expanding concern for thinking at the ecosystem level, and increased public participation. In addition, as shown in the policy-management vignettes, the legal remedies inherent in such policies as the American Indian Religious Freedom Act and the Endangered Species Act also shape managerial actions.

Recreation Opportunity Spectrum (ROS)

The Recreation Opportunity Spectrum[18] is a planning and management system that has been adopted by the U.S. Forest Service and Bureau of Land Management. The fundamental social value underlying ROS is the desire to provide diverse outdoor recreation opportunities ("from the paved to the primeval") for a diverse nation in which individual choice is a paramount value.

Integral to ROS is the concept that the level and character of biological, physical, social, and managerial conditions create various settings in which people can pursue opportunities for recreational experiences. Alternative combinations of these environmental, social, and managerial conditions are inventoried and delineated on maps as zones ranging in character from urban to remote. From these combinations or settings, visitors derive a variety of experiences and benefits.[19] The Forest Service and

BLM attempt to manage these zones to provide the types of recreation experiences indicative of their classifications.[20] However, visitors ultimately produce their own recreation experiences, not managers. Managers provide what they consider to be the appropriate settings and opportunities for those experiences. Thus, the ROS is at best an organizing or conceptual framework that requires a substantial amount of management judgment.[21] As was demonstrated in the policy-management vignettes at the beginning of this chapter, these judgments are tempered by both legal mandates and public participation in the decision-making process.

Agency policies are paramount in implementing the ROS. Coupled with the character of the resource (e.g., degree of human impact), policies direct the agency to concentrate its efforts on all or only a certain portion of the ROS. The Forest Service typically delineates four or five management zones for visitor experiences at the less developed end of the spectrum: primitive, semiprimitive, semiprimitive nonmotorized, semiprimitive motorized, roaded natural, and in some places, roaded modified. Minimum attention is given to such discrimination in the rural and urban categories of the spectrum. However, a county park system could develop and manage for finer gradations within the rural class, whereas a municipal government might focus on finer tuning within the urban category.[22] Whether federal, state, or local, the ROS encourages managers to focus on specific sections of the spectrum and then develop relevant policies and management strategies for each section.

Limits of Acceptable Change

Observers of American wildland recreation have long recognized that unregulated recreational use would destroy the areas and negate the human benefits they were intended to provide. Just as unregulated forest exploitation was brought under control of scientific, sustained-yield forestry, a scientific basis for regulating wildland recreation has long been sought. If park and wilderness areas were to provide people with the outdoor experiences considered central to our society and at costs that would not discourage participation, then some defensible approach to limiting use had to be found.

This line of reasoning prompted the development of a recreation management framework loosely described as "recreation carrying capacity."[23] The term carrying capacity was borrowed from range and wildlife management, and refers to the number of animals a given area can support on a sustained basis, so that healthy animals are produced without destroying or degrading their habitat. The first application of the carrying capacity framework to outdoor recreation came from wildlife biologist Lowell Sumner in 1942.[24] Thinking primarily in terms of recreation impacts on wilderness biota, Sumner advocated limiting each area's use to its "recreational saturation point" or carrying capacity. Sumner defined carrying capacity as "the maximum degree of the highest type of recreational use which a wilderness can receive, consistent with its long-term preservation."[25]

A moment's reflection on Sumner's definition will reveal some of the difficulties that have plagued the recreation carrying capacity idea. What does the "highest type of recreational use" mean? The range of possible wildland recreation activities is extensive, and each different behavioral wrinkle brings different impacts on the biophysical environment. What, exactly, is meant by "long-term preservation?" Absolute preservation dictates no human use whatsoever, and even then there is no way truly to preserve a landscape, since natural processes will bring changes in the absence of human intervention. If we are trying to preserve a landscape as it existed at some time, what will the baseline time be? To maintain Yosemite Valley as an open meadow, as it was when whites first discovered it, would require prescribed burns, tree removal and other measures to interrupt natural succession toward a mature forest environment. Finally, consider the information needed to fully implement Sumner's framework. Each area has its peculiar mix of plant and animal communities, landforms, and recreational uses. Each area thus demands tailor-made scientific study of how specific patterns of recreation lead to changes in the biophysical characteristics we are attempting to preserve.

In its earliest formulation, then, recreation carrying capacity was a complex planning tool involving judgment and requiring unavailable information. Soon, with the addition of social concerns, the concept became even more complex. From the beginning, the human dimension had been recognized, but it was not until 1959 that it was given equivalent status with biophysical considerations. In that year, the National Advisory Council on Regional Recreation Planning added the following statement to the widely accepted biophysical definition of recreation carrying capacity: "carrying capacity may also be the maximum human use that is compatible with the quality of the recreation experience desired by the user."[26]

The final element was definitively added in 1964.[27] In his monograph entitled "The Carrying Capacity of Wild Lands for Recreation," J. Alan Wagar emphasized the role of management objectives in determining an area's recreational carrying capacity. Wagar argued, "In every statement of carrying capacity there must be, at least implicitly, a statement of some management objective."[28] He went on to place land managers and their decisions in pivotal positions:

> People seek wildland recreation for the enjoyment and benefit it gives. Yet it is only one of the products and services they want from a limited supply of land. Just as material products tend to reach a market price according to supply and demand, for any set of circumstances there will be a limit to what other values people will sacrifice for quality recreation. Thus, for purposes of determining recreational carrying capacity, the objective of managing wild lands may be stated as sustained production of the highest quality recreation that is possible at acceptable costs. On public lands, which provide most wildland recreation, decisions as to what costs are acceptable will have to be made by public servants striving to achieve the public good.[29,30]

Thus, with Wagar's contribution, the three essential ingredients of the carrying capacity recipe had been identified: management objectives, visitor perceptions, and environmental impacts. In the 39 years since Wagar's paper, scores of research projects have sought to define the linkages between recreational use and impacts on the environment and the visitors. In hundreds of articles and papers, scholars and practitioners have presented findings and argued over everything from methods to theoretical principles. Along the way, much of value has been learned. What has not been found is the philosopher's stone many have sought, a technically clean and scientifically valid way of determining how much use is too much. As the author of a recent review of the carrying capacity literature concludes, "There is no single carrying capacity for an outdoor recreation area. Rather, every area has a range of capacities depending upon management objectives and indicators and standards of quality."[31]

In the 1980s, increasing dissatisfaction with the appealing simplicity of recreation carrying capacity led researchers to develop a somewhat different approach. This framework for recreation management is called "Limits of Acceptable Change," or LAC.[32] The LAC approach begins with the proposition that, since any recreational use produces changes in the environment and visitor experiences, the proper question is not "How much use is too much," but "How much change is acceptable?" LAC then suggests a series of decisions that must be made to manage areas. Essentially, managers and visitors are asked to identify aspects of the biophysical and social environments that are important and can be monitored for change as recreational use proceeds. If changes in these indicators exceed limits determined in advance, action to modify recreational use will be taken. Actions can range from "light-handed" approaches, which minimally constrain visitor freedom, to "heavy-handed" steps that regulate visitor behavior very directly.[33]

One of LAC's most important contributions is its insistence on the pivotal role of management objectives. Somehow, in the course of all the carrying capacity studies, many managers and researchers lost track of the fact that how we manage our wildlands depends on what we are trying to accomplish with them. As Wagar concluded in 1964:

> While research can provide various types of information for guidance, final definitions of recreational carrying capacity must be of an administrative nature. Ecological studies can show how biotic communities will change with use, but someone must decide how much change is acceptable. In a similar manner, use of research surveys and other tools from the social sciences can measure current public opinion and analyze human motivation. But such motivation and opinion will seldom be based on a thorough understanding of availability and productivity of the resource. Someone must decide which combination of needs and desires it is most desirable to satisfy from our limited resources.
>
> On public land, which provides much of our wildland recreation, policy decisions should be by legislative directives and by public servants striving to achieve the public good. Recreational quality gained by limiting use must be weighed against values lost when such limits reduce the number of people served. Present values must be weighed against values for future generations.
>
> As competition for land increases, the limitation and allocation of uses will leave many special interest groups unhappy. And much as public officials might wish to shift the burden to impersonal equations, the formulas devised by researchers can guide but not supplant human judgment.[34]

The Limits of Acceptable Change approach, therefore, brings management back to the central position it occupied in Wagar's treatise four decades ago. There is one significant change, however, that reflects the nation's collective experience between 1964 and the present. Whereas Wagar pointed the finger at public officials alone, LAC specifies that park, recreation, and wilderness managers must work with interested members of the public throughout—defining management objectives, selecting indicators of change, setting standards for change, and determining what managerial steps will be taken to control excessive change. For example, to plan for the Bob Marshall Wilderness complex, a task force composed of researchers, Forest Service personnel, and individuals representing organized and unorganized interests in the area was constituted. The purposes of the task force were as follows:

> The task force provides continuing public participation in the LAC process. It is a means of informing citizens about the process and gaining their understanding and support. A basic precept underlying formation of the task force is that a substantial, important body of expertise exists within the citizenry. Another precept is that without public understanding and support, the process is unlikely to succeed. This is a particularly important notion, for it is consistent with the growing realization that resource planning is ultimately a political rather than a technical process.[35]

The fourth policy-management vignette in this chapter, the Deam Wilderness in Indiana, underscores the lessons learned on the Bob Marshall. In the case of the Deam, the task force developed LAC restrictions that were even more stringent than those proposed by the managers.[36]

Forest Service planners who worked with the Bob Marshall task force think LAC succeeded in providing an overall framework for planning, and they believe the key to LAC's success is that it can be adapted to planning processes that involve collaborative work between managers and interested citizens and groups. Despite its origins as an expert-driven planning system, LAC has been used as a social choice and learning framework for decision-making. As exemplified by the Bob Marshall and Charles C. Deam wilderness cases, the LAC provides the context where knowledge from a variety of perspectives is considered and science is used to inform rather than dictate decisions.

Benefits-based Management

Benefits-based management (BBM) is part of a larger change in the way we think about providing recreation services.[37] Managers customarily pay primary attention to such things as acres of park land, budgets for personnel, and numbers of programs offered. BBM, on the other hand, asks managers to consider first the benefits derived from people's participation in outdoor recreation. In BBM, physical space, budgets, and programs are simply means to achieving benefits for individuals, communities, and the biophysical environment. Management's challenge is to optimize the net benefits produced by recreational opportunities.[38]

BBM identifies four broad categories of benefits: personal (e.g., reduced tension), social/cultural (e.g., community cohesion), economic (e.g., reduced health care costs), and environmental (e.g., ecosystem protection). Incorporating such a broad range of benefits clearly extends the impact of wildland recreation outside park boundaries. BBM seeks an understanding of both on-site benefits to individuals and off-site benefits to individuals, society, the economy, and the environment associated with the provision of public recreation opportunities.[39]

BBM is used to guide the management of park and recreation programs and resources. For example, managers work within a BBM framework to help communities identify and justify an array of recreation options aimed at providing a broad range of benefits to residents.[40] More specific applications involve identifying a strategic program or service aimed at reducing a specific social problem (e.g., low self-esteem among teens) or capturing a specific benefit (e.g., restoration of a natural area).[41]

Managers working with BBM employ scientific information whenever possible. For example, they may rely on the growing body of survey research to estimate the social benefits expected to derive from recreation participation at their particular areas. However, scientific information cannot get them off the policy hook. The scientific data they seek, and the ways they interpret it, still depend on their management objectives, the shaping influence of various publics, and available funds.

PAYING FOR WILDLAND RECREATION

Providing high-quality recreation opportunities involves multiple expenses. Money is needed for operation and maintenance, for research, for land acquisition, and for staff hiring and training. Funding, the "mother's milk of public programs," significantly enables or constrains management strategies. Funding for recreation management has been a chronic problem for resource management agencies. There has been a move in recent years to charge recreationists more for their use of wildland areas.

Current recreation budgets are inadequate, and future projections are not encouraging.[42] The combined budgets for the seven major federal resource management agencies amount to less than 1 percent of the federal budget, and the budgets for recreation management are only a fraction of that. For most of the 1980s and 1990s, the federal resource management agencies have faced flat to slightly declining constant-dollar budgets. They have had to curtail land acquisition and new development even in the face of growing demand, and they have been unable to address huge backlogs of maintenance and facility upgrade needs. At the same time budgets have been flat, increases in administrative and assessment costs at the highest levels mean that fewer and fewer funds are trickling down to the lowest, "hands-on" levels of resource and recreation management. Agencies have been unable to fill recreation management positions and have had to close some field offices, forcing existing staff to perform more duties with fewer funds. With limitations on professional staff, the agencies are relying more on volunteers and cost-sharing partnerships with public and private organizations to carry out day-to-day site maintenance and customer service. Federal resource management agencies are also increasing fees to cover some management costs.

Projections indicate that the trend of flat to shrinking budgets for federal recreation management will continue into the near future.[43] Requests for increased funding fly in the face of efforts to reduce non-defense federal spending. In addition, such requests do not play well before budget committees alarmed over the growth of the national debt and the need to shift budget priorities in reaction to the 2001 terrorist attacks and the war in Iraq. In seeking to reconcile the demand for more money with the prospect of less, a rapidly growing number of commentators are suggesting we shift the burden from the general taxpayer to wildland recreation visitors.

Through the Land and Water Conservation Fund, enacted in 1964, the federal government has provided billions of dollars for outdoor recreation. All levels of government (federal, state, and local) across the recreation spectrum (remote to urban) have benefited from the LWCF. Land and Water Conservation funds have allowed various units of government to acquire park and recreation lands, develop recreation facilities, and redevelop older recreation facilities.[44] Land and Water Conservation funds are dispersed widely on a competitive grant application basis. Fifty percent matches are required. Furthermore, LWCF monies may not be used for operations and maintenance. The upshot is that, as significant as the LWCF has been, it was not designed to, nor can it be expected to keep pace with growing recreation demands and impacts on infrastructure and agency budgets.

The inadequacy of federal wildland recreation management agency budgets is nothing new; rather, it represents the typical state of affairs. The problems arising from inadequate funding for wildland recreation have spurred a long and vigorous debate about user fees. Increasing use is the root cause of many of the problems facing the nation's wildland recreation resources. "We're loving our parks to death," is the memorable shorthand describing the problem, and many observers, including recreation professionals, apply it well to all our wildland recreation resources. If increasing use is the primary challenge we must address, one approach to reducing visitation pressure is to charge more realistic prices for the services rendered. Not only would the fee revenues provide essential funding for management, but they might dampen demand, especially for close-to-home parks and sites that are not well-known or used mostly by local communities.[45]

Arguments in Favor of User Fees

First, according to proponents, wildland recreation user fees will add substantially to the revenues needed for proper resource management. Recent experience gained in the federal fee demonstration program described below appears to confirm this notion.

Second, according to user fee proponents, fees will not significantly reduce recreation participation. A 1977 survey of over 800 households by the Bureau of Outdoor Recreation found that the majority of all demographic groups favored user charges over general tax revenues as a way of paying for outdoor recreation. In addition, most respondents said they would be willing to pay higher fees than those then in effect.[46] More recent studies, as well, have substantiated recreationists' willingness to pay for their experiences. In most of these studies the majority of users favor fees, especially when the fees are used for improvements at the areas where they are collected.[47]

Third, some tourism interests have joined in the call for higher fees. Those looking at camping from a business perspective, for instance, have noted that it is difficult for a private campground operator to compete with the subsidized facilities offered by the Park Service and Forest Service. As one observer quipped: "We cannot give away cake and expect people to rush into the bakery business at the same time."[48]

Fourth, some argue that user fees would place recreation on a more even footing with timber and other commodity resources. The argument is that on the national forests, wildland recreation is often subordinate to the other multiple uses and that if all the competing uses were unsubsidized, wildland recreation's status would improve markedly. If recreation paid its way, it would receive better treatment in multiple-use planning.[49] This argument was supported by a study published in 1997 that revealed that between 1986 and 1991, southern Appalachian forests received about 47 percent of their requested recreation budgets, as against 97 percent of their requested timber budgets.[50]

Finally, and most fundamentally, proponents of user fees argue that those who benefit from governmental services, not the public at large, should pay for them. The guiding principle is "the user pays." Except for fundamentally important services like national security, transportation, and public health, it is unfair to tax the public at large to provide benefits to special interests—including park and wilderness visitors. Those opposing fees must try to make the case that participation in wildland recreation offers societal benefits of such a magnitude that the principle should be over-ridden.

Arguments Against User Fees

Those who oppose user fees rest their case, finally, on the belief that wildland recreation provides benefits to participants and society that are sufficiently important to justify providing opportunities at public expense, so that all citizens may participate. Arguments along this line are called "merit goods" arguments. Common to all these merit goods arguments is the notion that recreation user fees are discriminatory, depriving those on the lower rungs of the socioeconomic ladder a fair chance to realize these benefits. In what follows, we review four such arguments.

First, wildland recreation is seen as contributing to American cultural heritage values. For Aldo Leopold, in his early wilderness advocacy, distinctive features of the American way of life were forged in the frontier experience, and that was sufficient reason to set aside large expanses of roadless land for public recreation. In our day this viewpoint is expressed in law professor Dan Tarlock's argument for preservation of the national parks.

> Like Mozart's operas, Milton's poems, and ancient Jerusalem, areas of awesome scenic grandeur are treasures of western civilization that must be passed on as intact as possible from generation to generation . . . For me . . . it is enough that certain national parks are irreplaceable and have occupied an important role in shaping this nation's perception of itself.[51]

Bringing this conception to bear directly on the fees issue, scholars have raised concerns that reliance on user charges will diminish the symbolic weight of our wildland recreation treasures. At some point they will become simply one more set of commodities vying for the attention of the consuming public.[52] In a downward spiral of privatization, an over-emphasis on fees may lead government to abandon its role in appropriating funds for wildland recreation, while encouraging public agencies to become income generators. Rising visitor expectations for comfort and convenience may require additional expenditures on facilities, programs, and services at the expense of funds for operations and maintenance. Agencies may become so dependent on fees that they will focus on the mechanics of collecting them and lose sight of the reasons for having recreation areas in the first place.

Second, fee opponents argue that wildland recreation is important to individual growth and development. Olmsted thought that nature had special powers to heal us mentally and physically and to lead us to transcendent states where we could gain perspective on our daily lives. In a related contemporary conception, numerous scholars have linked outdoor recreation with spirituality and the realization of human potential.[53]

Third, those opposing fees argue that wildland recreation is an important source of community solidarity. Once again, Olmsted's ideas provide a starting place. Based on the social class integration he found at Birkenhead Park, Olmsted came to see public parks as "engines of democracy." In our time, social psychologists have become cognizant of the "leisure social worlds" to which people voluntarily belong.[54] The forces of modernism have severely weakened traditional, geographically bounded communities. For many people, association with others interested in the same recreational pursuits provides their relevant community. Fees may serve as a barrier to social processes important to our national well-being.[55]

Fourth, fee opponents suggest that wildland recreation participation helps develop environmental stewardship. Thinkers in this vein focus on the value of wildland recreation areas for public education—our parks and public lands can help teach us to live in a world of limits. One of the best statements of this idea is found in William Brown's *Islands of Hope*. Brown suggests that our national parks have an important educational role to play in leading us toward an environmentally viable future. According to Brown, parks should convey to their visitors a message of environmental stewardship they can take back home with them.[56] If wildland recreation areas can help us face the future in ways that benefit all, the public should not be expected to pay directly for using them.

History of User Fees Debate

Park Service historian Barry Mackintosh has traced the legislative and administrative struggle over user charges during the last half-century. According to his account, Congress has been the source of most of the shifting over the years, reflecting changes in the national mood from liberal to conservative and back. While congressional sentiment has shifted over the years, executive branch leadership has consistently supported user charges. The Office of Management and Budget and its forerunner, the Bureau of the Budget, have steadfastly pressed agencies providing outdoor recreation services to charge for them.

Congressional sentiment in establishing the early parks was that they were to be self-supporting, with full pay-as-you-go recreation realized primarily through concessionaires. By the 1920s, key congressional leaders advocated free public recreation on the grounds that it represented the "real American theory," and that "the American idea is not that there is going to be somebody with a collection plate every time you turn around in a publicly owned enterprise."[57] In 1927, fee opponents in Congress succeeded in prohibiting the use of appropriations at any park or monument that charged fees for campground use; this law effectively prohibited fees.[58] With the rapid growth of park visitation in the 1960s, congress again supported user fees; in this they were aligned with the Outdoor Recreation Resources Review Commission. The result was that fees were to be a major element in the Land and Water Conservation Fund as initially conceived.[59] In the late 1970s, anti-fee forces again achieved superiority in Congress. Guided by Representative Phillip Burton, Congress in 1979 prohibited the Park Service from raising existing fees or instituting new ones.[60]

In 1985 conservative President Reagan used an executive order to create a new recreation commission. The President's Commission on Americans Outdoors (PCAO) was charged with reviewing and making recommendations about recreation policies, with the added direction that the recommendations were to be consistent with the administration's philosophy of fiscal restraint across all levels of government. Thus far, PCAO has not been as influential as its predecessor ORRRC.[61] For example, in terms of funding, the PCAO recommended the creation of a billion dollar trust fund for parks and recreation, which was considered but not enacted by Congress until recently, and in a greatly altered form. Congress also followed PCAO's recommendation and approved a 25-year extension of the Land and Water Conservation Fund—while providing minimal appropriations for the fund until recently.[62] PCAO's recommendation for user fees took more than a decade to play out.

In denying the agencies at all levels (federal, state, and local) a secure federal source of funds, Congress turned its attention once again to pay-as-you-go recreation. In 1987, Congress established a 1-year experimental program for expanded fee collection in the National Park System. Fees could not be collected at any NPS units where prohibited by law or at areas where multiple entry points make fee collection impracticable. Congress also set fee limits of $3 per person and $5 per car. In the early 1990s, Congress increased fees at national parks.[63]

In 1996 the recreation fee tide reached its peak. In that year, based on PCAO recommendations, Congress established a recreation fee demonstration program (P.L. 104–134). This program authorized four agencies (FS, NPS, BLM, and USFWS) to increase or establish new recreation fees on a trial basis in certain parks and recreation areas. The program allows 80 percent of the increased fee revenue to remain at the site where it was collected. This provision appears to have overcome historical resistance from site managers. Managers have long been concerned that they would have to bear the costs of collecting fees and possibly discouraging visitation, thereby jeopardizing budgetary support while at the same time having to give the fees collected to the agency's central office. The funds cannot be used to build new facilities, but they can be used to fund the backlog of repairs and maintenance of existing facilities, protect resources, and improve visitor services.[64]

Though the fee demonstration program was authorized to run for 3 years only, it continues to receive support within the agencies and Congress.[65] Noting that the fee program raised $6.5 million for Washington and Oregon national forests, almost double the amount raised during the first year of the program, the Seattle Times reported that in 2001 the Forest Service would again charge $5 for a day pass and $30 for an annual pass to visit national forests in the Pacific Northwest.[66] Extolling the many successes of the American fee demonstration program, an article in the official magazine of the National Recreation and Parks Association advocated a similar fee program in Canada.[67] The 107th Congress of the United States recently approved continuance of the fee program through FY 2004.

Funding Wildland Recreation—Conclusions

How we pay for wildland recreation is in a state of transition, as it has been since the origins of the system. It is impossible to predict with confidence the twists and turns that lie ahead. For now, both unappropriated (user fees) and appropriated (federal budget) sources of funds are increasing. The balance between the two is yet to be decided. The events of September 11, 2001, have made the funding situation for all federal programs, including wildland recreation, more uncertain than ever. Before September 11, the administration of George W. Bush, though meeting some resistance from Congress, recommended substantial increases in funding for the acquisition and development of parklands and open space and for reducing the backlog of maintenance and repairs. As this is written in 2003, presidential and congressional attention is now focused on international terrorism and the Iraq war. Given this focus, and with the present shakiness of the national economy, the debate about significant additional funding for wildland recreation is temporarily on hold. The irony is that this comes at the very time when Americans more than ever want safe, secure places for recreation, while heightened security concerns may dissuade many from international travel.

We began this book by discussing the value of wildland recreation in America. How much Americans value their wildland recreation estate will surely be put to the test in the months and years ahead. As our economy responds or fails to respond to the challenges of international trade, terrorism, and nation building, as our population's interests in wildland recreation evolve with its increasing age and ethnic diversity, as there are new advances in transportation and communication, and as other factors shape the national mindset, we will need to be more creative and diligent than in the past to find practicable and equitable ways of paying for wildland recreation.

PUBLIC PARTICIPATION AND COLLABORATIVE MANAGEMENT

Even if managers were equipped with perfect management systems, and even if funding problems were miraculously eliminated, those responsible for taking care of our wildland recreation resources could not simply rely on their professional expertise to make final decisions about natural resources. Public resource managers working in a democratic context must work with citizens and the many groups and organizations to which they belong. In the remainder of this chapter, we present concepts and frameworks for thinking about this critical dimension of the manager's job.

Management necessarily involves making choices, and those choices inevitably involve conflicting values held by various individuals and groups. Prior to the emergence of public participation in the 1960s, resource managers' decisions tended to be based on power and authority.[68] Experience, however, showed that these approaches frequently led to unsatisfactory, unsustainable results. As conflict resolution expert M. J. McKinney suggests, one problem with both power and rights-based approaches is that:

> . . . they are adversarial in nature and tend to result in winners, losers, and impaired relationships among the parties. In both cases decisions are made, but the underlying problems are rarely resolved and the losers do not "go away."[69]

For these reasons, a third way—public participation—has recruited a growing number of adherents in recent years.

We think of public participation broadly, including collaboration, consensus building, partnerships, and other ways agency experts work with those outside the agency to share resources, resolve disputes, and reconcile divergent interests. Federal, state, and local park and natural resource management agencies often rely on individuals and interested parties to provide assistance not only in facility development, natural resource protection, and management programs, but also in policy, planning, and decision-making activities.[70] Policy, planning, and decision-making activities include formal partnerships or other collaborative arrangements where the parties involved share power. Or, they may involve citizen task forces and councils where there are no formal power sharing arrangements, but the task force or council has a great deal of influence over decision-making.

While the definitions of participation vary, there is general agreement that participation involves a spectrum of activities, which is

> . . . anchored at one end by provision of labor for project implementation and at the other by projects where local communities control all project features from objectives to outcomes.[71]

Others define participation as a spectrum of behaviors that reflect the degree of citizen power over decision-making[72] In wildland recreation policy and management, these behaviors can be arrayed along a spectrum (Figure 11–1).

The spectrum ranges from simple participation in outdoor recreation activities at the one end (low power) to policy-making authority at the other (high power). In between are such behaviors as volunteering in activities directed by others (e.g., voluntary trail maintenance), responding to agency requests for comments on plans, and offering unsolicited advice to managers. Solicited feedback is the type of one-way public input that natural resource agencies obtain most frequently, typically in the form of public hearings or requests for written comments on draft plans. Unsolicited feedback, a type of advocacy or civil disobedience, may appear in a variety of oral or written communication forms, protests, or demonstrations. Policy-making authority involves the highest level of power and might involve such activities as serving on a formal board, commission, or task force in which there may be power-sharing arrangements.

By all indications, public participation in natural resource management is increasing.[73] Several broad forces are driving this trend. First is the reality of stable or declining wildland recreation budgets, as described earlier in this chapter. Because of budgetary restrictions, federal land management agencies during the 1980s and 1990s relied heavily on volunteers and cost-sharing partnerships to carry out day-to-day site maintenance and visitor service.

A second reason for increases in public participation in the natural resources field is age-old American public aversion to powerful and aloof government. Citizens thinking along these lines have low trust in government and demand ever-increasing accountability from public officials. The traditional ways public administrators and resource managers have dealt with the public—as all-knowing, all-powerful experts—are being

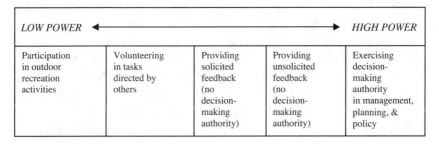

LOW POWER ←				→ HIGH POWER
Participation in outdoor recreation activities	Volunteering in tasks directed by others	Providing solicited feedback (no decision-making authority)	Providing unsolicited feedback (no decision-making authority)	Exercising decision-making authority in management, planning, & policy

Figure 11–1. Spectrum of Participation Behaviors in Wildland Recreation Management, Planning, and Policy-making

challenged, just as other traditional authority-based leadership in other realms of society is under fire.[74] Thus, there is growing pressure on public agencies to conduct resource management and planning activities in more transparent, inclusive, and collaborative ways.[75] A major precursor to more inclusive and collaborative resource management activities is citizen trust in agencies and organizations.[76] Trust, in turn, results in increased support for agency decisions.[77]

Collaborative Conservation—New Directions in Public Participation

The book, *Across the Great Divide: Explorations in Collaborative Conservation and the American West,* offers lessons about new directions in public participation that we believe can be applied to wildland recreation management across the country. The editors describe this approach to working with the public broadly, as follows:

> Often called "collaborative conservation," this new movement represents the new face of American conservation as we enter the twenty-first century. Although no single strategy, process, or institutional arrangement characterizes this movement, collaborative conservation emphasizes the importance of local participation, sustainable natural and human communities, inclusion of disempowered voices, and voluntary consent and compliance rather than enforcement by legal and regulatory coercion. In short, collaborative conservation reaches across the great divide connecting preservation advocates and developers, commodity production and conservation biologists, local residents, and national interest groups to find working solutions to intractable problems that will surely languish unresolved for decades in the existing policy system.[78]

Collaboration is viewed as growing out of the Alternative Dispute Resolution (ADR) efforts that were applied to environmental issues beginning in the mid-1970s. The goal of ADR was the resolution of difficult environmental issues through mediation, negotiation, and the building of formal agreements among adversaries. Professional facilitators with no particular interest in the dispute usually lead the process. While ADR typically focused on resolving disputes usually between two parties, collaborations involve multiple parties or groups of stakeholders.

> Collaboration was born largely of failure, the growing recognition that lawsuits, lobbying campaigns, administrative appeals, and other straight-line approaches to hard environmental issues are often narrow, usually expen-

sive (in more ways than one), and almost always divisive in ways that re-verberate beyond the immediate issue in dispute.[79]

In the American West, environmental conflicts not only are divisive, but they also tend to result in gridlock, with neither side being able to advance its agenda. However, in some cases it has been observed that environmental dispute resolution was possible once the affected parties were brought together and mutual interests examined. For adversaries frustrated from unsuccessful attempts at breaking political stalemates, collaboration offers something new. While the editors of *Across the Great Divide* make it clear that collaboration is no panacea and has its limitations, they also argue that certain characteristics (Table 11–1) make it amenable to solving the wicked problems involved in natural resource management.[80] Some myths of collaborative decision making are also highlighted in Table 11–1. These include the myths that collaboration always requires consensus, is place-based, and occurs only at the local level.

In drawing language and examples from *Across the Great Divide,* we do not want to give the mistaken impression that such actions are confined to or derived solely from the western experience. One of the most well-known examples of collaborative conservation in wildland recreation involves the Appalachian Trail Conference, a nonprofit organization that coordinates the management of the 2,168-mile Appalachian Trail. Since the trail traverses a great deal of private land, coordination and collaboration with private landowners are keys to successful management. The Appalachian Trail Conference (ATC), founded in 1925, relies on a confederation of 31 trail clubs with delegated authority to manage sections of the trail. In addition to the clubs, there are a number of other partners that supply resources necessary for trail maintenance:

- National Park Service (six national park units along the trail)
- U.S. Forest Service (eight national forests bisected by the trail)
- Numerous state parks, state forests, and gamelands from Maine to Georgia
- Various counties and cities along the trail

Overall trail management policies are established through joint meetings between the ATC Board and local and regional partners.[81]

A lesser-known, but precedent-setting example of collaborative management is Ebey's Landing National Historic Reserve (Washington), the

Table 11–1. Characteristics of Collaborative Conservation

CHARACTERISTICS	DESCRIPTION
"coalitions of the unalike"	They are groups of people who usually do not work to gether or have adversarial relationships. Sometimes these are last resort measures that arise when other methods of decision-making have failed.
"power circles"	Power is created when traditional opponents on a natural resource issue agree on a position.
"learning circles"	Members learn from each other's experience and expertise and grow from such shared knowledge. Even if a significant product or policy change does not emerge, this knowledge has longlasting value.
Seek innovation before compromise	The most successful collaboratives are those that were able to develop a solution in tandem that none of the members could have produced individually.
Meditative rather than polarizing leadership style	Mediative leadership tries to bring divergent people and interests together to identify common goals, whereas polarizing leadership tends to form a critical mass of support among a subset of the group so that "our side can win."
Informal in structure	This is one reason for their effectiveness. Informality gives the feeling that collaboration is voluntary and flexible and that decisions are not binding. This atmosphere allows for experimentation, allowing tentative members to decide how much they want to be involved in the early stages of the group's development.
Often nongovernmental in origin	While they may include government agents, their origin is typically outside of government. This is "one of the strongest features of collaborative problem solving" (p. 6).
Deal explicitly with questions of process, especially with regards to decision-making	Only some groups use formal consensus processes, which bind the group to some action. A wide range of less formal processes are also possible.
Place attachment is a strength but not a prerequisite	For example, statewide initiatives pertaining to clean water are sometimes often collaborative even though they are placeless (" 'statewide' is not a place": p. 7).
Often local or regional in scope	But, the idea that collaboration is always local is a myth; many examples of attempts at collaboration exist on the national level as well.

From: Snow, "Coming home: an introduction to collaborative conservation," pp. 6–7 in Brick et al., *Across the Great Divide . . .*

first unit of the NPS largely under private ownership. The National Park Service's role is primarily one of technical assistance. Administration and management is the responsibility of a local trust board, formed when the reserve was established by Congress in 1978. Seven residents, a representative from State Parks, and one from the National Park Service, serve on the Trust Board.[82]

Such collaborative arrangements are not unique. Other examples at both federal and international levels abound.[83]

No approach to public participation is perfect, and collaborative conservation has its opponents.[84] For example, one critic argues that the legal system is superior to collaboration, or local negotiation, as an approach to resolving public resource issues. He summarizes the flaws of collaboration as:

- Many of the underlying premises are unproven or untrue
- Collaboration can be a mask for cooptation
- Collaboration without the power of law is ineffective and unenforceable
- Local collaboration can undermine national plans and policies
- Collaboration abdicates legal responsibilities

These are similar to the arguments advanced by Michael McCloskey, former executive director of the Sierra Club, on several occasions. McCloskey particularly focuses on the fourth flaw, the potential undermining of national plans and policies. With the perspective of an organization that has fought long and hard for national controls over environmentally destructive local decision-making, McCloskey fears that local control will lower the effectiveness of such laws as the National Environmental Policy Act and the Endangered Species Act. McCloskey and others argue that there is plenty of evidence that left on their own, cities, states, and local citizens would not take the steps necessary to protect the environment.

There is little doubt that national or regional policies change, or devolve, as they pass through the implementation journey from the national to the local level.[85] By the time it is implemented at the local level, the policy may bear little resemblance to its original form. This transformation is exactly what Pressman and Wildavsky found in their classic study of federal aid to cities, *How Great Expectations in Washington are Dashed in Oakland.*[86] However, devolution does not necessarily undermine the intent or enforcement of the original policy.[87] In his study of several contentious environmental pollution cases, Edward Weber finds that "collaboration is appearing where we would least expect it—in the most combative of all regulatory arenas—pollution control politics."[88] And, in close to one hundred cases involving regulatory negotiation among diverse coalitions,

> . . . collaborative arrangements work within the larger framework of national laws, not in lieu of them, to prevent degradation; to provide long-term, holistic solutions to complex local problems; and to enhance the degree of local oversight and implementation expertise.[89]

Another argument against collaboration is offered by community planning scholar Maria Varela. She contends that, when it comes to the rights of the poor and the oppressed, collaboration often means pacification instead of justice. Varela refers to a case in New Mexico in which low income local residents were invited to the negotiation table regarding traditional uses of resources in nearby national forests. When it became clear that the locals would be denied access to these resources, the "have-nots" began viewing the collaborative process only as an act of charity, leading Varela to the conclusion that collaboration alone is insufficient without "economic justice and authentic cross-cultural learning."[90]

Supporters of collaboration agree that it is no panacea—that it is naïve to believe that interested parties sitting down and talking can solve all problems—and that national issues should be resolved through national not local processes.[91] The uncertainty of outcomes as policies devolve requires a fuller understanding of the conditions under which various forms of citizen participation and other regulatory arrangements work best.[92] Nonetheless, collaborative efforts can at least solve some of the problems, avoid some of the costs (social as well as financial) of litigation, propose innovations in public land management, and contribute to direct democracy.[93]

There are three important messages here. First, whether agencies or managers embrace it or not, public participation is a part of the formal policy process that we outlined in Chapter 2. It can be nurtured as part of the agency's culture. It can also be a reaction by citizens and parties to perceived flaws in the policy process. Secondly, public participation is a way to help wildland recreation managers solve particularly difficult problems, but it should not be thought of as a cure-all, as a means of pacification or as a way to relieve public managers of their obligations to make tough choices. Finally, collaboration and other forms of public participation involve powerful processes that wildland recreation managers are increasingly being called upon to facilitate. In the words of political scientist Robert Reich:

. . . the public manager's job is not only, or simply, to make policy choices and implement them. It is also to participate in a system of democratic governance in which public values are continuously rearticulated and recreated.[94]

CONCLUSIONS

We began this chapter with several policy-management vignettes to illustrate how today's public managers go about the complex task of policy implementation. By focusing on the interplay between policy and management, we tried to underscore a number of concepts and skills that we feel reflect the art and science of successful wildland recreation management in the twenty-first century. Carrying capacity, the recreation opportunity spectrum, and benefits-based management are concepts that direct thinking about how managers can best accomplish their agencies' missions in constantly changing ecological and cultural settings. These frameworks require traditional scientific skills in collecting, monitoring, and interpreting biological and social data. They also require some "art" in how they are applied in various situations, for there is no universal blueprint to follow. As federal and state agencies seek to stretch tight budgets, garner public support, and manage resources across multiple jurisdictions, collaboration and public participation will continue to be fundamental aspects of the wildland recreation manager's job. These fundamental democratic processes require advanced skills in interpersonal communications, teamwork, coordination, and social science methods. They do not take away the "science" from the manager's job, but the manner in which the results of science are applied and communicated takes on new dimensions as citizens increasingly expect a voice in decisions about how natural resources, including wildland recreation areas, are managed. As the policy-management vignettes displayed, managers are finding innovative ways to succeed in both the art and the science of their professions.

NOTES

1. Allen and Gould, "Complexity, Wickedness, and the Public Forests."
2. Ibid., p. 23.
3. We are indebted to several individuals for providing much of the information contained in the policy-management vignettes. *Vignette No. 1:* Therese

O'Rourke, Program Leader, Southern California Conservation Strategy (Southern California National Forests). Raina Fulton, Recreation Officer, Angeles National Forest (California). *Vignette No. 2:* Janna Larson, Landscape Architect and Recreation Planner, San Bernardino National Forest (California). She is now (2002) Deputy Director of the Sewee Visitor Center, Francis Marion National Forest. *Vignette No. 3:* Les Wadzinski, Recreation Program Manager, Hoosier National Forest (Indiana).

4. Stephenson, J.R., and Calcarone, G.M., 1999. Southern California mountains and foothills assessment: habitat and species conservation issues. General Technical Report GTR-PSW-172. Albany, CA: USDA, Forest Service, Pacific Southwest Research Station, 402 pp.

5. This case is consistent with statements made by John Phipps, Forest Supervisor of the Mt. Baker/Snoqualmie National Forest at a plenary session of the Society and Natural Resources Symposium in Bellingham, Washington (June 2000). When it was time for questions from the audience, one of the co-authors of this book asked him what he thought the effects of ecosystem thinking would be on outdoor recreation policy in the FS. He said that there would likely be no overall restrictions on a wide range of recreation uses, including motorized uses, but more restrictions on a site by site basis and he used the specific example of riparian zones. Protecting riparian zones from recreation development, roads, grazing, and other uses he argued, results in sustainability (e.g., a continuous supply of clean water). In the southern California case here, protecting riparian zones is intended to sustain populations of endangered species.

6. Cortner and Moote, "Ecosystem management: political challenges for managers and scientists"; Meffe et al., Chapter 2.

7. Cubbage et al., *Forest Policy,* p. 327.

8. Federal Register, 65(176): Sept. 11, 2000, 50 CFR Part 17, "Endangered and threatened wildlife and plants: Proposed designation of critical habitat for the California red-legged frog (*Rana aurora draytonii*)."

9. Meeting ADA requirements was one purpose of the redesign. The other purposes were to restore the fragile riparian habitat, provide a safe and healthy recreation experience, and meet the needs of increasing numbers of visitors and Latino users.

10. When Ms. Larson was interviewed, the Forest Service was in the process of developing universal access design standards for outdoor recreation facilities. These standards are now available for review and comment on-line at *http://www.fs.fed.us/recreation/programs/accessibility/.* Ms. Larson felt clear guidelines would greatly help overcome the challenge that this note refers to.

11. Wilkinson, *American Indians, Time and the Law,* pp. 21, 82–85; Clow and Sutton, *Trusteeship in Change: Toward Tribal Autonomy in Resource Management;* Spence, *Dispossessing the Wilderness,* pp. 6, 25–29,134–139;

Rudzitis, *Wilderness and the Changing American West,* p. 66; Burnham, *Indian Country, God's Country,* pp. 9–58.

12. P.L. 106–423, 106th Congress, "Timbisha Shoshone Homeland Act," January, 2000.

13. Burnham, *Indian Country, God's Country,* p. 6.

14. National Park Service, 2002. "Death Valley General Management Plan," p. 44.

15. Slover, "A mosaic of opinion: Collaborative planning for the Charles C. Deam Wilderness"; Wadzinski, L. Paper presented at 6th International Symposium on Society and Resource Management, June 5, 2002: "Capacity Management in the Charles C. Deam Wilderness."

16. For example, an entire workshop in 1997 was devoted to assessing the progress of and making recommendations for changes to the Limits of Acceptable Change planning process (McCool and Cole, compilers).

17. This is changing somewhat. Both Stankey ("The ROS and LAC Planning Systems," p. 181) and Driver and Bruns ("Concepts and Uses of the Benefits Approach to Leisure," p. 363) report initial attempts by the Forest Service, U.S. National Park Service, and Parks Canada to integrate these systems with broader, more holistic management and planning systems.

18. Clark and Stankey, 1979; Driver et al., 1987.

19. Stankey, "The ROS and LAC: A review . . . , p. 174.

20. For example, in a "primitive zone" emphasis is placed on maintaining the area's natural conditions with few management restrictions thus emphasizing opportunities for nonmotorized types of wilderness experiences gained from such activities as backpacking and hiking. In an "urbanized zone" large numbers of visitors and ensuing impacts are anticipated and facilities are "hardened" (e.g., paved trails) or managed to accommodate a wide range of mechanized and nonmechanized recreational activities.

21. Manning, "The Recreation Opportunity Spectrum," pp. 191–192.

22. Stankey ("The ROS and LAC Planning Systems: A Review of Experiences and Lessons," pp. 176–177) describes Australian and Danish attempts at applying the ROS at the urban end of the spectrum. He notes that in North America applications of the ROS continue to focus primarily on the "primitive" or "wilderness" end of the scale.

23. Hendee et al., *Wilderness Management,* Chapter 9, is a good overview of recreation carrying capacity.

24. Ibid, p. 215.

25. Sumner, 1942, The biology of wilderness protection, *Sierra Club Bulletin,* 27(8); 14–22.

26. Verburg, "The Carrying Capacity of Recreational Lands," p. 7.

27. Ibid., Verburg's is a good history of the emergence of the recreation carrying capacity idea.

28. Wagar, "The Carrying Capacity of Wild Lands for Recreation," p. 4.

29. Ibid., p. 5

30. We agree with Wagar about the role of public servants with one important caveat. As highlighted in this chapter's first policy-management vignette, managers' decisions frequently do not go unchallenged. If dissatisfied, environmental organizations may act quickly to ask the courts to set limits on acceptable costs in regards to recreation development. In the southern California national forest case, the unacceptable cost is loss of biological diversity.

31. Manning, *Studies in Outdoor Recreation,* 2nd edition, p. 79

32. Stankey et al., "The Limits of Acceptable Change (LAC) System for Wilderness Planning."

33. Following on the heels of LAC, other frameworks for applying carrying capacity emerged. According to Manning (1999), these include Visitor Impact Management (Graefe et al., 1990), Visitor Experience and Resource Protection (Manning et al., 1996, Hof and Lime, 1997, National Park Service, 1997), Carrying Capacity Assessment Process (Shelby and Heberlein, 1986), Quality Upgrading and Learning (Chilman et al., 1989, 1990), and Visitor Activity Management Process (Environment Canada and Park Service, 1991). All of these frameworks are variations of the LAC process. They incorporate Wagar's basic ideas but go a step further by providing structured processes for making carrying capacity decisions. Stankey (1999) reviews the overseas applications of the LAC and describes its shortcomings.

34. Conservation Foundation, *National Parks for a New Generation,* p. 57.

35. Stankey et al., "The Limits of Acceptable Change," p. 37.

36. Personal communications, Les Wadzinski, Recreation Program Manager, Hoosier National Forest, 6/14/02.

37. Benefits-based management (BBM) is part of a larger paradigm shift referred to as the Benefits Approach to Leisure, or BAL (Driver and Bruns, 1999). When it was first developed, BAL was called Benefits-based management (BBM). However, BBM implied a focus on management of inputs (e.g., labor and capital) instead of outputs (e.g., individual and societal benefits). BBM also was criticized for ignoring broader goals such as increasing political parity, encouraging more of a specific type of research, and influencing planning decisions. Thus, the developers of the system now refer to BBM as a specific application of BAL.

38. Driver and Bruns, "Concepts and Uses of the Benefits Approach to Leisure," pp. 349–350.

39. Anderson et al., "Planning to Provide Community and Visitor Benefits from Public Lands," p. 201.

40. For examples of the community-related benefits of recreation and pilot tests of the BBM system, see Stein et al. (1999) and Lee and Driver (1999).

41. For more examples of studies that link specific benefits to recreation, see Stein et al., 1995, and Driver and Bruns, 1999, p. 354.

42. For example, in "The parks are being loved to death . . ." (p. 56), More notes that the Forest Service has "accumulated an $812 million backlog of maintenance needs" and "has only enough money to maintain 17% of its roads."

43. Cordell and Betz ("Trends in outdoor recreation supply . . .") made this prediction before recent economic slowdowns, downward revisions of the size of the budget surplus, and the terrorist attacks in New York and Washington, DC.

44. According to the National Park Service, "Land and Water Conservation Fund" (*http://www.ncrc.nps.gov/programs/lwcf/fed_state.html,* accessed 6/19/02), over its first 30 years, the LWCF provided more than $8.8 billion to acquire new federal recreation lands and as grants to state and local governments. Federal government agencies received $5.5 billion in LWCF funds from 1965–1995, while state and local governments received $3.2 billion. From the stateside portion, 75% went to locally sponsored projects.

45. More and Stevens, "Do user fees exclude low-income people from resource-based recreation?" p. 343, and Manning, *Studies in Outdoor Recreation,* pp. 266–267, note that demand elasticity impacts the degree to which fee increases reduce use and cite relevant supporting studies. For close-to-home parks and sites that are not well-known or used mostly by local communities, studies indicate that demand is elastic and that use drops off steadily with increasing price. However, in cases where demand is inelastic (e.g., well-known U.S. national parks), overall visitation is not affected by fee increases.

46. Conservation Foundation, *National Parks for a New Generation,* p. 57.

47. Manning, *Studies in Outdoor Recreation;* More and Stevens, "Do user fees exclude low income people . . ."

48. Diamond, "The Role of the Private Sector," p. 172; LaPage, "New roles for government and industry in outdoor recreation."

49. Roggenbuck, "Subsidy Reduction Benefits Outdoor Recreation."

50. Morton, "Sustaining recreation resources . . ."

51. Tarlock, "For Whom the National Parks?" p. 262

52. Driver and Crandall, "Recreation on Public Lands."

53. Driver et al., *Nature and the Human Spirit: Toward an Expanded Land Management Ethic.*

54. Bryan, *Conflict in the Great Outdoors.*

55. Cockrell and Wellman, "Democracy and Leisure."

56. Brown, *Islands of Hope.*

57. MacIntosh, "Visitor Fees in the National Park System," p. 6.

58. Ibid., pp. 9–11

59. White, et al., "Trends in the Economics of Sustainable Outdoor Recreation and Tourism."

60. Ibid., p. 65.

61. Siehl, "U.S. Recreation Policies since World War II," notes that the PCAO's relative lack of influence as compared to ORRRC is probably because of limited involvement by Congress.

62. The FY 2002 Congressional appropriation was $140 million for the state side of the Land and Water Conservation Fund, a $50 million increase from FY 2001. The FY 2003 stateside appropriation is $94 million (*http://www.nps.gov/lwcf/fed_state.html* accessed 4/28/03).

63. Ibid.

64. Ibid., Gartner and Lime also note that the backlog of maintenance and repairs is currently (2000) $8 billion for the National Park Service alone.

65. Wilkinson, "Semipublic lands? Park user fees freeze out lower-income Americans," June 9, 2000, online, *www.csmonitor.com.*

66. Seattle Times, Sunday, Jan. 28, 2000, accessed online 2/16/01, archives. seattletimes.

67. Bates, "Paying to play: the future of recreation fees."

68. The roots of public participation, however, go back at least to 1946. Specifically, the Administrative Procedure Act of 1946 (60 Stat. 237) established the principle of public procedural rights in public policy and decision-making. Solomon et al., "Public Involvement under NEPA. . . ," p. 263, note that APA mandates federal agencies "to observe established procedural requirements set out in law, including public participation when required." Furthermore, "agency actions are not to be arbitrary, capricious, or an abuse of discretion by ignoring public input: and agency actions are not to be contrary to constitutional right, power, privilege, or immunity by formulating public policy without an opportunity for public comment or debate."

69. McKinney, in Brick et al., *Across the Great Divide,* pp. 33–40.

70. Tuler and Webler, "Public participation: Relevance and application in the National Park Service"; Wellman and Tipple, "Governance in the wildland-urban interface."

71. McDonough and Wheeler, *Toward School and Community Collaboration in Social Forestry,* p. 2.

72. Arnstein, "A ladder of citizen participation"; Wandersman, "User participation in planning environments"; Wandersman et al., "Who participates, who does not, and why?"

73. Brudney, "The effective use of volunteers . . ."; Propst et al., "Citizen participation trends and their educational implications . . ."; Propst and Bentley, "Trends in citizen participation . . ."; Putnam, "Bowling together."

74. See for example, Heifitz and Sinder, "Political leadership . . ."; Sirmon, "National leadership."; Wellman et al., "Governance in the wildland-urban in-

terface"; McCay and Jentoft, "From the bottom up . . ."; Roberts, "Public deliberation . . ." ; Snow, "Coming home: An introduction to collaborative conservation."

75. See for example, Wollondeck, "Public lands conflict and resolution . . ."; West and Brechin, *Resident peoples and national parks*; McDonough and Wheeler, *Toward school and community collaboration in community forestry;* Tuler and Webler, "Public participation: Relevance and application in the National Park Service"; Brick et al., *Across the Great Divide . . ."*

76. Smith and McDonough, "Beyond public participation . . . ," find that trust requires that the public participation process is perceived to be fair and that diverse viewpoints are actively solicited and considered at all stages of decision-making.

77. Lind and Tyler, *The social psychology of procedural justice*; Lauber and Knuth, "Measuring fairness in citizen participation"; Tyler and Degoey, "Collective restraint in social dilemmas . . ."

78. Snow, "Coming home . . . ," p. 2.

79. Ibid., pp. 3–4.

80. Allen and Gould, "Complexity, wickedness and public forests."

81. Appalachian Trail Conference, "Appalachian Trail Partners," online. *http://www.appalachiantrail.org/about/partners.html#sub2* accessed 6/19/02.

82. Lins, "Community development and the National Park Service" and "Ebey's Landing National Historical Reserve," *http://www.nps.gov/ebla/home.htm ,* accessed 6/19/02.

83. For example, see "Timucuan Ecological and Historic Preserve (Jacksonville, FL)," *http://www.nps.gov/timu/;* for further examples at the domestic level, see National Park Service, "Rivers, Trails and Conservation Assistance Program: What We Do," *http://www.ncrc.nps.gov/PROGRAMS/RTCA/WhatWeDo,* for a listing of 1000 miles of rivers, 700 miles of trails, and 30,000 acres of protected open space co-managed with grassroots groups and local governments in communities throughout the U.S. Also see case studies described in Knight and Landres (1998) and Brick et al. (2001). For numerous international examples, see West and Brechin (1991), McNeely et al. (1995), Saunier and Meganck (1995), Peterson and Johnson (1995), Furze et al. (1996), and McCay and Jentoft (1996).

84. For a recent critique from an international development perspective, see Cooke and Korhari (eds.), *Participation: The New Tyranny.*

85. Elmore, "Backward mapping: implementation research and policy decisions."

86. Pressman and Wildavsky, *Implementation: How Great Expectations in Washington are Dashed in Oakland.*

87. As a case in point, recall the outcome of the planning process related in the Deam Wilderness policy-management vignette in this chapter. Another case revolves around the Land and Water Conservation Fund Act. As a national

policy, this piece of legislation is responsible for distributing federal dollars to states for the purchase and/or development of open space and park lands. Some states have established mechanisms for further distributing a portion of their allocations to local units of government on a competitive basis. Using a variety of local citizen participation processes, local units of government develop priorities for acquisition and development, some of which are submitted to state governments as grant applications for Land and Water Conservation Fund monies. According to the National Park Service (*http://www.nps.gov/lwcf/fed_state.html*, accessed 4/28/03), this institutionalized devolution process has resulted in 37,000 grants to state and local governments over 30 years, or $3.2 billion, matched by local units of government on a 50/50 basis for a total of $6.4 billion. Seventy-five percent of the total funds obligated to the states have gone to locally sponsored projects to provide recreation opportunities close to where people live.

88. Weber, *Pluralism by the Rules,* p. 256.

89. Ibid., p. 257.

90. Varela, "Collaborative conservation: Peace or pacification?" p. 235.

91. Weber, *Pluralism by the Rules,* pp. 222, 264.

92. Ibid., p. 264.

93. Brick, "Finding a political niche for collaborative conservation," p. 173; Weber, *Pluralism by the Rules,* pp. 221–222.

94. Reich, *The Power of Public Ideas,* p. 124; Weber, *Pluralism by the Rules* (pp. 228–232), agrees with Reich's assessment.

CHAPTER 12

CONCLUSIONS

As we have seen, our wildland recreation resources are cultural creations born in conflicting value judgments about their purposes, and they are subject to a continuous process of redefinition as society changes. The policies we enact to govern our parks and wildland recreation areas are but temporary agreements among competing forces, and they are repealed, amended, and reinterpreted as a changing social environment demands. Public resource managers face the challenge of working within this turbulent environment to deliver societal benefits while protecting park resources. Our premise in writing this book is that understanding how wildland recreation resources and policies have come to be will help managers navigate the choppy waters they face in their jobs.

Today's context for wildland recreation policy has been formed by the conflict between utilitarian conservation and romantic preservation,[1] two central values at the turn of the nineteenth century, and by the deep-rooted organizational cultures of two agencies that reflect these values. The struggle between preservation and conservation continues to shape wildland recreation policy, but other important forces are also at work and professional managers must consider them.

Voices that have been largely overlooked are now joining the policy-making arena, both in terms of our evolving understanding of history and in terms of how we address contemporary issues. Recent scholarship has informed us of the contributions women made to the creation of wilderness and park areas and the protection of wildlife in the late 1800s and early 1900s. Scholars are helping us understand the role of working men and women in shaping urban parks and helping us understand how Native

Americans have enriched the story of humans' place in the environment. Through their work in environmental justice, scholars are also bringing out the perspectives and concerns of those who have traditionally been excluded from the wildland recreation policy conversation.

In this edition, we have sought to expand representation of those whose interests have been overlooked and whose voices have been silent. For public servants working in natural resource management, the implications of a narrow understanding of environmental history are serious. If agencies make policy decisions in an exclusionary fashion while, at the same time, the population of the United States continues to diversify, they cannot count on full public support, and they may draw antagonism.[2] Management strategies such as charging more and higher fees to make up for flat budgets may increasingly be seen as discriminatory by less privileged sectors of society. If agencies are to remain viable and credible, they must diversify their workforces and strongly encourage existing employees to get out from behind their desks and communicate with people who are not like them. As the conversation broadens, it will increasingly rewrite the traditional Muir vs. Pinchot wilderness narrative for wildland recreation.[3]

The agencies charged with caring for wildland recreation resources must change as society changes.[4] But agencies cannot and do not change easily. Like individuals, agencies must first survive, and that entails clarification of their mission and the delivery of services to clients interested in that mission. By clearly stating how the agency interprets its legislative mandate, by recruiting and retaining individuals who understand and support agency history and mission, and by meeting the needs of supporters in Congress and the public, agencies seek to ensure their survival.[5]

The USDA Forest Service and the National Park Service, the federal agencies most deeply involved in the evolution of American wildland recreation policy, both began institutional life with a strong sense of mission. Both agencies were products of the Progressive era, and their employees shared the assumptions of the age that governmental action was necessary to protect resources from special interests, that experts removed from politics should direct governmental efforts, and that the purpose of governmental action should be to use resources for the betterment of society. The Forest Service and Park Service both had charismatic early leaders who provided an indelible sense of purpose. This sense of purpose unified the agencies internally and solidified their external relations with Congress and the public.[6]

These two strong agencies have been aggressively challenged by the growth of the environmental movement in the last three decades. Environmentalists have always been present, of course, whether in the form of romantic preservationists like John Muir or ecologists like Aldo Leopold, and they have always challenged the agencies' progressive management philosophy. In the 1960s and 1970s, however, buoyed by a complex amalgam of social and economic conditions, the environmental coalition achieved unprecedented political strength. Now, in another swing of the pendulum, with environmentalist values well ingrained in American institutions, economic development interests are resurgent and are exerting countervailing pressure on the agencies.

Until recently, it has been very difficult to find ways to bring to the table the countervailing forces of environmentalism and economic development. With the advent of ecosystem management in recent years, a suitable conceptual framework may be emerging. Since human communities are part of ecological communities, the two must go hand-in-hand to achieve ecosystem management objectives.[7] This search for balance resembles the compromises that emerged from the use/preservation debate, but ecosystem management expands the geographic and temporal scales of the debate. Even though there is still much disagreement about the meaning and implications of ecosystem management, as an organizing concept it has become part of the everyday language of the natural resource management agencies. A quick perusal of agency websites will attest to this trend. The effects of ecosystem management thinking on wildland recreation management can be seen in many specific cases; our discussion of the four southern California forests in Chapter 11(policy-management vignette no. 1) is but one example.

Another conceptual framework that attempts to clarify both economic and environmental outcomes is benefits-based management. While ecosystem management pertains to natural resources in general, benefits-based management focuses on the human outcomes (economic and non-economic) associated with outdoor recreation. The Forest Service and Park Service have been less enthusiastic about adopting benefits-based management as a guiding framework than they have about ecosystem management, but wider acceptance may be only a matter of time. Two other agencies, the Corps of Engineers and Bureau of Land Management, are making notable attempts at making benefits-based management part of the organizational landscape for managers. As we have seen, interagency competition has often driven policy changes; if this pattern holds, the Forest Service and Park Service may soon follow the lead of the Corps and BLM in implementing benefits-based management in more than isolated cases.

Both ecosystem management and benefits-based management are leading to changes in the way in which the Recreation Opportunity Spectrum and Limits of Acceptable Change management frameworks are employed. ROS and LAC are being modified to address both ecosystem management goals and the broader social benefits of recreation.

Management agencies operate in the ebb and flow of social values and decision-making frameworks. Wildland recreation managers are in the hot seat, and the future likely will hold more conflict as expansion of the wildland recreation estate waxes and wanes, urban sprawl continues, participation in the diverse forms of outdoor recreation rises and falls, and the variety of recreation tastes increases. While there may occasionally be relief from restrictions on budgets and personnel, there is little doubt that wildland recreation managers will always be expected to do a lot with a little. Wildland recreation is important in American life, but not so important that we will lavish resources on it. Budgets have been flat throughout the 1980s and 1990s; there is a backlog of maintenance needs; and related laws (NEPA, ESA, ADA) and new concerns like "homeland security" have increased the responsibilities of public recreation providers without accompanying increases in staff or funds. Agencies have explored user fees to make ends meet, but this has raised concerns that millions of Americans will be denied access to public lands and waters and that government will shirk its responsibility to pay for equitable access to nature and open space.[8] For these and other reasons, wildland recreation management will be an increasingly demanding profession.

Even though public funding for wildland recreation management has never been abundant, we agree with Jeanne Clarke and Daniel McCool that Americans are well served by public resource management agencies and the men and women who staff them:

> The annual budgets for the Corps (of Engineers), the Forest Service, the National Park Service, the Natural Resources Conservation Service, the Bureau of Reclamation, the Bureau of Land Management, and the U.S. Fish and Wildlife Service combined add up to less than $16 billion, or less than 1 percent of the current (1996) $1.6 trillion federal budget. Americans thus enjoy a nation-wide system of parks and forests, an abundance of reasonably priced food, little scarcity of drinkable water, the opportunity to see

bald eagles, wolves and grizzlies in the wild, and much else, all for relatively little money. We think that this is quite a bargain.[9]

Furthermore, as pointed out in the introductory chapter, the wildland recreation estate continues to grow. The 2000 annual report of The Wilderness Society boasted the title, "Year 2000: The Best for American Land Protection in Twenty Years." Backing up this claim, the authors reported the following accomplishments:

- Establishment of eleven national monuments and expansion of two others, resulting in the protection of 5 million acres of public lands
- Addition of 1 million acres to the National Wilderness Preservation System
- Executive and administrative orders to leave 60 million roadless acres in national forests in their natural condition
- A significant increase in Congressional funding for land acquisition
- Actions to restore the Everglades, protect Hawaii's coral reefs, limit snowmobile use in national parks, and solve traffic gridlock problems in Yosemite and Zion National Parks

The Wilderness Society report notes that this list surpassed any year's efforts since the enactment of the Alaska Lands Act in 1980, which protected 105 million acres of public lands.[10] Not all of these accomplishments have survived, however. In its first three years, the George W. Bush administration overturned Clinton's executive order pertaining to the 60 million acres of unroaded lands in national forests (see Chapter 8) and reopened the issue of snowmobile restrictions. Nonetheless, most of the Year 2000 accomplishments have endured. More protected public lands generally mean more lands available for wildland recreation. More wildland recreation means an increased need for managers who can interpret the broad policies that establish these places and implement strategies to protect them.

Expansion of the wildland recreation estate is an important dimension of policy, but there are others. Enlightened policies also are needed to move toward such societal goals as:

- Funding the backlog of long overdue maintenance and repairs of the wildland recreation estate
- Diversifying the workforce of federal resource management agencies
- Making public participation part of agency organizational culture

- Encouraging creative partnerships between agencies, different levels of government, and the public and private sectors

Appropriations passed during the current Bush administration have added to the Land and Water Conservation Fund and enabled some progress on the backlog of maintenance and repairs. Policies that address diversity and public participation are beginning to occur, but more are needed, and there is ample room for gains in efficiency and effectiveness through partnerships.

There is a great need for leadership at all levels in all wildland recreation management agencies. Agency leaders help place issues on decision-makers' agendas, a fundamental step in the policy process (see Figure 2–2), and they also provide corrective feedback to policy-makers. Resource managers at all levels can function as policy entrepreneurs, or visionaries with the skills and enthusiasm needed to bring issues to the forefront for public debate and champion a cause.

THE POLICY PROCESS

In Chapter 2, we described the policy process. Here, we want to reaffirm two key points. First, the agency and its key actors—professional managers—are central to the policy process. They are in the "free fire zone" of policy implementation not only because they carry out the broad policies handed them by Congress and their superiors, but also because they create policies themselves and influence new policies.

Agencies are pivotal in another important way. As the histories of the Forest Service and National Park Service illustrate, interagency rivalry was key to the creation of a diverse supply of outdoor recreation resources in the United States. Ironically, at the present time interagency cooperation and partnerships are increasingly seen as indispensable to implementing ecosystem management, which involves managing across social, political, and ecological boundaries.

Agencies are increasingly being called upon to expand the public dialogue to include the powerless and to contribute to effective democratic practice. Failure to form partnerships, cooperate, and facilitate more than token public participation frequently stymies policy implementation. Instead, skillful interest groups use litigation and the threat of litigation to get what they want. But, as one concerned citizen at a legislative hearing so eloquently put it: "Litigation is a poor way to conduct public policy; all we wanted to do was sit down and work with the agency." The adroit manager can avoid getting to the point of litigation as a last resort.

Our second key point about the policy process is that it is anything but linear and predictably rational. The classic formal model we described in the second chapter should be considered only as an ideal, both as it applies to natural resource management and to public administration in general. Far from being neatly linear and rational, the policy process is complex, dynamic, cyclical, and value laden. It is subject to random events and chaos. Policies can be formed by single acts of key individuals, catastrophes like the fires at Yellowstone and Los Alamos, or an unpredictable series of seemingly inconsequential, incremental acts that combine to shift the course of action.

THE MANAGEMENT RESPONSE

Relating wildland recreation to the larger social context, while accounting for the uniqueness of their areas' resources and users, challenges wildland recreation managers with "wicked" problems.[11] Making the job doubly difficult is the fact that management must pursue national goals within the confines of particular settings.

All too often, wildland recreation managers, especially those trained in natural resources curricula, have tended to focus on the physical and biological attributes of their areas, while treating visitors as threats that must be managed to preserve the natural resources. While site-specific problems caused by human impacts are real, most areas receive mass use only on small portions of the land or water.[12] It is the manager's job to find ways to obtain the resources they need to protect natural resources during peak use times. As Alan Wagar explained in his reassessment of the carrying capacity concept in 1974: "From the viewpoint of society, the objective of all resource management is to create and maintain a flow of benefits for people . . . We must not forget that protecting and managing resources are means, not ends."[13]

Development of more definitive policy would do much to reduce the wickedness of the problems facing wildland recreation managers. For example, the National Forest Management Act narrowed the range of alternatives by setting restrictions on clearcutting, and in the *2000 Management Policies* manual the National Park Service attempted more clearly to define the term "resource impairment." This increased specificity over previous policy statements is intended to give managers a better basis for arguing for road closures and other management actions aimed at resource protection. Nevertheless, a high degree of policy clarity in future wildland recreation management should not be expected. Policies reflect compromises among competing interests and, therefore, they tend to contain ambiguities that reflect the incomplete settlement of the struggle that produced them. As writer Chris Anderson so succinctly phrases the issue in *Edge Effects: Notes from an Oregon Forest,* "No policy can be justified on the grounds that it is entirely pure."[14] Furthermore, even if Congress could spell out all decisions, it might hesitate to do so, realizing that social wants vary by location and can change quickly. For these reasons, legislation tends to be somewhat open-ended, leaving the administrative agencies, interested publics, and the courts to work out the details. One of the marks of creative management is finding ways to resolve the inevitable tension between focus and openness in particular issues.

If substantial policy clarification is not in the offing, what else can managers turn to in the face of increasingly wicked problems? Science can be a source of great help, and wildland recreation managers must have a working understanding of a range of scientific knowledge in order to be successful. More and more, as well, managers will need to be able to recognize the inevitable limitations of science, and that entails a solid grasp of the scientific method. However, as explained in the first chapter, science can only inform decisions; it cannot make them.[15] Decision-making is part of the complicated and unpredictable policy process that we have described throughout this book. As such, science is only the beginning.

Political competence is also requisite to successful policy implementation. As defined by Hanna Cortner and Merton Richards, political competence

... requires knowing the principal political actors and their beliefs, values, and motivations; the intensity with which they hold their preferences; the resources they have available to press their demands in the political arena; and possible areas of policy conflict and consensus. By examining the choices and preferences of important interest groups and the resources and strategies they have available to maximize their values, resource managers can pinpoint significant impediments to implementation of forest plans. Being aware of these possible political pitfalls is a way to avoid surprises.[16]

Interpersonal skills—including collaboration and communications—and a strong sense of purpose are key components of political competence. Interpersonal skills, particularly the political skills that are pivotal in dealing effectively with conflict, will come to the fore in future wildland recreation management. One aspect of management that is especially dependent on such skills is management planning, where conflicting interests must be reconciled.[17] The Yosemite Plan was one of many that began to open the wildland recreation planning process to the public. Another example of open planning involved the Bob Marshall Wilderness Complex in western Montana.[18] As described in Chapter 11, collaborative conservation is the early twenty-first century's version of open planning and management. Collaborative arrangements are unique to each situation, but the overall goal is to influence decisions on a wide variety of environmental issues (e.g., timber management, control of sprawl, land use, recreation and tourism development, pollution abatement) by bringing together diverse people who usually do not communicate with each other or are adversaries.[19]

In the case of collaborative conservation and other forms of public participation, representation of the various interests is critical to the validity of any plans produced. Given the heterogeneity of our population and the multiplicity of governmental planning exercises that must be undertaken, it is difficult to envision anything approaching perfect representation of the public interest in any working group. This leaves an essential role for those public servants who are knowledgeable and consistently concerned about wildland recreation areas—the managers—to represent the evolving public interest as best they can.[20]

Reconciling diverse public interests is only one of the many aspects of wildland recreation management demanding political competence. Good management entails more than sizing up interest groups accurately and mediating among them. It also involves building support via effective two-way communications, coordination, and collaboration.[21] If they are to participate effectively in the social choices that will be made for their areas, wildland recreation managers must understand the evolving purposes of the areas and the emerging missions of their agencies. Equally important, they must develop their own personal sense of purpose, which will help them articulate agency policy and challenge it when necessary. Wildland recreation management thus calls for a great deal of understanding—of the natural resources, the visitors, the interest groups, the agency, and, most importantly, oneself. Such understanding cannot be taught in a course or even in an entire college education. It arises slowly from the combination of formal education, self-education, and life experiences. Our goal in this book has been to set the foundation. The rest is up to you.

NOTES

1. There are also other essential, debatable, and perhaps unsolvable questions or values, including how society values aesthetics, biodiversity, and the spirituality of place; and the relative weights managers and society give to the consumptive demands of "outsiders" (nonresidents) rather than to local, sometimes subsistence-based, peoples. However, these seem to be current manifestations of the old debate.

2. Swinnerton, "Recreation and conservation: Issues and prospects."

3. Taylor, "Meeting the challenge of wild land recreation management."

4. Foresta, *America's National Parks and Their Keepers,* pp. 261–287; Twight, *Organizational Values and Political Power;* Maser, "The dysfunctional agency"; Freemuth, "The national parks: Professional versus political determinants of reality."

5. Kaufman, *The Forest Ranger,* Leman, "The Forest Ranger Revisited," and Tipple and Wellman, "Herbert Kaufman's Forest Ranger Thirty Years Later" are informative about the means by which coherence is brought to the apparently decentralized Forest Service; see also Clarke and McCool, *Staking Out the Terrain,* pp. 7–11.

6. According to Clarke and McCool (*Staking Out the Terrain*), another powerful agency, the Corps of Engineers, has characteristics similar to those of the USFS in terms of sense of mission, esprit de Corps, public identity as leaders in a well-recognized discipline (civil engineering), consistent and powerful clientele support, and so on. In other words, there are certain traits that powerful agencies share. While Clarke and McCool put the USFS and COE in the "superstar" category, and the NPS in the "Muddling Through" category, they also conclude that the NPS has been on the rise for some time and could become a "superstar" agency at some point.

7. Grumbine, "What is ecosystem management?"; Freemuth, "The emergence of ecosystem management"; Salwasser, "Ecosystem management: a new perspective for national forests and grasslands."

8. Cordell and Betz, "Trends in outdoor recreation supply . . . ," p. 89; More, "A functionalist approach to user fees."

9. Clarke and McCool, *Staking Out the Terrain,* p. 229.

10. The Wilderness Society, "Year 2000: The best for American land protection in twenty years." Washington, DC: The Wilderness Society, 21 pp. Available online at *www.wilderness.org.*

11. Allen and Gould, "Complexity, Wickedness, and the Public Forests."

12. Burch, "Much Ado about Nothing"; agreeing with Burch, More argues that the notion that the parks are being "loved to death" is one of the myths of recreation management ("The Parks are Being Loved to Death . . . ," pp. 59–61.

13. Wagar, "Recreational Carrying Capacity Reconsidered," p. 275. However, we acknowledge that current bio- or ecocentric worldviews might challenge Wagar's premise that resource protection is a means rather than an end. Since Wagar wrote, there has been increased recognition and acceptance that wildland resources have value to species other than humans. This acceptance helps explain why so many people commit time and energy to ecological restoration efforts. Furthermore, ecosystem management encourages the achievement of both bio- and anthropocentric goals.

14. Anderson, *Edge Effects . . .* , p. 29.

15. Sellars, *Preserving Nature in the National Parks,* provides numerous examples of policy reforms in the national parks that flew in the face of contradictory scientific evidence. In addition, see Allen and Gould; Wagar; Burch; Behan, "Political Dynamics of Wildlife Management"; and Burchfield, "Finding Science's Voice in the Forest."

16. Cortner and Richards, "The Political Component of National Forest Planning."

17. Susskind and Weinstein, "Towards a Theory of Environmental Dispute Resolution," is an excellent source on the application of social conflict theory to environmental issues. Since the first edition of this book, other useful sources of information about conflict resolution have appeared, including Wondolleck, *Public Lands Conflict and Resolution,* and Yaffee and Wondolleck, "Building Bridges Across Agency Boundaries."

18. Ashor et al., "Improving Wilderness Planning Efforts"; Brick et al., *Across the Great Divide . . .*

19. The Appalachian Trail Conference and the Greater Yellowstone Coalition are two of the most visible examples of collaborative management. We provide a smaller scale example in Chapter 11. Other examples are found in McNelly, *Expanding Partnerships in Conservation;* Knight and Landres, *Stewardship Across Boundaries;* Brick et al., *Across the Great Divide . . . ;* and Clark and Cromley, *Foundations of Natural Resources Policy and Management.*

20. Goodsell, *The Case for Bureaucracy;* Reich, *The Power of Public Ideas;* and Wamsley et al., *Refounding Public Administration.*

21. Shannon, "Resource Managers and Policy Entrepreneurs"; Yaffee, "Cooperation: A Strategy for Achieving Stewardship Across Boundaries."

APPENDIX

APPLICABLE LAWS, REGULATIONS, AND EXECUTIVE ORDERS FINAL YOSEMITE VALLEY PLAN/SEIS (2000)

This appendix describes the key pieces of legislation that form the legal context for development of the Final Yosemite Valley Plan/SEIS. These pieces of legislation have guided development of this document and would continue to guide its implementation.

NATIONAL PARK SERVICE ENABLING LEGISLATION

Act of June 30, 1864, 13 Stat. 325, 16 USC §48. Authorizes a grant to California for the "Yo-Semite Valley," and for land embracing the "Mariposa Big Tree Grove." This tract was "to be held for public use, resort, and recreation" by the state of California, and to "be inalienable for all time."

Act of August 25, 1916 (National Park Service Organic Act), PL 64-235, 16 USC §1 et seq. As amended. On August 15, 1916, Congress created the National Park Service with the National Park Service Organic Act. This act, as reaffirmed and amended in 1970 and 1978, establishes a broad framework of policy for the administration of national parks:

> "The Service thus established shall promote and regulate the use of the Federal areas known as National Parks, Monuments, and Reservations . . . by such means and measures as to conform to the fundamental purpose of the said Parks, Monuments, and Reservations, which purpose is to conserve the scenery and the natural and historic objects and the wild life therein and to provide for the enjoyment of the same in such manner and by such means as will leave them unimpaired for the enjoyment of future generations."

GENERAL LEGISLATION AND REGULATIONS

Americans with Disabilities Act, PL 101-336, 104 Stat. 327, 42 USC §12101. This act states that all new construction and programs will be accessible to individuals with disabilities. Additionally, National Park Service Special Directive 83–3 states that accessibility will be proportional to the degree of development (i.e., areas of intense development such as visitor centers, museums, drive-in campgrounds, etc., will be entirely accessible, and areas of lesser development such as backcountry trails and walk-in campgrounds may have fewer accessibility features). All development proposed in the Final Yosemite Valley Plan/SEIS must be consistent with this act.

Architectural Barriers Act of 1968, PL 90-480, 82 Stat. 718, 42 USC §4151 et seq. This act establishes standards for design/construction or alteration of buildings to ensure that physically disabled persons have ready access to and use of such buildings. The act excludes historic structures from the standards until they are altered. All development proposed in the Final Yosemite Valley Plan/SEIS must be consistent with this act.

California Wilderness Act of 1984 (PL 98–425). In 1984, Congress officially included most of Yosemite National Park in the National Wilderness Preservation System and named it the Yosemite Wilderness. Many other California wilderness areas were established or expanded with the passage of this act. Inclusion of an area in the National Wilderness Preservation System does not change the jurisdictional responsibility for the land. The National Park Service continues to manage the Yosemite Wilderness under the additional requirements for the Wilderness Act of 1964. Though the project area for the Final Yosemite Valley Plan/SEIS does not include designated Wilderness, indirect impacts on designated Wilderness have been evaluated.

Council on Environmental Quality Regulations for Implementing the Procedural Provisions of the National Environmental Policy Act (NEPA) (40 CFR Parts 1500-1508). The Council on Environmental Quality regulations for implementing the National Environmental Policy Act (NEPA) establish the process by which federal agencies fulfill their obligations under the NEPA process. The Council on Environmental Quality regulations ascertain the requirements for environmental assessments and environmental impact statements that document the NEPA process. The Council on Environmental Quality regulations also define such key terms as "cumulative impact," "mitigation," and "significantly" to ensure consistent application of these terms in environmental documents. This environmental impact statement was prepared as directed in the Council on Environmental Quality regulations.

National Environmental Policy Act (NEPA) of 1970. PL 91-190, 83 Stat. 852, 42 USC §4341 et seq. The NEPA process is intended to help public officials make decisions that are based on understanding of environmental consequences, and take actions that protect, restore, and enhance the environment. Regulations implementing NEPA are set forth by the Council on Environmental Quality. The NEPA process guides the overall planning process for the Final Yosemite Valley Plan/SEIS.

Rehabilitation Act of 1973, PL 93-112, 87 Stat. 357, 29 USC §701 et seq. As amended by the Rehabilitation Act Amendments of 1974, 88 Stat. 1617, this act sets forth a broad range of services and basic civil rights for individuals with disabilities. It prohibits discrimination against persons with visual, hearing, mobility, and mental impairments. All development proposed in the Final Yosemite Valley Plan/SEIS must be consistent with this act.

Wild and Scenic Rivers Act of 1968 as amended (PL 90-542; 16 USC 12371-1287). This act identifies distinguished rivers of the nation that possess remarkable scenic, recreational, geologic, fish and wildlife, historic, cultural, or other similar values; preserves the rivers' free-flowing condition; and protects their local environments. The Merced River in Yosemite National Park was designated a Wild and Scenic River in 1987. All actions proposed in this plan will protect and enhance the values that are recognized by the Merced Wild and Scenic River designation.

Wilderness Act of 1965 (PL 88-577). The Wilderness Act protects congressionally-designated wilderness areas from roads, dams, and other permanent structures; from timber cutting and the operation of motorized vehicles and equipment; and, since 1984, from new mining claims and mineral leasing. Though the Final Yosemite Valley Plan/SEIS does not directly impact designated Wilderness, indirect impacts on wilderness will be identified and addressed.

NATURAL RESOURCES LEGISLATION

Clean Air Act, as amended, PL Chapter 360, 69 Stat. 322, 42 USC §7401 et seq. Section 118 of the Clean Air Act requires all federal facilities to comply with existing federal, state, and local air pollution control laws and regulations. The National Park Service works in conjunction with the Mariposa County Air Pollution Control District to ensure that all construction activities meet requirements.

Federal Water Pollution Control Act (commonly referred to as the Clean Water Act) of 1977 (33 USC 1251 et seq.). The Clean Water Act provides for the restoration and maintenance of the physical, chemical, and biological integrity of the nation's waters. Section 404 of the act prohibits the discharge of fill material into navigable water of the United States, including wetlands, except as permitted under separate regulations by the U.S. Army Corps of Engineers and U.S. Environmental Protection Agency. The placement of fill in wetlands should be avoided if there are practicable alternatives. Compliance with Section 401 and 404 of the Clean Water Act will be completed as necessary prior to any new construction proposed in this plan.

Clean Water Act Amendments of 1987. The 1987 amendments to the act required that the Environmental Protection Agency establish regulations for the issuance of municipal and industrial stormwater discharge permits as part of the National Pollutant Discharge Elimination System. The final Environmental Protection Agency regulations were published in November 1990. These regulations apply to any construction activities that disturb more than five acres of land.

A Notice of Intent to comply with the state's General Construction Activity Stormwater Permit will be submitted to the State Water Resources Control Board, and a Stormwater Pollution Prevention Plan will be developed and approved for all proposed construction projects that affect more than 5 acres.

Comprehensive Environmental Response, Compensation, and Liability Act (commonly referred to as CERCLA or the Superfund Act) PL 96-

510, 94 Stat. 2767, 42 USC §9601 et seq. Congress enacted CERCLA to address growing concerns about the need to clean up uncontrolled, abandoned hazardous waste sites and to address future releases of hazardous substances into the environment. Applicable sites in Yosemite National Park are managed under the National Park Service CERCLA program.

Endangered Species Act of 1973, as amended, PL 93-205, 87 Stat. 884, 16 USC §1531 et seq. The Endangered Species Act protects threatened and endangered species, as listed by the U.S. Fish and Wildlife Service, from unauthorized take, and directs federal agencies to ensure that their actions do not jeopardize the continued existence of such species. Section 7 of the act defines federal agency responsibilities for consultation with the U.S. Fish and Wildlife Service and requires preparation of a Biological Assessment to identify any threatened or endangered species that is likely to be affected by the proposed action. The National Park Service initiated and maintained formal consultation with the U.S. Fish and Wildlife Service throughout the Final Yosemite Valley Plan/SEIS process and prepared a Biological Assessment (see Appendix K) in order to meet obligations under the Endangered Species Act.

Porter-Cologne Water Quality Control Act (California Water Code, Section 13020). Under the authority of the Porter-Cologne Act and federal Clean Water Act, Regional Water Quality Control Boards act as regional agencies for the State Water Resources Control Board and are responsible for regional enforcement of water quality laws and coordination of water quality control activities. The regional board for the Yosemite area is the Central Valley.

Resource Conservation and Recovery Act, as amended (RCRA), PL 94-580, 30 Stat. 1148, 42 USC §6901 et seq. This act establishes a regulatory structure for the management of solid and hazardous waste from the point of generation to disposal. In particular, applicable provisions include those that address underground storage tanks and sites contaminated with elements identified under Federal and State Resource Conservation and Recovery Act regulations.

CULTURAL RESOURCES LEGISLATION

Antiquities Act of 1906, PL 59-209, 34 Stat. 225, 16 USC §432 and 43 CFR 3. This act provides for the protection of historic or prehistoric remains, "or any antiquity," on federal lands. It protects historic monuments and ruins on public lands. It was superseded by the Archeological Resources Protection Act (1979) as an alternative federal tool for prosecution of antiquities violations in the National Park System.

Archeological Resources Protection Act of 1979, PL 96-95, 93 Stat. 712, 16 USC §470aa et seq. and 43 CFR 7, subparts A and B, 36 CFR. This act secures the protection of archeological resources on public or Indian lands and fosters increased cooperation and exchange of information between private, government, and the professional community in order to facilitate the enforcement and education of present and future generations. It regulates excavation and collection on public and Indian lands. It requires notification of Indian tribes who may consider a site of religious or cultural importance prior to issuing a permit. The act was amended in 1988 to require the development of plans for surveying public lands for archeological resources and systems for reporting incidents of suspected violations.

National Historic Preservation Act of 1966, as amended, PL 89-665, 80 Stat. 915, 16 USC §470 et seq. and 36 CFR 18, 60, 61, 63, 68, 79, 800. The National Historic Preservation Act requires agencies to take into account the effects of their actions on properties listed in or eligible for listing in the National Register of Historic Places. The Advisory Council on Historic Preservation has developed implementing regulations (36 CFR 800), which allow agencies to develop agreements for consideration of these historic properties. Yosemite National Park, in consultation with the Advisory Council, the California State Historic Preservation Officer (SHPO), American Indian tribes and the public, has developed a Programmatic Agreement for planning, design, construction, operations and maintenance activities. This Programmatic Agreement provides a process for compliance with National Historic Preservation Act, and includes stipulations for identification, evaluation, treatment, and mitigation of adverse effects for actions affecting historic properties. The National Park Service will follow stipulations of this Programmatic Agreement for all future planning and design projects, including development of the Indian Cultural Center and all out-of-Valley development described in the final plan. The Programmatic Agreement allows the National Park Service to implement standard mitigating measures for some actions, if the State Historic Preservation Officer and the public are notified and provided an opportunity to comment (see Appendix D).

American Indian Religious Freedom Act, PL 95-341, 92 Stat. 469, 42 USC §1996. This act declares policy to protect and preserve the inherent and constitutional right of the American Indian, Eskimo, Aleut, and Native Hawaiian people to believe, express, and exercise their traditional religions. It provides that religious concerns should be accommodated or addressed under NEPA or other appropriate statutes.

Native American Grave Protection and Repatriation Act, PL 101-601, 104 Stat. 3049, 25 USC §3001-3013. This act assigns ownership or control of Native American human remains, funerary objects, sacred objects, and objects of cultural patrimony that are excavated or discovered on federal lands or tribal lands to lineal descendants or culturally affiliated Native American groups.

EXECUTIVE ORDERS

Executive Order 11593: Protection and Enhancement of the Cultural Environment. This Executive Order instructs all federal agencies to support the preservation of cultural properties. It directs them to identify and nominate cultural properties under their jurisdiction to the National Register of Historic Places and to "exercise caution_ to assure that any federally owned property that might qualify for nomination is not inadvertently transferred, sold, demolished, or substantially altered."

Executive Order 11988: Floodplain Management. This Executive Order requires federal agencies to avoid, to the extent possible, adverse impacts associated with the occupancy and modification of floodplains, and to avoid development in floodplains whenever there is a practical alternative. If a proposed action is found to be in the applicable regulatory floodplain, the agency shall prepare a floodplain assessment, known as a Statement of Findings. A Statement of Findings has been prepared for the Final Yosemite Valley Plan/SEIS in accordance with National Park Service, Special Directive 93-4 (Floodplain Management Guideline) and is included as Appendix N.

Executive Order 11990: Protection of Wetlands. This Executive Order established the protection of wetlands and riparian systems as the official policy of the federal government. It requires all federal agencies to consider wetland protection as an important part of their policies and take action to minimize the destruction, loss or degradation of wetlands, and to preserve and enhance the natural and beneficial values of wetlands. Should adverse impacts on wetlands be identified, a Wetland Statement of Findings would be prepared and included in subsequent compliance (such as an environmental assessment or environmental impact statement) for the specific project.

Presidential Executive Order 12898: Federal Actions to Address Environmental Justice in Minority Populations and Low-Income Populations. This Executive Order requires all federal agencies to incorporate environmental justice into their missions by identifying and addressing disproportionately high and adverse human health or environmental effects of their programs and policies on minorities and low-income populations and communities. Impacts on minority and low-income populations have been identified and are addressed in Vol. Ia, Chapter 3, Affected Environment and Vol. Ib, Chapter 4, Environmental Consequences.

Presidential Executive Order 12902: Energy Efficiency and Water Conservation. This Executive Order directs each agency involved in the construction of a new facility to design and construct it to use energy efficiently, conserve water, and employ renewable energy technologies. The requirements of this Executive Order would be met during the design phase for any new facilities proposed in the Final Yosemite Valley Plan/SEIS.

Executive Order 13101: Greening the Government Through Waste Prevention, Recycling, and Federal Acquisition. This Executive Order requires that federal agencies increase the procurement of environmentally preferable or recovered materials. Agencies are directed to set annual goals to maximize the number of recycled products purchased relative to nonrecycled alternatives. In addition, each agency is to establish a program for promoting cost-effective waste prevention and recycling at each of its facilities. The requirements of this executive order would be met during development and implementation phases of the Final Yosemite Valley Plan/SEIS.

Executive Order No. 13112: Invasive Species. This Executive Order prevents the introduction of invasive species and directs federal agencies to not authorize, fund, or carry out actions that it believes are likely to cause or promote the introduction or spread of invasive species. Actions proposed in the Final Yosemite Valley Plan/SEIS include measures to prevent the introduction and spread of invasive species.

DEPARTMENT OF THE INTERIOR—DIRECTOR'S ORDERS

Director's Orders provide guidance for implementing certain aspects of National Park Service policy. Copies of those that have been completed may be obtained by contacting the NPS Office of Policy or by accessing the National Park Service web site. The following Director's Orders may be relevant to the Final Yosemite Valley Plan/SEIS planning process:

Completed Director's Orders

1. The Directives System
2. Park Planning
9. Law Enforcement Program
16A. Reasonable Accommodation for Applicants and Employees with Disabilities
17. National Park Service Tourism
18. Wildland Fire Management
20. Agreements
21. Donations and Fundraising
28. Cultural Resource Management
32. Cooperating Associations
41. Wilderness Preservation & Management
50B. Occupational Safety and Health
77–1. Wetland Protection
83. Public Health
National Park Service Guidelines
NPS-12 National Environmental Policy Act Guidelines
NPS-77 Natural Resources Management Guidelines

Yosemite National Park Home Page[ParkNet]
http://www.nps.gov/yose/planning/yvp/seis/vol_II/appendix_a.html
File created/updated Monday, 22-Jan-01 15:27:38
Yosemite National Park Web Manager

BIBLIOGRAPHY

Abbey, E. 1961. *Desert Solitaire*. Random House, New York.

Adams, D.A. 1993. *Renewable Resource Policy: The Legal-Institutional Foundations*. Island Press, Washington.

Allen, G., and E. Gould, Jr. 1986. Complexity, wickedness, and public forests. *Journal of Forestry,* 84:20–23.

Aley, J., W.R. Burch, B. Conover, and D. Field, editors. 1999. *Ecosystem Management: Adaptive Strategies for Natural Resources Organizations in the 21st Century.* Taylor and Francis, Philadelphia.

Allin, C.W. 1982. *The Politics of Wilderness Preservation*. Greenwood Press, Westport, CT.

Anderson, D.H., R. Nickerson, T.V. Stein, and M.E. Lee. 2000. Planning to provide community and visitor benefits from public lands. In *Trends in Outdoor Recreation, Leisure and Tourism*. Gartner, W.C. and D.W. Lime, editors. CABI Publishing, New York, pp. 197–212.

Anderson, J.E., D.W. Brady, C.S Bullock III, and J. Stewart, Jr. 1984. *Public Policy and Politics in America,* 2nd ed. Brooks/Cole, Monterey, CA.

Anderson, J.E. 1975. *Public Policy-Making*. Praeger, New York.

Ashor, J.C., S.F. McCool, and G.C. Stokes. 1985. Improving wilderness planning efforts: Application of the transactive planning approach. Paper presented at the National Wilderness Research Conference, Fort Collins, CO, July 23–26.

Baker, R.A. 1985. The conservation congress of Anderson and Aspinall, 1963–64. *Journal of Forest History,* 29:104–119.

Baldwin, D.W. 1972. *The Quiet Revolution: Grass Roots of Today's Wilderness Preservation Movement*. Prescott, Boulder, CO.

Bangs, E.E. and S.H. Fritts. 1996. Reintroducing the gray wolf to central Idaho and Yellowstone National Park. *Wildlife Society Bulletin,* 24(3):402–403.

Bates, N.A. 1999. Paying to play: the future of recreation fees. *Parks and Recreation Magazine,* July: 46–52.

Baumgartner, F.R., and B.D. Jones. 1993. *Agendas and Instability in American Politics*. University of Chicago Press. Chicago.

Berry, J.K., and J.C. Gordon, editors. 1993. *Environmental Leadership: Developing Effective Skills and Styles*. Island Press, Washington.

Betz, C.J., D.B.K. English, and H.K. Cordell. 1999. Outdoor recreation resources. In *Outdoor Recreation in American Life: A National Assessment of Demand and Supply Trends*. Cordell, H.K., C.J. Betz, J.M. Bowker, D.B.K. English, J.C. Bergstrom, R.J. Teasley, M.A.Tarrant, and J. Loomis, editors. Sagamore, Champaign, IL, pp. 39–183.

Beveridge, C.E., and D. Schuyler. 1983. *The Papers of Frederick Law Olmsted,* Supplementary Series, Volume III, *Creating Central Park, 1857–1961.* Johns Hopkins University Press, Baltimore.

Beveridge, C.E. and C. Hoffman. 1997. *The Papers of Frederick Law Olmsted,* Supplementary Series, Volume I, *Writings on Public Parks, Parkways, and Park Systems*. Johns Hopkins University Press, Baltimore.

Bode, C. 1981. *Introduction to The Portable Emerson*. Viking Penguin, New York.

Bode, C. 1947. *Introduction to The Portable Thoreau*. Viking Penguin, New York.

Bonnicksen, T. 1982. The development of forest policy in the United States. In *Introduction to Forest Science*. R.A. Young, editor. Wiley, New York, pp. 7–36.

Botkin, D.B. 2001. *No Man's Garden: Thoreau and a New Vision for Civilization and Nature*. Island Press, Washington.

Bratton, S. 1985. Battling Satan in the wilderness. Paper presented at the National Wilderncss Research Conference, Fort Collins, CO, July 22–26.

Brick, P., D. Snow, and S. Van de Wetering, editors. 2001. *Across the Great Divide: Explorations in Collaborative Conservation and the American West*. Island Press, Washington.

Brick, P. 2001. Of impostors, optimists, and kings: Finding a political niche for collaborative conservation. In *Across the Great Divide: Explorations in Collaborative Conservation and the American West*. P. Brick, D. Snow, and S. Van de Wetering, editors. Island Press, Washington, pp. 172–179.

Brockman, C.F., and L.C. Merriam, Jr. 1979. *Recreational Use of Wild Lands*. McGraw-Hill, New York.

Brown, W.E. 1971. *Islands of Hope*. National Recreation and Park Association, Arlington, VA.

Brudney, J.L. 1999. The effective use of volunteers: Best practices for the public sector. *Law and Contemp. Probs.* 62:219–225.

Brunson, M.W. 2000. Managing naturalness as a continuum: Setting limits of acceptable change. In *Restoring Nature: Perspectives from the Social Sciences and Humanities*. P.H. Gobster and R.B. Hull, editors. Island Press, Washington, pp. 220–244.

Bryan, H. 1979. Conflict in the great outdoors. Sociological Studies Monograph No. 4. University of Alabama Bureau of Public Administration. Tuscaloosa, AL.

Burch, W. R., Jr. 1986. Much ado about nothing—some reflections on the wilder and wilder implications of social carrying capacity. *Leisure Sciences*, 6:487–496.

Burnham, P. 2000. *Indian Country, God's Country: Native Americans and the National Parks*. Island Press, Washington.

Burton, P. 1983. Clear and present dangers. *Wilderness*, 46:20–24.

Butler, M.E. 1999. *Prophet of the Parks: The Story of William Penn Mott, Jr*. National Recreation and Parks Association, Ashburn, VA.

Cahn, R. 1985. Horace Albright remembers the origins. *National Parks*. 59:27–31.

Caro, R. 1974. *The Power Broker: Robert Moses and the Fall of New York*. Alfred A. Knopf, New York.

Catlin, G. 1976. North American Indians: Being letters and notes on their manners, customs, and conditions, written during eight years' travel amongst the wildest tribes in North America. R. Nash. In *The American Environment: Readings in the History of Conservation*. 2nd ed. Addison-Wesley, editors. Reading, MA, pp. 5–9.

Chase, A. 1986. *Playing God in Yellowstone: The Destruction of America's First National Park*. Atlantic Monthly Press, Boston.

Chase, A. 1983. The last bears of Yellowstone. In *Atlantic Monthly,* 240:63–73.

Chavez, D.J. 2001. Managing outdoor recreation in California: Visitor studies 1989–1998. In *Gen. Tech. Rep. PSW-GTR-180*. Pacific Southwest Research Station, U.S. Department of Agriculture, Albany, CA.

Chilman, K., J. Ladley, and T. Wikle. 1989. Refining existing recreational carrying capacity systems: emphasis on recreational quality. In *Proceedings of the 1988 Southeastern Recreation Research Conference*. University of Georgia, Athens, pp. 118–123.

Chilman, K., D. Foster, and A. Everson. 1990. Updating the recreational carrying capacity process: Recent refinements. In *Managing America's Enduring Wilderness Resource*. Minnesota Agricultural Experiment Station, St. Paul, pp. 234–238.

Clarke, J.N., and D.C. McCool. 1996. *Staking out the Terrain: Power Differentials among Natural Resource Management Agencies,* 2nd edition. State University of New York Press, New York.

Clark, R.N. and G.H. Stankey. 1979. The recreation opportunity spectrum: A framework for planning, management and research. In *General Technical Report PNW-98*. USDA Forest Service, Pacific Northwest Forest & Range Experiment Station, Portland, OR.

Clark, T.W., A.R. Willard, and C.M. Cromley. 2000. *Foundations of Natural Resources Policy and Management*. Yale University Press, New Haven.

Clawson, M. 1983. *The Federal Lands Revisited*. Resources for the Future, Washington.

Clawson, M., and R.B. Held. 1957. *The Federal Lands: Their Use and Management*. Johns Hopkins University Press for Resources for the Future, Baltimore.

Clawson, M., and Knetsch, J. L.1966. *Economics of Outdoor Recreation*. Johns Hopkins University Press for Resources for the Future, Baltimore.

Clow, R.L. & Sutton, I. 2001. *Trusteeship in Change: Toward Tribal Autonomy in Resource Management*. University Press of Colorado, Boulder.

Cockrell, D. E., and J.D. Wellman. 1985. Democracy and leisure: Reflections on pay-as-you-go outdoor recreation. In *Journal of Park and Recreation Administration,* 3:110.

1985. *National Parks for a New generation: Visions, Realities, Prospects*. Conservation Foundation, Washington.

Cooke, B. and U. Korhari. 2001. *Participation: The New Tyranny*. Zed Books. London.

Cordell, H.K., C.J. Betz, J.M. Bowker, D.B.K. English, J.C. Bergstrom, R.J. Teasley, M.A. Tarrant, and J. Loomis. 1999. *Outdoor Recreation in American Life: A National Assessment of Demand and Supply Trends*. Sagamore, Champaign, IL.

Cordell, H.K., and G.R. Super. 2000. Trends in Americans' outdoor recreation. In *Trends in Outdoor Recreation, Leisure and Tourism,* Gartner, W.C., and D.W. Lime, editors. CABI Publishing, Oxon, UK, pp. 133–145.

Cordell, H.K. and C.J. Betz. 2000. Trends in Outdoor Recreation Supply on Private and Public Lands in the U.S. In *Trends in Outdoor Recreation, Leisure and Tourism,* Gartner, W.C., and D.W. Lime, editors. CABI Publishing, Oxon, UK, pp. 75–90.

Cortner, H., M. Shannon, M. Wallace, S. Burke, and M. Moote. 1996. Institutional barriers and incentives for ecosystem management: A problem analysis. In *Gen. Tech. Rep. PNW-GTR-354*. USDA Forest Service, Pacific Northwest Research Station, Portland, OR.

Cortner, H., and M. Moote. 2000. Ecosystem management: Political challenges for managers and scientists. *Park Science,* 20(1):18–20.

Cortner, H.J., and M.T. Richards. 1983. The political component of national forest planning. *Journal of Soil and Water Conservation*. 38:79–81.

Cortner, H.J., and D.J. Schweitzer. 1981. Institutional limits to national public planning for forest resources: The Resources Planning Act. *Natural Resources Journal,* 21:203–222.

Cox, T.R. 1985. Americans and their forests: Romanticism, progress, and science in the late nineteenth century. *Forest History,* 29:156–168.

Crompton, J., and C. Lamb. 1986. *Marketing Government and Social Services.* John Wiley, New
York.

Cronon, W. 1983. *Changes in the Land: Indians, Colonists, and the Ecology of New England.* Hill
and Wang, New York.

Cronon, W. 1995. *Uncommon Ground: Toward Reinventing Nature.* W.W. Norton & Co., New York.

Cronon, W. 1995. The trouble with wilderness. *The New York Times Magazine,* Aug. 16, 1995,
section 6.

Cronon, W. 1996. Getting back to the wrong nature. *Utne Reader,* May–June 1996. 76–79.

Cubbage, F.W., J. O'Laughlin, and C.S. Bullock III. 1993. *Forest Resource Policy.* Wiley, New
York.

Dana, C. 1981. The curtain rises. In *Sixty-Fifth Anniversary National Park Service.* SW Parks and
Monuments Association and National Park Foundation, p. 2.

Dana, S.T. 1956. *Forest and Range Policy.* McGraw-Hill, New York.

Dana, S.T., and S.K. Fairfax. 1980. *Forest and Range Policy,* 2nd edition. McGraw-Hill, New York.

Deneke, F.J. 1978. Technical assistance, education, and research programs in urban forestry. In *Proceedings of the National Urban Forestry Conference.* USDA Forest Service and State University of New York, College of Environmental Science and Forestry. Washington. November
13–16, pp. 467–478

DeVoto, B. 1943. *Year of Decision: 1846.* Houghton Mifflin, New York.

Diamond, H.C. 1970. The role of the private sector in providing recreational opportunities. In *Elements of Outdoor Recreation Planning.* B.L. Driver, editor. The University of Michigan School
of Natural Resources, Ann Arbor, MI, pp. 171–176.

Dorman, R.L. 1998. *A Word for Nature: Four Pioneering Environmental Advocates, 1845–1913.*
The University of North Carolina Press, Chapel Hill, 256 pp.

Downs, A. 1972. Up and down with ecology—the issue-attention cycle. *The Public Interest*
28:38–50.

Driver, B., P. Brown, T. Gregoire, and G. Stankey. 1987. The ROS planning system: Evolution, basic concepts, and research needed. *Leisure Sciences.* 9(3): 203–214.

Driver, B.C., and D.A. Crandall. 1984. Recreation on public lands: Should the user pay? *American
Forests.* 90:10–11. 49–53.

Driver, B.L. 1996. Benefits-driven management of natural areas. *Natural Areas Journal,*
16(2):94–99.

Driver, B.L., P. Brown, and G. Peterson, 1991. *Benefits of Leisure.* Venture, State College, PA.

Driver, B.L., D. Dustin, T. Baltic, G. Elsner, and G. Peterson. 1996. *Nature and the Human Spirit:
Toward an Expanded Land Management Ethic.* Venture, State College, PA.

Driver, B.L. and D.H. Bruns. 1999. Concepts and uses of the Benefits Approach to Leisure. In *Leisure
Studies: Prospects for the 21st Century.* E.L. Jackson, and T.L Burton, editors. Venture State
College, PA, pp. 349–369.

Duddleson, W.J. 1975. National parks are beset by policy problems, Conservation Foundation Letter. July and August.

Dwyer, J.F., D.J. Nowak, M.H. Noble, and S.M. Sisinni. 2000. Connecting people with ecosystems
in the 21st century: An assessment of our nation's urban forests. In *Gen. Tech. Rep. PNW-GTR-*

490. U.S. Department of Agriculture, Forest Service, Pacific Northwest Research, Station. Portland, OR.

Elmore, R.P. 1989. Backward mapping: Implementation research and policy decisions. *Political Science Quarterly,* 94(4):601–616.

Emerson, R.W. *Nature.* C. Bode, editor. 1981. *The Portable Emerson.* Viking Penguin, New York.

Environment Canada and Park Service. 1991. *Selected Readings on the Visitor Activity Monitoring Process.* Environment Canada, Ottawa.

Everhart, W.C. 1985. *The National Park Service.* Westview Press, Boulder, CO.

Fischer, H. 1995. *Wolf Wars: The Remarkable Inside Story of the Restoration of Wolves to Yellowstone.* Falcon Press, Helena, MT.

Flader, S. 1974. *Thinking Like a Mountain: Aldo Leopold and the Evolution of an Ecological Attitude toward Deer, Wolves, and Forests.* University of Nebraska Press, Lincoln.

Foresta, R.A. 1984. *America's National Parks and Their Keepers.* Resources for the Future, Washington.

Forman, D. 1996. Islands of Doom. *Utne Reader,* May–June. pp. 81–84.

Fox, S. 1981. *John Muir and His Legacy.* Little Brown, Boston.

Fox, S. 1984. We Want No Straddlers. *Wilderness,* 48:5–19.

Frederick, K.D., and R.A. Sedjo. 1991. *America's Renewable Resources: Historical Trends and Current Challenges.* Resources For the Future, Washington.

Freemuth, J. 1989. The National Parks: Political vs. professional determinants of policy. *Public Admin. Review,* 49:278–286.

Freemuth, J. 1996. Emergence of ecosystem management: Reinterpreting the gospel? *Society and Natural Resources,* 9:411–417.

Frome, M. 1992. *Regreening the National Parks.* University of Arizona Press, Tucson.

Furze, B., T. DeLacy, and J. Birckhead. *Culture, Conservation and Biodiversity: The Social Dimension of Linking Local Development and Conservation through Protected Areas.* Wiley, Chichester, England.

Gartner, W.C., and D.W. Lime. 2000. *Trends in Outdoor Recreation, Leisure and Tourism.* CABI Publishing, New York.

Gartner, W.C., and D.W. Lime. 2000. The Big Picture: A Synopsis of Contributions. In *Trends in Outdoor Recreation, Leisure and Tourism.* W.C. Gartner and D.W. Lime, editors. CABI Publishing, Oxon, UK, pp. 1–15

Gilbert, B. 1985. *Westering Man: The Life of Joseph Walker.* University of Oklahoma Press, Norman, OK.

Gilligan, J.P. 1953. The development of policy and administration of forest service primitive and wilderness areas in the western United States, Unpublished PhD Dissertation, University of Michigan, Ann Arbor.

Gleick, J. 1987. National parks becoming morgues for many mammals. *Roanoke Times and World-News.* (Reprinted from *The New York Times,* Feb. 15.)

Glick, D.A., and T.W. Clark. 1998. Overcoming boundaries: The Greater Yellowstone ecosystem. In *Stewardship Across Boundaries.* R.L. Knight and P.B. Landres, editors. Island Press, Washington.

Gobster, P.H., and R.B. Hull. 2000. *Restoring Nature: Perspectives from the Social Sciences and Humanities.* Island Press, Washington.

Gobster, P.H. 1993. Managing urban and high-use recreation settings: Selected papers from the Urban Forestry and Ethnic Minorities Paper Sessions. *4th North American Symposium on Society and Resource Management,* May 17–20, 1992, University of Wisconsin, Madison. *Gen. Tech. Rep. NC-163.* St. Paul, MN: North Central Forest Experiment Station, U.S. Department of Agriculture.

Goodsell, C.T. 1985. *The Case for Bureaucracy: A Public Administration Polemic,* 2nd edition. Chatham House, Chatham, NJ.

Graefe, A., F. Kuss, and J. Vaske. 1990. *Visitor Impact Management: The Planning Framework.* National Parks Conservation Association, Washington.

Graefe, A.R., J.J. Vaske, and F.R. Kuss. 1984. Social carrying capacity: An integration and synthesis of twenty years of research. *Leisure Sciences.* 6:395–431.

Graham, F. Jr. 1978. *The Adirondack Park: A Political History.* Alfred A. Knopf, New York.

Graham, R. 1985. Erasing man's mark in the Everglades. *National Parks,* 59:14–16.

Grodzins, M. 1962. *The Many American Governments and Outdoor Recreation: Trends in American Living and Outdoor Recreation: A Report to the Outdoor Recreation Resources Review Commission.* USGPO, Washington.

Grumbine, R.E. 1994. What is ecosystem management? *Conservation Biology,* 8(1):27–38.

Hammitt, W., and D. Cole. 1998. *Wildland Recreation: Ecology and Management.* John Wiley, New York.

Hammond. J.L. 1977. Wilderness and life in cities. *Sierra Club Bulletin.* 62:12–14.

Hartzog, G.B., Jr. 1988. *Battling for the National Parks.* Moyer Bell Limited, Mt. Kisco, NY.

Hays. S.P. 1959. Conservation and the gospel of efficiency. In *The Progressive Conservation Movement 1890–1920.* Harvard University Press, Cambridge, MA.

Heisler, G.H. 1986. Energy saving with trees. *Journal of Arboriculture,* 12(5):113–125.

Hendee, J.C, and C.P. Dawson. 2002. *Wilderness Management: Stewardship and Protection of Resources and Values.* Fulcrum, Golden, CO.

Hendee, J., G. Stankey, and R. Lucas. 1990. *Wilderness Management,* 2nd edition. North American Press, Golden, CO.

Hendee, J.C., G.H. Stankey, and R.C. Lucas. 1978. Wilderness management. In *USDA Forest Service Miscellaneous Publication No. 1365.*

Hibbard, B.H. 1924. *A History of the Public Land Policies.* Macmillan, New York. Reprinted by the University of Wisconsin Press.

Hof, M., and D. Lime. 1997. Visitor experience and resource protection framework in the national park system: rationale, current status, and future direction. In *Proceedings—Limits of Acceptable Change and Related Planning Processes: Progress and Future Directions. Gen. Tech. Rep. INT-271.* USDA Forest Service, Intermountain Experiment Station, Ogden, UT. pp. 29–36.

Hope, J. 1971. Hassles in the park. *Natural History,* 80:20–23, pp. 82–86, 90–91.

Huth, H. 1957. *Nature and the American: Three Centuries of Changing Attitudes.* University of California Press, Berkeley, CA.

Ibrahim, H., and Cordes, K.A. 1993. *Outdoor Recreation.* Brown and Benchmark, Madison, WI.

Irland, L.C. 1979. *Wilderness Economics and Policy.* D.C. Heath, Lexington, MA.

Ise, J. 1961. *Our National Park Policy: A Critical History.* Johns Hopkins University Press, Baltimore.

Jenkins, W.I. 1978. *Policy Analysis: A Political and Organizational Perspective.* St. Martin's, New York.

Jones, C.O. 1977. *An Introduction to the Study of Public Policy,* 2nd edition. Duxbury Press, North Scituate, MA.

Kaplan, R., and S. Kaplan. 1989. *The Experience of Nature: A Psychological Perspective*. Cambridge University Press, Cambridge.

Kaplan, R., S. Kaplan, and R.L. Ryan 1998. *With People in Mind: Design and Management of Everyday Nature*. Island Press, Washington.

Kaufman, H. 1960. *The Forest Ranger: A Study in Administrative Behavior*. Johns Hopkins University Press, Baltimore.

Kaufman, P.W. 1996. *National Parks and the Woman's Voice: A History*. University of New Mexico Press, Albuquerque.

Kelly, J.R., and R.B. Warnick. 1999. *Recreation Trends and Markets: The 21st Century*. Sagamore, Champaign, IL.

Kingdon, J.W. 1995. *Agendas, Alternatives, and Public Policies*, 2nd edition. Little, Brown & Company, Boston.

Knight, R.L., and K.J. Gutzwiller. 1995. *Wildlife and Recreationists: Coexistence through Management and Research*. Island Press, Washington.

Knight, R.L. and P.B. Landres. 1998. *Stewardship across Boundaries*. Island Press, Washington.

Lacey. M.J. 1979. The mysteries of earth-making dissolve: A study of Washington's intellectual community and the origins of environmentalism in the late nineteenth centuty. Unpublished PhD Dissertation, George Washington University. 1979.

LaPage, W. 1976. New roles for government and industry in outdoor recreation. In *General Technical Report SE-9*. U.S. Department of Agriculture, Forest Service, Southeastern Forest Experiment Station, Asheville, NC, pp. 218–229.

Lauber, T.B. and B.A. Knuth. 1998. Measuring fairness in citizen participation. *Society and Natural Resources Journal*. 12 (1), 19–3.

Lee, M.E. and B.L Driver. 1999. Benefits-based management: A new paradigm for managing amenity resources. In *Ecosystem Management: Adaptive Strategies for Natural Resources Organizations in the 21st Century*. J. Aley, W.R. Burch, B. Conover, D. Field, editors. Taylor & Francis, Philadelphia, PA. Ch. 10

Leman. C.K. 1981. The forest ranger revisited: Administrative behavior in the U.S. forest service in the 1980s. Paper presented at the annual meeting of the American Political Science Association, New York. September 3–6.

LeMaster, D.C. 1984. *Decade of Change: The Remaking of Forest Service Statutory Authority During the 1970s*. Greenwood Press, Westport, CT.

Leopold, A. 1949. *A Sand County Almanac and Sketches Here and There*. Oxford University Press, New York.

Leopold. A. 1921. The Wilderness and Its Place in Forest Recreational Policy. *Journal of Forestry*, 29:718–721.

Limerick, P.N. 1987. *The Legacy of Conquest: The Unbroken Past of the American West*. Norton, New York.

Lind, E.A. and T.R. Tyler. 1988. *The Social Psychology of Procedural Justice*. Plenum Press, New York.

Lindblom, C. 1979. Still muddling, not yet through. *Public Administration Review*. Nov/Dec, pp. 517–526.

Lindblom, C.E. 1968. *The Policymaking Process*. Prentice-Hall, Englewood Cliffs, NJ.

Lins, S.A. 1991. Community development and the National Park Service. *Small Town,* July–August: 4–11.

Little, C.E. 1995. *Greenways for America*. Johns Hopkins University Press, Baltimore.

Little. C.A. 1975. Greenline parks: An approach to preserving recreational landscapes in urban areas. In *Report to the Environmental Policy Division*. Congressional Research Service, Library of Congress, Washington.

Loomis, J.B. 1993. *Integrated Public Lands Management: Principles and Applications to National Forests, Parks, Wildlife Refuges and BLM Lands*. Columbia University Press, New York.

Loomis, J., K. Bonetti, and C. Echohawk. 1999. Demand for and supply of wilderness. In *Outdoor Recreation in American Life: A National Assessment of Demand and Supply Trends*. H.K. Cordell, C.J. Betz, J.M. Bowker, D.B.K. English, J.C. Bergstrom, R.J. Teasley, M.A. Tarrant, and J. Loomis, editors. Sagamore, Champaign, IL. Ch. 7

Loomis, J. and R. Richardson. 2001. *Economic Values of Wilderness in the United States*. Dept. of Agriculture and Resource Economics, Colorado State University, Ft. Collins, CO.

Lowenthal, D. 1964. Introduction to 1965 reprinting of *G.P. Marsh, Man and Nature*. Harvard University Press, Cambridge, MA.

Lyden, F.J. 1975. Using Parson's functional analysis in the study of public organizations. *Administrative Science Quarterly*. 20:59–70.

Mackintosh, B. 1985. *Visitor Fees in the National Park System: A Legislative and Administrative History*. National Park Service History Division, Washington.

Mackintosh, B. 1991. *The National Parks: Shaping the System*. U.S. Dept. of the Interior, Washington.

MacLeish, W.H. 1994. *The Day Before America*. Houghton-Mifflin, Boston.

Mann, C.C. 2002. *1491. The Atlantic*, 289(3):41–53.

Manning, R. 1999. *Studies in Outdoor Recreation: Search and Research for Satisfaction*. 2nd edition. Oregon State University Press, Corvallis, OR.

Manning, R., D. Lime, and M. Hof. 1996. Social carrying capacity of natural areas: theory and application in the U.S. national parks. *Natural Areas Journal*, 16, 118–127.

March, J.G., and J.P. Olson. 1989. *Rediscovering Institutions: The Organizational Basis of Politics*. Free Press, New York.

Marsh, G.P. 1864. *Man and Nature: Or Physical Geography as Modified by Human Action*. Harvard University Press, Cambridge, MA.

Marshall, R. 1930. The Problem of the Wilderness. *The Scientific Monthly*, reprinted in *The Living Wilderness*, 40 (1976): 31–35.

Martin, M. 1983. Peshtigo: The fire a nation forgot. *American Forests*, 89:14–16, 53–55.

Marx, L. 1964. *The Machine in the Garden*. Oxford University Press, New York.

Maser, C. 1994. *Sustainable Forestry: Philosophy, Science and Economics*. St. Lucie Press, Delray Beach, FL.

McCay, B.J., and S. Jentoft. 1996. From the bottom up: Participatory issues in fisheries management. *Society and Natural Resources Journal*, 9(3), 237–250.

McCarthy, G.M. 1976. The forest reserve controversy: Colorado under Cleveland and McKinley. *Journal of Forest History*, 20:80–90.

McCool, S.F., and D.N. Cole. compilers. 1997. Proceedings—Limits of acceptable change and related planning processes: Progress and future directions. In *May 20–22, 1997, Missoula, MT. General Technical Report INT-GTR-371*. U.S. Department of Agriculture, Forest Service, Rocky Mountain Research Station, Ogden, UT.

McDonough, M.H., and C.W. Wheeler, 1998. *Toward School and Community Collaboration in Social Forestry: Lessons from the Thai Experience*. U.S. Agency for International Development, Washington.

McGeary, N.M. Gifford. 1970. *Pinchot: Forester, Politician.* Princeton University Press, Princeton, NJ.

McNeely, J.A. 1995. *Expanding Partnerships in Conservation.* Island Press, Washington.

McPhee, J. 1971. *Encounters with the Archdruid.* Farrar, Straus, and Giroux, New York.

McPhee, J. 1971. Ranger. *New Yorker,* 47:45, 89.

McPherson, E.G., D.J. Nowak, and R.A. Rowntree. 1994. Chicago's urban forest ecosystem: Results of the Chicago urban forest climate project. In *Gen. Tech. Rep. NE-186.* USDA Forest Service, Northeastern Forest Experiment Station, Radnor, PA.

McQuillan, A.G. 2001. American Indian timber management policy: Its evolution in the context of U.S. forest history. In *Trusteeship in Change: Toward Tribal Autonomy in Resource Management.* R.L. Clow, and I. Sutton, editors. University Press of Colorado, Boulder, CO, Chapter 4, pp. 73–102.

Meine, C. 1988. *Aldo Leopold: His Life and Work.* University of Wisconsin Press, Madison, Wisconsin.

Meltz, R., D.H. Merriam, and R.M. Frank. 1999. *The Takings issue: Constitutional Limits on Land Use Control and Environmental Regulation.* Island Press, Washington.

Merchant, C. 1985. The women of the progressive conservation crusade, 1900–1915. In *Environmental History: Critical Issues in Comparative Perspective.* K.E. Bailes, editors. University Press of America.

Merchant, C. 1993. *Major problems in American environmental history.* D.C. Heath and Company, Lexington, MA.

Merchant, C. 1985. Women and conservation. In *Major Problems in American Environmental History.* C. Merchant, editor. Heath and Co., Lexington, MA, pp. 373–382.

Merchant, C. 1995. *Earthcare: Women and the Environment.* Routledge, New York.

Meffe, G.K, L.A. Nielsen, R.L. Knight, and D.A. Schenborn. 2002. *Ecosystem Management: Adaptive, Community-based Conservation.* Island Press, Washington.

Miller, C. 2001. *Gifford Pinchot and the Making of Modern Environmentalism.* Island Press, Washington.

Mintron, M. 2000. *Policy Entrepreneurs and School Choice.* Georgetown University Press, Washington.

Mitchell, J.G. 1985. In wilderness was the preservation of a smile. *Wilderness,* 48:10–21.

Mitchell, J.G. 1978. The regreening of urban America. *Audubon,* 80:29–52.

More, T., and T. Stevens. 2000. Do user fees exclude low-income people from resource-based recreation? *Journal of Leisure Research,* 32(3):341–357.

More, T.A. 1999. A functionalist approach to user fees. *Journal of Leisure Research,* 31(3):227–244.

More, T.A. 2002. The parks are being loved to death and other frauds and deceipts in recreation management. *Journal of Leisure Research,* 34(1):52–78.

Morris, E. 1979. *The Rise of Theodore Roosevelt.* Ballantine, New York.

Morton, P. 1997. Sustaining recreation resources on southern Appalachian national forests. *Journal of Park and Recreation Administration,* 14(2):121–208.

Muir, J. 1916. *A Thousand-Mile Walk to the Gulf.* Houghton Mifflin, Boston.

Nash, A.E.K. 1981. Reflections on the exclusionary zoning of American nature. *Michigan Law Review,* 79:1299–1313.

Nash, R.F. 1990. *American Environmentalism: Readings in Conservation History.* McGraw-Hill, New York.

Nash, R. 1976. *The American Environment: Readings in the History of Conservation,* 2nd edition. Addison-Wesley, Reading, MA, 1976.

Nash, R. 1973. *Wilderness and the American Mind,* revised edition. Yale University Press, New Haven, CT.

National Park Service. 1997. *VERP: The Visitor Experience and Resource Protection (VERP) Framework—A Handbook for Planners and Managers.* National Park Service, Denver Service Center, Denver, CO.

National Parks Conservation Association. 2000. Private lands, public challenge: NPS continues its push to buy private land to protect parks. *National Parks Magazine,* Sept/Oct: 3–4.

Noble, D.W. 1968. *The Eternal Adam and the New World Garden: The Central Myth of the American Novel Since 1830.* George Braziller, New York.

Nowak, D.J., P.J. McHale, M. Ibarra (and others). 1998. Modeling the effects of urban vegetation on air pollution. In *Air Pollution Modeling and Its Application* XII. S.E. Gryning and N. Chaunerliac, editors. Plenum Press, New York, pp. 399–407.

Nye, R. 1966. *This Almost Chosen People: Essays in the History of American Ideas.* Michigan State University Press, East Lansing.

Odell. R. 1986. Congress tells it like it's supposed to be. Conservation Foundation letter, November–December.

Oelschlaeger, M. 1991. *The Idea of Wilderness: From Prehistory to the Age of Ecology.* Yale University Press, New Haven, CT.

Olmsted, F.L. 1953. The Yosemite Valley and the Mariposa Big Trees: A preliminary report, as reconstructed by L.W. Roper, *Landscape Architecture,* 44:12–25.

Olson, S. 1971. *The Depletion Myth: A History of Railroad Use of Tirnber.* Harvard University Press, Cambridge, MA.

Pecore, M. 1992. Menominee sustained yield management: A successful land ethic in practice. *Journal of Foresty,* July: 12–16.

Peterson, D.L., and D.R. Johnson.1995. *Human Ecology and Climate Change: People and Resources in the Far North.* Taylor and Francis, Washington.

Petty, R.O. 1974. Essay. In *Torkel Korling, Wild Plants in Flower 111: The Deciduous Forest.* Torkel Korling, Dundee, IL.

Pinchot, G. 1966. *The Fight for Conservation.* The University of Washington Press, Seattle.

Pressman, J.L., and A. Wildavsky. 1984. *Implementation: How Great Expectations in Washington are Dashed in Oakland; or, Why It's Amazing that Federal Programs Work at all, This Being a Saga of the Economic Development Administration as Told by Two Sympathetic Observers Who Seek to Build Morals on a Foundation of Ruined Hopes.* University of California Press, Berkeley, CA.

Propst, D.B., and S.C. Bentley. 2001. Trends in citizen participation in outdoor recreation management: Manager vs. citizen perspectives. In *Proceedings of Fifth Outdoor Recreation and Tourism Trends Symposium,* Sept. 17–20, 2000. Dept. of Park, Recreation & Tourism Resources, Michigan State University, East Lansing, Michigan, pp. 202–213.

Propst, D.B., J.D. Wellman, H.R. III Campa, and M.H. McDonough. 2000. Citizen participation trends and their educational implications for natural resource professionals. In *Trends in Outdoor Recreation and Tourism.* D.W. Lime, W.C. Gartner, and J. Thompson, editors. CAB International, Wallingford, Oxon, UK, Ch. 35.

Putnam, R.D. 2002. Bowling together. *TAP* (The American Prospect). 13(3):1–6, *http://www.prospect.org/print/V13/3/putnam-r.html*

Quinn, T. P. 1996. Recreation service enterprises on public lands: Policy, perceptions, and pricing—an analysis of whose interests counts. Unpublished PhD dissertation, Department of Forestry, Michigan State University, East Lansing.

Reich, R. B. 1988. *The Power of Public Ideas*. Harvard University Press, Cambridge, MA.

Rettie, D.F. 1995. *Our National Park System: Caring for America's Greatest Natural and Historic Treasures*. University of Illinois Press, Urbana and Chicago.

Reisner, N. 1984. Power, profit and preservation. *Wilderness,* 48:26–34.

Richardson, R.D. 1986. *Henry Thoreau: A Life of the Mind*. University of California Press, Berkeley, CA.

Ripley, R.B. 1975. *Congress: Process and Policy*. Norton, New York.

Risbrudt, C. 1986. The real issue in below-cost sales: Multiple-use management of public lands. *Western Wildlands,* 12:2–5.

Roberts, N. 1997. Public deliberation: an alternative approach to crafting policy and setting direction. *Public Administration Review,* 57(2):124–132.

Robinson, G.O. 1975. *The Forest Service*. Johns Hopkins University Press for Resources for the Future, Baltimore.

Rodgers, A.D. 1951. *Bernhard Edward Fernow: A Story of North American Forestry*. Princeton University Press, Princeton, NJ.

Roggenbuck, J.W. 1981. Subsidy reduction benefits outdoor recreation. Paper presented at the annual meeting of the National Recreation and Parks Association. Orlando, FL, October 22.

Roper, L.W. 1973. *FLO: A Biography of Frederick Law Olmsted*. Johns Hopkins University Press, Baltimore.

Rosenzweig, R., and Blackmar, E. 1992. *The Park and the People: A History of Central Park*. Cornell University Press, Ithaca, NY.

Roth, D.M. 1984. *The Wilderness Movement and the National Forests: 1964–1980*. USDA Forest Service, FS 391.

Rowntree, R.A., and J.L. Wolfe, compilers. 1980. Abstracts of urban forestry research in progress—1979. In *Gen. Tech. Rep. NE-60*. U.S. Department of Agriculture, Forest Service, Northeastern Forest Experiment Station, Broomall, PA.

Rudzitis, G. 1996. *Wilderness and the Changing American West*. Wiley, New York.

Runte, A. 1979. *National Parks: The American Experience*. University of Nebraska Press, Lincoln.

Runte, A. 1991. *Public Lands, Public Heritage: The National Forest Idea*. Roberts Rinehart, Niwot, CO.

Rybczynski, W. 1999. *A Clearing in the Distance: Frederick Law Olmsted and America in the Nineteenth Century*. Scribner, New York.

Sabatier, P.A. 1988. An advocacy coalition framework of policy change and the role of policy-oriented learning therein. *Policy Sciences,* 21:129–168

Salwasser, H. 1999. Ecosystem management: A new perspective for national forests and grasslands. In *Ecosystem management: Adaptive Strategies for Natural Resources Organizations in the 21st Century*. J. Aley, W.R. Burch, B. Conover, and D. Field, editors. Taylor and Francis, Philadelphia, PA, Ch. 6

Saunier, R.E., and R.A. Meganck. 1995. *Conservation of Biodiversity and the New Regional Planning*. Organization of American States and IUCN—The World Conservation Union. Washington.

Sax, J.L. 1976. America's national parks: their principles, purposes, and prospects. *Natural History.* 85:57–88.

Sax, J.L. 1980. *Mountains without Handrails: Reflections on the National Parks*. The University of Michigan Press, Ann Arbor.

Schenck, C.A. 1955. *The Biltmore Story: Reflections on the Beginning of Forestry in the United States*. Minnesota Historical Society, St. Paul.

Schiff, A.C. 1962. *Fire and Water: Scientific Heresy in the Forest Service*. Harvard University Press, Cambridge, MA.

Schrepfer, S. 1976. Perspectives on conservation: Sierra Club strategies in Mineral King. *Journal of Forest History*. 20:176–190.

Schroeder, H.W. 1989. Environment, behavior, and design research on urban forests. In *Advances in Environment, Behavior, and Design*, vol. 2. E.H. Zube and G.T. Moore, editors. Plenum Press, New York.

Schroeder, H.W. 1990. Perceptions and preferences of urban forest users. *Journal of Arboriculture*. 16(3):58–61.

Schroeder, H.W. and S.R. Ruffolo. 1996. Householder evaluations of street trees in a Chicago suburb. *Journal of Arboriculture*. 22(1):35–43.

Searle, R.N. 1977. *Saving Quetico-Superior: A Land Set Apart*. Minnesota Historical Society Press, St. Paul.

Sellars, R.W. 1992. The roots of National Park management. *Journal of Forestry*, 90(1):16–19.

Sellars, R.W. 1997. *Preserving Nature in the National Parks: A History*. Yale University Press, New Haven, CT.

Shabecoff, P. 1986. Outdoors proposal drawing objections from Reagan aides. *The New York Times*, Nov. 19.

Shands, W.E., P.R. Hagenstein, and M.T. Roche. 1979. *National Forest Policy: From Conflict Toward Consensus*. Conservation Foundation, Washington.

Shankland, R. 1951. *Steve Mather of the National Parks*. Alfred A. Knopf, New York.

Shannon, M.A. 1991. Resource managers as policy entrepreneurs: Governance challenges of the urban-forest interface. *Journal of Forestry*, June: 27–30.

Sharpe, G.W., C.H. Odegaard, and W.F. Sharpe. 1983. *Park Management*. Wiley, New York.

Sharpe, M.S. 1972. The National Parks and Young America. In *National Parks for the Future*. Washington: Conservation Foundation. pp. 197–212.

Shelby, B., and T. Heberlein. 1986. *Carrying Capacity in Recreation Settings*. Oregon State University Press, Corvallis, OR.

Siehl, G.H. 2000. U.S. recreation policies since World War II. In *Trends in Outdoor Recreation, Leisure and Tourism*. W.C. Gartner and D.W. Lime, editors. CABI Publishing, New York. Ch. 8.

Smith, H.N. 1950. *Virgin Land: The American West as Symbol and Myth*. Harvard University Press, Cambridge, MA.

Smith, J.N. 1972. The Gateways: Parks for whom? In *National Parks for the Future*. Conservation Foundation, Washington, pp. 213–236.

Smith, P.D., and M.H. McDonough. 2001. Beyond public participation: Fairness in natural resource decision making. *Society and Natural Resources*, 14:239–249.

Snow, D. 2001. Coming home: An introduction to collaborative conservation. In *Across the Great Divide: Explorations in Collaborative Conservation and the American West*. P. Brick, D. Snow, and S.V. De Wetering, editors. Island Press, Washington, pp. 1–11.

Socolow, R.H. 1976. Failures of discourse: Obstacles to the integration of environmental values into natural resource policy. In *When Values Conflict: Essays on Environmental Analysis, Dis-*

course, an Decision. L.H. Tribe, C.S. Schelling, and J. Voss, editors. Holt, Rinehart and Winston, New York.

Solomon, R.M., S. Yonts-Shepherd, and W.T. Supulski II. 1997. Public involvement under NEPA: trends and opportunities. In *Environmental Policy and NEPA: Past, Present, and Future.* R. Clark and L. Canter, editors. St. Lucie Press, Boca Raton, Florida. Ch. 16, pp. 261–276 .

Spence, M.D. 1999. *Dispossessing the Wilderness: Indian Removal and the Making of National Parks.* Oxford University Press, New York.

Stankey, G. 1985. The limits of acceptable change (LAC) system for wilderness planning. In *General Technical Report INT-176.* USDA Forest Service, Intermountain Research Station, Ogden, UT.

Stankey, G.H. 1999. The recreation opportunity spectrum and the limits of acceptable change planning systems: A review of experiences and lessons. In *Ecosystem Management: Adaptive Strategies for Natural Resources Organizations in the 21st Century.* J. Aley, W.R. Burch, B. Conover, and D. Field, editors. Taylor and Francis, Philadelphia, PA. Chapter 12.

Stankey, G.H., S.F. McCool, R.N. Clark, and P.J. Brown. 1999. Institutional and organizational challenges to managing natural resources for recreation: A social learning model. In *Leisure Studies: Prospects for the 21st Century.* E.L. Jackson and T.L. Burton, editors. Venture, State College, PA, CH. 26.

Stegner, W. 1962. *Beyond the Hundredth Meridian: John Wesley Powell and the Second Opening of the West.* Riverside Press, Cambridge, MA.

Stein, T.V., D.H. Anderson, and D. Thompson. 1999. Identifying and managing for community benefits in Minnesota state parks. *Journal of Park and Recreation Administration,* 17(4):1–19.

Sumner, E. Lowell. 1942. The biology of wilderness protection. *Sierra Club Bulletin,* 27(8):14–22.

Susskind, L., and A. Weinstein. 1980. Towards a theory of environmental conflict resolution. *Boston College Environmental Affairs Law Review,* 9:311–357.

Swain, D.C. 1966. The passage of the National Park Service Act of 1916. In *Wisconsin Magazine of History* 50:4–17.

Swinnerton, G. 1999. Recreation and Conservation: Issues and Prospects. In *Leisure Studies: Prospects for the 21st Century.* EL. Jackson, and T.L. Burton, editors. Venture, State College, PA, pp. 199–231.

Tarlock, A.D. 1952.For whom the national parks? *Stanford Law Review: The Wilderness World of John Muir.* Teale, E.W., editor. Houghton Mifflin, Boston, 34 (1981):255–274.

Taylor, D.E. 1998. The urban environment: The intersection of white middle-class and white working-class environmentalism (1820–1950s). *Advances in Human Ecology.* 7:207–292

Taylor, D.E. 1999. Central Park as a model for social control: Urban parks, social class and leisure behavior in nineteenth-century America. *Journal of Leisure Research,* 31(4):420–477.

Taylor, D.E. 2000. Meeting the challenge of wild land recreation management: Demographic shifts and social inequality. *Journal of Leisure Research,* 32(1):171–179.

Teale, W.W. 1952. *The Wilderness World of John Muir.* Houghton-Mifflin, Boston.

Thompson, R.C. 1963. Politics in the wilderness: New York's Adirondack Forest Preserve. *Forest History.* 6:14–23.

Thoreau, H.D. 1947. Civil disobedience. In *The Portable Thoreau.* C. Bode, editor. Viking, New York.

Thoreau, H.D. 1973. The Maine woods. In *The American Landscape: A Critical Anthology of Prose and Poetry.* J. Conron, editor. Oxford University Press, New York.

Thoreau, H.D. Walden. 1854. In *The Portable Thoreau.* C. Bode, editor. Viking, New York.

Tipple, T.J., and J.D. Wellman. 1991. Herbert Kaufman's forest ranger thirty years later: From simplicity and homogeneity to complexity and diversity. *Public Administration Review,* 51(5):421–428.

Tipple, T.J., J.D. Wellman, and G.L. Wamsley. 1990. Urban forestry administration in the Netherlands. *Society and Natural Resources,* 3:395–403.

Tipple, T.J., and J.D. Wellman. 1996. The living infrastructure: Managing the greenspace. In *Public Works Administration: Modern Public Policy Perspectives.* L. Brewer, editor. Sage, Thousand Oaks, CA, pp. 149–162.

Tucker, W. 1982. *Progress and Privilege: America in the Age of Environmentalism.* Anchor-Doubleday, Garden City, NY.

Tuler, S., and T. Webler. 1999. Voices from the forest: What participants expect of a public participation process. *Society and Natural Resources,* 12:437–453.

Tuler, S., and T. Webler. 2000. Public participation: Relevance and application in the National Park Service. *Park Science,* 20:24–26.

Turner, F.J. 1961. The significance of the frontier in American history (1893). In *American Social Thought.* R. Ginger, editor. Hill and Wang, New York.

Twight, B.W. 1983. *Organizational Values and Political Power: The Forest Service Versus the Olympic National Park.* Pennsylvania State University Press, University Park, PA.

Tyler, T., and P. Degoey. 1995. Collective restraint in social dilemmas: Procedural justice and social identification effects on support for authorities. *Journal of Personality and Social Psychology,* 69(3):482–497.

Udall, M., and M. Wallop. 1985. At issue: President's commission on Americans outdoors: What should it be and do? *American Forests,* 92:10 11, 52–53, 58–59.

Ulrich, R.S. 1993. Biophilia, biophobia and natural landscapes. In *The Biophilia Hypothesis,* S.R. Kellert, and E.O. Wilson, editors. Island Press. Washington, pp. 73–137.

U.S. Department of Agriculture. 2002. Budget Summary. *http://www.usda.gov/agency/obpa/Budget-Summary/2002/2002budsum.htm#nre,* accessed 10/24/01.

U.S. Department of Agriculture, Forest Service. 1975. Municipal watershed management: symposium proceedings. In *Gen. Tech. Rep. NE-13.* Northeastern Forest Experiment Station, Upper Darby, PA.

USGAO. 2001. Major management challenges and program risks: Department of the Interior. In *USGAO Performance and Accountability Series, GAO-01-249.* USGAO, Washington.

USGAO. 1994. *National Park Service: Activities outside park borders have caused damage to resources and will likely cause more.* GAO/RCED-94–59, Jan. 3.

USGAO. 1996. *National Park Service: Activities Within Park Borders Have Caused Damage to Resources.* GAO/RCED-96–202, Aug. 23.

USGAO. 1997. *National Park Service Needs Better Information to Preserve and Protect Resources.* GAO/T-RCED-97-76, Feb. 27.

U.S. Geological Survey. 1980. *Ferdinand Vandiveer Hayden and the Founding of Yellowstone National Park.* GPO, Washington, 1980-311-348-1.

Varela, M. 2001. Collaborative conservation: Peace or pacification? In *The View from Los Ojos: Across the Great Divide: Explorations in Collaborative Conservation and the American West.* P. Brick, D. Snow, and S.V. De Wetering, editors. Island Press, Washington, pp. 228–235.

Verberg, K. The carrying capacity of recreational lands: A review. Occasional Paper No. 1. Prairie Regional Office, Parks Canada.

Wagar, J.A. 1964. The carrying capacity of wild lands for recreation. *Forest Science Monograph 7.*

Wagar, J.A. 1974. Recreational carrying capacity reconsidered. *Journal of Forestry,* 72:274–278.

Wagner, F.H., R. Foresta, R.B. Gill, D.R. McCullough, M.R. Pelton, W.F. Porter, and H. Salwasser (Consultation on Law and Policy by J.L. Sax). 1995. Wildlife Policies in the U.S. National Parks. Island Press, Washington, DC.

Wamsley, G.L. 1990. *Refounding Public Administration.* Sage, Newbury Park, CA.

Wandersman, A. 1979. User participation in planning environments: A conceptual framework. *Environment and Behavior,* 11(4), 465–482.

Wandersman, A., P. Florin, R. Friedmann, and R. Meier, 1987. Who participates, who does not and why? An analysis of voluntary neighborhood organizations in the US and Israel. *Sociological Forum,* 2, 534–555.

Watkins, T.H. 1992. Father of the Forests. *Journal of Forestry,* January: 12–15.

Watkins, T.H. 1984. *The Terrible-Tempered Mr. Ickes.* Audubon 82:93–111.

Weber, E.P. 1998. *Pluralism by the Rules.* Georgetown University Press, Washington.

Wellman, J.D. 1987. *Wildland Recreation Policy.* Wiley, New York.

Wellman, J.D., and T.J. Tipple. 1992. *Working with the community: A conceptual framework for urban forest managers.* American Forests, Forest Policy Center Report, Washington, 92–93.

Wellman, J.D., and T.J. Tipple. 1993. Governance in the wildland-urban interface: a normative guide for natural resource managers. In *Culture, Conflict, and Communication in the Wildland-Urban Interface.* A.W. Ewart, D.J. Chavez, and A.W. Magill, editors. Westview Press, Boulder, CO, pp. 337–347.

West, P.C., and S.R. Brechin 1991. *Resident Peoples and National Parks: Social Dilemmas and Strategies in International Conservation.* University of Arizona Press, Tucson.

White, C.M., M. Cobus, R.E. Manning, J. Seffel, and T. More. 1995. Trends in the economics of sustainable outdoor recreation tourism: The future of outdoor recreation fees for the public sector. In *Proceedings of the Fourth International Outdoor Recreation and Tourism Trends Symposium,* May 14–17. J.L Thompson, D.W. Lime, B. Gartner, and W.M. Sames, editors. University of Minnesota, College of Natural Resources and Minnesota Extension Service, St. Paul.

Wilkinson, C.F. 1987. *American Indians, Time and the Law: Native Societies in a Modern Constitutional Democracy.* Yale University Press, New Haven, CT.

Winter, P.L., L.J. Palucki, and R.L. Burkhardt. 1999. Anticipated responses to a fee program: The key is trust. *Journal of Leisure Research,* 31(3):202–226.

Wirtz, R.A. 2000. Roadless initiative more complex than knuckle-dragging loggers vs. spotted owls. *Fedgazette,* 12(2):12–17.

Wondolleck, J. 1988. *Public Lands Conflict and Resolution: Managing National Forest Disputes.* Plenum, New York.

Worster, D. 2001. *A River Running West: The Life of John Wesley Powell.* Oxford University Press, New York.

Yaffee, S.L. 1998. Cooperation: A strategy for achieving stewardship across boundaries. In *Stewardship Across Boundaries.* R.L. Knight, and P.B. Landres, editors. Island Press, Washington, Ch. 14, pp. 299–326.

Zimmerman, E.W. 1951. *World Resources and Industries.* Harper and Row, New York.

Zube, E. 1995. No park is an island. In *Expanding Partnerships in Conservation.* J.A. McNeely, editor. Island Press, Washington, Ch. 20.

INDEX